APPLIED MULTIDIMENSIONAL SCALING

Editors' Series in Marketing

Paul E. Green, Philip Kotler, consulting editors

P. E. Green and V. R. Rao: **Applied Multidimensional Scaling: A Comparison of Approaches and Algorithms**

T. S. Robertson: **Innovative Behavior and Communication**

PAUL E. GREEN *Wharton School of Finance and Commerce*
University of Pennsylvania

Graduate School of Business
and Public Administration
VITHALA R. RAO *Cornell University*

APPLIED MULTIDIMENSIONAL SCALING

A Comparison of Approaches and Algorithms

Holt, Rinehart and Winston, Inc.
New York   Chicago   San Francisco   Atlanta
Dallas   Montreal   Toronto   London   Sydney

Copyright © 1972 by Holt, Rinehart and Winston, Inc.
All rights reserved
Library of Congress Catalog Card Number: 70-159398
ISBN: 0-03-080271-7
Printed in the United States of America
5 4 3 2   038   1 2 3 4 5 6 7 8 9

Editor's Foreword

The development and rapid diffusion of new methodology frequently leads to claims and counterclaims regarding which technique is suitable for which problem. Multidimensional scaling methodology currently appears to be in this state. Paul E. Green and Vithala R. Rao have worked in this field for a number of years and are mindful of the many diverse approaches and algorithms that can be used to scale psychological data.

This book provides, for the first time, an intensive and extensive comparison of various conceptual approaches and scaling algorithms applied to a common data base. All basic data and summary computer outputs have been included, enabling the new practitioner to replicate the results in the process of developing his own background and skills in the area. In addition, the mathematical details of each algorithm are described.

In short, this is a book for the technician and the potential user of multidimensional scaling. Professors Green and Rao provide a vehicle by which the applied researcher can accomplish this objective in a systematic and operationally based manner.

Philip Kotler

Preface

New developments in methodology that undergo rapid diffusion in the scientific community usually lack documentation on how the techniques are being used and on how they should be used. In the behavioral and administrative sciences, multidimensional scaling methodology has undergone such rapid diffusion, and relatively little detailed recording of current practice has been made, let alone standardization of that practice.

While it seems premature to discuss standardization, it is appropriate to discuss documentation of current practice, which is what we have attempted to do in this text. In brief, we analyze a small data bank consisting of responses by forty-two subjects to questions about relative similarities, attribute ratings, and preference ranking tasks for a set of fifteen breakfast food items. A large variety of approaches and algorithms are compared conceptually and empirically in terms of this common data bank.

Thus this text has been prepared for the current, or potential, practitioner who already knows something about multidimensional scaling and wishes to become more versed in the detailed application of these techniques. Chapter 1 describes our objectives in detail and provides an overview for the rest of the book.

Insofar as classroom use is concerned, the text is best suited for graduate-level students in marketing or behavioral research. As background we assume that the reader has already examined the classic books by W. S. Torgerson (*Theory and Methods of Scaling*, Wiley, 1958) and C. H. Coombs (*A Theory of Data*, Wiley, 1964). It would be helpful if the student has also read P. E. Green and F. J. Carmone's *Multidimensional Scaling and Related Techniques in Marketing Analysis* (Allyn and Bacon, 1970). However, we emphasize the specialized scope of the present text; realistically it probably will be used by students interested in scaling and data analysis within some broader research context.

To our knowledge, the text represents the most comprehensive multidimensional scaling analysis of a single set of empirical data that has so far been attempted. But we hope its value is measured less in the volume of computer output (a stack about four feet high, if one counts false starts and check runs) and more in terms of our desire to contrast a diversity of approaches and computer algorithms that have been proposed for multidimensional scaling.

Since our substantive field is marketing, our choice of data bank and kinds of comparative analyses reflects this background. We hope, however, that this text will appeal to applied researchers in other segments of the behavioral and administrative sciences, as well as to marketing researchers.

Acknowledgments

Few authors have the opportunity to obtain such comprehensive and knowledgeable reviews of their work as we have had of ours. Specifically, we greatly appreciate the incisive and careful technical reviews provided by Drs. J. Douglas Carroll and Myron Wish, both of Bell Laboratories, who have not only contributed substantially to the methodological development of multidimensional scaling, but are also mindful of the potential applicability of these methods to fields outside their own field of psychology. Professor Philip Kotler, of Northwestern University, provided a thorough appraisal of the book from the viewpoint of the marketing academic. If residual errors or inadequacies remain, they are clearly our responsibility.

We are also indebted to our respective institutions for the financial support received from the Computing Centers of the University of Pennsylvania and Cornell University. Miss Najma Khalid provided valuable assistance in many of the computer runs. Finally, the indispensable help of Miss Mollie Horowits, long used to the unreasonable demands of authors, is gratefully recognized.

In retrospect, that four-foot-high stack of computer output does not appear so formidable (or impressive) at this writing. Probably, that reflection is associated with how most studies end—and, perhaps, how new studies should begin.

Philadelphia, Pennsylvania   Paul E. Green
Ithaca, New York   Vithala R. Rao
November 1971

Contents

Editor's Foreword   v

Preface   vii

CHAPTER 1   **INTRODUCTION AND OVERVIEW**   1
Study Objectives   3
The Data Bank   3
Alternative Conceptual Approaches   5
Alternative Algorithms   11
Additional Comments on the Data Base   12
Format of Subsequent Chapters   14
Summary   16

CHAPTER 2   AGGREGATE-LEVEL ANALYSIS OF
               DISSIMILARITIES DATA   17
               Outline of the Analysis   18
               Alternative Data Collection Procedures and Preprocessing Steps   22
               Ratings Data Scaling   34
               Congruence Testing   41
               Summary   48

CHAPTER 3   DISAGGREGATE-LEVEL ANALYSIS OF
               DISSIMILARITIES DATA   49
               Outline of Analysis   50
               Approaches to Individual Differences   53
               INDSCAL Analysis at the Total Group Level   55
               Analysis of Respondent Differences in Perception   62
               INDSCAL Analysis at the Subgroup Level   65
               Property Fitting at the Subgroup Level   66
               Summary   76

CHAPTER 4   INTERNAL ANALYSIS OF PREFERENCE DATA   78
               Outline of the Analysis   79
               Alternative Procedures in the Internal Analysis of
                   Preference Data   81
               Internal Analysis of Overall Preferences   83
               Tests for Congruence with INDSCAL Stimulus Space   90
               Summary   103

CHAPTER 5   EXTERNAL ANALYSIS OF PREFERENCE DATA   104
               Outline of Analysis   105
               External Analysis and Market Segmentation   106
               The PREFMAP Algorithm   108
               External Analysis of Overall Preferences   109
               Summary   132

CHAPTER 6   SUMMARY OF FINDINGS AND FUTURE
               RESEARCH AREAS   133
               Summary of Methodological Findings   134
               Summary of Substantive Findings   138
               Potential Research Areas   141
               Towards a Schema for the Design of Predictive Studies   147
               Summary   150

APPENDIX A   QUESTIONNAIRE AND BASIC DATA OF STUDY   152

APPENDIX B   **DETAILS OF THE PROGRAM USED**   181

TRICON   182

DISTAN   187

M-D-SCAL V   188

TORSCA 8   192

PARAMAP   196

Johnson Hierarchical Cluster Program   199

C-MATCH   200

INDSCAL   203

Howard-Harris Cluster Program   207

PROFIT   210

MDPREF   212

PREFMAP   214

APPENDIX C   **SUPPORTING MATERIAL FOR CHAPTER DISCUSSIONS**   219

CHAPTER 2

Table C.1   Basic Data on Directly Judged Dissimilarities from TRICON for First Three Subjects (see Table 2.2)   220

Table C.2   Basic Data on Derived Distances (DISTAN) from Ratings for First Three Subjects (see Table 2.3)   221

Table C.3   Stimulus Coordinates from Metric Scaling of Direct Dissimilarities in Two and Three Dimensions (see Figure 2.2)   222

Figure C.1   Shepard Diagram from Metric Scaling of Direct Dissimilarities in Two and Three Dimensions (see Figure 2.3)   222

Table C.4   Stimulus Coordinates from M-D-SCAL V Analysis of Direct Dissimilarities in Two and Three Dimensions (see Figure 2.4)   223

Figure C.2   Shepard Diagram from M-D-SCAL V Analysis of Direct Dissimilarities in Two and Three Dimensions (see Figure 2.5)   223

Table C.5   Stimulus Coordinates from TORSCA 8 Analysis of Direct Dissimilarities in Two and Three Dimensions (see Figure 2.6)   224

Figure C.3   Shepard Diagram from TORSCA 8 Analysis of Direct Dissimilarities in Two and Three Dimensions (see Figure 2.7)   224

Table C.6   Stimulus Coordinates from Parametric Mapping of Direct Dissimilarities in Two and Three Dimensions (see Figure 2.8)   225

Figure C.4   Shepard Diagram from Parametric Mapping of Direct
Dissimilarities in Two and Three Dimensions (see
Figure 2.9)   225

Table C.7   Stimulus Coordinates from Metric Scaling of Derived
Dissimilarities in Two and Three Dimensions (see
Figure 2.11)   226

Figure C.5   Shepard Diagram from Metric Scaling of Derived Dissimilarities in Two and Three Dimensions (see
Figure 2.12)   226

Table C.8   Stimulus Coordinates from M-D-SCAL V Analysis of
Derived Dissimilarities in Two and Three Dimensions
(see Figure 2.13)   227

Figure C.6   Shepard Diagram from M-D-SCAL V Analysis of
Derived Dissimilarities (see Figure 2.14)   227

Table C.9   Stimulus Coordinates from TORSCA 8 Analysis of
Derived Dissimilarities in Two and Three Dimensions
(see Figure 2.15)   228

Figure C.7   Shepard Diagram from TORSCA 8 Analysis of Derived
Dissimilarities in Two and Three Dimensions (see
Figure 2.16)   228

Table C.10   Stimulus Coordinates from Parametric Mapping of
Derived Dissimilarities in Two and Three Dimensions
(see Figure 2.17)   229

Figure C.8   Shepard Diagram from Parametric Mapping of Derived
Dissimilarities in Two and Three Dimensions (see
Figure 2.18)   229

Table C.11   Stimulus Coordinates from Discriminant Analysis
of Ratings Data in Three Dimensions (see Figure
2.20)   230

Table C.12   Canonical Weights from Discriminant Analysis of
Ratings Data in Three Dimensions (see Figure 2.20)   230

Table C.13   Two-Space Stimulus Coordinates Orthogonally Rotated
to Best Congruence with Metric Scaling Configuration
Obtained from Dissimilarities (see Figure 2.21)   231

CHAPTER 3

Table C.14   Individual-subject Correlation Coefficients from
Aggregate-level INDSCAL Analysis of Direct Dissimilarities in Two and Three Dimensions (see Table 3.1)   232

Table C.15   Individual-subject Dimension Saliences from Aggregate-
level INDSCAL Analysis of Direct Dissimilarities
in Two and Three Dimensions (see Figure 3.3)   233

Table C.16   Stimulus Coordinates from Aggregate-level INDSCAL
Analysis of Direct Dissimilarities in Two and Three
Dimensions (see Figure 3.4)   234

Table C.17   Results of Max "r" Property Fitting of Average Ratings
in the Three-dimensional INDSCAL Stimulus Space of
Direct Dissimilarities Data   234

Table C.18   Individual-subject Correlation Coefficients from
Aggregate-level INDSCAL Analysis of Derived Dis-
similarities in Two and Three Dimensions (see
Table 3.2)   235

Table C.19   Individual-subject Dimension Saliences from Aggregate-
level INDSCAL Analysis of Derived Dissimilarities in
Two and Three Dimensions (see Figure 3.5)   236

Table C.20   Stimulus Coordinates from Aggregate-level INDSCAL
Analysis of Derived Dissimilarities in Two and Three
Dimensions (see Figure 3.6)   237

Table C.21   Means, Standard Deviations, and Pairwise Correlation
Matrix of the 10 Background Characteristics (see
Table 3.4)   237

Table C.22   Euclidean Distances Based on Direct Dissimilarities
between Husbands and Wives   238

Table C.23   Subgroup Compositions at 10 Levels of Hierarchical
Clustering of the 42 Respondents (see Table 3.7)   239

Table C.24   Individual-subject Correlation Coefficients from Group
A and B INDSCAL Analysis of Direct Dissimilarities
in Two Dimensions (see Table 3.9)   240

Table C.25   Individual-subject Dimension Saliences and Stimulus
Coordinates from Group A INDSCAL Analysis of Direct
Dissimilarities in Two Dimensions (see Figure 3.8)   241

Table C.26   Individual-subject Dimension Saliences and Stimulus
Coordinates from Group B INDSCAL Analysis of Direct
Dissimilarities in Two Dimensions (see Figure 3.9)   242

Table C.27   Average Ratings on the 10 Rating Scales for Group A   243

Table C.28   Average Ratings on the 10 Rating Scales for Group B   243

Table C.29   Stimulus Coordinates from Group A and Group B INDSCAL
Analysis of Average Ratings Data in Two Dimensions
(see Figure 3.16)   243

CHAPTER 4

Table C.30   Stimulus and Subject Coordinates from MDPREF Analysis
in Two and Three Dimensions (see Figure 4.2)   244

Table C.31   Stimulus and Subject Coordinates from Rational Starting
Configuration M-D-SCAL V Analyses in Three Dimensions
(see Figures 4.3 and 4.5)   246

Table C.32   Stimulus and Subject Coordinates from M-D-SCAL V Analysis
(Row Split Option) in Two and Three Dimensions (see
Figure 4.3)   247

Figure C.9   Shepard Diagram Based on Three-Space Solution from
M-D-SCAL V Row Split Analysis (see Figure 4.4)   249

Figure C.10   Shepard Diagram Based on Three-Space Solution from
M-D-SCAL V Row Comparability Analysis (see Figure 4.6)   249

Table C.33   Stimulus and Subject Coordinates from M-D-SCAL V Analysis
(Row Comparability Option) in Two and Three Dimensions
(see Figure 4.5)   250

Table C.34   Stimulus Coordinates for Rational Starting Configuration
from Parametric Mapping Analysis in Two and Three
Dimensions (see Figure 4.7)   252

Table C.35   Stimulus Coordinates from Parametric Mapping in Two
and Three Dimensions (see Figure 4.7)   252

Figure C.11   Shepard Diagram Based on Three-Space Solution from
Parametric Mapping (see Figure 4.8)   253

Table C.36   First Eight Subjects' Dissimilarities in Overall
Preference Rankings (see Figure 4.10)   253

Table C.37   Stimulus Coordinates from TORSCA 8 Analysis in Two
and Three Dimensions (see Figure 4.10)   254

Figure C.12   Shepard Diagram Based on Three-Space Solution from
TORSCA 8 Analysis (see Figure 4.11)   255

Table C.38   Product-Moment Correlations by Subject from Three-Way
CANDECOMP Analysis in Two and Three Dimensions (see
Figure 4.12)   255

Table C.39   Stimulus Coordinates from Three-Way CANDECOMP Analysis
in Two and Three Dimensions (see Figure 4.12)   256

Table C.40   Dimension "Loading" Matrices, Subjects, and Scenarios
from Three-Way CANDECOMP Analysis in Two and Three
Dimensions (see Figure 4.12)   256

CHAPTER 5

Table C.41   Ideal-point Coordinates and Dimension Weights for
Group A Overall Preferences (see Figure 5.2)   258

Table C.42   Ideal-point Coordinates and Dimension Weights for Group B Overall Preferences (see Figure 5.4)   259

Table C.43   Vector Model Direction Cosines for Group A and Group B Overall Preferences (see Figures 5.3 and 5.5)   260

Table C.44   Supporting Output for Four-way Discriminant Analysis, Perceptual-Preference Segments versus Background Characteristics (see Figure 5.6)   261

Table C.45   Multiple Correlation Coefficients and F-Ratios between Phases for the Linear Model of Group A Scenario-dependent Preferences   262

Table C.46   Multiple Correlation Coefficients and F-Ratios between Phases for the Linear Model of Group B Scenario-dependent Preferences   262

Table C.47   Multiple Correlation Coefficients and F-Ratios between Phases for the Monotone Model of Group A Scenario-dependent Preferences   263

Table C.48   Multiple Correlation Coefficients and F-Ratios between Phases for the Monotone Model of Group B Scenario-dependent Preferences   263

Table C.49   Ideal-point Coordinates and Dimension Weights for Group A Scenario-dependent Preferences (see Figure 5.7)   264

Table C.50   Ideal-point Coordinates and Dimension Weights for Group B Scenario-dependent Preferences (see Figure 5.8)   264

Table C.51   Vector Model Direction Cosines for Group A and Group B Scenario-dependent Preferences (see Figures 5.7 and 5.8)   264

Table C.52   Subject Saliences and Stimulus Coordinates from INDSCAL Analysis of Groups a and b in Two Dimensions (see Figures 5.9 and 5.10)   265

Table C.53   Multiple Correlation Coefficients and F-Ratios between Phases for the Monotone Model of Group a Scenario-dependent Preferences   266

Table C.54   Multiple Correlation Coefficients and F-Ratios between Phases for the Monotone Model of Group b Scenario-dependent Preferences   267

Table C.55   Ideal-point Coordinates and Dimension Weights for Group a Scenario-dependent Preferences   268

Table C.56   Ideal-point Coordinates and Dimension Weights for Group b Scenario-dependent Preferences   269

Table C.57   Vector Model Direction Cosines for Group a and b Scenario-dependent Preferences (see Figures 5.11 and 5.12)   270

CHAPTER 6

Table C.58   Correlation Matrix of Interpoint Distances across 17 Pseudosubjects (see Table 6.1)   271

Table C.59   Stimulus Coordinates from INDSCAL Analysis of Group Stimulus Space in Two Dimensions (see Figure 6.1)   272

Table C.60   Pseudosubject Saliences of INDSCAL Scaling of 17 Algorithm-Data Set Combinations in Two Dimensions (see Figure 6.2)   272

References   273

Index   285

APPLIED MULTIDIMENSIONAL SCALING

CHAPTER 1

INTRODUCTION AND OVERVIEW

In the eight years since R.N. Shepard [120] published the first computer-based procedure for nonmetric analysis, the field of multidimensional scaling has increased markedly in depth and scope. While the roots of this methodology go back at least 33 years [164] and reflect the contributions of eminent psychometricians like Torgerson [138], Guttman [60], and Coombs [27], the nonmetric approaches have sparked new interest. Not only have many behavioral scientists become curious about the procedures but researchers in the life sciences and business disciplines have shown interest as well.

In the field of marketing, for example, a number of multidimensional scaling studies already have been conducted. While the findings of these early efforts are scanty and ill documented, an increasing number of marketing researchers [39, 53, 57, 105] are experimenting with these procedures. At this stage in development it is not surprising that a variety of approaches and algorithms have been applied and that substantive applications often appear to lack the coherence and cumulative impact associated with more mature methodologies.

One of the deterrents to more widespread application of multidimensional scaling has been the lack of suitable documentation and intermethod comparisons of the computer algorithms. Over the past five years an intensive investigation of the applicability of multidimensional scaling techniques to marketing analysis has been under way at the Wharton School of Finance and Commerce. During this time the authors and their colleagues have had the opportunity (and sometimes frustration) of working with these techniques at both pilot and field data levels.

This book has grown out of our conviction that applied researchers in marketing and other fields would benefit from a report directed to them as the potential *users* of these techniques. We felt that a worthwhile contribution could be made by analyzing a common data bank in depth. In this way we could contrast differences in conceptual approaches and computer algorithms, while providing all basic input data and enough computer output so that other researchers could reproduce our results in the course of becoming familiar with the methodology.

No detailed discussion of the conceptual aspects of the methodology has been attempted here. We assume the reader is familiar with its theoretical underpinnings—at least at the level discussed by Green and Carmone [48]—and has perused the classic background books by Torgerson [141] and Coombs [29]. We also assume that he would like to delve more deeply into the operational features of the methodology and benefit from the experiences of those who (often by more trial and error than desired) have used it.

The newness of the methodology and its still-evolving nature preclude any attempt to spell out a comprehensive analytical procedure or a detailed account of algorithmic specifications. Virtually all the programs discussed in this book probably will be modified, if not by their original developers, then by future applications researchers. It would be naive to assume that the illustrations selected here will possess much permanence. Indeed, our hope lies in the opposite direction—that dissemination of these approaches to a wider audience will accelerate the methodological changes already anticipated in multidimensional scaling.

STUDY OBJECTIVES

Several motivations underlie the preparation of this book. The main objectives are summarized as follows:

1. To contrast various conceptual approaches to the multidimensional scaling of similarities and preference data
2. To contrast a variety of algorithms designed for more or less similar purposes
3. To provide brief descriptions of various computer run preparations (including specification of key control parameters), capsule descriptions of programs, and sufficient output so that our miniature data bank may be used as a sample problem, if desired[1]
4. To discuss a number of substantive problems arising in the analysis of the data bank used in this study
5. To suggest a variety of content areas in which multidimensional scaling could be applied in future research

In brief, we will analyze a set of data obtained from 42 respondents regarding their dissimilarities judgments, stimulus construct ratings, and preferences for 15 food items used at breakfast and snack time. The stimulus set and respondent group were chosen mainly for convenience. While we discuss a number of substantive questions, our primary motivation is methodological—to use this single data bank as a vehicle for applying the various approaches and algorithms.

THE DATA BANK

Data for this study were obtained during February 1970 from 21 Wharton School MBA students and their wives (a total of 42 respondents). Subsequent chapters describe the complete experimental design. Individual responses were obtained for the following classes of data:

1. Directly judged dissimilarities of 15 food items, whose names are in Table 1.1
2. Numerical ratings of each of the 15 food items on each of 10 bipolar scales, using a 7-point equal-interval scale; the list of bipolar scales is also shown in Table 1.1
3. Rankings of the 15 food items, according to six preference "scenarios," the first being for overall preference and the remainder for menus and serving occasions; these are listed in Table 1.2
4. Respondent background information; these characteristics also appear in Table 1.2

[1]Card decks containing all basic data used in this study are available, on request, from the authors.

Table 1.1   Food Items and Bipolar Scales Used in Pilot Study

Food Item	Plotting Code	Bipolar Scales
1. Toast pop-up	TP	1. Easy to prepare/Hard to prepare
2. Buttered toast	BT	2. Simple flavor/Complex flavor
3. English muffin and margarine	EMM	3. Mainly for adults/Mainly for kids
4. Jelly donut	JD	4. High calories/Low calories
5. Cinnamon toast	CT	5. Artificial flavor/Natural flavor
6. Blueberry muffin and margarine	BMM	6. Dry texture/Moist texture
7. Hard rolls and butter	HRB	7. Expensive/Inexpensive
8. Toast and marmalade	TMd	8. Highly filling/Not highly filling
9. Buttered toast and jelly	BTJ	9. Mostly eaten by itself/Mostly eaten with other foods
10. Toast and margarine	TMn	10. Simple shape/Complex shape
11. Cinnamon bun	CB	
12. Danish pastry	DP	
13. Glazed donut	GD	
14. Coffee cake	CC	
15. Corn muffin and butter	CMB	

Table 1.2   Preference Scenarios and Respondent Background Data

Preference Scenario	Plotting Code
1. Overall preference	Q
2. "When I'm having a breakfast, consisting of juice, bacon and eggs, and beverage"	R
3. "When I'm having a breakfast, consisting of juice, cold cereal, and beverage"	S
4. "When I'm having a breakfast, consisting of juice, pancakes, sausage, and beverage"	T
5. "Breakfast, with beverage only"	U
6. "At snack time, with beverage only"	V

Respondent Background Data

1. Sex
2. Age
3. Marital status (not used in subsequent analyses)
4. Number of children
5. Overweight?
6. If so, by what percentage of normal weight?
7. What does your typical weekday breakfast consist of?
8. What does your typical weekend breakfast consist of?
9. Regular coffee drinker, that is, at least once a day?
10. Regular tea drinker, that is, at least once a day?
11. Regular milk drinker, that is, at least once a day?

While not exhaustive of the classes of responses to which the methodology can be applied, these sets of data are illustrative of the types of judgments frequently obtained in applied multidimensional scaling studies. Moreover, these data are sufficient for contrasting a variety of approaches and algorithms.

ALTERNATIVE CONCEPTUAL APPROACHES

Considering the embryonic development of multidimensional scaling, applied researchers' differing approaches to its problems are not surprising. This is certainly true in marketing, where a number of alternative research strategies can be identified from the literature. Such differences exist in the scaling of *similarities* (more generally, "proximities") data as well as in the scaling of *preference* (or other kinds of "dominance") data.

ALTERNATIVE APPROACHES TO THE
SCALING OF SIMILARITIES DATA

An examination of the kinds of applied work going on in multidimensional scaling reveals that at least three descriptors are important in differentiating alternative conceptual approaches to the scaling of similarities data:[2]

1. Respondent task: overall similarities (or dissimilarities) responses to unspecified criteria versus ratings on prespecified constructs followed by computation of some derived measure of similarity
2. Experimenter emphasis: scaling of aggregate or group data versus methods that retain individual differences
3. Scaling method: metric versus nonmetric scaling algorithms

In the case of descriptor 1, the solicitation of *direct* judgments of overall similarity allows the respondent and the stimuli jointly to evoke the appropriate frame of reference. If prespecified attributes are used, however, the researcher usually computes a *derived* measure of similarity (or dissimilarity) for each stimulus pair across "scores" on the prespecified constructs.

Alternatively, he may use some form of factor analysis, metric or nonmetric, to obtain a stimulus-attribute space from rankings involving *two* sets of entities.[3]

---

[2]This classification is by no means exhaustive. For example, direct judgments of similarity could be obtained under tasks in which the respondent is given (a) prespecified constructs by which pairs of stimuli are to be judged for relative similarity or (b) a set of conditions (for example, buying a gift for a friend) under which similarity judgments are to be made.

[3]By "two sets of entities" we mean ordering items versus ordered items. For example, if a set of brands are ranked according to each of several attributes, the data matrix could be represented spatially by a set of points (brands) and vectors (attributes) in a common space. This configuration of points and vectors in this space could be developed so that the rank orders of projections of points onto each vector best reproduce, for a specified dimensionality, the manifest data rankings.

Thus, while it is not necessary to compute (and subsequently scale) *derived* similarity measures from ratings-type data, many researchers have adopted this approach.[4]

In the case of descriptor 2, some applied researchers use similarities data that have been aggregated or averaged across individuals as input to a multi-dimensional scaling procedure. They assume, explicitly or implicitly, that perceptions are homogeneous for members of the response group. The computer output is a *single* configuration of points representing stimuli whose distances reflect the relative similarities between the stimuli indicated in the aggregated data matrix.

Other researchers, however, are concerned with differences among individuals as well as stimuli. They keep the similarities data from different individuals intact and apply scaling techniques that provide for different points of view, in terms of the evoked dimensions, their relative importance, stimulus scale separations along dimensions, or the ordering of stimuli along the dimensions. In these instances, generally more than one perceptual map is determined from the subjects' similarities data.

As for descriptor 3, some applied researchers use metric models which assume that the similarities are measured on at least an interval scale (unique up to a linear transformation). Others prefer nonmetric algorithms which assume only that the rank order of the similarities is known.

Table 1.3 shows the resulting eightfold classification.[5] To illustrate the variety of approaches we could say that Johnson's *n*-way discriminant procedure

Table 1.3   Alternative Conceptual Approaches to the Scaling of Similarities Data

	Direct Similarity Measures		Derived Similarity Measures	
Aggregate (group) Scaling	Metric	Nonmetric	Metric	Nonmetric
Individual Differences Scaling	Metric	Nonmetric	Metric	Nonmetric

[4]This point raises the question of defining multidimensional scaling. A narrow definition would require that the input represent some measure of proximity for each stimulus pair. The broader definition adopted here is based on *output* considerations, that is, any method that could lead to multidimensional scales.

[5]As can be noted, the descriptors direct versus derived refer to task and/or preparation of the data prior to scaling. Aggregate versus disaggregate analysis refers to *both* data preprocessing and scaling model, while metric versus nonmetric refers only to scaling procedure.

[74] entails a metric scaling of aggregate data utilizing derived distance measures. Howard and Sheth [70] advocate the metric scaling of derived measures of similarity using methods that retain individual differences. Stefflre [133] and Greenberg [56] have used nonmetric approaches on directly judged similarities at the aggregate level only. The present authors [54] prefer the combined use of metric and nonmetric methods on direct judgments of similarity by methods retaining individual differences.

Direct versus Derived Similarities

The question of direct versus derived similarities is an important one in the development of a conceptual approach to the scaling of similarities judgments. The major problems associated with the use of ratings on prespecified constructs are (a) obtaining a reasonably exhaustive set of scales, (b) determining the weights to apply to each scale in obtaining a derived similarity measure, and (e) the presupposition that the subject views all scales as unidimensional.

While we shall not examine these disadvantages in detail at this point, it seems that the primary advantage of direct judgment similarity scaling is that the techniques do *not* force the respondent to confine his responses to criteria prespecified by the researcher. Indeed, direct judgment scaling can be used to determine the most salient constructs for stimulus discrimination. However, ratings judgments on prespecified constructs can be useful in *interpreting* configurations developed from direct judgments of similarity. We prefer to relegate ratings data to this latter role, rather than making them the primary basis for deriving overall similarities.

Although not included in our three-way classification, another potential descriptor considers the *form* of the dissimilarity or similarity measure, for example, Euclidean distance, city block distance, correlation or covariance measure, matching coefficient. In a sense the "weighting" of scales is part of the more general problem of choosing appropriate proximity measures. Thus, we emphasize the special case of direct versus derived measures of similarity from the standpoint of reflecting applied practice rather than from the viewpoint of conceptual generality.

Aggregate versus Disaggregate Analysis

Aggregate versus disaggregate analysis also seems to be an important conceptual issue, since it is reasonable to suppose that people *do* perceive the world in different ways. While multidimensional scaling techniques can be used on a single respondent's data, in practical cases the researcher is likely to be interested in *some* aggregation. We favor methods that are capable of retaining individual differences, but we attempt pragmatically to develop a *limited* number of points of view, or subgroup configurations.

Analyzing data at the disaggregate level has two major advantages. First, the researcher may be able to correlate individual or subgroup differences in perceptual judgments with other characteristics of the respondents, for example, personality, life style, socioeconomic, demographic, or product usage variables. Such information could be useful for market segmentation. Second, if preference data for the respondents were later analyzed, differences in preference would not be confounded with differences in perception, since the respondents would *already* be in subgroups according to homogeneity of perception. In our view these advantages usually outweigh the additional computing and analytical time associated with disaggregate levels of analysis.

Metric versus Nonmetric Algorithms

While the choice of metric or nonmetric algorithms has probably represented the most controversial issue at both the theoretical and applied levels, it seems to us the least important, because both methods may be easily used in tandem.

The greater generality of nonmetric methods must be weighed against the disadvantages of their possibly yielding locally optimal or even degenerate solutions. And metric approaches often yield solutions that are close to those found by nonmetric algorithms. Rather than choose only one of these approaches, we utilize both, primarily for comparative purposes. Again, the benefits must be weighed against the costs of additional computer and interpretive time.

Comparative Analysis

Contrasting the various conceptual approaches summarized in the eightfold classification of Table 1.3 seems a useful way to gain some perspective regarding their similarities and differences in terms of a set of real data. Hence, the framework of Table 1.3 will be followed in the analyses of dissimilarities data in Chapters 2 and 3.

ALTERNATIVE APPROACHES TO THE
SCALING OF PREFERENCE DATA

In contrast to their differences of opinion regarding the homogeneity of respondents' similarities judgments, all applied researchers recognize the tendency of preference judgments to be heterogeneous across people. (Indeed, many of the techniques which we will discuss are based on the presupposition of preference heterogeneity.) Moreover, since preferences for a specific respondent generally entail a unidimensional ordering of the stimuli, the question of direct versus derived measures of preference is not germane.

The three descriptors that appear to distinguish alternative analyses of preference data are:

1. Completeness of data: internal analysis of preferences alone versus external analysis of preferences using spaces already developed from similarities data[6]
2. Type of representation: for example, point-point models versus point-vector models
3. Scaling method: metric versus nonmetric algorithms

In the case of descriptor 1, internal approaches to the multidimensional scaling of preference data [130] attempt to develop *simultaneously* a joint space of stimuli and "person points" (or vectors) from the preference data alone. On the other hand, external approaches [19] usually utilize both similarities and preferences in constructing the joint space of stimuli and people. The person points (or vectors) are fitted into a space already obtained from a prior analysis of the similarities data.

In the case of descriptor 2, some joint-space models represent both stimuli and persons as points in a common attribute space. The person points, as in unfolding analysis [29], are assumed to be hypothetical stimuli that possess the combination of dimension levels the respondent would most prefer. Other joint-space models [127] portray persons' preferences as vector directions; the scale values of a respondent's preference function are represented by the projections of the real stimuli onto his "preferred" direction in the joint space of stimulus points and person vectors.

As for descriptor 3, the applied researcher again has a choice of metric or nonmetric approaches. As we shall show in subsequent chapters, various other generalizations of the simple (Coombsian) ideal-point and vector models also are possible.

Table 1.4   Alternative Conceptual Approaches to the Scaling of Preference Data

	Point-Point Representation		Point-Vector Representation	
Internal Analysis Scaling	Metric	Nonmetric	Metric	Nonmetric
External Analysis Scaling	Metric	Nonmetric	Metric	Nonmetric

[6]The labels "internal" versus "external" analysis of preference (or other dominance) data were first suggested by J.D. Carroll [13]. However, it should be mentioned that external analysis, as discussed by Carroll, does *not* require the prespecified space in which representations of preference are embedded to be based on similarities data. Physical or other dimensions not involving scaled judgments of similarity could be used if relevant to a particular investigation.

Table 1.4 shows the resulting eightfold classification. Again, to illustrate the variety of approaches, Slater's model [130] can be cited as an example of internal analysis of preference data using a metric approach and a point-vector representation. Kruskal and Carmone's M-D-SCAL V program [87] permits an unfolding analysis of preference data using a nonmetric approach to develop a point-point representation. Carroll and Chang's PREFMAP approach [13] utilizes both metric and nonmetric methods in the context of external analysis and provides both point-point and point-vector representations.

Internal versus External Analysis

The choice of internal versus external analysis entails the trading-off of additional data collection (under external analysis) against the additional information provided by the similarities data. In our view, external analysis is clearly preferable in most instances, if only because the analysis of preference data alone is likely to confound differences in perception with differences in preference. Moreover, external analysis permits the researcher to gather additional information, such as the salience of perceptual dimensions, in accounting for preference as one moves from a perceptual space to an evaluative space. It seems that the importance (or salience) of some dimensions may change markedly as one moves from a perception-cognition set to an evaluative one.[7]

Point-Point versus Point-Vector Representation

While the question of representing preference (or other types of dominance) judgments is an important one theoretically, in practice a hierarchy of models can be fitted, particularly if external analysis is used. Since the vector model is a special case of the ideal-point model (as will be shown in subsequent chapters), algorithms like PREFMAP permit us to see if more elaborate preference models—including generalizations of the simple ideal-point model—are justified by significantly better fits to the data. In practice, of course, we would use the simpler models if they provided reasonable descriptions of the manifest data.

Metric versus Nonmetric Algorithms

In scaling preference data it seems appropriate to apply both metric and nonmetric algorithms in order to obtain comparative information. Here, as in the context of similarities data, we feel that the controversy between metric and nonmetric applications neglects the fact that the procedures can be used in tandem.

---

[7]Another reason, more pragmatic in nature, is that current internal analysis procedures (of the nonmetric variety, particularly) are still subject to computational difficulties involving local minima and possible solution degeneracy. It is important to mention, however, that external analysis assumes that no dimensions relevant to preference are not also relevant to perception.

Comparative Analysis

We have now stated our own positions on each of the descriptors for analyzing not only similarities data but also preference data. For comparative purposes, however, analyses in subsequent chapters will cover most of the cells in the eightfold classifications of both Table 1.3 and Table 1.4. In this way the reader can reach his own conclusions regarding correspondences and divergences among alternative conceptual approaches.

ALTERNATIVE ALGORITHMS

Assuming that the researcher can settle on a conceptual approach for scaling similarities and preference data, a variety of scaling algorithms are available for implementing many of these approaches. And it goes almost without saying that computer-based algorithms are a requirement for implementing any work in multidimensional scaling.

Although we shall discuss these alternative algorithms in detail in subsequent chapters, it seems appropriate here to describe briefly why certain algorithms are employed in this study and others are not. Our selection of algorithms was based on

1. Our own familiarity and experience with the procedures
2. A feeling that the algorithms selected are representative of the major ways (currently available) to analyze similarities and preference data
3. A conviction that most of the algorithms omitted from consideration would yield results quite similar—if used for the same tasks—to the ones described here
4. Lack of relevance of some algorithms to the data collected in this study

While we have used the terms *metric* and *nonmetric* to distinguish between the basic linear or nonlinear functions under which the algorithms operate, several gradations of "metricity" are involved. These can be listed as follows:

1. Metric, analytic algorithms.[8]
2. Iterative algorithms with prespecified functional form. This function typically is of polynomial form, ranging, for example, from the first to the fourth degree (that is, Kruskal's simple scaling [87] procedure).
3. Quasi-nonmetric algorithms where monotone transformations are involved, but the criterion on any specific iteration is metric.
4. Monotone (nonmetric) algorithms without prespecified functional form.
5. Continuity methods where "smoothness" replaces the monotone criterion.

---

[8]We shall call metric factor analytic methods analytic, even though the solutions involve an iterative approach.

Continuity methods tend to preserve local monotonicity, but the programs are not based on this principle. An example is Carroll and Chang's Parametric Mapping program [126].

Table 1.5 shows the major algorithms classified for similarities and preference data separately in the above categories.[9] Some algorithms like M-D-SCAL V, PREFMAP, and INDSCAL contain alternative versions that are applicable to more than a single category. Indeed, algorithms such as TORSCA 8 and 9 and M-D-SCAL V are useful in the analysis of both similarities and preference data.

A number of algorithms used for ancillary tasks of property vector fitting, rotation of matrices to agreement, canonical decomposition, and clustering will be discussed as we work through the analyses; the characteristics of the algorithms selected for further study will be examined in detail.

The major programs excluded for study are those of Guttman and Lingoes [91], McGee [94, 95], Roskam [116], and de Leeuw [36, 37]. While we have used many of these programs in the past, space limitations and our own comparative lack of familiarity have prompted us to concentrate here on a subset of the available computer programs which we feel is nonredundant and representative of the algorithmic universe.

ADDITIONAL COMMENTS ON THE DATA BASE

As mentioned earlier, the miniature data bank used in this study consists of a variety of judgments on 15 breakfast and snack items by a group of 42 respondents, 21 Wharton MBA students and their wives. The questionnaire was self-administered separately by husband and wife. All subjects independently filled out the same questionnaire and received compensation for their efforts. The questionnaire and the basic data of each subject appear in Appendix A.

DISSIMILARITIES DATA

Each respondent provided a set of direct judgments of dissimilarity by means of n-dimensional rank order [141]. In this procedure each of the n stimuli serves, in turn, as a reference item. The remaining $n - 1$ items are then ranked strictly in terms of increasing dissimilarity to the reference item. Such tasks yield conditional proximity judgments that can be scaled immediately [87] or preprocessed [10] by triangularization [29]. The latter procedure is followed in this book. This step produces a set of 15 X 15 dissimilarities matrices, one for each respondent; these data are referred to as direct judgments of (overall) dissimilarity.

[9]In addition to the scaling procedures mentioned in Table 1.5, a number of ancillary techniques—canonical correlation, orthogonal matrix matching, linear and nonlinear regression, canonical decomposition of n-way matrices, and cluster analysis (metric and nonmetric)—are used. The relevance of each of these techniques to the problem will be discussed in subsequent chapters.

Table 1.5   Alternative Algorithms Appropriate for Various Types of Multidimensional Scaling

Similarities Data	Preference Data
Metric	Metric
Torgerson's Classical Scaling*	Principal Components Analysis*
n-way Discriminant Analysis*	Tucker's Preference Model
Carroll and Chang's INDSCAL*	Carroll and Chang's MDPREF*
Tucker's 3-mode Factor Analysis	Carroll and Chang's PREFMAP*
	Schonemann's Metric Unfolding Analysis
Iterative, Prespecified Functional Form	Bechtel, Tucker, and Chang's Preference
Kruskal's M-D-SCAL V Simple Scaling*	Model
Quasi-nonmetric	Iterative, Prespecified Functional Form
Young and Torgerson's TORSCA 8	Carroll's Polynomial Factor Analysis
(first stage)*	M-D-SCAL V Simple Scaling*
TORSCA 9 (first stage)	
NINDSCAL	Quasi-nonmetric
	TORSCA 8 (first stage)*
Monotone Methods	TORSCA 9 (first stage)
TORSCA 8 (second stage)*	
TORSCA 9 (second stage)	Monotone Methods
M-D-SCAL V*	Shepard-Kruskal Nonmetric Factor
McGee's EMD, CEMD-DEMD programs	Analysis
Roskam's MINI programs	TORSCA 8 and 9 (second stage)
De Leeuw's NMSPOM program	M-D-SCAL V*
Guttman and Lingoes' SSA series	PREFMAP*
	Guttman and Lingoes' SSAR series
Continuity Methods	MINI programs
Carroll and Chang's Parametric Mapping*	
	Continuity Methods
	Parametric Mapping*

*Used in this study, but are not exhaustive of the various algorithms employed here.

RATINGS DATA

Each respondent rated the 15 food items on 10 bipolar scales, according to a 7-point equal-interval scale. In this case *derived* dissimilarities were obtained by computing Euclidean distances for each pair of stimuli in ratings "space." Again, a separate 15 X 15 dissimilarities matrix was obtained for each respondent; these data are referred to as *derived* judgments of dissimilarity.

In addition, and in accord with our earlier comments, the rating scales also were assumed to be (unidimensional) property vectors that could be fitted into a multidimensional space obtained by scaling either the whole set of derived dissimilarities or the direct dissimilarities obtained by means of the *n*-dimensional rank-order step.

PREFERENCE DATA

Each respondent was asked for his or her overall (strict) preference ranking of the 15 food items. In addition, preference rankings were obtained from each respondent for five occasion/menu scenarios. Thus, a 6×15 matrix of rank-order preference data for each subject was available for analysis.

BACKGROUND DATA

As shown in Table 1.2, each respondent was asked to report a small amount of background data; and each respondent was coded according to marriage partner. Given the nature of the sample, the respondents would be expected to be rather homogeneous in age and cultural background; hence, no claim is made for the generality of the results of this study to nonstudent populations.

FORMAT OF SUBSEQUENT CHAPTERS

In the following chapters we try to adhere to the eightfold classifications of Tables 1.3 and 1.4. Not all combinations are explored, but enough conceptual alternatives are covered to give the reader some idea of their similarities and differences. In each chapter devoted to data analysis a standard format is followed. First, the appropriate part of the data base and the scaling objectives are described. Then the approaches and algorithms adopted are discussed at a conceptual level, and a flow diagram of the analysis is supplied. The methodological results and substantive implications are reported. Appropriate computer program descriptions and additional computer input and output appear in Appendixes B and C.

Chapters 2 and 3 deal with the analysis of dissimilarities data. In Chapter 2 we emphasize aggregate, or group, analysis and examine both direct and derived dissimilarities judgments by metric and nonmetric approaches. Congruence tests are then made within and across each class of solution. In Chapter 3 we emphasize the scaling of disaggregate data, again according to direct and derived dissimilarities. In addition, a variety of property-fitting procedures utilizing the rating scales as "outside" vectors are illustrated as approaches to dimension interpretation. We also present analyses of the relationships between individual differences in dissimilarities judgments and respondent background data. Finally, the similarities data are partitioned, using a clustering procedure, into homogeneous perceptual segments.

Chapters 4 and 5 are concerned with the analysis of preference data. Chapter 4 emphasizes the internal analysis of overall preferences. Both point-point and point-vector models are utilized, and both metric and nonmetric algorithms are employed. The derived stimulus configurations are then compared to the group stimulus space obtained in the individual differences analysis of Chapter 3, and differences in preference are related to respondent background data.

Chapter 5 is primarily concerned with external analyses of the preference data, again by metric and nonmetric point-point and point-vector models. Both overall and scenario-dependent preferences are analyzed by type of perceptual-preference segment.

Chapter 6 presents a summary of findings and considers the implications for future research in alternative conceptual and algorithmic approaches to the scaling of similarities and preference data. In addition, a number of substantive problem areas—market segmentation, new product concept testing, evaluation of persuasive communications, and so on—are discussed as possible application areas for multidimensional scaling methods.

Listings of the basic data, computer program descriptions, and supplementary computer outputs are presented in Appendixes A, B, and C. These key in with the text to provide the reader with sufficient material to replicate the results of this study as he learns how to use the programs and checks out their characteristics on his own computer hardware. Basic references, referred to by number in the text, follow the Appendixes.

CONCLUDING COMMENTS ON SCALING ANALYSIS

We have already indicated that our analyses of the miniature data bank do not utilize all the computer algorithms available for multidimensional scaling. Additional limitations of a more general nature should also be stated at this point.

First, we have not attempted an exhaustive substantive analysis of the data bank used in this study. We have limited most of our discussion to two- and sometimes three-dimensional solutions. While we do use algorithms that retain individual differences, we usually avoid subsequent scalings at the individual-respondent level. And we have omitted a variety of internal analyses that could be made of combined dissimilarities and preference data. Also, in scaling scenario-dependent preferences we have elected to work largely at the average-subject level in order to conserve space.

Second, we have not tried to provide extensive discussions of the theoretical bases of the algorithms employed. Overviews appear in Appendix B and elsewhere [48]. More detailed descriptions can be found in the original papers referred to in this book.

Third, our selection of control parameters, for example, number of iterations, goodness-of-fit cutoff values, has been somewhat arbitrary. However, we have tried to be consistent in parameter value selection when several programs are used for more or less the same purposes.

In short, our purpose has been to contrast a variety of approaches and algorithms that are *illustrative* of how a set of dissimilarities and preferences can be analyzed, without claiming superiority for our strategy. We feel that most of the major ways of analyzing these data have been covered, though in less detail than would suit analysts who are highly experienced in the application of this methodology.

SUMMARY

In this introductory chapter we have given an overview and stated our objectives and rationale for the comparative analysis of alternative conceptual approaches and algorithms to the multidimensional scaling of similarities and preference data. In this regard two classification schemes were presented to illustrate alternative approaches. In subsequent chapters a variety of approaches and algorithms will be applied to a common data bank using the frameworks established here.

The miniature data bank to be utilized was also described briefly. We concluded with a description of material to be covered in depth in the following chapters.

CHAPTER 2

AGGREGATE-LEVEL ANALYSIS OF DISSIMILARITIES DATA

In this chapter we focus on scaling the dissimilarities data obtained from the 42 subjects who supplied the miniature data bank used throughout this study. In this chapter all analyses are performed at the aggregate, or group, level.

As noted in Chapter 1, the basic data covering dissimilarity judgments (see questionnaire in Appendix A) consisted of each respondent's

1. Conditional rank orders of the remaining stimuli from each of the 15 food items serving, in turn, as the reference item[1]
2. Set of integer-valued ratings (on a 7-point equal-interval scale) for each of the 15 food items on each of 10 bipolar scales

Thus, the basic three-way data matrices were of the order 42 × 15 × 15 and 42 × 15 × 10, respectively. Table 1.1 lists the 15 stimuli (food items) and the 10 bipolar scales used in the questionnaire.

OUTLINE OF THE ANALYSIS

The approaches considered in the treatment of aggregate dissimilarities data are:

1. An analysis of direct measures of dissimilarity by
   a. Metric algorithms
   b. Nonmetric algorithms
2. An analysis of derived measures of dissimilarity by
   a. Metric algorithms
   b. Nonmetric algorithms

PREPROCESSING STEPS

Since both the conditional rank-order and the ratings data[2] required preprocessing to develop a complete[3] order of dissimilarities, we describe these procedures first. We discuss the preprocessing steps in the more general context of comparing alternative methods for collecting similarities data. The TRICON program [10] was used to preprocess the conditional rank-order data, yielding a symmetric matrix of dissimilarities for each subject. The entries of these 42 respondent matrices were then averaged cell by cell to obtain the 15 × 15 *group* matrix of direct dissimilarities.

In the case of the ratings data a derived measure of dissimilarity—squared Euclidean distance—was computed in ratings "space" for each respondent separately, after each of his ratings across stimuli had been standardized to

---

[1]In the preprocessing of these data, self-similarities received rank 1, thus providing a 15 × 15 matrix of ranks.

[2]The bipolar scales themselves were developed by means of a repertory grid [76] procedure on an independent sample of subjects. The 10 scales used here were drawn from an original set of 22, as obtained from the repertory grid technique.

[3]It should be mentioned that it is possible to scale the conditional rank-order data directly, e.g., by Kruskal's M-D-SCAL V program [87]. However, we elected to "triangularize" the data first. (For a synthetic data analysis comparing the two approaches, see [52].)

zero mean and unit standard deviation.[4] This was accomplished by the DISTAN program. The 42 15 × 15 matrices, whose entries are squared distances, were then averaged cell by cell and finally the square root of each averaged entry was computed. The result, again, was a 15 × 15 *group* matrix of derived dissimilarities.

SCALING THE DIRECT MEASURES OF DISSIMILARITY

The 15 × 15 matrix of direct measures of dissimilarity (as originally obtained on an individual level from the TRICON program) was scaled at the group level using four multidimensional scaling algorithms:

1. Metric method: a "classical" analysis [138] of dissimilarities converted to scalar products using the first iteration (that is, a principal components analysis) of the TORSCA 8 [163] program[5]
2. Prespecified function method: a "simple scaling" analysis [87] using an iterative procedure that incorporates a linear model
3. Monotone method: TORSCA 8 [163] program[6]
4. Continuity method: Parametric Mapping [126]

In each case solutions were sought in three and two dimensions.

As a check on the adequacy of low-dimensional solutions (for example, two dimensions) to approximate the original dissimilarity relationships, the same 15 × 15 input matrix was submitted to Johnson's hierarchical clustering program [75]. Selected cluster contours (for Johnson's "diameter" option) were then embedded, illustratively, in the TORSCA monotone two-space solution. Since the clustering procedure is dimension-free, it provided a rough visual check on the adequacy of the low-dimensional solutions.

SCALING THE DERIVED MEASURES OF DISSIMILARITY

Each of the preceding steps, including the clustering analysis, also was performed on the 15 × 15 group matrix of dissimilarities as derived from the

---

[4]While equalizing the scales to zero mean does not affect the squared distances, standardization to unit variance has the effect of placing all ratings scales on a common basis as normalized variates.

[5]We are using the terms *classical* or *metric* advisedly, since the principal components part of the TORSCA program (used to compute a starting configuration) does *not* estimate an additive constant to "convert" dissimilarities to distances, converting these to scalar products, and factor analyzing the scalar products matrix.

[6]Actually both the quasi-nonmetric (first stage) and nonmetric (second stage) features were used in tandem. Since the first-stage procedure was employed only for refinement of the starting configuration, obtained from the metric (principal components) analysis, the combined effect is monotone.

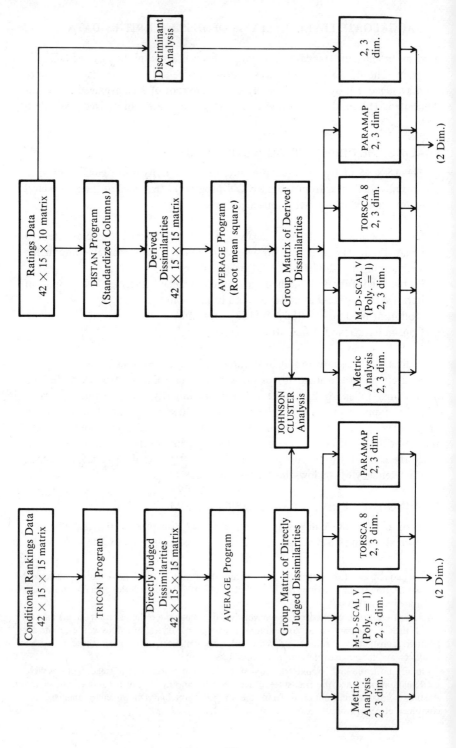

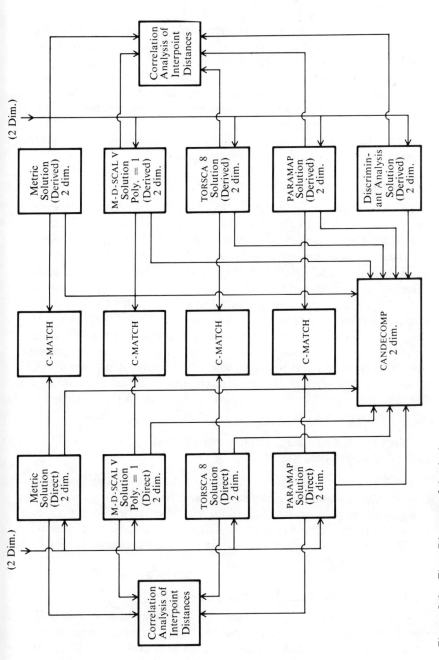

Figure 2.1   Flow Diagram of Analysis

21

ratings data. Again, scaling solutions were sought in three and two dimensions and selected cluster contours, found from a clustering of stimuli based on the derived measures, were embedded in the TORSCA monotone two-space solution. In short, a full replication of the preceding analysis was performed.

In addition, the original ratings data were analyzed in group standardized form by a (metric) linear discriminant analysis [74]. In this procedure each food item was treated as a group, and the 10 bipolar scales served as "predictor" variables. The axes of this reduced space were the discriminant functions that maximize among-groups to within-groups variance.

COMPARING THE CONFIGURATIONS

Each pair of scaling configurations (based on direct versus derived measures) was compared—illustratively for the two-space solutions—by means of C-MATCH, Cliff's orthogonal matching approach [22]. In this case the configurations were constrained to be related by a similarity transform, that is, translation of origin, rotation, reflection, and central dilation (a uniform stretching or contraction of the axes).

In addition, all nine scaling configurations (including that obtained from the 15-group discriminant analysis) were submitted to a CANDECOMP analysis [15] after having been orthogonally rotated to maximal congruence with a target matrix (the metric solution applied to direct dissimilarities). This procedure enabled us to develop a synthesized "master" configuration and set of weights which show how each of the separate configurations (and a set of original dimensions) is related to the synthesized configuration. A flow diagram of the full analysis appears in Figure 2.1.

ALTERNATIVE DATA COLLECTION PROCEDURES AND PREPROCESSING STEPS

To obtain direct and derived dissimilarities data for the data bank we used two procedures, respectively, the method of n-dimensional rank order [141] and ratings judgments on prespecified constructs. Since a large variety of other procedures for collecting dissimilarities data also are available to the researcher, it will be helpful to consider their nature before we discuss the preprocessing steps employed in the study.

ALTERNATIVE DATA COLLECTION METHODS

Inasmuch as distance-type models are typically used as the primary representation of dissimilarities data, the basic unit of input data is the tetrad, or pair-by-pair comparison such as stimulus pair AB versus stimulus pair CD. After the possible estimation of an additive constant, metric methods assume that the input data are ratio-scaled distances possibly subject to error. Nonmetric methods of the type used here assume only that the various dissimilarities can be at least partially ordered. With n stimuli there exist $1/2\, n\, (n-1)$ distinct pairs. The number of implied tetradic comparisons is given by the expression $1/8\, (n)\, (n+1)\, (n-1)\, (n-2)$. Of these comparisons, $1/2\, (n)\, (n-1)\, (n-2)$ represent conjoint tetrads, each pair of pairs having a stimulus in common; and $1/8\, (n)\, (n-1)\, (n-2)\, (n-3)$ represent disjoint tetrads, having no stimuli in common.

Disjoint and Conjoint Tetrads

Tetradic data may be obtained using (a) rank order of pairs, (b) direct comparisons of pairs of pairs, (c) magnitude estimation, and (d) subjective grouping. Since more comparisons (disjoint as well as conjoint tetrads) are involved, these data collection procedures generally require more effort on the part of the respondent than conditional-ordering methods. However, they yield more information directly, since comparative judgments can be obtained for all distinct tetrads. Magnitude estimation, in particular, is quite useful because the respondent is asked only to estimate the degree of similarity of each stimulus pair on, say, a 9-point scale ranging from "almost identical" to "extremely dissimilar." Only the rank order of these dissimilarities is needed for nonmetric procedures.

Conjoint Tetrads

Conjoint data collection methods [29] entail fewer judgments by the respondent, but result in a partial rather than a complete ordering of the dissimilarities. Possible methods for use are (a) n-dimensional rank order, (b) triads [141], (c) picking k out of $n-1$ items that are most similar to the reference item, (d) ordering k out of $n-1$ items in terms of relative similarity to the reference item. However, the procedure to be used entails a subsequent decision regarding

1. Scaling the conditional proximities directly, or
2. "Upgrading" the data by procedures like triangularization [29].

In this study we have employed the conjoint data collection technique of n-dimensional rank order, followed by conversion of the data (via triangularization) to yield a complete (but weak) rank order.

Our choice of the conjoint data collection approach was based on the comparatively large number of stimuli involved—15 food items. A disjoint data collection procedure would have entailed 5460 implicit comparisons versus the 1365 comparisons implied by the n-dimensional ranking procedure.

By triangularizing the directly obtained partial order we upgrade the quality of the data by assuming that transitivity holds over all inferred disjoint comparisons, none of which is given directly by the respondent. This is the price paid to obtain a complete (but not necessarily unique) order of pairs—hence, more monotone constraints—for entry into the multidimensional scaling programs.

Profile Data

In the ratings data of this study, a dissimilarity measure for each pair of food items was computed in ratings "space" by treating the ratings of each food item as profile data. This approach enabled us to develop a derived measure in tetradic form (both conjoint and disjoint comparisons) and a complete rather than partial order.

It should also be mentioned that the results of many methods that lead to direct conjoint measures (for example, picking k out of $n-1$ for each of the n reference items) can also be treated as profiles in developing a kind of "second-order" measure of dissimilarity, similar in computation to that described in the preceding paragraph. In this case, the set of "final" dissimilarities would again be a complete order.

PREPROCESSING THE CONDITIONAL RANK-ORDER DATA

The program used in this study to convert the conditional rank-order data (obtained from the n-dimensional ranking procedure) was TRICON [10], which is described more fully in Appendix B. Essentially, the program takes conditional rank-orders as input data and embeds them in a complete but not necessarily unique order. In general, the complete order will be a weak order (that is, it will contain ties). The output of the program consists of a half-matrix (or vector of stimulus pairs in standard order) of dissimilarities.

The program uses Coombs' triangularization procedure [29] and includes the following steps:

1. Conditional rank orders are transformed to matrices of order $1/2\, n\, (n-1) \times 1/2\, n\, (n-1)$, in which each pair is compared to every other pair.
2. All original conjoint comparisons are represented by a series of 1s and 0s. That is, if row pair is more dissimilar than column pair, a 1 is placed in the i, jth cell and, correspondingly, a 0 is placed in the j, ith cell.
3. The rows and columns of pairs are permuted to place row sums in decreasing order.
4. In the case of tied blocks of rows, an exhaustive within-block search is made to find the permutation of rows that minimizes the number of 1s appearing below the diagonal of the matrix of permuted rows and columns.
5. The positions of 1s appearing below the diagonal (representing intransitivities) are then noted, and the number and locations of such intransitivities are printed.
6. Intransitivities are removed by one of two procedures.

7. If desired, the resulting (transitive and triangular) matrix can then be powered to find all rth order disjoint comparisons (assuming that transitivity holds over all derived inequalities).

In analyses of synthetic data we have found excellent recoveries [52] using the TRICON procedure, even in the presence of moderate amounts of noise. Although the complete order resulting from this application generally was not unique, in practice it was quite close to the original (complete) rank order.

For the 15 food items, the TRICON program was applied to each of the 42 15 × 15 matrices of conditional rank orders. The results of this preprocessing step, shown illustratively as half-matrices of dissimilarities for the first three respondents, appear in Appendix Table C.1. A tabulation of the frequency of intransitivities appears in Table 2.1.

Table 2.1   Frequency of Intransitivities from the TRICON Program

Class Interval	Frequency
≤ 50 intransitivities	3
51-100	11
101-150	21
151-200	6
≥ 201	1
Total	42

Out of 1365 implied comparisons, the smallest number of observed intransitivities was 29, and the largest was 239. In general, the incidence of intransitivities did not exceed 10 percent, as can be noted from Table 2.1. Although not shown here, neither did we find that the incidence of intransitivities was associated with the respondent's sex.

The next step in the analysis was to average the half-matrices on a cell-by-cell basis. The averaged direct dissimilarities (shown in Table 2.2) constitute the first set of primary input data for this chapter.

PREPROCESSING THE DERIVED DISSIMILARITIES DATA

Preprocessing of the ratings data proceeded in an analogous manner. First, each subject's individual 15 × 10 ratings matrix was standardized by columns to zero mean and unit standard deviation. Next, squared Euclidean distances were computed for each stimulus pair in the (standardized) ratings space. This step resulted in 42 15 × 15 squared distance matrices. (Table C.2 presents these data for the first three respondents.)

As a final step, the squared distance matrices were averaged cell by cell across the 42 subjects and square roots were taken of each cell value, following a suggestion made by Horan [66]. The averaged derived dissimilarities data (shown in Table 2.3) represent the second set of primary input data for this chapter.

SCALING THE DIRECT DISSIMILARITIES

We now focus on the direct dissimilarities data of Table 2.2. This input matrix was scaled in three and two dimensions by the following:

Table 2.2   Input Matrix of Direct Dissimilarities from the TRICON Program

	Stimulus*						
	1	2	3	4	5	6	7
1	0.0	59.130	62.420	43.640	36.010	60.210	78.010
2	59.130	0.0	30.790	83.890	44.150	60.940	27.020
3	62.420	30.790	0.0	82.370	57.760	23.800	26.850
4	43.640	83.890	82.370	0.0	65.460	53.330	93.710
5	36.010	44.150	57.760	65.460	0.0	64.110	72.920
6	60.210	60.940	23.800	53.330	64.110	0.0	50.490
7	78.010	27.020	26.850	93.710	72.920	50.490	0.0
8	34.570	36.360	52.440	55.350	32.870	59.690	64.230
9	32.100	32.290	50.180	49.110	36.290	55.830	61.550
10	61.520	8.490	25.290	85.640	48.960	58.730	31.520
11	51.260	78.350	72.210	32.680	21.650	47.420	78.210
12	46.650	84.550	76.140	21.400	49.300	46.980	83.700
13	55.170	83.820	78.070	7.830	55.700	55.000	88.850
14	53.670	83.010	70.680	30.560	49.870	47.080	78.130
15	72.170	48.130	21.870	73.620	62.490	15.250	33.370

	Stimulus*						
	8	9	10	11	12	13	14	15
1	34.570	32.100	61.520	51.260	46.650	55.170	53.670	72.170
2	36.360	32.290	8.490	78.350	84.550	83.820	83.010	48.130
3	52.440	50.180	25.290	72.210	76.140	78.070	70.680	21.870
4	55.350	49.110	85.640	32.680	21.400	7.830	30.560	73.620
5	32.870	36.290	48.960	21.650	49.300	55.700	49.870	62.490
6	59.690	55.830	58.730	47.420	46.980	55.000	47.080	15.250
7	64.230	61.550	31.520	78.210	83.700	88.850	78.130	33.370
8	0.0	5.520	37.940	64.230	59.800	60.380	63.770	63.520
9	5.520	0.0	38.320	61.300	57.480	65.850	65.560	64.490
10	37.940	38.320	0.0	80.140	86.420	83.860	84.240	52.930
11	64.230	61.300	80.140	0.0	20.310	23.330	23.100	58.260
12	59.800	57.480	86.420	20.310	0.0	20.540	10.700	62.460
13	60.380	65.850	83.860	23.330	20.540	0.0	24.760	66.770
14	63.770	65.560	84.240	23.100	10.700	24.760	0.0	54.170
15	63.520	64.490	52.930	58.260	62.460	66.770	54.170	0.0

*See Table 1.1 for stimulus identification.

Table 2.3   Input Matrix of Derived Dissimilarities from the Ratings Data

	Stimulus*						
	1	2	3	4	5	6	7
1	0.0	1.710	1.590	1.560	1.540	1.650	1.850
2	1.710	0.0	1.060	1.680	1.230	1.520	1.180
3	1.590	1.060	0.0	1.460	1.160	1.140	1.250
4	1.560	1.680	1.460	0.0	1.470	1.420	1.860
5	1.540	1.230	1.160	1.470	0.0	1.260	1.540
6	1.650	1.520	1.140	1.420	1.260	0.0	1.510
7	1.850	1.180	1.250	1.860	1.540	1.510	0.0
8	1.530	0.970	1.120	1.450	1.090	1.360	1.330
9	1.520	1.060	1.140	1.330	1.090	1.310	1.460
10	1.680	0.780	1.110	1.740	1.270	1.550	1.250
11	1.540	1.690	1.460	1.200	1.410	1.360	1.660
12	1.830	2.040	1.680	1.320	1.730	1.460	1.970
13	1.490	1.730	1.470	0.990	1.450	1.390	1.780
14	1.780	1.890	1.540	1.460	1.600	1.390	1.770
15	1.640	1.290	1.040	1.560	1.270	1.100	1.230

	Stimulus*						
	8	9	10	11	12	13	14	15
1	1.530	1.520	1.680	1.540	1.830	1.490	1.780	1.640
2	0.970	1.060	0.780	1.690	2.040	1.730	1.890	1.290
3	1.120	1.140	1.110	1.460	1.680	1.470	1.540	1.040
4	1.450	1.330	1.740	1.200	1.320	0.990	1.460	1.560
5	1.090	1.090	1.270	1.410	1.730	1.450	1.600	1.270
6	1.360	1.310	1.550	1.360	1.460	1.390	1.390	1.100
7	1.330	1.460	1.250	1.660	1.970	1.780	1.770	1.230
8	0.0	0.770	1.020	1.480	1.810	1.550	1.670	1.280
9	0.770	0.0	1.170	1.430	1.750	1.470	1.660	1.270
10	1.020	1.170	0.0	1.760	2.080	1.750	1.910	1.350
11	1.480	1.430	1.760	0.0	1.110	1.020	1.160	1.390
12	1.810	1.750	2.080	1.110	0.0	1.110	1.010	1.610
13	1.550	1.470	1.750	1.020	1.110	0.0	1.220	1.440
14	1.670	1.660	1.910	1.160	1.010	1.220	0.0	1.410
15	1.280	1.270	1.350	1.390	1.610	1.440	1.410	0.0

*See Table 1.1 for stimulus identification.

1. The metric or "classical" analysis in which the data of Table 2.2 were first converted to scalar products[7]
2. Kruskal's simple scaling procedure, using a linear model applied directly to the data of Table 2.2

[7]It should also be mentioned that the classical Torgerson procedure [141] is a two-stage method. The purpose of the first stage is to convert a matrix of $_iP_{jk}$ (proportion of times $d_{ij} > d_{ik}$) to unit normal deviates, and then to scale the resulting deviates $_iZ_{jk}$ by Thurstone's comparative judgment method.

3. A monotone analysis of the data of Table 2.2, using the first and second stages of the TORSCA 8 program

4. A Parametric Mapping analysis of the data of Table 2.2

These procedures can be viewed as making successively weaker assumptions about the nature of the data relations. As an additional step, the data of Table 2.2 were cluster analyzed by Johnson's nonmetric procedure [75].

METRIC ANALYSIS

The metric analysis of direct dissimilarities data indicated that the first two components accounted for 81.4 percent of the variance and the first three components for 90.2 percent. In all, eight nonzero eigenvalues were obtained.[8]

Figure 2.2 shows the two-space stimulus configuration, and Figure 2.3 the accompanying Shepard diagram of dissimilarities versus distances.[9] Two-space and three-space coordinate values and the Shepard diagram accompanying the three-space solution appear, respectively, in Table C.3 and Figure C.1.

The configuration of Figure 2.2 is oriented arbitrarily in terms of principal components. With this caveat in mind, notice that sweet items like jelly donut, cinnamon bun, and glazed donut appear on the left side of the horizontal axis, while nonsweet items like buttered toast, toast and margarine, and hard rolls and butter appear on the right side. We also note clusters of items, for example, toast pop-up with cinnamon toast; toast and marmalade with buttered toast and jelly.

The metric analysis indicates that, in terms of accounted-for variance, a two- or possibly three-dimensional solution appears adequate to portray the relationships in the group data. From the Shepard diagram of Figure 2.3 we see that the scatter around the fitted linear function is low, which suggests that the metric solution may be close to the still-to-be computed nonmetric solutions.[10]

SIMPLE SCALING ANALYSIS

Kruskal's M-D-SCAL V program was next applied as a means of "simple scaling" [87], in which a linear function was employed in the fitting process.

---

[8]The program used for the metric analysis involved a single iteration of the first-stage portion of the TORSCA 8 program. As previously indicated, in this phase of the program the (metric) scaling does *not* involve estimation of an additive constant. That is, the dissimilarities are treated as ratio-scaled distances.

[9]A Shepard diagram (a term coined by Guttman) is a scatter plot of input data (e.g., dissimilarities) versus (a) distances computed by the algorithm and/or (b) best fitting "distances," that is, the numbers closest to the computed distances that are monotone with the input data. In some plotting routines both (a) and (b) appear on the same diagram and are represented by different plotting symbols. Here, only the computed distances appear.

[10]Of course, in other applications the Shepard diagram may not be found to contain a strong linear component. In these cases [156] the metric and nonmetric scaling solutions may not agree well.

Again, solutions were sought in three and two dimensions. The three-dimensional solution from the foregoing metric analysis was used as a "rational" starting configuration with this program, which was set for a maximum of 50 iterations.

A minimum stress of 0.101 (stress formula 2 [87]) was reached at the end of 26 iterations for the three-dimensional solution, and a minimum stress of 0.162 was found at the end of 16 iterations for the two-dimensional solution. The latter configuration is plotted in Figure 2.4, and its associated Shepard diagram appears in Figure 2.5. Supporting information is in Table C.4 and Figure C.2 of Appendix C.

Given that the starting configuration was obtained from the metric analysis and a linear version of simple scaling was used, it is not surprising that the two-dimensional solution of Figure 2.4 is very similar to that of Figure 2.2.

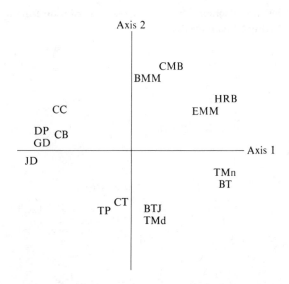

Figure 2.2   Two-space Configuration from Metric Scaling of Direct Dissimilarities

Key

TP	Toast pop-up		BTJ	Buttered toast and jelly
BT	Buttered toast		TMn	Toast and margarine
EMM	English muffin and margarine		CB	Cinnamon bun
JD	Jelly donut		DP	Danish pastry
CT	Cinnamon toast		GD	Glazed donut
BMM	Blueberry muffin and margarine		CC	Coffee cake
HRB	Hard rolls and butter		CMB	Corn muffin and butter
TMd	Toast and marmalade			

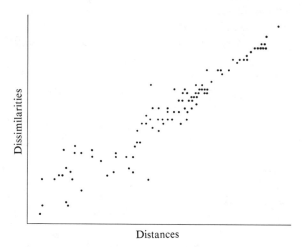

Figure 2.3   Shepard Diagram Based on Two-space Solution from Metric Scaling of Direct Dissimilarities

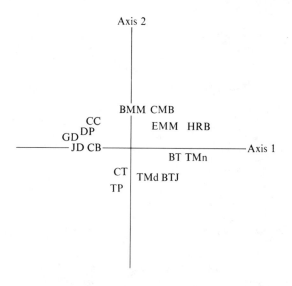

Figure 2.4   Two-space Configuration from M-D-SCAL V Analysis of Direct Dissimilarities (See Figure 2.2 for key.)

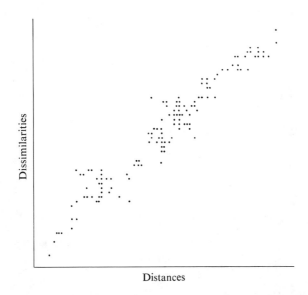

**Figure 2.5   Shepard Diagram Based on Two-space Solution from M-D-SCAL V
Analysis of Direct Dissimilarities**

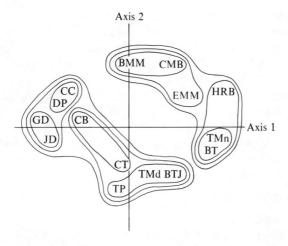

**Figure 2.6   Two-space Configuration from TORSCA 8 Analysis of Direct
Dissimilarities (See Figure 2.2 for key.)**

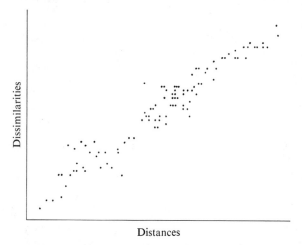

Figure 2.7   Shepard Diagram Based on Two-space Solution from TORSCA 8 Analysis of Direct Dissimilarities

NONMETRIC ANALYSIS

Young and Torgerson's TORSCA 8 program was next applied to the input data of Table 2.2. In this run the algorithm was set for 25 first-stage and 25 second-stage iterations, again using metric solutions in the three space and two space, respectively, as starting configurations.[11]

A minimum stress of 0.045 (stress formula 1 [84]) was reached at the end of 4 first-stage iterations and 25 second-stage iterations in three dimensions. A stress value of 0.079 was found at the end of 4 first-stage iterations and 23 second-stage iterations in two dimensions. The two-dimensional configuration is shown in Figure 2.6, and the associated Shepard diagram in Figure 2.7. Supporting information is in Table C.5 and Figure C.3.

Casual observation of Figure 2.6 again shows how similar the configuration is to the preceding ones. Not surprisingly, the strong linear component of the monotone function of Figure 2.7 affirms the fact that all three solutions, thus far, are quite close to each other.

PARAMETRIC MAPPING ANALYSIS

The last scaling algorithm used in this series was Carroll and Chang's Parametric Mapping or PARAMAP program. In this algorithm the "smoothness" of the function relating recovered distances to input data replaces the monotonicity criterion of the second-stage of the TORSCA program. While

---

[11]The TORSCA 8 program automatically computes its starting configuration (using principal components) regardless of whether stage one or stage two is employed. As stated earlier, stage one of the program is quasi-nonmetric but stage two is nonmetric. As such, the combined use of stages one and two is viewed as nonmetric in this book.

Parametric Mapping tends to preserve at least local monotonicity, it is not based on the monotonicity principle.

The same type of rational starting configuration used previously was employed here, and the program was set for a maximum of 50 iterations. The badness-of-fit measure in Parametric Mapping is Carroll's kappa value, whose minimum achievable value is unity.

Kappa values of 1.055 and 1.050 were obtained for three and two dimensions, respectively. (Apparently no solution improvement resulted in going from two to three dimensions.) In both cases the program utilized all 50 iterations.

Figures 2.8 and 2.9 show the two-dimensional configuration and Shepard diagram, respectively. (Supporting detail appears in Table C.6 and Figure C.4.) Again we note a configuration quite close to those obtained previously. Thus, the metric, iterative-linear, monotone, and smoothness (continuity) approaches *all* appear to yield quite similar configurations in this case.

NONMETRIC CLUSTER ANALYSIS

As a supplementary step, the input data of Table 2.2 were submitted to Johnson's nonmetric clustering program. This algorithm develops dimension-free hierarchies by the methods of single linkage ("connectedness option") or complete linkage ("diameter option"). In this problem the program was employed to determine how well the low-dimensional scaling solutions preserved the original relationships in the input data.

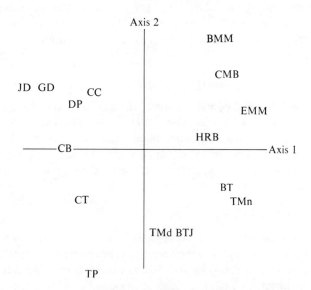

Figure 2.8   Two-space Configuration from Parametric Mapping of Direct Dissimilarities (See Figure 2.2 for key.)

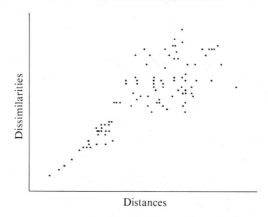

Figure 2.9   Shepard Diagram Based on Two-space Solution from Parametric Mapping of Direct Dissimilarities

Figure 2.10 shows the resulting hierarchies for both the connectedness and diameter options. Despite some disparaties in cluster composition, the diameter option generally leads to more compact clusters.

We now can plot selected cluster contours obtained from the hierarchical grouping program in the reduced space solutions in order to see how much violence has been done to the original relationships by dimensional compression via the scaling algorithms. This is done, illustratively, for the TORSCA 8 monotone solution (Figure 2.6) using the cluster composition found by the diameter option. We see that the contours plot quite regularly in two space, suggesting that two dimensions summarize much of the information in the input data.

CONFIGURATION INTERPRETATION

As Figures 2.2, 2.4, 2.6, and 2.8 show, the configurations obtained from all four algorithms are quite similar. Our tentative interpretation of the horizontal axis as a type of "sweetness" or "caloricness" dimension appears to be borne out in all configurations. The vertical axis appears more difficult to interpret, but we can view it tentatively as a type of "toast/nontoast" axis as based on the extent of required preparation.[12]

RATINGS DATA SCALING

As discussed earlier, derived dissimilarities obtained from the $42 \times 15 \times 10$ three-way matrix of ratings data were scaled at the group level by the procedures used in the previous section. Table 2.3 shows the root mean squared distances derived from the ratings data.

[12] In Chapter 3 we shall review this tentative interpretation by means of property fitting procedures and an INDSCAL analysis of individuals' data.

Connectedness Method

```
Grouping                        Stimulus Number
 Value      5  4 13 11 12 14  1  8  9  7  2 10  3  6 15
 5.52       •  •  •  •  •  •  •  X X X  •  •  •  •  •  •
 7.83       •  X X X  •  •  •  •  X X X  •  •  •  •  •  •
 8.49       •  X X X  •  •  •  •  X X X  •  X X X  •  •  •
10.70       •  X X X  •  X X X  •  X X X  •  X X X  •  •  •
15.25       •  X X X  •  X X X  •  X X X  •  X X X  •  X X X
20.31       •  X X X  X X X X X  •  X X X  •  X X X  •  X X X
20.54       •  X X X X X X X X X  •  X X X  •  X X X  •  X X X
21.65     X X X X X X X X X X X  •  X X X  •  X X X  •  X X X
21.87     X X X X X X X X X X X  •  X X X  •  X X X  X X X X X
25.29     X X X X X X X X X X X  •  X X X  •  X X X X X X X X X
26.85     X X X X X X X X X X X  •  X X X  X X X X X X X X X X
32.10     X X X X X X X X X X X  X X X X X  X X X X X X X X X X
32.29     X X X X X X X X X X X  X X X X X X X X X X X X X X X X
32.87     X X X X X X X X X X X X X X X X X X X X X X X X X X X X
```

Diameter Method

```
Grouping                        Stimulus Number
 Value      1  8  9  5 11  4 13 12 14  7  2 10  3  6 15
 5.52       •  X X X  •  •  •  •  •  •  •  •  •  •  •  •
 7.83       •  X X X  •  •  X X X  •  •  •  •  •  •  •  •
 8.49       •  X X X  •  •  X X X  •  •  •  X X X  •  •  •
10.70       •  X X X  •  •  X X X  X X X  •  X X X  •  •  •
15.25       •  X X X  •  •  X X X  •  X X X  •  X X X  •  X X X
21.65       •  X X X  X X X  X X X  X X X  •  X X X  •  X X X
23.80       •  X X X  X X X  X X X  X X X  •  X X X  X X X X X
30.56       •  X X X  X X X  X X X X X X X  •  X X X  X X X X X
31.52       •  X X X  X X X  X X X X X X X  X X X X X  X X X X X
34.57     X X X X X  X X X  X X X X X X X  X X X X X  X X X X X
60.94     X X X X X  X X X  X X X X X X X  X X X X X X X X X X
64.23     X X X X X X X X X  X X X X X X X  X X X X X X X X X X
65.85     X X X X X X X X X X X X X X X X X  X X X X X X X X X X
93.71     X X X X X X X X X X X X X X X X X X X X X X X X X X X X
```

Figure 2.10   Tree Diagrams, by Method, from Hierarchical Grouping Algorithm of Direct Dissimilarities

In addition, after standardization of the ratings across stimuli and respondents to mean-zero and unit-standard deviation, the original three-way data matrix was scaled by means of the linear discriminant model [74], consisting of 15 groups, 10 predictor variables, and 42 cases per group. This technique is equivalent to a metric scaling of Mahalanobis D^2.

Control parameters for the metric scaling, simple scaling, TORSCA 8, and Parametric Mapping algorithms were identical to those described earlier. Again, solutions were sought in three and two dimensions. (Numerical coordinates and ancillary Shepard diagrams for these computer runs are given in Tables C.7-C.10 and Figures C.5-C.8.)

Figures 2.11 through 2.18 show the configurations and associated Shepard diagrams of the four scalings in two dimensions.

Insofar as the metric solution is concerned, 14 nonzero eigenvalues were obtained. However, the first three components accounted for 59.3 percent of the variance, and the first two for 50.1 percent. These values are less than their counterpart values obtained under the metric scaling of directly obtained dissimilarities. Figure 2.11 indicates that when rotated approximately 180 degrees, the configuration is roughly similar to Figure 2.2, although there are some differences.

The M-D-SCAL V simple scaling solution, yielding stress values of 0.089 and 0.146 on 24 and 16 iterations for three space and two space, respectively, is also quite close to that obtained from the metric scaling solution (see Figure 2.11).

The TORSCA 8 monotone program took 6 first-stage iterations and 25 second-stage iterations for the three-space solution; the final stress was 0.042. In the two-space solution 3 first-stage iterations and 19 second-stage iterations were involved; the resulting stress was 0.066.

The PARAMAP program used 49 iterations for the three-space solution and 27 for the two-space run; the corresponding kappa values were 1.01 and 1.02.

The other three configurations (Figures 2.13, 2.15, and 2.17) are quite close to Figure 2.11. Thus, we can say that differences across algorithms as applied to derived dissimilarities are relatively minor. Similarly, we can recall that differences across algorithms as applied to direct dissimilarities data were also rather small. Of course, we should have expected this, given the strong linear component of the function (shown in the Shepard diagrams) linking dissimilarities with derived distances.

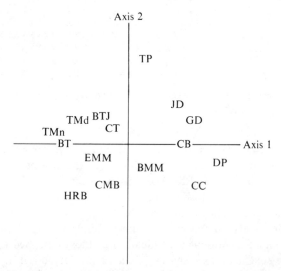

Figure 2.11   Two-space   Configuration   from   Metric   Scaling   of   Derived Dissimilarities (See Figure 2.2 for key.)

HIERARCHICAL CLUSTER ANALYSIS

In replicating the analysis of direct dissimilarities data, Johnson's clustering program was applied to the derived dissimilarities of Table 2.3. The results of the connectedness and diameter procedures are shown in heirarchical form in Figure 2.19.

As before, selected cluster contours were plotted, illustratively, in the

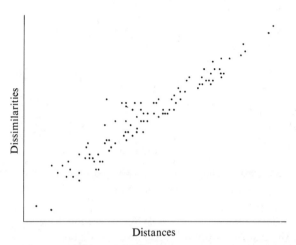

Figure 2.12   Shepard Diagram Based on Two-space Solution from Metric Scaling of Derived Dissimilarities

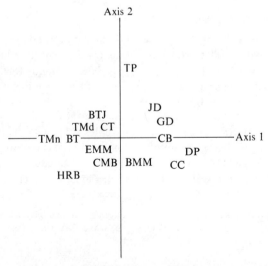

Figure 2.13   Two-space Configuration from M-D-SCAL V Analysis of Derived Dissimilarities (See Figure 2.2 for key.)

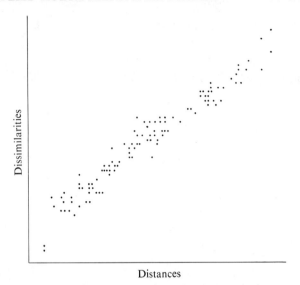

Figure 2.14   Shepard Diagram Based on Two-space Solution from M-D-SCAL V Analysis of Derived Dissimilarities

two-space solution obtained from the TORSCA 8 monotone analysis, using the results from the diameter option.[13] As shown in Figure 2.15, the contours are fairly regular, indicating that the two-space representation is a reasonably faithful one. However, it is interesting that toast pop-up remains as an isolate through most of the clustering hierarchy.

DISCRIMINANT ANALYSIS

As a last step in scaling the ratings data at the aggregate level, the original $42 \times 15 \times 10$ matrix (after standardization across subjects and stimuli) was scaled by linear discrimination analysis [74]. This technique treated the stimuli as 15 groups and permitted the metric scaling of a derived dissimilarities matrix whose entries are Mahalanobis D^2.

A plot of the stimulus "centroids" in discriminant function space is shown in Figure 2.20. (Supporting detail appears in Tables C.11 and C.12.) Allowing for reflection of the configuration about the horizontal axis (compared to Figures 2.11, 2.13, 2.15, and 2.17) we note its high correspondence to the preceding configurations from the scaling of derived dissimilarities data.

---

[13]We note some differences in the clustering solutions. For example, stimuli 8 and 9 merge with 2 and 10 under the connectedness method, while they first merge with stimulus 5 under the diameter method.

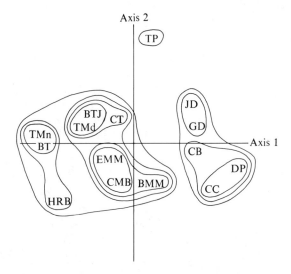

Figure 2.15   Two-space Configuration from TORSCA 8 Analysis of Derived Dissimilarities (See Figure 2.2 for key.)

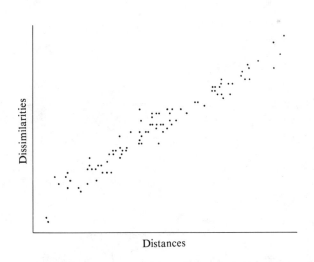

Figure 2.16   Shepard Diagram Based on Two-space Solution from TORSCA 8 Analysis of Derived Dissimilarities

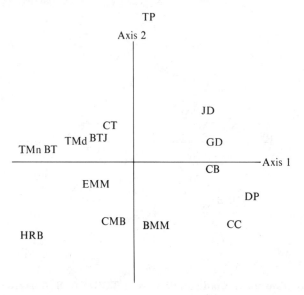

Figure 2.17   Two-space Configuration from Parametric Mapping of Derived Dissimilarities (See Figure 2.2 for key.)

Figure 2.18   Shepard Diagram Based on Two-space Solution from Parametric Mapping of Derived Dissimilarities

Connectedness Method

```
 Grouping                     Stimulus Number
  Value      1  11  4  13  12  14  7  6  5  8  9  2  10  3  15
  0.77       •   •  •   •   •   •  •  •  •  X  X  X   •  •   •
  0.78       •   •  •   •   •   •  •  •  •  X  X  X  X X X  •  •
  0.97       •   •  •   •   •   •  •  •  •  X  X  X  X  X  X  X  • •
  0.99       •   •  X X X  •   •   •  •  •  X  X  X  X  X  X  X  • •
  1.01       •   •  X X X  X X X   •  •  •  X  X  X  X  X  X  X  • •
  1.02       •   X X X X X  X X X  •  •  •  X  X  X  X  X  X  X  • •
  1.04       •   X X X X X  X X X  •  •  •  X  X  X  X  X  X  X  X X X
  1.06       •   X X X X X  X X X  •  •  •  X X X X X X X X X X
  1.09       •   X X X X X  X X X  •  •  X X X X X X X X X X X
  1.10       •   X X X X X  X X X  •  X X X X X X X X X X X X X
  1.11       •   X X X X X X X X X  •  X X X X X X X X X X X X X
  1.18       •   X X X X X X X X X  X X X X X X X X X X X X X X
  1.33       •   X X X X X X X X X X X X X X X X X X X X X X X X X
  1.49       X X X X X X X X X X X X X X X X X X X X X X X X X X
```

Diameter Method

```
 Grouping                     Stimulus Number
  Value      1  4  13  11  12  14  7  2  10  5  8  9  6  3  15
  0.77       •  •   •   •   •   •  •  •   •  X  X  X   •  •   •
  0.78       •  •   •   •   •   •  X X X  •  X  X  X   •  •   •
  0.99       •  X X X  •   •   •  X X X  •  X  X  X   •  •   •
  1.01       •  X X X  •  X X X  •  X X X  •  X  X  X   •  •   •
  1.04       •  X X X  •  X X X  •  X X X  •  X  X  X   •  X X X
  1.09       •  X X X  •  X X X  •  X X X  X X X X X  •  X X X
  1.13       •  X X X  •  X X X  •  X X X  X X X X X X X X X
  1.16       •  X X X  X X X X X  •  X X X  X X X X X  X X X X X
  1.25       •  X X X  X X X X X  X X X X X  X X X X X  X X X X X
  1.36       •  X X X  X X X X X  X X X X X  X X X X X X X X X X
  1.46       •  X X X X X X X X X  X X X X X  X X X X X X X X X X
  1.55       •  X X X X X X X X X  X X X X X X X X X X X X X X X X
  1.83       X X X X X X X X X X X  X X X X X X X X X X X X X X X
  2.08       X X X X X X X X X X X X X X X X X X X X X X X X X X X
```

Figure 2.19   Tree Diagrams by Method, from Hierarchical Grouping Algorithm of Derived Dissimilarities

CONGRUENCE TESTING

At this stage in the analysis we visually noted two main results:

1. A correspondence of the two-space configurations, across algorithms, for direct and derived dissimilarities considered separately.

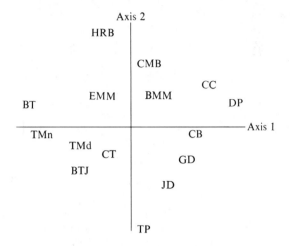

Figure 2.20   Stimulus Configuration from First Two Dimensions of Linear Discriminant Analysis of Ratings Data (See Figure 2.2 for key.)

2. Differences between the configurations based on direct dissimilarities and those based on derived dissimilarities. Although the dimension labels of "sweetness" and "toast/nontoast" appear appropriate for each, the scale separations differ somewhat across scaling solutions associated with the two sets of data. Also, the orientations of the two sets of configurations are different (involving in most instances a rotation of approximately 180 degrees).

At this point our interest focuses on how well the various two-space configurations agree with each other.

The visual evidence of two-space configuration congruence across algorithms was tested for each class of dissimilarities separately by computing interpoint distance correlations between all pairs of solutions.[14] The results of this analysis are shown in Table 2.4.

As can be seen from Table 2.4, the correspondences are generally excellent. The Parametric Mapping solution (direct dissimilarities) is the only case in which the product moment correlation is less than 0.9.[15] Thus we can conclude that for this particular data bank the within-data set solutions are largely invariant

---

[14] Another way of comparing the configurations involves the principal components of a "supermatrix" whose columns are the dimensions obtained from all configurations.

[15] The relatively poor performance of Parametric Mapping appears to be due to the fact that the function relating solution to input data departs substantially from smoothness. In other instances Parametric Mapping may yield parsimonious solutions where methods requiring monotonicity do not [126].

Table 2.4   Product-Moment Correlations of Interpoint Distances by Algorithm within Data Set

Algorithm	Direct Dissimilarities			
	1	2	3	4
1. Metric Scaling	1.000			
2. M-D-SCAL V	0.980	1.000		
3. TORSCA 8	0.982	0.999	1.000	
4. Parametric Mapping	0.815	0.840	0.840	1.000

Algorithm	Derived Dissimilarities				
	1	2	3	4	5
1. Metric Scaling	1.000				
2. M-D-SCAL V	0.979	1.000			
3. TORSCA 8	0.981	0.999	1.000		
4. Parametric Mapping	0.966	0.993	0.993	1.000	
5. Discriminant Analysis	0.953	0.922	0.929	0.920	1.000

over scaling algorithm.[16] Given the large linear component of the function relating input data to computed distances, this is not surprising.

Of particular interest is the fact that the discriminant analysis yielded a solution that closely resembled the classical solution based on ordinary Euclidean distances. That is, rescaling the relative potencies of the components (the Mahalanobis D^2s based on a common covariance matrix) produced little difference in results. But this should not be construed as a general finding. Ordinarily we would expect the solution based on ordinary Euclidean distances (in squared form) to be related not by a similarity transform, but by a more general affine or linear transform.

Next, we were interested in configuration congruence *across* the two data sets, with type of algorithm held constant. And in matching the pairwise configurations, we wished to make only a similarity transform—translation of origin, rotation, reflection, and central dilation of the axes.

Second, we wished to compare all nine configurations (including that obtained from the linear discriminant analysis) in terms of a somewhat more general transformation, which would permit differential stretching along (unique) dimensions of a common (group) space. Such a generalized canonical correlation is embodied in Carroll and Chang's CANDECOMP program [15], which provides the group stimulus space as output as well as a set of dimension stretching factors showing how each configuration is related to the group space.

---

[16]Solutions for different algorithms within type of data—direct versus derived dissimilarities—correlate more highly with each other than solutions within a specific algorithm do across the two data sets (see Table C.58).

CONGRUENCE TESTING VIA ORTHOGONAL ROTATION

The first step in configuration matching utilized Cliff's method [22], C-MATCH. This program (designed by Pennell and Young [108]) takes two configurations after standardization of each to an origin at the centroid and a mean distance to the origin of unity and orthogonally rotates either or both to congruence by maximizing their sum of cross-products. In addition, the version used here computes two ancillary congruence measures:

1. Product-moment correlations of interpoint distances
2. Average-cosine measure between pairs of vectors in the matched space

The first measure is invariant under similarity transformations. The second measure permits a somewhat more general transformation involving differential stretching of the vectors after rotation. While we emphasize the first measure, we discuss both in the interest of completeness.

For illustrative purposes Cliff's algorithm was applied to only the two-space solution sets of direct versus derived dissimilarities for each algorithm separately. This algorithm enables one to

1. Fit a second matrix to a "target" matrix.
2. Rotate both matrices to a common orientation.

In this particular application we elected to follow the first procedure. The two-space configuration obtained from the analysis of direct dissimilarities was held fixed, and the second configuration (scaled from derived dissimilarities) was fitted to it. As a preliminary step, both matrices were uniformly scaled and rotated (when necessary) to a principal components orientation.

As conjectured, the best-fitting rotation of the second configuration to the first involved a rotation of almost 180 degrees. Table 2.5 shows the direction cosines of the best-fitting orthogonal transformations for each type of algorithm and indicates that the best-fitting rotations are virtually identical across all four algorithms.

Goodness-of-fit measures are summarized in Table 2.6, again by type of algorithm; column 2 shows the product-moment correlation between interpoint distances which is the most appropriate measure for appraising goodness of fit. With the exception of the Parametric Mapping solution, the product-moment correlations are slightly over 0.8.

If we neglect differences in vector length and use the average cosine between pairs of vectors in the matched space, the goodness of fit increases to values ranging from 0.922 to 0.953.[17]

---

[17]However, restriction of configuration comparisons to a similarities transformation is now no longer assumed.

Table 2.5   Orthogonal Transformation Matrices Applied to Configurations Based on Derived Dissimilarities for Best Congruence with Target (Direct Dissimilarities) Matrices

| | Metric Scaling | | M-D-SCAL V | |
Axis	1	2	1	2
1	−0.993	0.117	−0.995	0.098
2	−0.117	−0.993	−0.098	−0.995

| | TORSCA 8 | | Parametric Mapping | |
	1	2	1	2
1	−0.995	0.095	−0.991	0.130
2	−0.095	−0.995	−0.130	−0.991

Table 2.6   Goodness-of-fit Measures Obtained from the Orthogonal Congruence Analysis

Algorithm	Average Cosine	Interpoint Distance Correlation
Metric Scaling	0.950	0.804
M-D-SCAL V	0.948	0.801
TORSCA 8	0.953	0.805
Parametric Mapping	0.922	0.633

In brief, the results so far indicate that the configurations obtained from the direct and derived dissimilarities data are reasonably close to each other, after appropriate rotation. Apparently the specific bipolar scale choices and the assignment of equal manifest weight in their contribution to overall derived dissimilarity have not exerted a marked effect on the resulting configuration's congruence with the one obtained by analyzing the direct dissimilarities data.

CANONICAL DECOMPOSITION ANALYSIS

The preceding analysis was performed on a pairwise basis; that is, only two configurations at a time were compared for congruence. We might inquire, however, about the congruence of *all* of the configurations (including the one obtained by application of multiple discriminant analysis). Carroll and Chang's canonical decomposition, or CANDECOMP, model provides a way to examine configuration congruence that is not restricted to pairwise comparisons.

Again, the two-dimensional coordinates of the nine scaling solutions were used as input data. The CANDECOMP program finds a group stimulus configuration and a set of weights that indicate how each input configuration is related to the group stimulus configuration. In addition, a set of weights is obtained for each dimension of the input configurations. That is, an input configuration can be decomposed into three matrices: (a) a group stimulus matrix, (b) a "loading" matrix of input configuration weights, and (c) a "loading" matrix of weights for each original dimension; and both the (b) and (c) sets of weights can be applied to the uniquely oriented axes of the group stimulus matrix.

The program was set for 15 iterations using an arbitrary starting configuration.[18] A solution was sought in two dimensions only, using the option that solves simultaneously for all matrices. Figure 2.21 shows the group stimulus space, as obtained from all nine input matrices. Table 2.7 shows the appropriate sets of "weights" for the nine input matrices and the original two-space coordinates as well as goodness-of-fit measures.

Examining Figure 2.21 first, we note that the horizontal dimension continues to represent a caloricness axis.[19] The vertical dimension again seems to separate the toasted from the nontoasted items, but it also may be viewed as separating items predominantly associated with breakfast from items such as hard rolls, corn muffin, and blueberry muffin, less highly associated with breakfast. Thus, all nine types of data-algorithms appear to represent essentially the same configuration after we allow for differential stretching along the axes of Figure 2.21. Table 2.7 supports this conclusion as well.[20]

Now we examine the axis weights for the nine input configurations. The correspondence between data type and algorithm is quite high. In each case we note that axis 2 receives slightly higher relative weight (within algorithm) for the derived versus direct dissimilarities.[21] This suggests the type of differential stretching discussed earlier. The original axis weights also show the closeness of the CANDECOMP orientation to the original orientations of the other configurations.[22]

---

[18] However, the program required only 5 iterations to reach a solution. Input matrices were *first* orthogonally rotated to best congruence with (illustratively) the metric scaling solution of direct dissimilarities data (Figure 2.2). This step is recorded in Table C.13. A certain arbitrariness is associated with the orientation of Figure 2.21; an alternative procedure for performing this type of congruence test (and one that is *not* dependent on starting orientation) is described in Chapter 3. However, overall goodness of fit is not affected by these alternative approaches.

[19] Interestingly enough, however, the configuration of Figure 2.21 involves a reflection about the vertical axis, as compared to that of Figure 2.2.

[20] In using the CANDECOMP feature of INDSCAL, note that this procedure assumes all solutions to have the same dimensionality and that dimensions are comparable from solution to solution. In subsequent chapters the INDSCAL procedure is used for congruence purposes in other ways, for example, where the input data consist of distances rather than stimulus coordinates.

[21] An exception to this tendency is noted in the Parametric Mapping solutions.

[22] In this application the original axis weights should be considered in terms of their absolute value.

Overall, the two-space solution accounts for 95 percent of the variance in the original scalar products matrices. Moreover, with the exception of one of the Parametric Mapping solutions, the individual product-moment correlations are all in the high 90s.

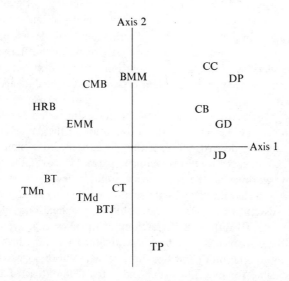

Figure 2.21   Group Stimulus Configuration from CANDECOMP analysis of Nine Input Matrices (See Figure 2.2 for key.)

Table 2.7   "Weights" Matrices and Goodness-of-fit Values for Nine Input Configurations and Two-Space Coordinates

| | Dimension Weight | | Goodness of Fit |
	Axis 1	Axis 2	(Correlation)
Input Configuration			
Metric Scaling (direct)	3.35	2.15	0.975
Metric Scaling (derived)	3.45	2.35	0.985
M-D-SCAL V (direct)	3.47	2.05	0.982
M-D-SCAL V (derived)	3.48	2.38	0.984
TORSCA 8 (direct)	3.45	2.10	0.984
TORSCA 8 (derived)	3.46	2.40	0.984
Parametric Mapping (direct)	2.91	2.43	0.919
Parametric Mapping (derived)	3.37	2.50	0.987
Discriminant Analysis	3.12	2.66	0.972
Original Coordinates			
Axis 1	−0.99	0.08	
Axis 2	−0.13	1.00	

SUMMARY

In this chapter we have analyzed at the aggregate, or group, level two types of dissimilarities data: (a) directly judged dissimilarities (obtained from the TRICON procedure) and (b) derived dissimilarities (obtained from the ratings of the stimuli on each of 10 bipolar scales). In both cases four different algorithms were used, covering metric (classical) scaling, simple scaling, monotone, and continuity scaling. In addition, a linear discriminant analysis was performed on the ratings data, and clustering methods were used on both the direct and derived dissimilarities data. Scaling solutions were then compared across algorithms within data type, across data types within algorithm, and, finally, on an overall basis.

In general it was found that two- or three-dimensional solutions were appropriate in portraying most of the information in the data. Within type of input data—direct or derived—all algorithms produced quite similar configurations when the two-space solutions were compared. Moreover, little appeared to be gained by working at the three-space solution level. Interpoint distance correlations across algorithms and data sets were generally good, indicating that the derived dissimilarities were reasonable approximations of the direct dissimilarities data. (If differential stretching of the axes using average cosine or CANDECOMP congruence is permitted, the congruence is quite high.)

Tentative interpretation of the two-dimensional solution suggests a sweetness or caloricness label for one dimension and a toasted-nontoasted label for the other.

In the next chapter we return to the interpretability of the dissimilarities data using an individual differences analysis.

CHAPTER 3

DISAGGREGATE-LEVEL ANALYSIS OF DISSIMILARITIES DATA

A rough analogy can be drawn between descriptive statistics and the multidimensional scaling of data. Chapter 2's approach of obtaining group scaling solutions to describe dissimilarities judgments, may be compared to the approach of describing data by a measure of central tendency, for example, the mean. But information on mean alone usually does not adequately summarize the behavior under study; we must often include some measure of dispersion, such as the standard deviation, among the sample entities.

In a similar manner it is easy to argue that group solutions are generally inadequate in providing complete descriptions of individual perceptions. Procedures that retain some form of individual differences enable the researcher to preserve as much of the original data as practical, thereby providing a deeper understanding of perceptual behavior.

This chapter is concerned with scaling dissimilarities data in ways that retain individual differences. The analysis is again based on two sets of data, namely, direct and derived measures of dissimilarity for each respondent. The preprocessing procedures for arriving at these data have been discussed in Chapter 2. The data on direct measures consist of a three-way 42 X 15 X 15 matrix obtained by the TRICON procedure [10], while the corresponding data on derived measures were obtained by the DISTAN program [110].

OUTLINE OF ANALYSIS

In Chapter 1 we discussed the major descriptors—aggregate versus individual differences scaling, direct versus derived dissimilarity measures, metric versus nonmetric algorithms by which approaches to the multidimensional scaling of dissimilarities data can be classified. Here we emphasize disaggregate-level analysis, first discussing the rationale and techniques for scaling individual differences and then analyzing the data bank of food item dissimilarities at the level of individual differences.

TOTAL GROUP-LEVEL ANALYSIS

The full three-way 42 X 15 X 15 matrix of directly judged dissimilarities was first analyzed according to the INDSCAL model [15] and solutions were computed in three and two dimensions. A similar procedure was used for the three-way matrix of derived dissimilarities. The two-dimensional group stimulus spaces obtained for these two kinds of data were then tested for congruence and also compared to the group solutions in Chapter 2. Further analysis was then confined primarily to the INDSCAL results of the *directly* judged dissimilarities.[1]

At the total group level (that is, using all 42 respondents' direct dissimilarities data) individual differences were analyzed in three ways. First, the respondents' background characteristics were related to their perceptual differences as represented by the saliences the respondents assigned to each dimension of the three-dimensional group stimulus configuration. This was done using canonical correlation.

Second, the direct dissimilarities data were used to test for significant relationships that might exist between the perceptions of husbands and wives. A 42 X 42 matrix of intersubject distances was first computed from the 42 X 105

---

[1] We prefer these data as the focal point of analysis because the respondent is free to choose his own criteria or frame of reference for discriminating among the stimuli.

matrix of subjects by direct dissimilarities judgments (with each subject's dissimilarities expressed in row-vector form). The distance of every husband to his wife was then compared with his average distance to all other females in the sample. The null hypothesis that husband-wife perceptual distances do not differ from husband-other female distances was tested, using the nonparametric sign test. A similar comparison was made for wives in the sample.

Third, the three-dimensional saliences of each respondent as obtained from the INDSCAL analysis of direct dissimilarities were submitted to the numerical clustering program developed by Howard and Harris [71]. This method enabled us to form groups of respondents who shared similar perceptual structures.[2] To illustrate disaggregate-level analysis, a two-group clustering of subjects was used in subsequent analysis, with these subgroups identified as A and B.

The flow diagram of the analysis at the total-sample level is shown in Figure 3.1.

SUBGROUP ANALYSIS

Analysis at the subgroup level was done separately for groups A and B, using both the directly judged dissimilarities (TRICON data) and the basic data obtained from the 10 bipolar rating scales. But since the procedures were identical for the two subgroups, they are elaborated only for A.

First, the direct dissimilarities data of group A were submitted to the INDSCAL program, and a group stimulus space was found in two dimensions. To correspond to A's direct dissimilarities data, a subgroup ratings 10 X 15 matrix (10 scales by 15 stimuli) was computed by simply averaging the individual ratings judgments of group A members, cell by cell. This matrix of average ratings was used as an "outside" property matrix (consisting of scale values on 10 properties) and its relationship to group A's average-subject stimulus space was examined by three methods:

1. Max "r" linear regression [102]
2. Monotone regression procedure [13]
3. Nonlinear correlation procedure [16]

These methods fitted the 10 property vectors individually in the stimulus space using the respective criteria of maximum linear correlation, maximum monotone correlation, and maximum nonlinear (and possibly nonmonotonic) correlation. These methods of property fitting helped in interpreting the dimensions of each subgroup stimulus space in terms of linear combinations of the basic dimensions satisfying the specific correlation measures noted above. Separate analyses of A and B provided an opportunity to study subgroup differences. A comparison of

---

[2]This procedure represents a highly promising means of segmentation (based on cognitive behavior) in fields such as marketing.

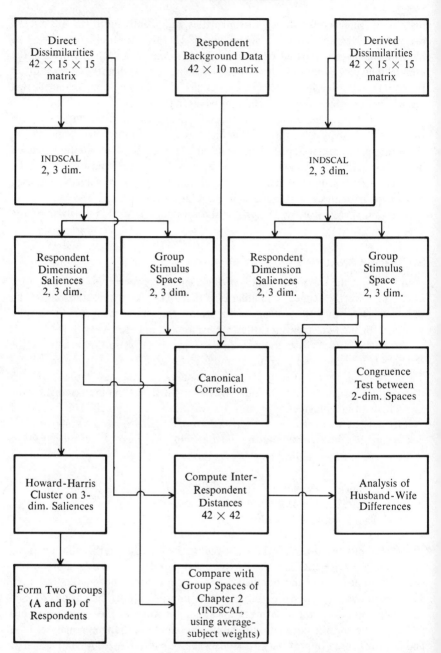

Figure 3.1   Flow Diagram of Analysis at the Total-Group Level

the three methods within each subgroup enabled us to examine differences among property-fitting algorithms as applied to a common set of data.

As a final step, differences that might exist in A's and B's bipolar ratings were also examined, but only at the average-subject level. These steps are shown as a flow diagram in Figure 3.2.

APPROACHES TO INDIVIDUAL DIFFERENCES

Both metric and nonmetric methods are available to scale dissimilarities data in models retaining individual differences. In the limiting case, metric or nonmetric methods (as discussed in Chapter 2) can be used to scale judgments of *each* subject separately. However, this procedure does not take into account any communality that might exist among individuals; nor does it supply a means of connecting the solutions obtained at the individual level.[3] One recourse would be to make pairwise comparisons between individuals' configurations, but, at the least, this method would be very cumbersome and tedious, particularly when a large number of individuals were involved.

A possible alternative procedure is as follows. First, a set of *g* groups of subjects can be formed on the basis of their *overall* association in respect to dissimilarities judgments. (One procedure for performing such clustering is the Points of View model of Tucker and Messick [146].) The data of the average subject or the actual subject closest to the centroid in each group could then be scaled, either metrically or nonmetrically. Even with this procedure, the researcher has no convenient way of interrelating the different scaling solutions of the groups.[4]

The INDSCAL model developed by Carroll and Chang [15] offers a more elegant approach to scaling individual differences. This model assumes a common, or group stimulus, space, with differential weighting of (uniquely oriented) axes for each subject of the group. The subject weights or saliences on each dimension are idiosyncratic and can be used to estimate each subject's private perceptual space. The method solves for both the common (group stimulus) space and the dimension weights for each subject. Thus, communalities among individuals provide greater stability in the stimulus configuration. Our INDSCAL analyses, however, are restricted to only the metric version of the

---

[3]Also, data from individual subjects not infrequently lack sufficient reliability to make individual differences stable enough for interpretation.

[4]While a Tucker-Messick Points of View analysis could have been made, this was not attempted here in view of space limitations and the fact that the INDSCAL procedure provides more information (for example, a unique orientation of the stimulus space).

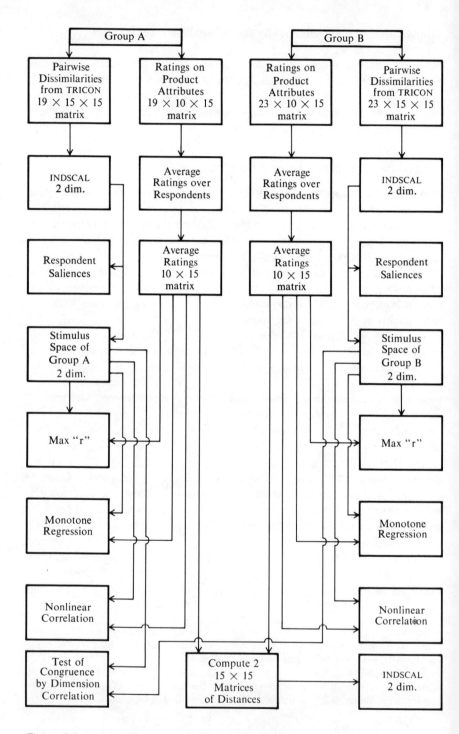

Figure 3.2   Flow Diagram of Analysis at the Subgroup Level

algorithm.[5] Thus, approaches corresponding to the individual differences-nonmetric cells (Table 1.3) are not covered.

INDSCAL ANALYSIS AT THE TOTAL GROUP LEVEL

As noted earlier, the INDSCAL model estimates both the subject saliences and the group stimulus space for any prespecified dimensionality. In the most general solution provided by INDSCAL, no constraint is built into the model to yield uncorrelated dimensions in the stimulus space. The program computes a global measure of goodness of fit, namely, the proportion of variance in the scalar products matrix (computed from the input data) accounted for by the model. For each subject, however, the correlation coefficient between scalar products computed from the coordinates of the subject's estimated private configuration and his original data (also converted to scalar products) can be used as a measure of individual goodness of fit.

DIRECT DISSIMILARITIES ANALYSIS

Table 3.1 shows the global measures of goodness of fit, the average of the subjects' correlation coefficients, and the correlations between the dimensions of the group stimulus space (for three- and two-dimensional solutions) obtained from the analysis of the $42 \times 15 \times 15$ matrix of respondents' directly judged dissimilarities. (The individual-subject correlation coefficients computed as noted above for two and three dimensions are shown in Appendix Table C.14.)

Table 3.1 Summary Statistics from INDSCAL Analysis of Directly Judged Dissimilarities in Three and Two Dimensions

Statistic	3 Dimensions	2 Dimensions
Percentage of Variance Accounted for by the INDSCAL Model	59.6	49.4
Average Correlation Coefficient across Subjects	0.763	0.688
Correlation between Axes		
1 and 2	0.043	0.043
1 and 3	−0.440	
2 and 3	−0.330	

Improvement at the global level by going from two to three dimensions is of the order of 10 percentage points of additional variance accounted for. However, the third dimension in the three-dimensional case is rather highly correlated with

[5]The reasons for this are primarily pragmatic. First, no computer program incorporating the nonmetric feature is generally available. Second, earlier tests on an experimental version of Carroll and Chang's quasi-nonmetric algorithm did not result in substantially different configurations from those obtained metrically (personal communications from J.D. Carroll).

the other two dimensions. As noted in Table C.15, the pattern of three-dimensional saliences suggests that most subjects were attending primarily to only one or two dimensions. Thus, a three-dimensional solution would appear to represent a useful *group* summary, although most subjects' private spaces seemed to be one- or two-dimensional. In accord with the format in Chapter 2, we emphasize the two-dimensional stimulus solution, although analysis of subject differences was carried out in the more accurate three-dimensional space.

The two- and three-dimensional stimulus coordinates are presented in Table C.16. The two-dimensional subject space is shown in Figure 3.3, and the corresponding group stimulus space in Figure 3.4.

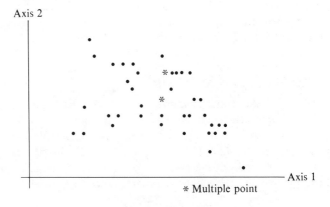

Figure 3.3   Plot of Two-space Subject Saliences Obtained from INDSCAL Analysis of Direct Dissimilarities

The two-dimensional group stimulus space—adjusted by the program to unit sums of squares axis projections—lends itself to an interpretation parallel to those in Chapter 2. In Figure 3.4, the horizontal dimension turns out to be a type of sweetness dimension. Nonsweet hard rolls and butter and English muffin and margarine are positioned at the extreme left, while sweet items like jelly donut and glazed donut are shown on the extreme right. The vertical axis again appears to be a toast/nontoast dimension. The toasted food items are positioned on the lower portion of the chart, while the nontoast items are positioned in the upper portion and are well separated from the toasted category.[6]

In passing, we note that the first two dimensions of the three-dimensional stimulus space (whose coordinate values appear in Table C.16) are almost

---

[6]The characteristics of the various clusters that emerge in this, and other, analyses are of interest. The toasts can be subdivided into buttered toast and toast and margarine; toast and marmalade and buttered toast and jelly; toast pop-ups and cinnamon toast. In the roll-muffin grouping there is some distinction between blueberry muffin and corn muffin versus rolls and English muffin. Finally, cinnamon bun, Danish pastry, glazed donut, jelly donut, and coffee cake can all be characterized as pastry or cake-like items.

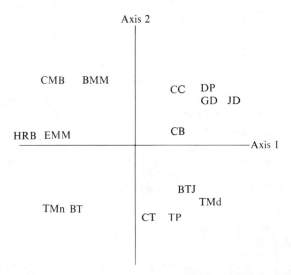

Figure 3.4   Two-space Stimulus Configuration from INDSCAL Analysis of Direct Dissimilarities (Projections scaled to unit sums of squares)

Key

TP	Toast pop-up	BTJ	Buttered toast and jelly
BT	Buttered toast	TMn	Toast and margarine
EMM	English muffin and margarine	CB	Cinnamon bun
JD	Jelly donut	DP	Danish pastry
CT	Cinnamon toast	GD	Glazed donut
BMM	Blueberry muffin and margarine	CC	Coffee cake
HRB	Hard rolls and butter	CMB	Corn muffin and butter
TMd	Toast and marmalade		

identical to corresponding axes of the two-dimensional solution space shown in Figure 3.4. No simple interpretation seems appropriate for the third dimension, which is, we suspect, (in concert with the first) more interpretable from a clustering point of view.[7]

DERIVED DISSIMILARITIES

Application of the INDSCAL model to the derived dissimilarities data yielded

[7]Further analysis was done to see whether the third dimension could be easily interpreted. Respondent ratings on the 10 product attributes were averaged, yielding 10 property vectors. Each of these vectors was fitted in the three-dimensional stimulus space, using the max "r" procedure. Results of this analysis (presented in Table C.17) do not provide any clear dimensional interpretation of the third dimension. What *can* be noted in the one-three plane (see Table C.16) of the three-dimensional solution is the separation of butter/margarine spreads (second quadrant) from sugar/cinnamon coatings (fourth quadrant). That is, a clustering interpretation, rather than a dimensional one, appears appropriate in this case.

similar results.[8] This is not surprising in light of the high degree of correspondence between these two sets of data in Chapter 2. The summary statistics describing goodness of fit and correlation between dimensions for three- and two-dimensional solutions are given in Table 3.2. (Individual correlation coefficients are presented in Table C.18.) The summary results are very similar to those obtained for directly judged dissimilarities with one exception: the high (absolute) correlation between axes 1 and 2 of the group stimulus space.

Table 3.2   Summary Statistics from INDSCAL Analysis of Derived Dissimilarities in Three and Two Dimensions

Statistic	3 Dimensions	2 Dimensions
Percentage of Variance Accounted for by the INDSCAL Model	58.2	46.3
Average Correlation Coefficient across Subjects	0.753	0.668
Correlation between Axes		
1 and 2	−0.288	−0.288
1 and 3	−0.463	
2 and 3	0.439	

The two- and three-dimensional subject saliences and stimulus coordinates for the derived dissimilarities are shown in Tables C.19 and C.20. The two-dimensional configuration of saliences and the group stimulus space are shown in Figures 3.5 and 3.6, respectively.

The two-dimensional group stimulus space of Figure 3.6 may be interpreted as follows. The horizontal axis can be thought of as a toast/nontoast dimension, while the vertical axis appears to be a sweet/nonsweet dimension. The axes of this space represent a permutation of those found for directly judged dissimilarities. A similar type of axis permutation (which is permissible under all of the scaling methods used here) was found in Chapter 2 when solutions obtained from direct dissimilarities were contrasted with those obtained from derived dissimilarities.

CONGRUENCE TESTING

At this point the two INDSCAL configurations of Figures 3.4 and 3.6 can be compared for congruence. In addition, the nine stimulus configurations obtained by the various algorithm-data combinations in Chapter 2 can be compared in this new context. Since the INDSCAL algorithm provides a unique orientation of the

[8]These data were entered into the INDSCAL program as Euclidean distances, in contrast to the TRICON data entered as dissimilarities.

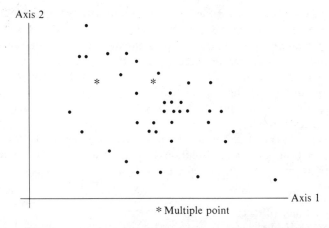

Figure 3.5   Plot of Two-space Subject Saliences from INDSCAL Analysis of Derived Dissimilarities

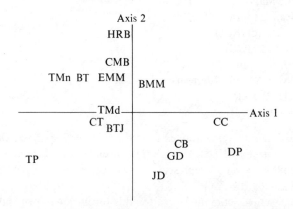

Figure 3.6   Two-space Stimulus Configuration from INDSCAL Analysis of Derived Dissimilarities (Projections scaled to unit sums of squares) (See Figure 3.4 for key.)

configuration, we do not wish to rotate the solution along the lines followed in Table 2.5. Instead, we want to stretch the axes of Figures 3.4 and 3.6 differentially (in accord with the square roots of the average subject's saliences), since the configurations of Chapter 2 are based on subject averages. As will be recalled, the configurations of Figure 3.4 and 3.6 are currently in standard (unit sums of squares) form insofar as axis projections are concerned.

However, congruence tests can be carried out using the INDSCAL procedure itself. That is, we assume that the INDSCAL group space obtained from the analysis of direct dissimilarities (Figure 3.4) represents the target matrix. We first stretch the axes of this space differentially in accord with the square roots of the average subject's saliences (see Table C.15). We then enter this solution as a *fixed* target configuration in the INDSCAL program and have the program solve for sets of dimension saliences for each of the other solutions relative to it. As described earlier, the INDSCAL program also computes a goodness-of-fit measure, the product-moment correlation between original data (converted to scalar products), and the private space distances of each pseudosubject (also converted to scalar products).

The analysis was undertaken using the differentially stretched configuration of Figure 3.4 as the target solution and the following two-dimensional configurations, expressed (insofar as input data are concerned) as interstimulus Euclidean distances:

1. Metric Scaling (direct)
2. M-D-SCAL V (direct)
3. TORSCA 8 (direct)
4. Parametric Mapping (direct)
5. Metric Scaling (derived)
6. M-D-SCAL V (derived)
7. TORSCA 8 (derived)
8. Parametric Mapping (derived)
9. Discriminant Analysis (derived)
10. INDSCAL (direct)
11. INDSCAL (derived)

The first nine data sets were obtained from the Chapter 2 analyses. Data set 10 is the average subject's INDSCAL solution itself (entered merely for check purposes), while data set 11 represents the average subject's INDSCAL solution for derived dissimilarities.[9]

The average-subject stimulus space for this run is not shown, since it is just like Figure 3.4 except that the horizontal axis is slightly differentially stretched relative to the vertical axis. The pseudosubject space of saliences is shown in Figure 3.7, and Table 3.3 shows the results in numerical form as well as the goodness-of-fit measure of each pseudosubject to the average-subject's INDSCAL configuration based on direct dissimilarities.

Looking first at Table 3.3, we note that the product-moment correlations for all cases involving directly judged dissimilarities are about 0.85, which suggests

---

[9]The two-dimensional INDSCAL solution for the group A cluster of respondents and the two-dimensional INDSCAL solution for the group B cluster of respondents, both expressed as Euclidean distances, were also entered as two additional data sets. Here, as well, the subgroup configurations were differentially stretched in accord with the square roots of the saliences of their respective average subjects. We comment on these input data in a subsequent section of the chapter dealing with subgroup analysis. Plotting codes (Figure 3.7) are A and B for cases 10 and 11, above, and C and D for groups A and B, respectively.

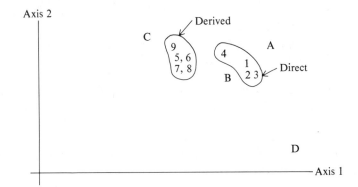

Figure 3.7 Plot of Two-space Pseudosubject Saliences from INDSCAL Congruence Analysis

that the INDSCAL target configuration is reasonably close to the configurations found at the aggregate level of analysis. Solutions based on the scaling of derived dissimilarities are generally lower in goodness of fit, but still are about equal to each other. This latter observation is in accord with the within-set algorithmic comparisons made in Chapter 2.

From Figure 3.7 (supported by the entries of Table 3.3), we note first that weights for data sets 1 through 4 are tightly clustered, and their square roots exhibit the effect of slight differential stretching of the horizontal axis relative to the vertical axis. Weights for data sets 5 through 9 are approximately equal to each other and, again, are tightly clustered. Data set 11 (the INDSCAL solution

Table 3.3 Pseudosubject Dimension Weights and Goodness-of-Fit Values Obtained from the INDSCAL Congruence Analysis

Pseudosubject	Dimension Weight 1	2	Goodness of Fit (Correlation)
1. Metric Scaling (direct)	0.735	0.482	0.879
2. M-D-SCAL V (direct)	0.727	0.447	0.854
3. TORSCA 8 (direct)	0.724	0.455	0.856
4. Parametric Mapping (direct)	0.648	0.529	0.837
5. Metric Scaling (derived)	0.503	0.538	0.737
6. M-D-SCAL V (derived)	0.508	0.515	0.724
7. TORSCA 8 (derived)	0.510	0.515	0.726
8. Parametric Mapping (derived)	0.518	0.540	0.749
9. Discriminant Analysis	0.453	0.587	0.742
10. INDSCAL (direct)	0.825	0.563	1.000
11. INDSCAL (derived)	0.656	0.436	0.788
12. Group A INDSCAL (direct)	0.377	0.611	0.719
13. Group B INDSCAL (direct)	0.903	0.102	0.909

obtained from derived dissimilarities) weights the horizontal axis somewhat more heavily than the vertical.

We conclude that the aggregate-level scaling of Chapter 2 produces results reasonably consistent with the disaggregate-level analysis of both direct and derived dissimilarities. Accordingly, it seems appropriate to call the uniquely oriented group space of Figure 3.4 *the* stimulus space for this data bank, as expressed in normalized (unit sums of squares) form. Its orientation, incidentally, is quite similar to that in Figure 2.21, the latter being synthesized, at the aggregate level, over the nine algorithm-data combinations considered in the previous chapter. This finding further supports our earlier interpretation of the (uniquely oriented) axes as sweet/nonsweet and toast/nontoast.

ANALYSIS OF RESPONDENT DIFFERENCES IN PERCEPTION

The weights assigned to the three-dimensional INDSCAL solution, as obtained from scaling direct judgments of dissimilarity (see Table C.15) can be used as respondent measures of dimension salience. An analysis of the relationship of these perceptual measures to respondent background characteristics was done using canonical correlation. The 10 characteristics chosen are shown in Table 3.4. The means, standard deviations, and correlation matrix among all pairs of the 10 predictors are shown in Table C.21. The results of the canonical analysis are presented in Table 3.5. The common variance between the two sets of variables, that is, the 3 dimension saliences and the 10 background characteristics, is only 25.1 percent, and none of the latent

Table 3.4   The 10 Background Characteristics

Variable Number	Name	Description and Codes
1	SEX	Male = 1, Female = 0
2	AGE	Actual age in years
3	NCHILD	Number of children; actual number as reported
4	OVERWGT	Whether the respondent considers himself or herself overweight; Yes = 1, No = 0
5	PCTOWT	Percent overweight; actual percentage as reported (0 percent for those not overweight)
6	WDAYBF	Weekday breakfast type; Light = 1, Heavy = 0 (any combination of juice or fruit, beverage, toast or other bakery item, cheese, or cereal is coded as "light" breakfast)
7	WENDBF	Weekend breakfast type; Light = 1, Heavy = 0 (same definition as above)
8	COFFEE	Coffee drinking; Regularly = 1, Otherwise = 0 ("Regularly" here and below is defined as one or more times per day)
9	TEA	Tea drinking; Regularly = 1, Otherwise = 0
10	MILK	Milk drinking; Regularly = 1, Otherwise = 0

Table 3.5   Results of Canonical Correlation between Three-Dimensional Saliences and Respondent Background Data

Summary Measure	Latent Root Number		
	1	2	3
Canonical Correlation	0.621	0.462	0.249
Wilks Lambda	0.453	0.738	0.938
Chi Square	27.685	10.632	2.246
Degrees of Freedom	30	18	8
Probability Less than	0.587	0.909	0.972

roots is statistically significant. This analysis of the data indicates that differences in dimension saliences are not significantly related to respondent background characteristics.

HUSBAND-WIFE DIFFERENCES

It will be recalled that the data of this study were collected from 21 married couples. We take advantage of this feature of the research design to examine husband-wife differences in perceptions. A 42 X 42 matrix of interrespondent Euclidean distances was computed using the 42 X 105 matrix of direct dissimilarities. (The 21 X 21 submatrix of distances between husbands and wives is in Table C.22.) The distance of every husband to his wife was first compared with his average distance to all other females in the sample. A sign test between these two statistics was made across the 21 husbands in the sample. The procedure was then repeated for the 21 wives.

These two sets of distances are presented in Table 3.6. The observed number of positive differences in both tests turned out to be 6. The expected value under the null hypothesis is 10.5. In both cases the test statistic is significant at the 5 percent alpha level. Thus, we can conclude that at the overall dissimilarities data level, the perceptions of husbands and wives differed from those of "random" pairings. That is, husband-wife combinations tended to perceive the food items more similarly than other male-female pairings.[10]

SEGMENTATION BASED ON DIMENSION SALIENCES

The three-dimensional saliences for each subject (obtained from the INDSCAL analysis of direct dissimilarities) were next used to form segments of respondents with different perceptions. This was accomplished by the Howard-Harris [71] numerical clustering algorithm.[11] In this program the

[10]The above analysis also was replicated by computing appropriate distances in the INDSCAL salience space (Figure 3.3); the findings were qualitatively similar to those shown above; the null hypothesis was rejected at the 5-percent level.

[11]The three-dimensional INDSCAL saliences (shown in Table C.15) were submitted to this program with no standardization (by columns) of the 42 X 3 data matrix.

Table 3.6   Husband-Wife Distances Compared to Husband-Other Female and
            Wife-Other Male Distances for Direct Dissimilarities Data

Pair	Distance of Every Husband (Wife) to Wife (Husband) (1)	Average Distance of Husband to All Other Females (2)	Average Distance of Wife to All Other Males (3)	Sign of (1) - (2)	Sign of (1) – (3)
1	22.81	29.40	29.64	-	-
2	21.83	28.06	27.60	-	-
3	31.82	27.66	32.81	+	-
4	28.33	29.12	28.89	-	-
5	27.13	31.91	27.52	-	-
6	20.02	30.33	28.16	-	-
7	25.77	29.25	29.14	-	-
8	30.79	30.94	28.14	-	+
9	18.03	29.14	29.12	-	-
10	32.85	38.56	28.97	-	+
11	33.65	26.60	32.75	+	+
12	22.69	28.39	28.68	-	-
13	33.69	31.67	35.39	+	-
14	34.79	32.14	29.41	+	+
15	15.07	30.29	29.59	-	-
16	35.68	37.78	33.48	-	+
17	13.75	30.43	29.16	-	-
18	25.58	34.81	30.47	-	-
19	29.58	29.55	32.51	+	-
20	43.00	28.25	41.82	+	+
21	27.69	28.46	29.51	-	-

criterion used for forming clusters is the minimum within-group sum of squares.
The values of this criterion at each of 10 cluster levels are shown in Table 3.7.
The subgroup compositions at these levels are shown in Table C.23.

Further analysis in this chapter was done at the disaggregated level of two
subgroups.[12] The respondent numbers falling into these two subgroups, labeled
A and B, are shown in Table 3.8.[13] (Appendix A shows the procedure used in
coding respondents.)

[12]The reasons for this selection are twofold: (a) the three-level grouping resulted in groups
of small size (12, 15, and 15) compared with 19 and 23 at the two-group level and (b) the
improvement in the criterion value from the two-level to three-level clustering did not
appear large enough to warrant further division.

[13]Alternative methods exist for forming segments of respondents on the basis of perceptual
behavior. For example, the degree to which each individual conforms to the INDSCAL
model (in a prespecified dimensionality) can be used to form subgroups. This alternative is
used in part of the analysis of Chapter 5.

Table 3.7   Within-Group Sum of Squares at 10 Levels of Grouping

Grouping Level	Within-group Sum of Squares	Percentage of Total Sum of Squares	Grouping Level	Within-group Sum of Squares	Percentage of Total Sum of Squares
1	3.290	100	6	0.686	21
2	1.904	58	7	0.595	19
3	1.353	41	8	0.512	16
4	1.039	31	9	0.452	14
5	0.830	25	10	0.392	12

Table 3.8   Subjects Assigned to Group A and Group B

Group A		Group B	
041	151	011	072
082	152	012	081
092	161	021	091
101	162	022	131
102	181	031	132
111	182	032	142
112	191	042	171
121	201	051	172
122	202	052	192
141		061	211
		062	212
		071	

INDSCAL ANALYSIS AT THE SUBGROUP LEVEL

To probe further into the differences between the perceptual judgments of groups A and B, we submitted the directly judged dissimilarities data of each group (and its average subject) *separately* to the INDSCAL program and obtained two-dimensional solutions. Table 3.9 shows the statistics describing degree of fit and the dimension correlations; these results provide some support for separation of the 42 respondents into groups A and B.[14] It is of interest that the dimension correlations are −0.36 for group A versus −0.63 for group B.

The stimulus spaces for groups A and B are displayed in Figures 3.8 and 3.9, respectively. (The individual correlations, saliences, and coordinate values are presented in Tables C.24 through C.26.) These subgroup stimulus configurations may be interpreted in a manner similar to the configuration of all 42 subjects. In group A the horizontal dimension turns out to be a sweet/nonsweet axis. In group B the vertical dimension appears to be a sweetness dimension. The vertical

[14]It should be pointed out that group B's improvement in accounted-for variance (see Table 3.1 for contrast) is considerably greater than group A's.

Table 3.9   Summary Statistics of the Fit from the INDSCAL Analysis of Directly Judged Dissimilarities for Groups A and B in Two Dimensions

Statistic	Group A	Group B
Percentage of Variance Accounted for by Model	54.7	60.5
Average Correlation Coefficient across Subjects	0.724	0.771
Correlation between Axes 1 and 2	−0.355	−0.634

axis of group A appears to represent a toast/nontoast dimension. The horizontal axis of group B is a bit more equivocal, but separates breakfast items from snack items. Moreover, positions of the stimuli vary somewhat between the two configurations. The linear relationship between the two configurations can be discerned by a simple correlation analysis. The pairwise dimension correlations of the two-space solutions are presented in Table 3.10.

We note from Table 3.10 that axis 1 of group A is highly correlated negatively ($r = -0.955$) with axis 2 of group B. Thus, both subgroups exhibit high communality for the sweetness dimension.[15] And by looking back at Figure 3.7 and Table 3.3 we observe that the groups are highly separated in the subject space; this, of course, is to be expected, given the manner in which the groups were constructed.

Table 3.10   Pairwise Correlations between Axes of Group A and B Two-space Configurations

Group A	Group B	
	Axis 1	Axis 2
Axis 1	0.596	−0.955
Axis 2	0.119	0.369

PROPERTY FITTING AT THE SUBGROUP LEVEL

It is now of interest to examine the way in which the 10 bipolar scale ratings (see Table 1.1 for scale descriptions) related to the stimulus configurations of groups A and B, as obtained from the scaling of direct judgments of dissimilarity. This part of the analysis employed three methods of property fitting, namely, max "r" linear regression, monotone regression, and nonlinear regression. Each method was used separately for the two subgroups. The input data in each case consisted of the average scale ratings of one of the two subgroups and the corresponding INDSCAL stimulus coordinates for the average

[15] Although not shown here, group A and group B subjects also differ on the third dimension in terms of subject saliences for the dimensions of the total-group INDSCAL solution (see Table C.15).

subject of each group. That is, these spaces are similar to Figures 3.8 and 3.9 except for differential stretching according to the square roots of the average-subject saliences (see Tables C.25 and C.26). The average ratings (that is, property matrices) for groups A and B are shown in Tables C.27 and C.28.

The property-fitting methods assist in further interpretation of the stimulus spaces, making possible a more intensive study of the differences in the configurations of groups A and B. The results of each method are discussed in turn.

MAX "r" LINEAR REGRESSION PROCEDURE

The max "r" procedure of property fitting finds the best direction in the stimulus space for each property scale so that the projections of the stimuli onto the fitted vector maximally correlate linearly with the original ratings on the property. This method amounts to a multiple linear regression with each property scale serving, in turn, as a criterion variable. The resulting multiple correlation (degree of fit) for each fitted vector and the direction cosines are tabulated for groups A and B in Table 3.11. The fitted vectors are graphically portrayed in Figure 3.10 for group A and in Figure 3.11 for group B.

The multiple correlation coefficients in Table 3.11 indicate how well the construct represented by the property scale is linearly related to the dimensions of the configuration. The root mean squares of the correlations are 0.74 and 0.77, respectively, for group A and group B. Also, the patterns of individual fits

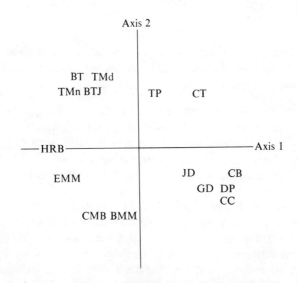

Figure 3.8   Two-space Stimulus Configuration of Group A from INDSCAL Analysis of Direct Dissimilarities (Projections scaled to unit sums of squares) (See Figure 3.4 for key.)

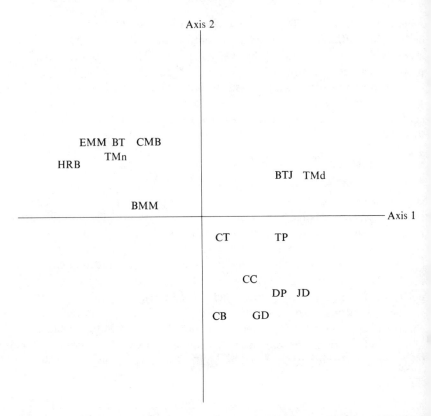

Figure 3.9   Two-space Stimulus Configuration of Group B from INDSCAL Analysis of Direct Dissimilarities (Projections scaled to unit sums of squares) (See Figure 3.4 for key.)

of the 10 rating scales are quite similar for the two groups. We note that properties 1 and 6, representing, respectively, the constructs "difficulty of preparation" and "texture" are not highly correlated with the perceptual configuration. Apparently these constructs are not relevant for the two-dimensional configurations under discussion; the correlations in each case are less than 0.6.

A comparison of Figures 3.10 and 3.11 reveals some differences in the configurations of groups A and B.[16] First, consider the fitted vector positioned close to the horizontal dimension of group A's configuration, that is, the one labeled "mostly eaten with other foods." However, the same vector is positioned in B's configuration closer to the vertical dimension. But, as mentioned earlier, group B's vertical axis projections are highly correlated (negatively) with group A's horizontal axis projections.

[16]These differences are interesting to note since the INDSCAL procedure using the simultaneous method of estimation produces configurations that are uniquely oriented.

Table 3.11   Results of Max "r" Linear Regression for Groups A and B

| Property Vector | Group A | | | Group B | | |
	Correlation Coefficient	Direction Cosine Axis 1	Axis 2	Correlation Coefficient	Direction Cosine Axis 1	Axis 2
1. Easy to prepare/ Hard to prepare	0.437	−0.814	−0.581	0.412	−0.888	0.461
2. Simple flavor/ Complex flavor	0.811	0.870	−0.493	0.816	0.505	−0.863
3. Mainly for adults/ Mainly for kids	0.614	0.933	0.360	0.706	0.987	0.162
4. High calories/ Low calories	0.738	−0.915	0.405	0.936	−0.454	0.891
5. Artificial flavor/ Natural flavor	0.643	−0.977	0.212	0.827	−0.733	0.680
6. Dry texture/ Moist texture	0.077	−0.299	0.954	0.544	0.996	0.084
7. Expensive/Inexpensive	0.894	−0.728	0.686	0.804	0.011	0.999
8. Highly filling/ Not highly filling	0.912	−0.451	0.893	0.782	0.206	0.979
9. Mostly eaten by itself/ Mostly eaten with other foods	0.803	−0.991	0.133	0.895	−0.106	0.994
10. Simple shape/ Complex shape	0.974	0.351	−0.936	0.762	−0.412	−0.911
Root Mean Square	0.738			0.765		

MONOTONE REGRESSION PROCEDURE

The monotone regression procedure finds the best possible monotone function to relate the original ratings on the property scale to the projections of the stimuli on the fitted vector. Thus, this method of property fitting can be considered to be a monotone analogue of the max "r" procedure. The results obtained from this method (whose theory is discussed in Appendix B) are presented numerically in Table 3.12 and graphically in Figure 3.12 for group A and Figure 3.13 for group B.

The correlation coefficients of Table 3.12 for the monotone fit and Table 3.11 for the max "r" procedure can be directly compared. Not surprisingly, the degree of fit is higher in the monotone case for every property vector fitted; the root mean square is 0.85 for group A and 0.90 for group B, compared to 0.74 and 0.77, respectively, under the linear model. However, the positions of most of the fitted vectors in the stimulus space are not altered very much.

NONLINEAR CORRELATION PROCEDURE

In contrast to the max "r" and monotone regression methods, the index of nonlinear correlation, Carroll and Chang's kappa procedure [16], fits a nonlinear, and possibly nonmonotonic function to the ratings on each property.

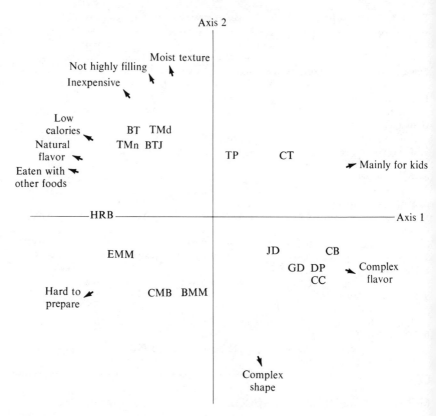

Figure 3.10   10 Property Vectors Fitted in the Average-subject Stimulus Space of Group A Using Max "r" Method

Key

TP	Toast pop-up		BTJ	Buttered toast and jelly
BT	Buttered toast		TMn	Toast and margarine
EMM	English muffin and margarine		CB	Cinnamon bun
JD	Jelly donut		DP	Danish pastry
CT	Cinnamon toast		GD	Glazed donut
BMM	Blueberry muffin and margarine		CC	Coffee cake
HRB	Hard rolls and butter		CMB	Corn muffin and butter
TMd	Toast and marmalade		→	Ends of vectors

The procedure involves extracting the smallest eigenroot, called kappa, associated with each property of a matrix derived from the ratings and the stimulus coordinates. (See Appendix B for a theoretical discussion of the procedure.) The results of this method are presented in Table 3.13. For each group and each property are shown (linear) correlation coefficients (between original and fitted vector) and also the direction cosines of the fitted vector in the original stimulus

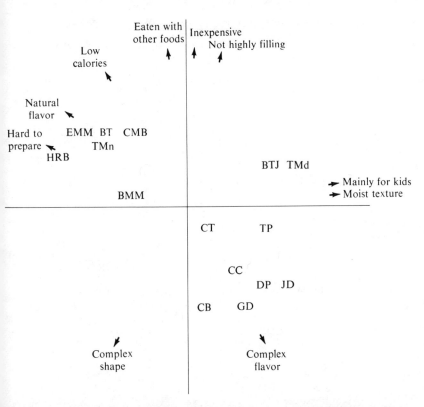

Figure 3.11   10 Property Vectors Fitted in the Average-subject Stimulus Space of Group B Using Max "r" Method (See Figure 3.4 for key.)

Table 3.12   Results of Monotone Regression for Groups A and B

Property Vector	Group A Correlation Coefficient*	Group A Direction Cosine Axis 1	Group A Direction Cosine Axis 2	Group B Correlation Coefficient*	Group B Direction Cosine Axis 1	Group B Direction Cosine Axis 2
1	0.674	−0.561	−0.828	0.593	−0.985	0.175
2	0.911	0.950	−0.313	0.889	0.472	−0.882
3	0.706	0.997	0.083	0.838	0.963	0.183
4	0.863	−0.980	0.200	0.991	−0.440	0.898
5	0.835	−0.913	0.408	0.954	−0.770	0.638
6	0.466	0.417	0.909	0.862	0.892	0.452
7	0.947	−0.723	0.691	0.948	0.172	0.985
8	0.963	−0.261	0.965	0.913	0.227	0.974
9	0.942	−0.982	0.188	0.974	−0.055	0.999
10	0.999	0.332	−0.944	0.933	−0.304	−0.953
Root mean square	0.846			0.896		

*These *linear* correlations between fitted scale values and monotonely transformed property scale values are used only for comparison purposes with Table 3.11.

71

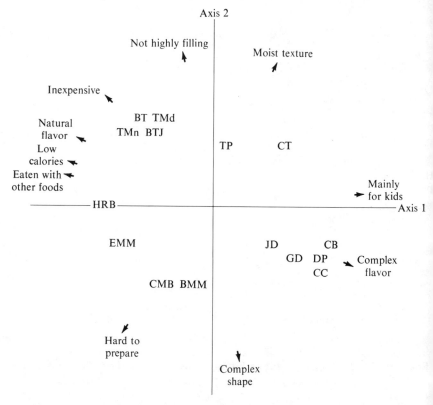

Figure 3.12   10 Property Vectors Fitted in the Average-subject Stimulus Space of Group A Using Monotone Regression Method (See Figure 3.4 for key.)

space. The fitted vectors are shown graphically in Figures 3.14 and 3.15 for the two subgroups. With the exception of a few of the properties, the fitted vectors are positioned quite closely to their counterparts found by the max "r" linear and the monotone regression procedures.

These results support our interpretation of the horizontal dimension of group A and vertical dimension of group B as a sweetness dimension. The root mean squares of 0.69 and 0.75 for group A and group B, respectively, are about the same as those found by the max "r" linear procedure.

In brief, we have noted that all three property-fitting procedures yield quite similar results with respect to fitted vector directions. Moreover, most of the fitted vectors represent composites of the INDSCAL dimensions, rather than being collinear with either the horizontal or vertical axes.

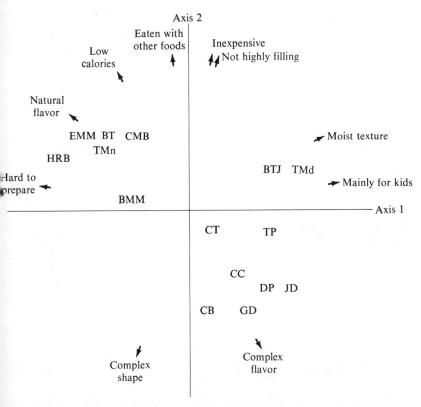

Figure 3.13   10 Property Vectors Fitted in the Average-subject Stimulus Space of Group B Using Monotone Regression Method (See Figure 3.4 for key.)

FURTHER ANALYSIS OF SUBGROUP DIFFERENCES BASED ON RATINGS DATA

It is also interesting to extend the analysis at the subgroup level to the ratings data. With this objective, two 10×15 matrices of *average* ratings were analyzed using the INDSCAL procedure.[17] First, derived interstimulus distances were computed for group A and group B separately. The resulting three-way matrix ($2 \times 15 \times 15$) was submitted to the INDSCAL program, and a two-dimensional solution was obtained.

[17] A more extensive approach not pursued here would have entailed a full CANDECOMP analysis of the three-way $42 \times 10 \times 15$ matrix of original ratings data followed by a multivariate analysis of variance (two-groups) of the resulting subject saliences. Our more limited approach is shown for descriptive purposes only.

Table 3.13 Results of Nonlinear Correlation Procedure for Groups A and B

Property Vector	Group A			Group B		
	Correlation Coefficient*	Direction Axis 1	Cosine Axis 2	Correlation Coefficient*	Direction Axis 1	Cosine Axis 2
1	0.437	−0.813	−0.582	0.345	−0.006	1.000
2	0.758	1.000	0.005	0.815	0.460	−0.888
3	0.387	0.684	−0.730	0.705	0.976	0.218
4	0.698	−0.999	−0.042	0.933	−0.317	0.949
5	0.588	−0.671	0.742	0.781	−0.175	0.985
6	0.054	−0.989	0.151	0.483	0.889	0.459
7	0.799	−0.776	0.631	0.804	−0.055	0.999
8	0.909	−0.541	0.841	0.783	0.204	0.979
9	0.802	−0.980	0.197	0.892	0.013	1.000
10	0.947	0.305	−0.953	0.743	−0.241	−0.971
Root mean square	0.691			0.749		

*These linear coefficients between fitted scale values and transformed property scale values are used only for comparison purposes with Table 3.11. The nonlinear correlation technique is *not* based on maximizing these values.

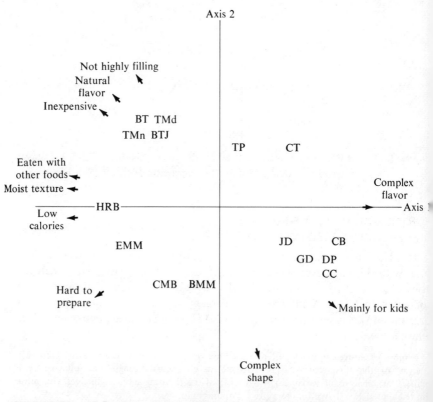

Figure 3.14   10 Property Vectors Fitted in the Average-subject Stimulus Space of Group A Using Index of Nonlinear Correlation (See Figure 3.4 for key.)

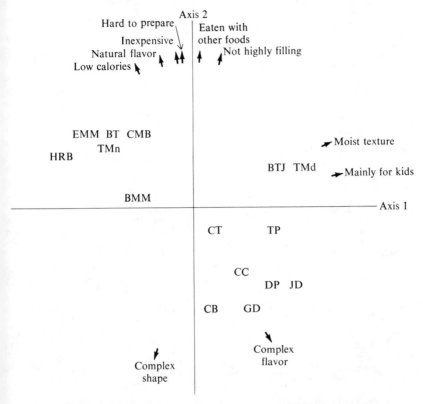

Figure 3.15   10 Property Vectors Fitted in the Average-subject Stimulus Space of Group B Using Index of Nonlinear Correlation (See Figure 3.4 for key.)

The model accounted for over 90 percent of the variance in the average ratings data for the two subgroups. The dimensions of the stimulus space turned out to be highly correlated; the value of the correlation coefficient was −0.72. This indicates that the rating scales are highly interdependent at the average-subject level. (The stimulus coordinates estimated from this analysis are presented in Table C.29.)

The saliences assigned by the two pseudosubject groups A and B provide a means for examining subgroup differences. The dimensional saliences for the pseudosubjects were almost identical; the values for dimensions 1 and 2, respectively, were 0.226 and 0.821 for group A and 0.221 and 0.805 for group B. Thus, the two subgroups do *not* appear to differ in terms of their average ratings on the bipolar scales.

Figure 3.16 shows the group stimulus space resulting from this step; and

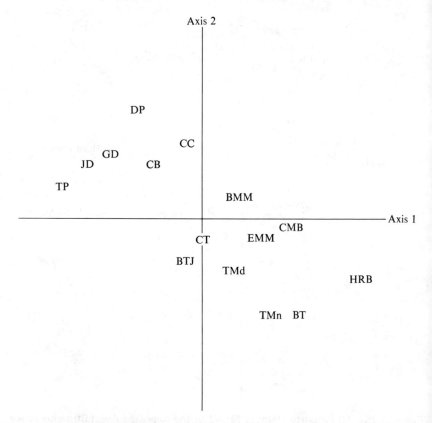

Figure 3.16   Group Stimulus Configuration Obtained from INDSCAL Analysis of Group A and B Averaged Ratings (projections scaled to unit sums of squares) (See Figure 3.4 for key.)

correlation of the axes is evident.[18] The most interesting finding, however, is that subject partitioning based on direct dissimilarities analysis results in subgroups (group A versus group B) that do not appear to differ in regard to configurations obtained from derived distances based on averaged ratings.[19]

SUMMARY

In this chapter we have analyzed at the disaggregate level (a) directly judged dissimilarities and (b) dissimilarities derived from the ratings data. In each case

[18]The rather weak correspondence in orientation between the configurations of Figures 3.6 and 3.16 appears to be due to the fact that only two pseudosubjects are used in the latter analysis. In general the fewer (and less dispersed) the subjects, the less "determinate" is the orientation provided by the INDSCAL method.

[19]Individual pseudosubject goodness-of-fit measures (correlation coefficients) were 0.959 and 0.941 for group A and group B average subjects, respectively.

only the metric version of the INDSCAL algorithm was used. The first part of the analysis resulted in estimates of both the saliences assigned by all respondents to a common (group) stimulus space and the coordinates of that space. The group stimulus spaces based on the two types of dissimilarities data were found to be highly congruent. The two main dimensions of the group stimulus spaces were interpreted as sweet/nonsweet and toast/nontoast.

Next we examined respondent differences in dimension saliences. The subject saliences from the more accurate three-dimensional stimulus space of directly judged dissimilarities were canonically correlated with the 10 background characteristics. This analysis did not show any significant relationship. However, an analysis of the direct similarities judgments between husbands and wives showed interesting results. Husband-wife pairs tended to perceive the food items more similarly than did other male-female pairings.

Using the three-dimensional saliences of directly judged dissimilarities, and the Howard-Harris clustering program, 10 levels of respondent clusters were formed. The two-level grouping, consisting of 19 and 23 respondents, was selected for further analysis. For these two subgroups, labeled group A and group B, INDSCAL solutions in two dimensions only were obtained using direct judgments of dissimilarity as input. The subgroup stimulus spaces differed in both orientation and stimulus projections, although the groups appeared to exhibit one dimension in common.

The average ratings data for the two subgroups were fitted to their respective average-subject INDSCAL solutions, using three methods of property fitting; max "r" linear regression, monotone regression, and nonlinear correlation. In general it was found that the 10 fitted vectors tended to be composites of the INDSCAL dimensions. Moreover, the property-fitting methods were found useful in interpreting only one of the two dimensions. Still, the average degree of fit for the group of scales in all three methods was fairly high. In most cases fitted vector directions did not vary markedly over the three procedures.

Finally, the average ratings data for groups A and B were analyzed, again using the INDSCAL procedure. This step showed no apparent difference in the ratings assigned by the two subgroup averages. Thus, groups A and B, while differing on judgments of direct dissimilarities, appear on the average to yield quite similar ratings judgments. (However, this does *not* have to be the case for specific individuals in either group.)

CHAPTER 4

INTERNAL ANALYSIS
OF PREFERENCE DATA

In this chapter we turn to the internal analysis of preference data. By this we mean the development of joint spaces—configurations of stimulus points *and* "person" points (or vectors) in a common space—solely from preference or other kinds of dominance data. We work primarily with the data on overall preferences, although one experimental internal analysis involving scenario-dependent preferences is included for completeness.

The main input data, then, consist of a 42×15 matrix of the 42 respondents' overall preference rankings of the 15 food items, whose names appear initially in Table 1.1.

OUTLINE OF THE ANALYSIS

As described in Chapter 1, the multidimensional scaling of preference orderings can be classified in terms of (a) internal versus external analysis, (b) point-point versus point-vector representations, and (c) metric versus nonmetric algorithms. Dealing only with internal analysis in this chapter, we fit point-point and point-vector models to the 42×15 matrix of overall preference data. In so doing we compare the various *derived* stimulus configurations with that obtained directly from the INDSCAL analysis of dissimilarities data described in Chapter 3.

Three methods are used in the first part of this analysis:

1. Carroll and Chang's MDPREF algorithm [17]. This method performs a metric analysis of the 42×15 overall preference matrix in terms of a point-vector representation. The stimuli are represented by points and the respondents by vectors in a common space.
2. Kruskal's M-D-SCAL V algorithm [87], as used for unfolding analysis. This method performs a nonmetric analysis of the 42×15 matrix in terms of a point-point representation; that is, both stimuli and respondents are represented as points in a common space. A program option that allows a different monotone function (relating stimulus preference to subject-stimulus distances) and one that constrains all respondents to the same monotone function (thus assuming intersubject comparability) are used.
3. Carroll and Chang's Parametric Mapping algorithm [126]. This method performs a continuity analysis of the data and yields a stimulus configuration only. The underlying model allows for idiosyncratic differences in individuals' utility functions, including the possibility of nonmonotonicity in the function relating preference to distance of stimuli from the ideal point.

After determining the joint-space configurations by means of the above algorithms, we compare, in various ways, the stimulus configurations "contained in" the preference data with the total group stimulus space obtained, illustratively, by the INDSCAL [15] analysis of direct judgments of dissimilarity (Chapter 3). In this way we can appraise the extent to which the perceptual information of the INDSCAL configuration is retained in the preference data. Several different procedures are used to measure this congruence.

In the next section, we turn to an obverse analysis of the overall preference data. A 42×42 matrix of interperson distances is first derived from the original 42×15 matrix of preferences. This latter matrix is then scaled nonmetrically,

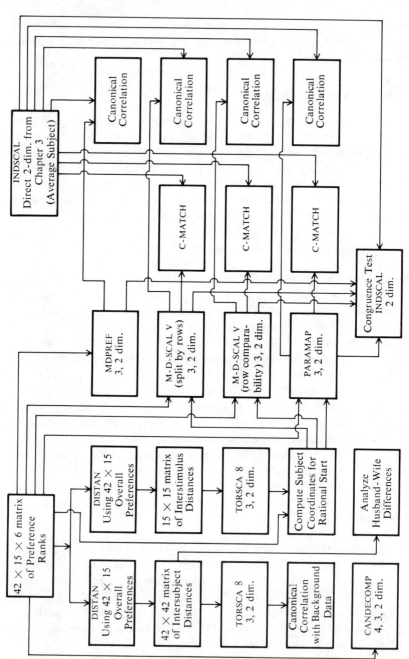

Figure 4.1   Flow Diagram of Internal Analysis

leading to a subject space only. The respondent background data are canonically correlated with the subject coordinates in order to see if communality of preference is related to other characteristics of the respondents. This step is analogous to the respondent background analyses performed in Chapter 3. We also examine, by means similar to Chapter 3, the communality of husband and wife preferences.

In the concluding section of this chapter we examine the relationships among scenario-dependent preferences, including "overall" preference. This type of internal analysis is accomplished by canonical decomposition [15] of the 42 X 15 X 6 three-way matrix of subjects' food item preferences under each of the 6 scenarios described in Table 1.2. This step produces a group stimulus configuration of the 15 food items and loading matrices for both subjects and scenarios.

Figure 4.1 is a flow diagram of the analysis followed in this chapter.

ALTERNATIVE PROCEDURES IN THE INTERNAL ANALYSIS OF PREFERENCE DATA

As already discussed, the internal analysis of preference data must assume communality of perception if differences in preference are not to be confounded with differences in perception.[1] Here we refer to "perception" in the context of evaluation. This implies that (a) the (common) perceptual dimensions continue to constitute the *arguments* of each respondent's utility (or value) function, but (b) the *saliences* of the perceptual dimensions may be altered as one moves from the context of dissimilarities judgments to preference judgments. That is why we use the term *evaluative*, rather than *perceptual*, space. We further assume the perceptual saliences are common to all respondents; that is, the (unknown) perceptual configuration is rotated and differentially stretched in the *same* way by all respondents (as discussed in [47]) before evaluative judgments are made.[2]

We also assume that vectors (or ideal points) *do* differ across subjects; otherwise we would not be able to determine a joint space configuration,

---

[1]An alternative point of view would be to regard the "group" evaluative space (to be solved for) as the appropriate reference configuration. We do not find this type of assumption very appealing, however. Finally, one *could* consider a type of weighted unfolding model [13] in which other techniques could be used for internal analysis [14]. Still, one must contend with the confounding of perceptual and preference saliences under any purely internal analysis procedure.

[2]Some care should be taken in the interpretation of these assumptions. When we assert that the similarities dimensions are relevant for preferences, we refer, conceptually, to the unknown "master" space, only a subspace of which may be obtained from the collection of either overall similarities or overall preference data. It is probable that *no* single task and/or scenario underlying the collection of similarities or preferences provides this "master" perceptual space.

metrically or nonmetrically. This assumption appears quite reasonable from a substantive standpoint.

Finally, the models used here are "deterministic" in that they assume (a) the positions of the stimulus points and person points (or vectors) are "fixed" in the common space (rather than random variables), and (b) it is the job of the algorithms to find the points or vectors whose relationships best reproduce the manifest data relations in specified ways.

POINT-VECTOR MODELS

Point-vector or scalar product models of preference structures represent one of the earliest types of internal analysis. Metric versions have been proposed by Tucker [143] and Slater [130], among others. The metric models derive from principal components procedures in which an $N \times n$ data matrix is approximated, in least squares sense, by the product of two matrices of order $N \times r$ and $r \times n$. The first matrix is usually called the component score matrix and can be represented geometrically as a set of N unit-length vectors (person vectors) in r dimensions. The $r \times n$ matrix consists of n points (the stimuli) in the same r (orthogonal) dimensions. This latter matrix is typically called a component-loading matrix.

More recent versions of the point-vector model such as those by Shepard and Kruskal [127] and Roskam [116] are nonmetric analogues of the factor model. That is, they find stimulus points and person vectors (in a common space) whose projections of points onto vectors best reproduce, for a specified dimensionality, the manifest data *orderings*, simultaneously for all persons.

Mention should also be made of Carroll and Chang's MDPREF model [17], the point-vector procedure used in this chapter. The algorithm also can be used in the analysis of paired comparison data. While the model is metric in utilizing Eckart-Young decomposition, it does not make the types of distributional assumptions often associated with factor analytic methods.

In using point-vector models to represent preference data, we assume, at a minimum, that utility increases monotonely with increases along each dimension (when dimensions are appropriately reflected). The cosines of the angle which a person vector makes with the reference axes represent the tradeoffs that the individual is assumed to make among changes in the "score" or level along each stimulus attribute (axis).

POINT-POINT MODELS

Point-point models, as the name suggests, represent both stimuli and individuals as points in a common space. A person point can be thought of as coinciding with a hypothetical stimulus that combines the dimension scores the person would prefer to all other combinations, that is, his ideal point. Earlier versions of this model assumed that utility would decline monotonically and symmetrically in all directions from the ideal point.

A fully nonmetric version of the point-point representation in multidimensional space has been suggested by Bennett and Hays [5]; in this case, however, one can find only the rank order of point projections, not the joint-space configuration itself.

More recently, Schonemann [118] has proposed a metric version of the unfolding (point-point) representation in which a joint-space configuration can be obtained. But the most important algorithmic advances probably have been made in nonmetric methods. Kruskal [87], Lingoes and Guttman [92], and Roskam [116] have all developed nonmetric approaches that accept rank-order preference data but yield metric joint space configurations. If comparability across persons' rank orders is assumed, Young's procedure [161] should be added to this list.

Finally, recent developments by Carroll and Chang [14, 126] have generalized the above models to allow for utility functions that need not be monotonic.[3] Carroll's polynomial factor analysis model and method [14] allows for quite general prespecified forms, while Carroll's and Chang's Parametric Mapping approach [126] is probably the most general of all and yields only a stimulus configuration. Then, if desired, the preference data can be entered again in conducting an external analysis of the type discussed in Chapter 5.

INTERNAL ANALYSIS OF OVERALL PREFERENCES

The 42 × 15 matrix of overall preferences constitutes the principal data set in this chapter. We first discuss the application of a point-vector model, Carroll and Chang's MDPREF approach, and then give applications of point-point models.

MDPREF ANALYSIS

The MDPREF method can be used to scale either individual subjects' paired comparisons data (including the cases of missing data and indifference relations) or their ranked data. In our case the data on overall preferences are already expressed as ranks in Table 4.1.

As indicated, the MDPREF scaling algorithm utilizes Eckart-Young decomposition (a principal components analysis) in which stimuli are represented as points and subjects as vectors in the same space. In this application the program was set to yield three- and two-dimensional solutions. Figure 4.2 shows the two-dimensional solution, and Appendix Table C.30 records supporting detail for both the three- and two-dimensional computer runs.

---

[3]In this context it should be mentioned that Kruskal's simple scaling method [87] permits the use of prespecified functional forms relating preference to distance from the ideal point that need not be monotone.

Table 4.1   Overall Preference Rankings by Individual Subject

	Stimulus*														
Subject	1	2	3	4	5	6	7	8	9	10	11	12	13	14	15
011	13	12	7	3	5	4	8	11	10	15	2	1	6	9	14
012	15	11	6	3	10	5	14	8	9	12	7	1	4	2	13
021	15	10	12	14	3	2	9	8	7	11	1	6	4	5	13
022	6	14	11	3	7	8	12	10	9	15	4	1	2	5	13
031	15	9	6	14	13	2	12	8	7	10	11	1	4	3	5
032	9	11	14	4	7	6	15	10	8	12	5	2	3	1	13
041	9	14	5	6	8	4	13	11	12	15	7	2	1	3	10
042	15	10	12	6	9	2	13	8	7	11	3	1	5	4	14
051	15	12	2	4	5	8	10	11	3	13	7	9	6	1	14
052	15	13	10	7	6	4	9	12	11	14	5	2	8	1	3
061	9	2	4	15	8	5	1	10	6	7	11	13	14	12	3
062	11	1	2	15	12	3	4	8	7	14	10	9	13	5	6
071	12	1	14	4	5	6	11	13	2	15	10	3	9	8	7
072	13	11	14	5	4	12	10	8	7	15	3	2	6	1	9
081	12	11	8	1	4	7	14	10	9	13	5	2	6	3	15
082	15	12	4	14	5	3	11	9	7	13	6	8	1	2	10
091	7	10	8	3	13	6	15	12	11	9	5	1	4	2	14
092	7	12	6	4	10	1	15	9	8	13	5	3	14	2	11
101	2	9	8	5	15	12	7	10	6	11	1	3	4	13	14
102	10	11	15	6	9	4	14	2	13	12	8	1	3	7	5
111	12	1	2	10	3	15	5	6	4	13	7	11	8	9	14
112	14	12	10	1	11	5	15	8	7	13	2	6	4	3	9
121	14	6	1	13	2	5	15	8	4	12	7	10	9	3	11
122	10	11	9	15	5	6	12	1	3	13	8	2	14	4	7
131	15	8	7	5	9	10	13	3	11	6	2	1	12	4	14
132	15	13	8	5	10	7	14	12	11	6	4	1	3	2	9
141	11	3	6	14	1	7	9	4	2	5	10	15	13	12	8
142	6	15	3	11	8	2	13	9	10	14	5	7	12	1	4
151	15	7	10	2	12	9	13	8	5	6	11	1	3	4	14
152	15	10	7	2	9	6	14	12	8	11	5	3	1	4	13
161	11	4	9	10	15	8	6	5	1	13	14	2	12	3	7
162	9	3	10	13	14	11	1	2	4	5	15	6	7	8	12
171	15	8	1	11	10	2	4	13	14	9	6	5	12	3	7
172	15	8	3	11	10	2	4	13	14	9	6	5	12	1	7
181	15	6	10	14	12	8	2	4	3	5	11	1	13	7	9
182	12	2	13	11	9	15	3	1	4	5	6	8	10	7	14
191	5	1	6	11	12	10	7	4	3	2	13	9	8	14	15
192	15	11	7	13	4	6	9	14	8	12	1	10	3	2	5
201	6	1	12	5	15	9	2	7	11	3	8	10	4	14	13
202	14	1	5	15	4	6	3	8	9	2	12	11	13	10	7
211	10	3	2	14	9	1	8	12	13	4	11	5	15	6	7
212	13	3	1	14	4	10	5	15	6	2	11	7	12	8	9

*See Table 1.1 for stimulus identification. Cell entries are ranks. Rank "1" indicates most preferred stimulus.

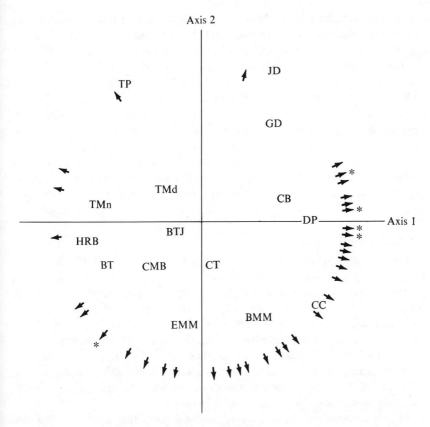

Figure 4.2   Two-space Point-Vector Configuration from MDPREF Analysis

Key

TP	Toast pop-up		BTJ	Buttered toast and jelly
BT	Buttered toast		TMn	Toast and margarine
EMM	English muffin and margarine		CB	Cinnamon bun
JD	Jelly donut		DP	Danish pastry
CT	Cinnamon toast		GD	Glazed donut
BMM	Blueberry muffin and margarine		CC	Coffee cake
HRB	Hard rolls and butter		CMB	Corn muffin and butter
TMd	Toast and marmalade		→	Ends of vector
			→ *	Multiple terminus

When we compare Figure 4.2 with the INDSCAL configuration of Figure 3.4, we note changes in the derived stimulus space. The MDPREF solution, as shown in the arbitrary principal components orientation, evidences some rotation and differential stretching of the INDSCAL configuration.[4] However, it should be noted that the MDPREF method defines solutions *only* up to an affine transform. Hence, the stimulus configuration could be translated, reflected, rotated, and differentially stretched (with an accompanying transform of subject vectors) for appropriate congruence with the INDSCAL configuration.

We first note that the horizontal axis (with the major exceptions of corn muffin and butter and hard rolls and butter) separates the toasted from nontoasted items rather well. The vertical axis is much more difficult to interpret, but in the positioning of the person vectors we observe a preponderance of vector locations in the fourth quadrant. This finding suggests higher preferences, in general, for the sweet items (Danish pastry, glazed donut, and so on). Still, we note that some vectors appear in each quadrant, suggesting that preferences for these food items are quite heterogeneous across the 42 subjects.

M-D-SCAL V ANALYSES

Kruskal's M-D-SCAL V algorithm was applied to the data of Table 4.1. This program is representative of nonmetric unfolding methods that lead to a point-point representation of stimuli and respondents. That is, two sets of points are positioned in a common space in a way that best preserves the manifest rank order for each subject point (defined as an ideal point). Thus, it is assumed that preference declines monotonically and symmetrically with increasing distance between each stimulus point and each ideal point.

If the model holds, we can *deduce* between-subject and between-stimulus relations, although the original monotone constraints are based only on subject-stimulus rankings for each subject in turn.

In this analysis two options were used for unfolding purposes. The first option uses the "split-by-rows" feature to allow for *individual* monotone functions relating distances from the (to-be-solved-for) ideal point for each subject to his manifest rank order. The second option assumes interrow comparability in the data of Table 4.1 and, therefore, obtains only *one* monotone function linking dissimilarities with distance. However, this option still determines individualized ideal point positions.

A rational starting configuration (see Table C.31) was compiled before use of the preceding options.[5] First, the columns of Table 4.1 were treated as profile data and a 15×15 matrix of Euclidean distances was computed between all

---

[4]It would have been possible to use property-fitting procedures (similar to those used in Chapter 3) with the ratings scales serving as criterion variables to aid in the interpretation of the stimulus space of Figure 4.2. In view of subsequent analyses made in this chapter this step was not undertaken.

[5]Employment of a rational starting configuration is quite important, as is the use of stress formula 2, in applying M-D-SCAL V to nonmetric unfolding problems. Finally, as suggested by Wish (personal communication), the rational starting configuration itself can be viewed as a type of metric solution (for the stimuli only).

pairs of stimuli. This distance matrix was then transformed to scalar products and factored by principal components; the first three components were retained. Starting coordinate values for the 42 subjects were obtained by computing the centroid of the three most preferred stimuli in each respondent's preference ranking. While this procedure was arbitrary, it provided a reasonable starting configuration, which, of course, was modified during the application of the M-D-SCAL V algorithm.

Row Split Option

The data of Table 4.1 were then scaled by M-D-SCAL V in three and two dimensions, utilizing a maximum of 50 iterations as a program control parameter, under the split-by-rows option. In actuality the program used all 50 iterations in the three-space solution and only 36 iterations in the two-space solution.

Stress values were extremely poor in both computer runs; stress for the three-space solution was 0.361, while stress for the two-space solution was 0.405 (stress formula 2 [87]). Supporting details of the output are shown in Table C.32 and Figure C.9.

Figures 4.3 and 4.4 show, respectively, the two-space configuration of stimuli and ideal points and the associated Shepard diagram. In Figure 4.3 the stimuli with the exception of toast pop-up appear to fall roughly on the circumference of a circle. Ideal-point concentrations are noted in the third and fourth quadrants, suggesting some polarization between groups of respondents who prefer sweet items and those who prefer nonsweet items. However, the poor goodness-of-fit values suggest that (a) either the program was unable to find an appropriate representation in low dimensionality or (b) the simple unfolding model is inadequate to account for these data.[6] We return to this question later in the chapter.

Row Comparability Option

The M-D-SCAL V program was used next in a replication run of the preceding analysis. In this case the split-by-rows feature was omitted, so that only one monotone function was obtained, rather than a separate function for each subject. The rational starting configuration described above was used, and all other control parameters were identical to those used earlier.

The three-space solution required 25 iterations as compared with 26 in the two-space solution. Stress values, respectively, were 0.475 and 0.562—again extremely poor fits of model to data. Figures 4.5 and 4.6 show the resulting

---

[6]In this regard a second run of the data was made, using the three-space solution of the first run as a new starting configuration. Neither the three-space nor two-space configuration was changed appreciably. Moreover, stress values were practically the same as before.

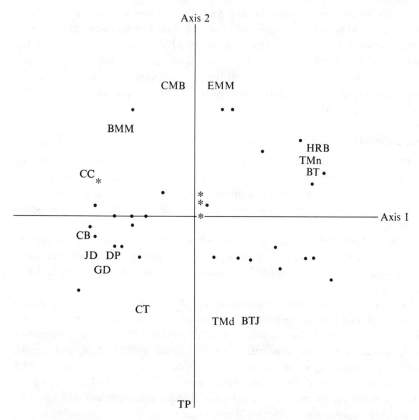

Figure 4.3 Two-space Configuration from M-D-SCAL V Row Split Analysis

Key

TP	Toast pop-up	BTJ	Buttered toast and jelly
BT	Buttered toast	TMn	Toast and margarine
EMM	English muffin and margarine	CB	Cinnamon bun
JD	Jelly donut	DP	Danish pastry
CT	Cinnamon toast	GD	Glazed donut
BMM	Blueberry muffin and margarine	CC	Coffee cake
HRB	Hard rolls and butter	CMB	Corn muffin and butter
TMd	Toast and marmalade	•	Ideal point
		*	Multiple point (ideal)

two-space configuration and the accompanying Shepard diagram, while supporting detail is shown in Table C.33 and Figure C.10.

A comparison of Figure 4.5 to Figure 4.3 shows that the derived stimulus configuration in Figure 4.5 is reflected about the horizontal axis of Figure 4.3. This reflection, of course, is quite permissible under the methods used here. Moreover, some stimuli, for example, cinnamon toast, are positioned consider-

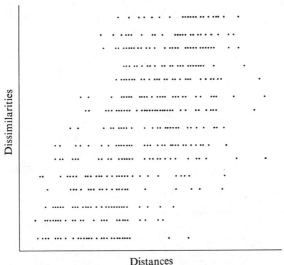

**Figure 4.4   Shepard Diagram Based on Two-space Solution from M-D-SCAL V
Row Split Analysis**

ably far from their (reflected) positions in Figure 4.3. Again we note some polarization among preferences, with tendencies to favor either the sweet or nonsweet items.

As before, the stress values are so poor as to limit severely any attempt at interpretation, but it seems possible that both M-D-SCAL V runs encountered problems of local minima.[7]

PARAMETRIC MAPPING ANALYSIS

The last unfolding algorithm used to analyze Table 4.1 was Carroll and Chang's Parametric Mapping. This program is based on continuity rather than monotonicity. Thus, it can handle individual differences in utility functions; indeed, the functions need not be monotone nor symmetric to an ideal point, but should be reasonably smooth. Only a stimulus configuration is obtained, but external analysis (described in Chapter 5) can be used to fit either ideal points or vector directions to the stimulus space obtained from this internal analysis.

The same type of rational starting configuration (see Table C.34) used in the M-D-SCAL V runs, above, was used for Parametric Mapping. The program was set for a maximum of 25 iterations; and both the three-space and two-space runs required this number of iterations. Carroll's kappa measures for the three-space

[7]A second run was made of these data as well, using the three-space solution of the first run as a starting configuration for the second. Again, neither configurations nor stress values were altered in any appreciable way.

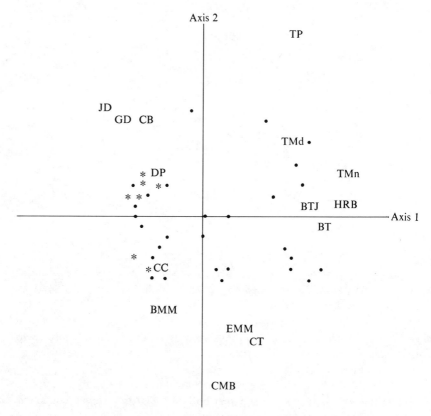

Figure 4.5   Two-space Configuration from M-D-SCAL V Row Comparability Analysis (See Figure 4.3 for key.)

and two-space solutions [126] were 1.011 and 1.022, respectively; both may be considered good fits. Figures 4.7 and 4.8 show the two-space configuration and accompanying Shepard diagram, while ancillary output appears in Table C.35 and Figure C.11.

We note in Figure 4.7 that toasted items are separated from nontoasted items on the horizontal axis (with the exception of corn and English muffins). However, the configuration of Figure 4.7 requires rotation before the stimulus-space interpretations of Chapters 2 and 3 can be applied readily.

TESTS FOR CONGRUENCE WITH INDSCAL STIMULUS SPACE

At this point the internal analysis of preference data has yielded four joint-space configurations, Figures 4.2, 4.3, 4.5, and 4.7. The MDPREF solution is based on a metric approach utilizing a point-vector representation, the two

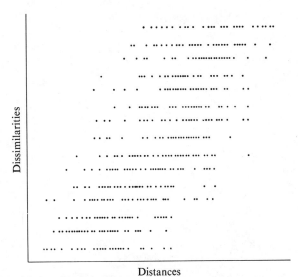

Figure 4.6   Shepard Diagram Based on Two-space Solution from M-D-SCAL V
Row Comparability Analysis

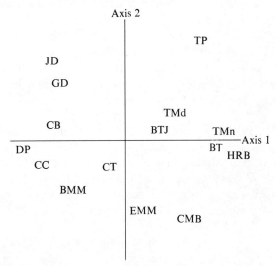

Figure 4.7   Two-space Configuration from Parametric Mapping

Key

TP	Toast pop-up	BTJ	Buttered toast and jelly
BT	Buttered toast	TMn	Toast and margarine
EMM	English muffin and margarine	CB	Cinnamon bun
JD	Jelly donut	DP	Danish pastry
CT	Cinnamon toast	GD	Glazed donut
BMM	Blueberry muffin and margarine	CC	Coffee cake
HRB	Hard rolls and butter	CMB	Corn muffin and butter
TMd	Toast and marmalade		

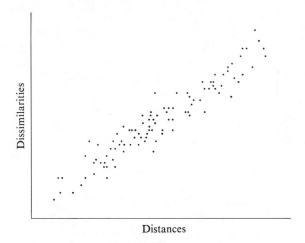

Figure 4.8   Shepard Diagram Based on Two-space Solution from Parametric Mapping

M-D-SCAL V solutions on monotone assumptions, and the Parametric Mapping algorithm on a continuity approach.

The *derived* stimulus configurations of each solution now constitute our focus of interest. To what extent has the INDSCAL group stimulus space (Figure 3.4) of the preceding chapter been revealed through analysis of the overall preferences data? In attempting to answer this question, three congruence procedures are followed:

1. An orthogonal matching procedure [22] similar to that used in Chapter 2
2. A more general affine transformation, as provided by canonical correlation
3. An INDSCAL analysis involving the determination of "subject" weights, given the stimulus configuration of Figure 3.4, differentially stretched using average-subject weights, that best account for the scalar products of each stimulus configuration derived from the preference data

As a first step in applying these three approaches, the stimulus coordinates (15 X 2) from Figures 4.2, 4.3, 4.5, and 4.7 were culled from the internal analyses. These coordinates and the INDSCAL coordinates of Figure 3.4 (now differentially stretched to reflect dimension saliences of the average subject) are shown in Table 4.2.

ORTHOGONAL ROTATION TO CONGRUENCE

The orthogonal rotation procedure used here is similar to that in Chapter 2. In this case all of the matrices of Table 4.2 (except the one obtained from MDPREF) were translated to a centroid of zero and rotated to principal components; vector lengths were adjusted to result in a mean distance from the origin of unity. The INDSCAL solution, differentially stretched according to square roots of the saliences of the average subject, was then used as a target and

Table 4.2   Two-space Stimulus Configurations Derived from Internal Analyses of Overall Preference Data and INDSCAL Average-subject Coordinates

Stimulus	INDSCAL (Target)*		MDPREF		M-D-SCAL V Row Split	
	Axis 1	Axis 2	Axis 1	Axis 2	Axis 1	Axis 2
1†	0.111	−0.244	0.264	0.465	0.033	−2.021
2	−0.240	−0.226	0.322	−0.135	1.251	0.413
3	−0.291	0.043	0.054	−0.377	0.264	1.288
4	0.295	0.141	−0.249	0.502	−1.093	−0.464
5	0.047	−0.243	−0.015	−0.145	−0.518	−1.038
6	−0.175	0.224	−0.189	−0.324	−0.799	0.917
7	−0.331	0.037	0.376	−0.085	1.250	0.692
8	0.209	−0.174	0.130	0.113	0.416	−1.134
9	0.193	−0.164	0.083	−0.042	0.547	−1.066
10	−0.236	−0.213	0.335	0.089	1.282	0.513
11	0.127	0.073	−0.263	0.075	−1.143	−0.205
12	0.213	0.171	−0.383	−0.014	−0.957	−0.499
13	0.219	0.170	−0.245	0.320	−1.006	−0.579
14	0.133	0.193	−0.381	−0.292	−1.055	0.369
15	−0.273	0.211	0.162	−0.150	−0.230	1.333

Stimulus	M-D-SCAL V Row Comparability		Parametric Mapping	
	Axis 1	Axis 2	Axis 1	Axis 2
1	0.980	1.861	0.146	0.213
2	1.259	−0.144	0.193	−0.013
3	0.399	−1.178	−0.001	−0.156
4	−0.982	1.116	−0.151	0.165
5	0.531	−1.324	−0.012	−0.063
6	−0.454	−1.029	−0.126	−0.107
7	1.500	0.106	0.216	−0.029
8	1.063	0.727	0.086	0.054
9	1.102	0.158	0.060	0.021
10	1.528	0.488	0.218	0.010
11	−0.680	1.036	−0.139	0.027
12	−0.533	0.445	−0.248	−0.015
13	−0.770	1.021	−0.142	0.120
14	−0.720	−0.449	−0.202	−0.065
15	0.146	−1.744	0.100	−0.161

*These coordinates represent the differentially stretched space of Figure 3.4 using square roots of the average-subject's weights shown in Table C.15.

†See Table 1.1 for stimulus identification.

Table 4.3   Transformation Matrices and Goodness of Fit of Internal Solutions Orthogonally Matched to Average-Subject INDSCAL Target (Two-space Configurations)

Algorithm Used in Internal Analysis of Unfolding Solutions	Axis	Transformation Matrix		Goodness-of-Fit Measure	
		1	2	Interpoint Distance Correlation	Average Cosine
M-D-SCAL V	1	−0.977	0.215	0.779	0.911
Row Split	2	−0.215	−0.977		
M-D-SCAL V	1	0.866	−0.499	0.467	0.760
Row Comparability	2	−0.499	−0.866		
Parametric Mapping	1	−0.695	−0.719	0.568	0.729
	2	0.719	−0.695		

the three stimulus configurations based on unfolding models were orthogonally rotated to it according to the rotation algorithm's criterion of maximizing the sums of cross products. Because the MDPREF procedure defines a solution only up to an affine transform, the stimulus matrix found by this method was *not* used in this set of congruence analyses. However, a general linear transform, in which the INDSCAL dimensions served as criterion variables yielded a root mean square correlation of 0.77.

Table 4.3 summarizes by type of internal analysis solution the transformation matrices required to bring each unfolding solution into best congruence with the target INDSCAL solution, and the goodness-of-fit measures that the program provides as output.[8]

As can be noted from Table 4.3, the derived stimulus configurations show differences, both among themselves and in terms of the reference configuration, the (rotated) average-subject INDSCAL solution. The product-moment correlations of interpoint distance pairs range from 0.467 to 0.779, suggesting that limitation of permissible transformations to a similarity transform is not sufficient to "recover" the (assumed latent) stimulus configuration underlying the preference judgments.

On the other hand, if more general types of transformations such as differential stretching of the axes *after* rotation, are permitted, the fits are improved somewhat (a range of 0.729 to 0.911) as evinced in the average cosine measure.

The average-subject INDSCAL stimulus space obtained in the Chapter 3

---

[8]The preliminary principal components analysis of the INDSCAL solution (utilized in the orthogonal matching program) has nullified the uniqueness of the orientation observed (in unit sums of squares form) in Figure 3.4. This, of course, has no adverse effect on the maintenance of interpoint distances and, hence, is quite appropriate for the congruence test used here.

analysis of direct dissimilarities appears tentatively relevant as the "argument" of the preference functions for the three unfolding models.[9] However, when viewed in the context of preference, this space appears to require rotation and some differential stretching. The INDSCAL configuration as such, is *not* preserved by a similarities transform.

CANONICAL CORRELATION

The second procedure used for congruence testing was canonical correlation. This procedure allows for a more general affine transformation, including translation, reflection, rotation, and differential stretching. In each case the average-subject's INDSCAL two-space coordinates (see Table 4.2) served as the criterion set, and the four internal analysis solutions served, in turn, as the predictor set. At most, two pairs of linear compounds can be obtained for this particular problem. Since canonical correlation involves affine transformations, the MDPREF solution is included in this set of congruence tests.

Appropriate output, consisting of canonical correlations, canonical weights, and statistical significance levels is shown in Table 4.4.

The results of the canonical correlation, which allows both the INDSCAL and derived stimulus spaces to rotate after differential axis stretching and translation, appear uniformly good across the four procedures used in the internal analysis. Canonical correlations for the first linear compound are all above 0.9. Despite the poor stress values observed in the M-D-SCAL V solutions earlier, we now note a high congruence between direct and derived stimulus spaces, given the possibility of a general linear transformation of each.

INDSCAL CONGRUENCE

The INDSCAL procedure itself was next applied as a type of congruence test to the data of Table 4.2. Given the uniqueness of the INDSCAL stimulus orientation, this congruence check appears to be the most relevant of the three. A preliminary step in the analysis involved the computation of interpoint distances between all pairs of stimuli for each internal analysis configuration of Table 4.2. The resulting $4 \times 15 \times 15$ three-way distance matrix was entered as input with the average-subject INDSCAL two-space coordinates shown in Table 4.2. In this case we selected the option of INDSCAL that allows a given matrix (in this case the average-subject INDSCAL coordinates) to be fixed and finds dimensional weights for the pseudosubjects (that is, the four internal analysis configurations) whose fitted scalar products best reproduce their interpoint distance data also converted to scalar products.

Figure 4.9 shows the unchanged stimulus space from Table 4.2 and the

---

[9]In some cases the postrotation ordering of the stimuli is not fully preserved. Hence, we suspect that the similarities and preference dimensions are not identical, but do appear closely related.

Table 4.4   Transformation Matrices and Canonical Correlations of Internal
Solutions Compared by General Linear Matching to Average-Subject
INDSCAL Target Two-Space Configurations

	Axis	Canonical Weight		Canonical Correlation	$p <$
		Criterion	Predictor		
MDPREF					
Compound 1	1	−0.822	0.918	0.946	0.0001
	2	−0.535	−0.397		
Compound 2	1	0.571	0.397	0.534	0.0404
	2	−0.846	0.918		
M-D-SCAL V Row Split					
Compound 1	1	−0.818	−0.057	0.937	0.0001
	2	0.611	1.077		
Compound 2	1	−0.576	1.011	0.867	0.0001
	2	−0.793	−0.104		
M-D-SCAL V Row Comparability					
Compound 1	1	−0.589	0.984	0.917	0.0001
	2	−0.783	−0.160		
Compound 2	1	0.810	0.181	0.620	0.0137
	2	−0.623	0.987		
Parametric Mapping					
Compound 1	1	−0.856	0.899	0.931	0.0001
	2	−0.481	−0.437		
Compound 2	1	0.519	0.437	0.663	0.0072
	2	−0.878	0.899		

pseudosubject weights. The overall goodness of fit (product-moment correlation) was 0.68, while individual goodness-of-fit measures were, respectively, 0.62, 0.82, 0.59, and 0.68 for MDPREF, M-D-SCAL V row split, M-D-SCAL V row comparability, and Parametric Mapping.[10]

As can be noted from Figure 4.9, the pseudosubject weights are grouped together quite closely and suggest an approximately equal weighting on each of the axes. This evidence appears to confirm that the arguments of the preference functions appear to be the dimensions of the INDSCAL configuration of the average subject, as obtained from direct dissimilarities data. But the size of the product-moment correlations between scalar products of the input data and model suggests that the correspondence is far from perfect.

In line with the limited information provided by internal preference analysis

[10] It is useful to note (and in Tables 4.3 and 4.4 as well) that the row-split option of M-D-SCAL V leads to higher congruence with the INDSCAL target than the row comparability option. This suggests that the preferences of different subjects are *not* all described by a single monotone function relating preference rankings to person-stimulus distances.

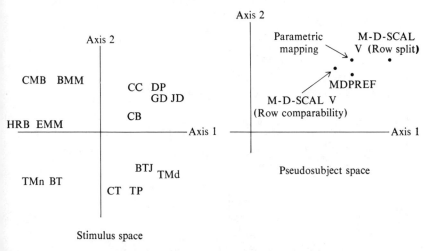

Figure 4.9   Average-subject Stimulus Configuration and Pseudosubject Space from INDSCAL Congruence Analysis

	Key		
TP	Toast pop-up	BTJ	Buttered toast and jelly
BT	Buttered toast	TMn	Toast and margarine
EMM	English muffin and margarine	CB	Cinnamon bun
JD	Jelly donut	DP	Danish pastry
CT	Cinnamon toast	GD	Glazed donut
BMM	Blueberry muffin and margarine	CC	Coffee cake
HRB	Hard rolls and butter	CMB	Corn muffin and butter
TMd	Toast and marmalade	•	Pseudosubject coordinates in subject space

we are now assuming homogeneity of perception, even though we know from the results of Chapter 3 that individual differences *are* found in the respondents' direct judgments of dissimilarity. In Chapter 5 we shall examine the preference-similarities relationships in terms of external analyses of more homogeneous subgroups (groups A and B of Chapter 3).

INDIVIDUAL DIFFERENCES IN OVERALL PREFERENCES

In this section we turn to *interperson* differences in overall preferences. From the original 42×15 matrix of preference data (Table 4.1) Euclidean distances were computed between each pair of subjects in stimulus space. (These distances appear illustratively in Table C.36.)

The resulting 42×42 matrix of dissimilarities was then scaled in three and two dimensions by the TORSCA 8 algorithm. A maximum of 10 first-stage iterations and 15 second-stage iterations were used as parameter values in each case. The stress value was 0.118 for the three-space solution and 0.167 for the two-space solution. Figure 4.10 shows the two-space configuration and Figure

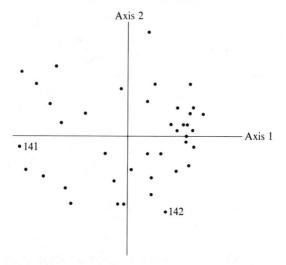

Figure 4.10   Two-space Person Configuration from TORSCA 8 Analysis of Preference Data

Key

• Subject points developed from preference Dissimilarity

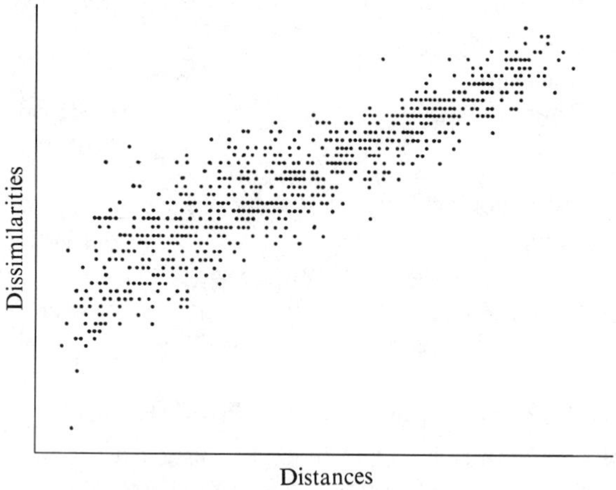

Figure 4.11   Shepard Diagram Based on Two-space Solution from TORSCA 8 Person Configuration

4.11 its accompanying Shepard diagram. Supporting output for both runs appears in Table C.37 and Figure C.12.

In this phase of the analysis we were interested in the relationship of individual differences in overall preferences to respondent background.[11] Figure 4.10 shows that respondents differed in overall preferences; subject 142's preferences (lower right quadrant) were considerably different from subject 141's preferences (lower left quadrant), as evinced by their large separation in the space.

A direct measure of the relationship of individual differences in overall preferences to respondent background data can be made by canonically correlating the coordinate values of the subject space with the respondents' background data: sex, age, number of children, and so on. (Table C.21 shows the mean values of the 42 subjects on each of the background variables, which are described in Table 3.4.)

The somewhat more accurate three-space coordinate values from the TORSCA 8 run were used as the criterion set and each respondent's 10-component vector of background data was used as the predictor set. The canonical correlation (Table 4.5) indicated that only the first of the three possible pairs of linear compounds was statistically significant at the 0.05 alpha level. The associated canonical correlation was 0.692, not particularly high.

Table 4.5 also shows the canonical weights for the first linear compound. Insofar as the criterion set is concerned, the third axis receives the highest weight. The three highest weights in absolute value for the predictor set are associated in descending order with "percentage overweight," the "overweight" dummy variable, and the "weekend breakfast" dummy variable. As might be imagined, subjects who were overweight tended to prefer sweet items more than those who were not overweight. Given the low canonical correlation, however, and subsequent results (reported in Chapter 5) we do not ascribe much importance to this finding.

HUSBAND-WIFE ANALYSIS

The husband-wife analysis was conducted in a fashion similar to that in Chapter 3. Using the three-space TORSCA 8 solution (subject space) as input data, we computed Euclidean distances between husband and wife versus each husband and all other females, and, similarly, between each wife and all other males. Table 4.6 shows the resulting tabulation. In 13 out of 21 cases husband-wife distances were less than husband-other female distances, and in 12 out of 21 cases wife-husband distances were less than wife-other male distances.

---

[11]The above scaling procedure appears closely related to the "subject space" obtained by a metric unfolding analysis [118]. J.D. Carroll (personal communication) has conjectured that if the scaling of interpoint distances were done metrically, the results would be essentially the same, up to an affine transform. Since canonical correlation allows for such affine transforms, it would seem that the correlation results would be quite close to those obtained from employing a metric-unfolding type of subject space. We have not tested this conjecture, however.

Table 4.5   Transformation Matrices and Canonical Correlations of
Subject Coordinates and Background Variables, for
First Linear Compound

Variable	Canonical Weight		Canonical Correlation	$p <$
	Criterion	Predictor		
1	0.025	−0.113	0.692	0.035
2	0.040	−0.373		
3	0.999	0.370		
4		−0.858		
5		1.030		
6		−0.002		
7		0.688		
8		−0.028		
9		0.268		
10		−0.353		

Table 4.6   Husband-Wife Distances Compared to Husband-Other Female and
Wife-Other Male Distances for Preference Data

Pair	Distance of Every Husband (Wife) to Wife (Husband) (1)	Average Distance of Husband to All Other Females (2)	Average Distance of Wife to All Other Males (3)	Sign of (1) − (2)	Sign of (1) − (3)
1	14.56000	16.67596	22.63843	−	−
2	18.75999	20.12193	20.44093	−	−
3	18.32999	21.09193	21.35695	−	−
4	19.64999	19.71194	23.81644	−	−
5	15.94000	17.36996	20.41444	−	−
6	29.42999	25.92194	21.91844	+	+
7	15.56000	20.43243	22.71594	−	−
8	13.56000	19.31244	20.89496	−	−
9	13.19000	15.99697	21.74896	−	−
10	21.90999	22.08095	21.41045	−	+
11	19.89999	25.84041	22.42143	−	−
12	14.97000	21.33145	20.95692	−	−
13	24.00000	20.53195	22.56642	+	+
14	23.48999	23.61394	22.22246	−	+
15	25.60999	24.71394	21.55695	+	+
16	27.89000	26.55794	20.51396	+	+
17	22.00000	19.23596	22.09042	+	−
18	28.90999	26.00142	21.54094	+	+
19	30.12999	25.83891	24.34044	+	+
20	26.07999	23.68443	23.25244	+	+
21	18.10999	25.12692	22.37544	−	−

The expected number in each case is 10.5. However, a sign test indicated that neither result was significant at the 0.05 level.

Thus, in contrast to the results of the Chapter 3 analysis of husband-wife correspondences in dissimilarities judgments, a significant association is not found between husband and wife preferences for these food items.

CANONICAL DECOMPOSITION OF SCENARIO-DEPENDENT PREFERENCES

Up to this point our attention has focused on the slice of the $42 \times 15 \times 6$ three-way matrix of preference rankings representing overall preferences. However, Carroll and Chang's INDSCAL program [15] also permits analysis via canonical decomposition of multiway *rectangular* matrices. That is, it is possible to obtain a group stimulus space of the 15 food items across subjects and scenarios. (An application of this feature was described in Chapter 2.)

Canonical decomposition assumes that any entry in the $42 \times 15 \times 6$ three-way matrix (obtained from Appendix A) of scenario-dependent preferences is a multiplicative combination of a subject-loading matrix, a group stimulus space of food items, and a scenario-loading matrix. As before, the group stimulus space is uniquely oriented.

In this chapter canonical decomposition represents another type of internal analysis of preference data and can be used when subjects express preferences under a variety of scenarios. Unlike the previous internal analysis procedures, canonical decomposition via INDSCAL results in a unique orientation of the group stimulus space.

Given the rather experimental nature of this approach, we elected to run the analyses in four, three, and two dimensions. However, since the respective accounted-for variances in the three-way scalar products matrix were 0.88, 0.87, and 0.85, only the two-dimensional results are described here. Supporting data for the three-dimensional results (loadings, stimulus coordinates, and individual subject correlations) are shown in Tables C.38, C.39, and C.40.

Canonical decomposition applied to rectangular matrices results in a set of coordinate values for each data mode, that is, subjects, stimuli, and scenarios. In this problem the coordinate values for subjects and scenarios can be viewed as types of factor loadings for each of the dimensions.

Figure 4.12 shows the two-dimensional group stimulus space and scenario space. Supporting numerical data for these spaces and also for the subject space are shown in Tables C.38, C.39, and C.40.

We examine the group stimulus space of Figure 4.12 first. The most striking characteristic of this configuration is the high correlation between stimulus dimensions. We also note that the sweetness dimension is especially dominant. However, a little reflection suggests that the sweetness dimension *would* be most salient in differentiating scenarios. As can be noted from Table 1.2, the scenarios range from heavy breakfasts to light breakfasts and snacks. As might be

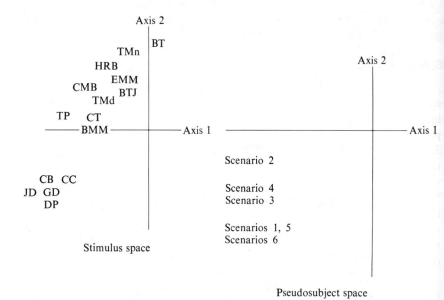

Figure 4.12   Two-space Stimulus Configuration and Pseudosubject Space from CANDECOMP Analysis of Three-way Preferences Matrix

Key

TP	Toast pop-up	BTJ	Buttered toast and jelly
BT	Buttered toast	TMn	Toast and margarine
EMM	English muffin and margarine	CB	Cinnamon bun
JD	Jelly donut	DP	Danish pastry
CT	Cinnamon toast	GD	Glazed donut
BMM	Blueberry muffin and margarine	CC	Coffee cake
HRB	Hard rolls and butter	CMB	Corn muffin and butter
TMd	Toast and marmalade		

surmised, the perceived sweetness of the food items (rather than toast/nontoast) is probably most appropriate in distinguishing among items that "go with" heavy versus light breakfasts or snacks.

This observation appears to be reinforced by the scenario loadings also shown in Figure 4.12. Here we note separations among (a) the egg-type entree (scenario 2), (b) the other heavy breakfast entrees (scenarios 3 and 4), and (c) the very light breakfast and/or snack (scenarios 5 and 6). Interestingly enough, overall preference (scenario 1) plots closest to scenarios 5 and 6; this suggests that our subjects were evaluating the stimuli in isolation, not in combination with other foods.

Because of the experimental character of this three-way canonical decomposition, we do not explore it further. However, this feature of INDSCAL might be quite useful in future studies of multimode rectangular data matrices of the sort illustrated here.[12]

SUMMARY

In this chapter we have focused on the internal analysis of preference data and the relationships of derived stimulus spaces to the space obtained from an independent analysis of dissimilarities data. In so doing we have ignored the perceptual configurations already available from the analyses of Chapters 2 and 3. Four algorithms involving linear, monotonic, and continuity assumptions were used to derive stimulus spaces (and in three of the four cases person points, or vectors) from the group's preference data. A comparison of these spaces with the "known" stimulus configuration of direct dissimilarities data obtained from the INDSCAL analysis demonstrated that the perceptual dimensions represent arguments of the preference function. However, the derived stimulus configurations require rotation and some differential stretching of the axes in order to fit the reference INDSCAL configuration.

An anlysis of interperson differences in preferences identified the predominant background variable as degree of overweight. While overweight respondents tended to prefer sweet items, the canonical correlation was not compellingly high. No association was noted among husband-wife preferences for this group of stimuli. The three-way scenario-dependent preference analysis indicated that the sweetness dimension was most salient in differentiating among different types of breakfast and/or snack entrees.

---

[12] A possibly superior approach to this type of analysis would involve *separate* scalings of each set of scenario-dependent preferences (via M-D-SCAL V or Parametric Mapping), followed by an INDSCAL analysis of interpoint distances computed between *stimulus* pairs (only) in the separate derived spaces.

CHAPTER 5

EXTERNAL ANALYSIS
OF PREFERENCE DATA

This chapter extends the discussion of Chapter 4 to external analysis. That is, the preference data are fitted into stimulus spaces found from *prior* analyses of dissimilarities data obtained from the same subjects for the same set of stimuli. The main input data consist of the following:

1. Two perceptual configurations, labeled group A and group B, obtained from an INDSCAL analysis of the direct dissimilarities of Chapter 3. We maintain

the separateness of these two configurations throughout the analyses of this chapter.

2. A 42 × 15 × 6 three-way matrix of each respondent's scenario-dependent preferences, including the case of overall preferences. Descriptions of the scenarios appear in Table 1.2.
3. Respondent scores on background variables, also as described in Table 1.2.

OUTLINE OF ANALYSIS

In Chapter 3 we first partitioned the 42 subjects on the basis of communality of perception, as obtained by the application of the INDSCAL model to direct judgments of dissimilarity. This led to group A, consisting of 19 subjects, and group B, consisting of 23 subjects. This partitioning of respondents was not introduced in Chapter 4, since the internal models of that chapter assume total-group homogeneity of perception in order to avoid confounding differences in perception with differences in preference.

However, in this chapter exploring models of external analysis, we maintain the separateness of groups A and B. We know from the analyses of Chapter 4 that on a *total-group* basis:

1. The arguments of the preference functions appear to be similar to perceptual dimensions found in both the aggregate (Chapter 2) and disaggregate (Chapter 3) analyses of dissimilarities data.
2. The dimensions of the arbitrarily oriented derived stimulus spaces of Chapter 4 require rotation and some differential stretching to be made congruent with the average-subject INDSCAL solution found in the Chapter 3 analysis of direct dissimilarities data.

For point 1, congruence tests permitting general linear transformations (such as canonical correlation) of each space indicated that the derived configurations could be matched rather closely with the average-subject INDSCAL solution of Chapter 3 (which in turn is closely related to the group solutions of Chapter 2). As point 2 suggests, transformation which involves a fixed-target matrix entails some rotation followed by differential stretching of the axes of the derived configurations along the uniquely oriented INDSCAL axes. This type of congruence test, in which the INDSCAL space is fixed, was also conducted in Chapter 4.

In this chapter we examine in some depth both the metric and nonmetric versions of Carroll and Chang's PREFMAP algorithm [13]. For the two-dimensional perceptual spaces of group A and group B separately, we:

1. Fit overall preferences, at the individual level, to the average-subject INDSCAL solutions by means of the metric and nonmetric versions of Carroll and Chang's PREFMAP algorithm.

2. Relate intergroup differences in perceptions and preferences to respondent background data by means of multiple discriminant analysis.
3. Fit scenario-dependent preferences, at the within-group average-subject level, by means of the metric and nonmetric versions of Carroll and Chang's PREFMAP algorithm.
4. Partially replicate step 3 at the *individual* respondent level for subsets of groups A and B made up of the six best-fitting subjects obtained from the INDSCAL subgroup analyses of Chapter 3 (Figures 3.8 and 3.9).

These steps are shown as a flow diagram in Figure 5.1.

Before conducting these analyses we comment on the general characteristics of methods for dealing with the external analysis of preference or other dominance data. We then try to show how external analysis represents a natural procedure in the development of a hierarchy of market segments.

EXTERNAL ANALYSIS AND MARKET SEGMENTATION

In Chapter 4 we distinguished between the descriptors of internal and external analysis of preference data and also enumerated the assumptions underlying internal analysis.

External analysis, while requiring the collection of *both* dissimilarities and preference data, allows the researcher to identify market segments in a structured, hierarchical fashion:

1. Through the use of an individual differences approach to the scaling of dissimilarities data (for example, the INDSCAL model), respondents *first* can be partitioned on the basis of communality of perception, and subgroups of subjects can be identified and respondent background data related to segments formed on the basis of perceptual communality.
2. Preference data for the subgroups thus identified can then be included in an external analysis, permitting the identification of two levels of preference-type segments based on:
   a. Communality in regard to dimension rotation or saliences (now in the context of preference) and, given this communality,
   b. Communality of ideal-point (or vector) location in the respondents' differentially stretched perceptual (or what may now be called "perceptual-evaluative") space. These "higher-level" segments can also be related to respondent background data.
3. Thus, two types of dimension saliences are permitted:
   a. Dimension saliences relating individual subjects to the group stimulus (perceptual) space.
   b. Dimension saliences associated with perceptual-evaluative space *after* a subgroup's configuration has already been differentially stretched in accord with the INDSCAL model.

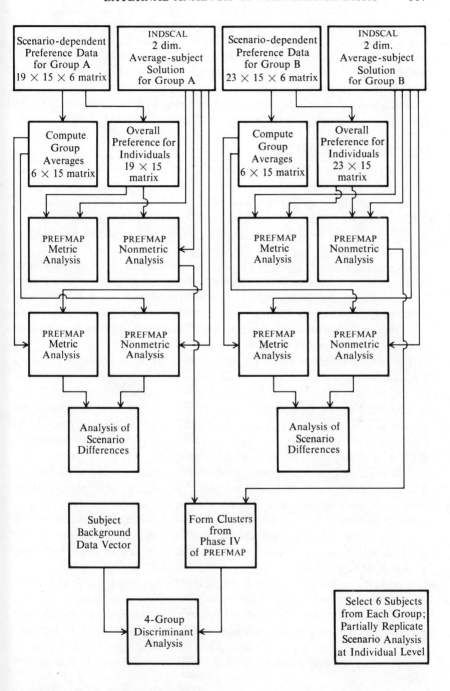

Figure 5.1   Flow Diagram of Analysis

We do not recommend that such an elaborate procedure always be followed in practice. We merely suggest that this type of procedure *can* be followed, assuming the anticipated gains of defining more detailed segments justify the additional costs of analysis. In principle this "meta-problem" of determining level of disaggregation also could be solved; in practice we suspect applied researchers will employ more subjective procedures in determining the type and degree of detail to pursue in the characterization of marketing segments.

THE PREFMAP ALGORITHM

Carroll and Chang's PREFMAP method is well suited for point 2. The *metric* version of the algorithm assumes that a respondent's preferences are related linearly to weighted squared distances in his perceptual space. Through various modifications of this basic formulation, a hierarchy of models ranging from a point-vector model to various point-point models can be handled by the same program.

The simplest model (applied in what is called phase IV in the computer program) is the vector model in which subjects' preferences are represented as scale values along unit-length vectors in the perceptual space obtained from some other analysis (usually a multidimensional analysis of dissimilarities data). As such, this model performs an external analysis analogous to the internal analysis of MDPREF discussed in Chapter 4.

The next most simple model (applied in phase III of the computer program) is a variant of Coombs' unfolding or distance model, which assumes preferences are linearly related to squared distances from each subject's ideal point (in the possibly rotated and differentially stretched perceptual-evaluative space of the average subject). The procedure also permits different kinds of ideal points to be fitted. In addition to the traditional positive ideal point, where preferences decrease with increasing distance of the stimuli from the ideal, the procedure permits negative ideal points, where preferences increase with increasing distance from the ideal, and even positive-negative or mixed ideal points, where preferences increase with distances along some dimensions and decrease with distances from the ideal along other dimensions. However, it is assumed that all subjects share the same perceptual-evaluative space and weight the axes of this space equally. This model represents an external analysis (and metric) analogue of M-D-SCAL V unfolding (using the off-diagonal, row split option).

Next in the hierarchy is the weighted ideal-point model (applied in phase II of the computer program) in which individual preferences are assumed to be linearly related to *weighted* squared distances of stimuli from a subject's ideal point. Weights for each individual are allowed to be idiosyncratic and are applied to the reference space, a possibly rotated and differentially stretched perceptual-evaluative space of the average subject.[1] The most complete model in the

---

[1] As mentioned in Chapter 4, J.D. Carroll has also developed, in a special case of polynomial factor analysis [14], an internal-analysis analogue to this model.

hierarchy (applied in phase I of the computer program), in addition to the above, also permits idiosyncratic rotation of the group stimulus space, as obtained originally from a previous analysis of the subjects' dissimilarities data.

The *nonmetric* version of the PREFMAP model is conceptually identical to the metric version except that monotonicity between preferences and squared distances (or vector projections) replaces the linearity assumption of the metric version. The nonmetric version performs a series of monotone regressions on the preference values, as first estimated by the metric version. The resulting modified parameter values (regression coefficients) are then reparameterized, according to procedures used in the metric version.

UTILIZATION OF PREFMAP
FOR SEGMENT IDENTIFICATION

Returning to the substantive point of identifying segments by communality of perception and preference, it should now be clear that the segments can be based on a number of different considerations:

1. Communality of subjects in perception saliences (as obtained from an INDSCAL analysis of dissimilarities data).
2. Communality of axis orientation of the stimulus configuration, now viewed in a preference or other dominance context. The resulting configuration can now be termed a perceptual-evaluative space.
3. Communality of dimension saliences of the possibly rotated perceptual dimensions; this includes as a special case the simple ideal-point model, in which the axes are equally weighted.
4. Communality of class of ideal-point model, including the vector model as a special case as ideal points become infinitely distant. For the general case this includes positive ideal points, negative (or anti-ideal) points and various combinations.
5. Communality of ideal-point or vector position, given class of ideal point.

As noted earlier, we generally would not desire to segment dissimilarities and preferences in as complete detail as shown. Fortunately, the metric version of the PREFMAP procedure provides some statistical guidance on the level of precision required to segment respondents in regard to preference communality.

EXTERNAL ANALYSIS OF OVERALL PREFERENCES

We first examine the nature of overall preference judgments by means of the PREFMAP method. Our basic input data consist of:

1. Two 15×2 matrices of coordinate values for the average subjects of group A and group B separately, as obtained from Chapter 3's INDSCAL analysis (see Figures 3.8 and 3.9). These matrices appear in Table 5.1 and are identical to

Table 5.1   Average-Subject Coordinates from INDSCAL Analysis for Groups A and B in Two Dimensions

Stimulus*	Group A		Group B	
	Axis 1	Axis 2	Axis 1	Axis 2
1	0.0529	0.1756	0.1702	−0.0521
2	−0.2000	0.2393	−0.2232	0.2072
3	−0.2604	−0.1275	−0.2314	0.2230
4	0.1778	−0.0980	0.2266	−0.2233
5	0.2086	0.1940	0.0351	−0.0560
6	−0.0852	−0.2452	−0.1447	0.0422
7	−0.2836	−0.0148	−0.3248	0.1733
8	−0.1703	0.2437	0.2296	0.1361
9	−0.2071	0.2196	0.2096	0.1336
10	−0.2274	0.2076	−0.2233	0.2009
11	0.3198	−0.0897	0.0420	−0.2896
12	0.2707	−0.1443	0.1881	−0.2186
13	0.2537	−0.1487	0.1172	−0.2898
14	0.2735	−0.1707	0.0981	−0.2118
15	−0.1232	−0.2409	−0.1692	0.2247

*See Table 1.1 for stimulus identification.

Table 5.2   Overall Preference Rankings for Groups A and B at the Individual-Subject Level

Subject	Stimulus*														
	1	2	3	4	5	6	7	8	9	10	11	12	13	14	15
Group A															
041	9†	14	5	6	8	4	13	11	12	15	7	2	1	3	10
082	15	12	4	14	5	3	11	9	7	13	6	8	1	2	10
092	7	12	6	4	10	1	15	9	8	13	5	3	14	2	11
101	2	9	8	5	15	12	7	10	6	11	1	3	4	13	14
102	10	11	15	6	9	4	14	2	13	12	8	1	3	7	5
111	12	1	2	10	3	15	5	6	4	13	7	11	8	9	14
112	14	12	10	1	11	5	15	8	7	13	2	6	4	3	9
121	14	6	1	13	2	5	15	8	4	12	7	10	9	3	11
122	10	11	9	15	5	6	12	1	3	13	8	2	14	4	7
141	11	3	6	14	1	7	9	4	2	5	10	15	13	12	8
151	15	7	10	2	12	9	13	8	5	6	11	1	3	4	14
152	15	10	7	2	9	6	14	12	8	11	5	3	1	4	13
161	11	4	9	10	15	8	6	5	1	13	14	2	12	3	7
162	9	3	10	13	14	11	1	2	4	5	15	6	7	8	12
181	15	6	10	14	12	8	2	4	3	5	11	1	13	7	9
182	12	2	13	11	9	15	3	1	4	5	6	8	10	7	14
191	5	1	6	11	12	10	7	4	3	2	13	9	8	14	15
201	6	1	12	5	15	9	2	7	11	3	8	10	4	14	13
202	14	1	5	15	4	6	3	8	9	2	12	11	13	10	7

Table 5.2   (Continued)

Subject	Stimulus*														
	1	2	3	4	5	6	7	8	9	10	11	12	13	14	15
Group B															
011	13†	12	7	3	5	4	8	11	10	15	2	1	6	9	14
012	15	11	6	3	10	5	14	8	9	12	7	1	4	2	13
021	15	10	12	14	3	2	9	8	7	11	1	6	4	5	13
022	6	14	11	3	7	8	12	10	9	15	4	1	2	5	13
031	15	9	6	14	13	2	12	8	7	10	11	1	4	3	5
032	9	11	14	4	7	6	15	10	8	12	5	2	3	1	13
042	15	10	12	6	9	2	13	8	7	11	3	1	5	4	14
051	15	12	2	4	5	8	10	11	3	13	7	9	6	1	14
052	15	13	10	7	6	4	9	12	11	14	5	2	8	1	3
061	9	2	4	15	8	5	1	10	6	7	11	13	14	12	3
062	11	1	2	15	12	3	4	8	7	14	10	9	13	5	6
071	12	1	14	4	5	6	11	13	2	15	10	3	9	8	7
072	13	11	14	5	4	12	10	8	7	15	3	2	6	1	9
081	12	11	8	1	4	7	14	10	9	13	5	2	6	3	15
091	7	10	8	3	13	6	15	12	11	9	5	1	4	2	14
131	15	8	7	5	9	10	13	3	11	6	2	1	12	4	14
132	15	13	8	5	10	7	14	12	11	6	4	1	3	2	9
142	6	15	3	11	8	2	13	9	10	14	5	7	12	1	4
171	15	8	1	11	10	2	4	13	14	9	6	5	12	3	7
172	15	8	3	11	10	2	4	13	14	9	6	5	12	1	7
192	15	11	7	13	4	6	9	14	8	12	1	10	3	2	5
211	10	3	2	14	9	1	8	12	13	4	11	5	15	6	7
212	13	3	1	14	4	10	5	15	6	2	11	7	12	8	9

*See Table 1.1 for stimulus identification.
†Cell entries are ranks; rank "1" indicates most preferred.

the stimulus coordinates of Figures 3.8 and 3.9 except that the axes have been differentially stretched in accord with the square roots of the average-subject saliences, as recorded in Appendix Tables C.25 and C.26.

2. Two matrices, 19 × 15 and 23 × 15, showing the overall preference rankings of the 19 subjects of group A and the 23 subjects of group B. These matrices appear in Table 5.2.

As stated earlier, our purpose here is to examine individual differences in overall preferences for the 15 food items. We do this separately for perceptual groups A and B, using both metric and nonmetric versions of the PREFMAP method.

METRIC ANALYSIS—ALL PHASES

The first step in the external analysis of preference data, for group A and group B separately, was to fit the metric version of PREFMAP to the perceptual configurations whose coordinate values appear in Table 5.1. All four phases of

PREFMAP were applied—from the most general model, which permits idiosyncratic rotation and differential axis stretching, to the simple vector model, which fits vectors in the rotated and differentially stretched space of the average subject.

By applying the most general model first, one can get some guidance on the level of complexity that represents an adequate fit of model to data. In this instance we wished to see if the *unique orientation* provided by the INDSCAL algorithm in the context of perception remained unique in the context of preference. A way to examine this question is to see how much better the most general model of PREFMAP (applied in phase I) does than the more restricted model (applied in phase II) that constrains all subjects to share the rotation of the average subject.

Table 5.3 shows the multiple correlation coefficients (goodness of fit) for all four phases of PREFMAP, ranging from the most general to the most specific model:

Table 5.3   Multiple Correlation Coefficients for Various Phases of Metric Analysis of Groups A and B

	Group A					Group B			
	Correlation Coefficient for Phase					Correlation Coefficient for Phase			
Subject	I	II	III	IV	Subject	I	II	III	IV
041	0.8680	0.8673	0.8669	0.8662	011	0.7348	0.7103	0.7070	0.6981
082	0.7656	0.7271	0.5862	0.5010	012	0.6636	0.6548	0.6413	0.6399
092	0.5756	0.5505	0.5241	0.5231	021	0.8771	0.7078	0.7077	0.4905
101	0.7467	0.4159	0.3119	0.3118	022	0.9638	0.9637	0.9612	0.9582
102	0.8202	0.7004	0.6068	0.5850	031	0.3462	0.3275	0.2650	0.0885
111	0.7379	0.6826	0.4663	0.4521	032	0.9265	0.9253	0.9205	0.9112
112	0.8281	0.8263	0.7924	0.7329	042	0.7234	0.6924	0.6887	0.6712
121	0.6899	0.5655	0.2371	0.0632	051	0.4005	0.3903	0.3816	0.3786
122	0.6091	0.3671	0.2802	0.1237	052	0.5931	0.5876	0.5854	0.5534
141	0.9551	0.8648	0.7604	0.7600	061	0.9490	0.9383	0.9339	0.9304
151	0.7873	0.7703	0.6455	0.3258	062	0.6182	0.5923	0.5923	0.5840
152	0.8034	0.7938	0.7865	0.7213	071	0.3496	0.3036	0.2542	0.2538
161	0.6212	0.6193	0.5520	0.3056	072	0.7807	0.7779	0.7684	0.7659
162	0.8346	0.7987	0.7668	0.6168	081	0.8126	0.8072	0.7987	0.7987
181	0.7576	0.7538	0.7487	0.4340	091	0.8187	0.7800	0.7802	0.7743
182	0.9227	0.8751	0.8714	0.6514	131	0.4561	0.4560	0.3772	0.3755
191	0.8979	0.8775	0.8456	0.8256	132	0.7936	0.7480	0.7057	0.7001
201	0.7283	0.5682	0.3774	0.3562	142	0.5499	0.5457	0.5013	0.1995
202	0.8739	0.8546	0.7031	0.6842	171	0.7121	0.7114	0.7100	0.7103
					172	0.6986	0.6972	0.6938	0.6931
					192	0.8500	0.8435	0.8161	0.5814
					211	0.7917	0.7657	0.6987	0.6850
					212	0.7030	0.6814	0.6787	0.6780

1. Idiosyncratic rotation *and* differential axis weighting (phase I).
2. Idiosyncratic differential axis weighting in rotated space of average subject (phase II).
3. Ideal-point model with equal axis weighting in rotated and stretched space of average subject (phase III).
4. Vector model in rotated and stretched space of average subject (phase IV).

Table 5.4 shows the corresponding F-ratios, which can be used to ascertain the statistical significance of adding the additional parameters required by the more general versions of PREFMAP.[2]

At this point our interest turns to a comparison of phase I, which applies the model that permits idiosyncratic rotation, with phase II, which applies the model that forces all respondents to share the rotation of the average subject. The root mean squares of the individual goodness-of-fit measures (multiple correlations) for phase I, the most general phase, are 0.787 and 0.723 for groups A and B, respectively. These values drop to only 0.726 and 0.701, respectively, in phase II, suggesting that relatively little appears to be gained (particularly for group B) by allowing idiosyncratic rotation. This result is highly confirmatory of the unique axis orientation afforded by the INDSCAL method.

On an individual-subject level, a comparison of phase I with phase II shows that only subject 141 of group A (and no subject of group B) exhibits an F-value (16.84) that exceeds the conservative critical F-value of 10.56 (with 1 and 9 degrees of freedom) required for significance at the 0.01 level. That is, the data of only 1 out of 42 subjects appear to be significantly better fitted by the most general, phase I, model in the PREFMAP hierarchy.

As a matter of interest, relatively little appears to be gained by going beyond the simple (equal-axis weighting) ideal-point model in the rotated and differentially stretched space of the average subject. In no case does the comparison of phase II with phase III show F-values exceeding the critical value of 10.04 (with 1 and 10 degrees of freedom) required for significance at the 0.01 level.

At this stage, then, it seems reasonable to suppose that most subjects' preference data can be fitted reasonably well by either the simple ideal-point or vector model with no need for idiosyncratic axis rotation or differential stretching of the average-subject stimulus spaces obtained from the INDSCAL analyses of Chapter 3. The respective root mean squares of phases III and IV are 0.649 and 0.564 for group A and 0.686 and 0.653 for group B.

However, this is still a conjecture. Specifically, we next wished to see if the INDSCAL average-subject spaces should be differentially stretched according to

[2]In a few cases one may note slightly negative F-ratios (due to rounding error in the computation of product-moment correlations) in the preceding, and subsequent, tables. These should be interpreted as zero values.

Table 5.4   F-Ratios between Phases for Metric Analysis of Groups A and B

| | F-Ratio between Phases I, J | | | | | |
| | F 1,2 | F 1,3 | F 1,4 | F 2,3 | F 2,4 | F 3,4 |
Subject D.F.*1 9	2 9	3 9	1 10	2 10	1 11
Group A						
041	0.0399	0.0334	0.0372	0.0298	0.0397	0.0544
082	1.2487	2.6364	2.4286	3.9264	2.9453	1.5514
092	0.3813	0.3816	0.2592	0.4071	0.2113	0.0163
101	7.8238	4.6818	3.1214	0.9152	0.4578	0.0004
102	5.0113	4.1879	3.0308	2.4012	1.4563	0.4536
111	1.5549	3.2323	2.2408	4.6517	2.4480	0.1833
112	0.0817	0.8270	1.4177	1.7314	2.2966	2.6835
121	2.6820	3.6040	2.7017	3.8744	2.3212	0.6088
122	3.3811	2.0930	1.6969	0.6500	0.6904	0.7547
141	16.8366	17.1218	11.4360	6.7374	3.3811	0.0164
151	0.6291	2.4064	4.0550	4.3450	5.9902	5.8550
152	0.3902	0.3396	1.0592	0.3077	1.4841	2.8392
161	0.0330	0.5944	1.4285	1.2795	2.3538	3.3431
162	1.7406	1.6098	3.1248	1.3770	3.5537	5.5405
181	0.1208	0.1418	2.7152	0.1785	4.3993	9.3158
182	5.1882	2.7914	8.6267	0.2780	7.2919	15.3106
191	1.6835	2.1223	1.9319	2.3971	1.9246	1.2884
201	3.9764	3.7175	2.5774	2.6652	1.4472	0.1990
202	1.2695	5.1310	3.7537	8.7565	4.8647	0.5705

*Degrees of freedom.

the average subject's preference data *before* application of either phase III or phase IV. This can be checked by entering the PREFMAP program at the phase-II level—which produces a differentially stretched perceptual-evaluative space of the average subject as input to phases III and IV—versus entering phase III directly with the original INDSCAL average-subject configurations. For contrast, this step was done using the nonmetric version of PREFMAP.

Accordingly, the data of Tables 5.1 and 5.2 were reprocessed through PREFMAP. However, this time phases II, III, and IV were utilized in one run and phases III and IV in a second run using the nonmetric version.

NONMETRIC ANALYSIS—PHASES II, III, AND IV
VERSUS PHASES III AND IV

Tables 5.5 and 5.6, respectively, show the results of this step for groups A and B in terms of the multiple correlation (goodness-of-fit) measures; in this case the criterion variable is the best-fitting monotone transformation.[3] Root mean squares for phases III and IV, respectively, are 0.836 and 0.766 under group A; corresponding values for group B are 0.845 and 0.823, given no differential

---

[3]In the nonmetric version of the program, the maximum number of iterations was set at 15 and the critical cutoff value (see Appendix B) at 0.0001.

Table 5.4   (Continued)

		F-Ratio between Phases I, J									
		F 1,2		F 1,3		F 1,4		F 2,3		F 2,4		F 3,4
Subject	D.F.*1	9	2	9	3	9	1	10	2	10	1	11

Subject	F 1,2 (1, 9)	F 1,3 (2, 9)	F 1,4 (3, 9)	F 2,3 (1, 10)	F 2,4 (2, 10)	F 3,4 (1, 11)
Group B						
011	0.6932	0.3916	0.3433	0.0928	0.1737	0.2775
012	0.1880	0.2344	0.1656	0.3057	0.1680	0.0323
021	10.4716	5.2390	6.8780	0.0033	2.6095	5.7355
022	0.0061	0.3095	0.4521	0.6805	0.7495	0.8431
031	0.1289	0.2537	0.3819	0.4147	0.5569	0.7383
032	0.1481	0.3522	0.5976	0.6080	0.8989	1.2336
042	0.8290	0.4629	0.4582	0.0985	0.2775	0.4973
051	0.0860	0.0792	0.0610	0.0797	0.0534	0.0295
052	0.0902	0.0632	0.2106	0.0398	0.2980	0.6093
061	1.8146	1.2805	1.0525	0.6901	0.6208	0.5675
062	0.4571	0.2290	0.1998	0.0010	0.0751	0.1642
071	0.3078	0.2952	0.1975	0.3036	0.1529	0.0024
072	0.1003	0.2195	0.1755	0.3721	0.2342	0.1021
081	0.2317	0.2953	0.1974	0.3887	0.1952	0.0018
091	1.6882	0.8398	0.6433	−0.0080†	0.1131	0.2577
131	0.0009	0.3735	0.2539	0.8289	0.4226	0.0166
132	1.7120	1.6026	1.1321	1.3939	0.7862	0.1724
142	0.0596	0.3296	1.1295	0.6620	1.8372	3.1080
171	0.0191	0.0272	0.0160	0.0392	0.0160	−0.0079†
172	0.0342	0.0583	0.0445	0.0913	0.0549	0.0202
192	0.3554	0.9165	4.1565	1.5795	6.4744	10.8003
211	0.9743	1.6703	1.2659	2.3724	1.4153	0.4074
212	0.5333	0.2985	0.2045	0.0668	0.0420	0.0187

*Degrees of freedom.
†Minus value is due to program rounding error and should be read as zero.

stretching of the INDSCAL solutions. If differential stretching from phase II is utilized, the root mean squares found in phase III (0.837 and 0.836 for group A and group B, respectively) remain virtually unchanged.[4] While phase II shows higher fits, given *idiosyncratic* stretching, the gain in the multiple correlation coefficients does not appear large enough to justify the added complexity of this model.[5]

Figure 5.2 shows the joint-space configuration (simple ideal-point or vector model) for group A subjects; Figure 5.3 shows the corresponding configuration for group B. Both figures utilize the original average-subject INDSCAL

[4] Aside from small computational differences, it should be noted that phase IV results (utilizing the vector model) would *not* be affected by either rotation or rotation followed by differential axis stretching.

[5] Strictly speaking, the F-ratios between phases are *not* appropriate for the nonmetric analysis and should be confined to descriptive purposes only.

Table 5.5   Multiple Correlation Coefficients and F-Ratios between Phases from the Nonmetric Analysis of Group A

	Correlation Coefficient for Phase			F-Ratios between Phases I, J			Correlation Coefficient for Phase		F-Ratio between Phases I, J F 3,4
Subject	II	III	IV	F 2,3 1 * 10	F 2,4 2 * 10	F 3,4 1* 11	III	IV	1 * 11
041	0.9416	0.9417	0.9379	−0.0148†	0.3117	0.7030	0.9414	0.9379	0.6410
082	0.9334	0.9171	0.6314	2.3484	18.3593	30.6171	0.9174	0.6315	30.7543
092	0.8130	0.7320	0.7313	3.6953	1.8624	0.0237	0.7315	0.7311	0.0120
101	0.8181	0.7654	0.7044	2.5236	2.6182	2.3828	0.7654	0.7044	2.3828
102	0.9622	0.8326	0.8077	31.3254	18.4197	1.4677	0.8325	0.8077	1.4587
111	0.9420	0.7444	0.6958	29.5683	17.8900	1.7269	0.7472	0.6962	1.8343
112	0.8911	0.8908	0.8843	0.0264	0.2910	0.6096	0.8907	0.8843	0.6049
121	0.9174	0.7459	0.4037	17.9998	21.4161	9.7557	0.7462	0.4037	9.7752
122	0.7344	0.6366	0.4971	2.9096	3.1717	2.9259	0.6368	0.4971	2.9319
141	0.9636	0.9186	0.8840	11.8337	10.2706	4.3869	0.9184	0.8843	4.3202
151	0.7193	0.7117	0.7115	0.2240	0.1158	0.0081	0.7117	0.7115	0.0056
152	0.9190	0.9017	0.8909	2.0256	1.6369	1.1417	0.9022	0.8909	1.2020
161	0.7470	0.7268	0.6878	0.6735	0.9620	1.2887	0.7267	0.6878	1.2855
162	0.9031	0.8987	0.8620	0.4233	1.9664	3.7036	0.8989	0.8620	3.7166
181	0.9762	0.9638	0.7061	5.1227	48.3115	66.5560	0.9634	0.7061	65.7774
182	0.9701	0.9218	0.8216	15.5284	22.6184	12.8011	0.9218	0.8219	12.7449
191	0.9520	0.9488	0.9434	0.6546	0.8660	1.1123	0.9491	0.9434	1.1799
201	0.7218	0.6458	0.6355	2.1686	1.2216	0.2481	0.6462	0.6352	0.2680
202	0.9294	0.9337	0.8692	−0.5920†	3.9783	9.9951	0.9008	0.8692	3.2657

*Degrees of freedom.
†Minus value is due to program rounding error and should be read as zero.

coordinates of groups A and B (Table 5.1) as suggested by the findings of the previous paragraph.[6]

We consider the analysis underlying Figure 5.2 first. From Table 5.5 we first note that group A phase III goodness-of-fit values markedly exceed those of phase IV for only four subjects: 082, 121, 181, and 182. That is, F-ratios between phases III and IV exceed the critical F-ratio of 9.65 (associated with the 0.01 significance level for 1 and 11 degrees of freedom) only for these four subjects. Since a nonmetric approach is being utilized, we continue to adopt a very conservative significance level and assign only these four subjects to a simple ideal-point model.

But, as indicated earlier, phase III permits negative ideal points as well as positive ideals. From Table C.41 we note that the dimension weights for these four subjects are all negative; preference increases with increasing squared

[6]Tables C.41, C.42, and C.43 show ideal-point and vector model parameter values for all subjects, as fitted by each model separately.

Table 5.6   Multiple Correlation Coefficients and F-Ratios between Phases from the Nonmetric Analysis of Group B

Subject	Correlation Coefficient for Phase II	III	IV	F-Ratios between Phases I, J — F 2,3 1 * 10	F 2,4 2 * 10	F 3,4 1 * 11	Correlation Coefficient for Phase III	IV	F-Ratio between Phases I, J F 3,4 1 * 11
011	0.8392	0.8386	0.8267	0.0330	0.3516	0.7348	0.8262	0.8266	−0.0209†
012	0.8205	0.7886	0.7890	1.5716	0.7764	−0.0179†	0.8205	0.7886	1.7262
021	0.9061	0.8277	0.7996	7.5948	5.0752	1.5977	0.8920	0.7996	8.4123
022	0.9990	0.9987	0.9987	3.4863	1.5802	−0.2658†	0.9992	0.9989	4.1199
031	0.7076	0.6997	0.4194	0.2226	3.2518	6.7587	0.5764	0.5509	0.4730
032	0.9801	0.9807	0.9807	−0.3042†	−0.1532†	−0.0026†	0.9799	0.9807	−0.4134†
042	0.8561	0.8560	0.8561	0.0063	0.0010	−0.0047†	0.8558	0.8559	−0.0087†
051	0.6755	0.6538	0.6430	0.5320	0.3941	0.2677	0.6671	0.6427	0.6309
052	0.8163	0.7751	0.7590	1.9636	1.3522	0.6811	0.7908	0.7591	1.4421
061	0.9827	0.9746	0.9740	4.6067	2.4764	0.2606	0.9804	0.9736	3.7543
062	0.8093	0.8078	0.7924	0.0688	0.3917	0.7807	0.7985	0.7924	0.2929
071	0.5772	0.5641	0.5365	0.2237	0.3396	0.4902	0.5733	0.5361	0.6772
072	0.9197	0.9211	0.9181	−0.1682†	0.0948	0.4003	0.9182	0.9184	−0.0194†
081	0.9305	0.9259	0.9254	0.6326	0.3551	0.0803	0.9304	0.9254	0.7534
091	0.9686	0.9429	0.9420	7.9090	4.1026	0.1820	0.9633	0.9419	6.2389
131	0.7117	0.6633	0.6594	1.3488	0.7264	0.1007	0.7124	0.6595	1.6211
132	0.9681	0.9267	0.9035	12.4901	9.6284	3.3096	0.9588	0.9038	13.9446
142	0.7488	0.5836	0.3949	5.0100	4.6073	3.0813	0.7463	0.6850	2.1796
171	0.8923	0.8912	0.8883	0.0937	0.1724	0.2736	0.8888	0.8883	0.0441
172	0.8922	0.8912	0.8883	0.0833	0.1675	0.2746	0.8889	0.8883	0.0507
192	0.9029	0.9032	0.7779	−0.0285†	5.6863	12.5771	0.7732	0.7781	−0.2096†
211	0.8908	0.8082	0.8083	6.7932	3.3933	−0.0043†	0.8855	0.8082	6.6746
212	0.8091	0.8091	0.8007	0.0003	0.1959	0.4306	0.8086	0.8019	0.3417

*Degrees of freedom.
†Minus value is due to rounding error and should be read as zero.

distance from the ideal point. Hence, this interpretation should be placed on the four ideal points plotted in Figure 5.2.

The remaining 15 subjects of group A were assigned to the vector model, as applied in phase IV. These subjects appear as vector directions in Figure 5.2; direction cosines of the vectors appear in Table C.43. Hence, subjects of group A were assigned to the vector model *unless* their improvement in goodness of fit exceeded the conservative level of significance (alpha equal to 0.01) used for model assignment purposes.

An identical procedure was used for assigning group B subjects to the simple ideal point or the vector model. In this case only one subject (subject 132, as noted in Table 5.6) was "significantly" better fitted by the simple ideal-point model. Again this subject's dimension weights were negative. Accordingly,

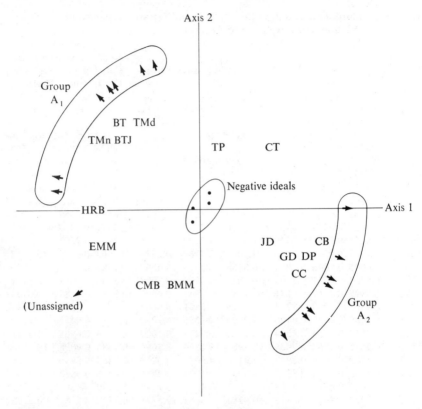

Figure 5.2   Joint-space Configuration of Group A Subjects

Key

TP	Toast pop-up	BTJ	Buttered toast and jelly
BT	Buttered toast	TMn	Toast and margarine
EMM	English muffin and margarine	CB	Cinnamon bun
JD	Jelly donut	DP	Danish pastry
CT	Cinnamon toast	GD	Glazed donut
BMM	Blueberry muffin and margarine	CC	Coffee cake
HRB	Hard rolls and butter	CMB	Corn muffin and butter
TMd	Toast and marmalade		

Figure 5.3 represents one subject by a (negative) ideal point and the remaining 22 subjects by vector directions (see Tables C.42 and C.43).

At this point it seems useful to recapitulate the results of the preceding analysis:

1. Using the metric version of PREFMAP we first established that the stimulus space orientations (provided by the INDSCAL average-subject analyses of Chapter 3) also remain reasonably unique in the context of overall preference

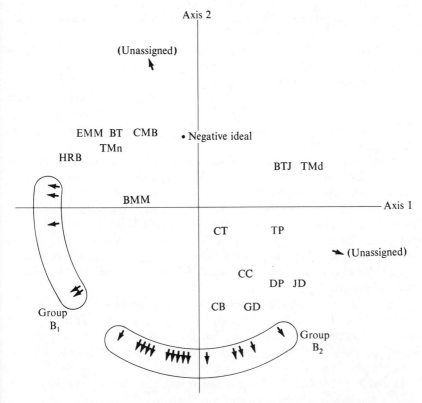

Figure 5.3   Joint-space Configuration of Group B Subjects (See Figure 5.2 for key.)

judgments. This was evinced by the fact that the most general PREFMAP model, allowing idiosyncratic rotation, provided little improvement over the more restrictive model requiring all subjects to share the orientation of the average subject.

2. Using the nonmetric version of PREFMAP we next explored the following alternatives:

a. A simple ideal-point (or vector) model, utilizing the original average-subject INDSCAL space, versus

b. A simple ideal-point (or vector) model fitted to the INDSCAL space that is differentially stretched (in the context of evaluation) according to preferences of the average subject.

In this case it appeared that little would be gained through differential stretching of the average-subject INDSCAL spaces. (In addition, little improvement would be effected by allowing idiosyncratic axis stretching.) Accordingly, we assume that the overall preferences of group A and group B can be adequately represented by simple ideal-point or vector models, in the *original* average-subject INDSCAL spaces.

3. The 19 subjects of group A and 23 subjects of group B were next partitioned into ideal-point types versus vector-model types on the basis of whether phase III goodness-of-fit values "significantly" exceeded those of phase IV. A significance level of 0.01 was used. Four subjects of group A and 1 subject of group B were assigned to negative ideal-point models. These joint-space configurations are shown in Figures 5.2 and 5.3 for group A and group B, respectively.

Accordingly, the four (negative) ideal-point subjects of group A and one (negative) ideal-point subject of group B were set aside as being quite disparate from the remaining subjects.

The 15 remaining (vector-model) subjects of group A and the 22 remaining (vector-model) subjects of group B (Figures 5.2 and 5.3) appeared to fall into two main clusters each, insofar as vector position is concerned. The group assignments shown in Figures 5.2 and 5.3 were made rather arbitrarily, leading to one unassigned vector-model subject for group A and two unassigned vector-model subjects for group B.

Thus, four reasonably homogeneous subgroups of vector-model subjects were defined and designated as A_1, A_2, B_1, and B_2 (as noted in Table 5.7). For illustrative purposes we elected to deal only with these four subgroups in subsequent analysis related to perceptual-preference segments and background characteristics.

Insofar as interpretation of ideal point or vector positions is concerned, both

Table 5.7   Subjects in Subgroups Obtained from PREFMAP Analysis

Group A			Group B		
Group A_1	Group A_2	Unassigned	Group B_1	Group B_2	Unassigned
111	041	082*	062	011	061
122	092	121*	171	012	132*
141	101	161	172	021	142
162	102	181*	211	022	
191	112	182*	212	031	
201	151			032	
202	152			042	
				051	
				052	
				071	
				072	
				081	
				091	
				131	
				132	

*Assigned to negative ideal-point model.

Figures 5.2 and 5.3 show a fair amount of heterogeneity. Figure 5.2 shows that group A vector-model subjects break down into two groups: those who prefer toast-like items (assigned to A_1) and those who like sweet, cake-like items (assigned to A_2). The negative ideal-point subjects, plotting near the center of the configuration, appear to like some members of both types of food items.

Similarly, rather high heterogeneity is noted among group B vector-model subjects, as shown in Figure 5.3. The B_2 segment tends to prefer sweet, cake-like items, while the B_1 segment displays higher preference for bread-like items like toast, rolls, or muffins. Thus, while group A and group B clusters were originally selected on the basis of within-group perceptual similarity, there remains considerable heterogeneity *within* segment insofar as ideal point location or vector direction is concerned.

DISCRIMINANT ANALYSIS

Having identified these four subgroups, our attention next turned to whether these assignments were related to respondent background characteristics. An appropriate procedure to use here is multiple discriminant analysis in which the 10-component background vectors (see Table 1.2) are used as a set of predictor variables. Group sizes were as follows:

> group A_1: 7 respondents
>
> group A_2: 7 respondents
>
> group B_1: 5 respondents
>
> group B_2: 15 respondents
>
> unassigned: 8 respondents (not included in discriminant analysis)

The four-way discriminant analysis [38] yielded rather poor results. As shown by the classification matrix of Table 5.8, only 20 of the 34 respondents used in this part of the analysis were correctly classified, a "hit" ratio of 59 percent. Moreover, the canonical correlation associated with the first discriminant function was only 0.676 (see Table C.44). While the first discriminant function is significant at the 0.05 level, the discrimination is not high enough from a practical standpoint to warrant interpretation.

Figure 5.4 shows a plot of respondents in discriminant function space (based on the first two linear compounds). As expected, we note only a modest separation of the group means along each axis. Thus, we conclude that the perceptual-preference segments found here are not highly associated with respondent background characteristics.

SCENARIO-DEPENDENT PREFERENCES

Respondents were also asked for preference rankings according to a set of entree-occasion scenarios. This set of six scenarios (including overall preferences as scenario 1) is described in Table 1.2. For purposes of illustration, these

Table 5.8 Classification Matrix Obtained from Discriminant Analysis of Groups A_1, A_2, B_1, and B_2

	Predicted Group				
Actual Group	A_1	A_2	B_1	B_2	Total
A_1	4	1	1	1	7
A_2	1	4	2	0	7
B_1	0	1	3	1	5
B_2	1	5	0	9	15
	6	11	6	11	34

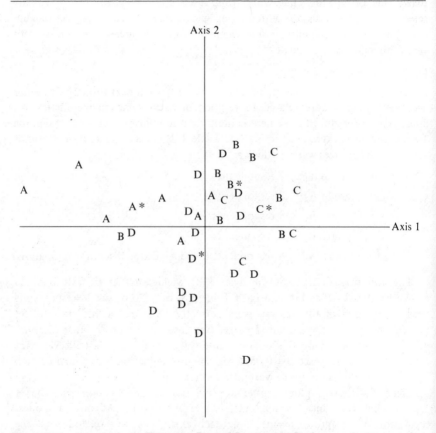

Figure 5.4   Discriminant Function Plot of Perception-Preference Segments of First Two Linear Compounds

Key
A. Group A_1 members
B. Group A_2 members
C. Group B_1 members
D. Group B_2 members
*   Group means

122

preferences are first treated at the *average-subject* level for group A and group B separately. We then partially replicate the analysis at the individual-subject level for group A and group B subsets, consisting of six members each. Table 5.9 shows the set of average-subject preference ranks. The group A and group B INDSCAL average-subject coordinates of Table 5.1 and the average ranks of Table 5.9 constituted the primary input data for this phase of the analysis.[7]

These sets of data were again analyzed by PREFMAP, following the same procedure discussed in the preceding section. That is, the metric version of PREFMAP was first used to fit the full hierarchy of models; then the nonmetric version was employed to examine the adequacy of more restrictive (but simpler) models.

The multiple correlation results associated with the metric analysis using all four preference models, and the accompanying F-ratios, are reported in Tables C.45 and C.46. In the case of group A the root mean squares of the individual-scenario multiple correlations are 0.842 and 0.835, respectively, for the most general model (applied in phase I) and the model that constrains all subjects to share the same orientation of the space (applied in phase II). Analogous values of 0.675 and 0.671 are found for group B. We conclude that little is gained by permitting idiosyncratic rotation; in other words, the *unique* orientations of the average-subject INDSCAL solutions appear to be retained in the context of scenario-dependent preferences as well.

The nonmetric version of PREFMAP was employed next. In this case we wished to see if either the simple ideal-point or vector model was adequate in accounting for the preference data. Again the alternatives of differential stretching of the INDSCAL average-subject space and use of the original coordinates (Table 5.1) were compared. The appropriate individual-scenario multiple correlations are reported in Tables C.47 and C.48. The root mean squares for phase III applied to the original INDSCAL spaces were 0.893 and 0.818 for groups A and B, respectively. Phase III fits, if preceded by differential stretching of the axes, based on preferences under the average scenario, were 0.895 and 0.825 for groups A and B, respectively. Even phase 2 fits, allowing idiosyncratic axis stretching, were only 0.909 (group A) and 0.844 (group B). Hence, fitting preferences to the *original* INDSCAL average-subject space does about as well as the more general models that allow either idiosyncratic or total-group stretching of the INDSCAL average-subject coordinates in the context of preference.

Given these results, we again elected to contrast the simple ideal-point model with the vector model (fitted to the original INDSCAL coordinates of Table 5.1).

When the simple ideal-point model was compared to the vector model for group A's data (see Table C.47) the correlation coefficients, which could only be

[7]An approach not attempted here would have involved an MDPREF and M-D-SCAL V analysis of the 12 × 15 matrix of Table 5.9, similar to the analyses made in Chapter 4.

Table 5.9   Average-Subject Scenario Dependent Preferences for Groups A and B

Scenario†	Stimulus*									
	1 11	2 12	3 13	4 14	5 15	6	7	8	9	10
Group A										
1	10.84 8.21	6.63 5.89	7.79 7.47	9.00 6.79	9.00 10.68	7.58	8.79	6.26	6.00	9.05
2	11.26 10.89	2.79 9.00	6.53 9.79	11.53 9.95	9.05 9.32	9.32	6.53	4.58	4.63	4.84
3	10.84 9.11	5.79 7.63	7.00 7.89	10.16 7.89	8.79 9.42	7.95	9.26	5.84	5.16	7.26
4	10.63 9.53	4.47 8.95	6.84 9.79	10.11 9.74	8.53 8.79	8.16	8.74	4.58	4.58	6.58
5	10.63 8.05	8.42 5.42	7.89 7.89	8.11 6.11	9.47 9.84	6.05	10.32	6.11	6.16	9.53
6	10.53 8.00	8.84 3.58	8.58 5.58	6.58 3.89	9.00 9.89	7.53	10.74	9.00	7.53	10.74
Group B										
1	12.43 5.87	9.00 4.13	7.04 7.61	8.04 3.87	7.61 9.48	5.22	9.87	10.35	8.70	10.78
2	11.87 9.35	2.87 11.00	4.87 12.09	11.61 10.00	6.65 8.22	6.61	8.04	7.17	4.91	4.74
3	11.39 8.22	5.70 7.52	7.04 9.57	9.78 7.13	7.83 9.39	6.91	9.87	7.00	5.39	7.26
4	11.91 8.13	5.26 7.57	7.26 8.83	8.87 7.39	7.43 9.70	7.17	9.74	7.91	6.26	6.57
5	11.57 5.43	8.87 3.22	7.96 7.13	8.04 3.57	8.48 9.78	6.39	10.65	10.78	8.74	9.39
6	11.17 5.52	10.48 4.30	8.39 5.13	5.74 4.30	8.74 8.84	6.00	10.09	10.43	9.65	11.22

*See Table 1.1 for stimulus identification.
†See Table 1.2 for scenario description.

used descriptively in the monotone version, differed appreciably from each other (using the earlier criterion of 0.01 significance) in all but one case (scenario 6). For simplicity, we represented all of group A's scenario-dependent preferences as an ideal-point model. The appropriate joint-space configuration is shown in Figure 5.5, in which all ideal points are "anti-ideals," (see Table C.49), that is, preference *increases* directly with squared distance from the ideal, at least within the range of these stimuli. Note also that the ideal points are clustered closely around the origin of the stimulus configuration.

In group B's data, however, only one scenario (scenario 6) appeared to be better represented by an ideal-point model (see Table C.48). However, this point was close to the "rim" of the stimulus configuration, suggesting that a vector model might provide a good approximation to an ideal-point model. In the light of these findings we elected to portray all of group B's data as a vector model

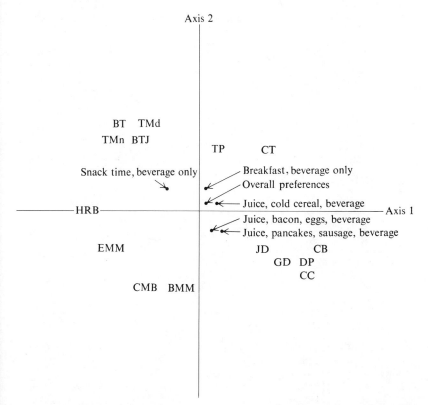

Figure 5.5   Joint-space Configuration of Group A Averaged Scenario-dependent Preferences (See Figure 5.2 for key.)

(see Tables C.50 and C.51). The appropriate joint-space configuration is shown in Figure 5.6.

Focusing first on the negative ideal-point model of Figure 5.5, we note that all points are clustered near the origin of the configuration. However, there are subgroupings of scenarios 2 and 4 (heavier breakfasts) and scenarios 3 and 5 (lighter breakfasts).

Figure 5.6, representing the vector model of group B is examined next. Here also preferences on the average seem to be dependent upon scenario. Scenarios 1, 5, and 6 (overall and light breakfast or snack) cluster rather closely. The heavier breakfasts represent another cluster that emphasizes less sweet, toasted items. Interestingly enough, on an overall basis group B subjects tend to favor the same sweet items that are preferred under light breakfast and snack scenarios.

In practice, of course, we would not ordinarily analyze the scenario-dependent preferences only at the average-subject level. It is quite possible that

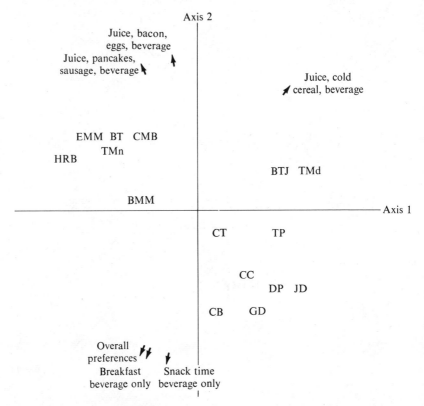

Figure 5.6   Joint-space Configuration of Group B Averaged Scenario-dependent Preferences (See Figure 5.2 for key.)

individual subjects could depart quite substantially from the preceding aggregate-level findings. Fortunately, the PREFMAP hierarchy of preference models is capable of fitting preference data at the individual-subject level, where scenario-dependent preferences can be treated as "subjects," analogous to the analyses made at the overall preference level discussed earlier in this chapter. This step is followed, on a small-scale basis, in the concluding section of the chapter.

A PARTIAL REPLICATION AT THE INDIVIDUAL LEVEL

In order to demonstrate the analysis of scenario-dependent preference data on an individual basis, the preceding steps were partially replicated on two subsets (of six subjects each) drawn from group A and group B. We called these subsets group a and group b.

Each subset was formed by finding in each group the six subjects who displayed the highest product-moment correlation in the INDSCAL disaggregate-

Table 5.10 Best-fitted Subjects in Original INDSCAL Analyses of Groups A and B

Subject	Original Correlation	Revised Correlation when Analyzed Separately
Group A		
092	0.800	0.824
112	0.832	0.869
121	0.806	0.839
151	0.786	0.806
152	0.782	0.777
182	0.856	0.629
Group B		
021	0.886	0.849
022	0.890	0.887
051	0.876	0.860
061	0.879	0.915
091	0.912	0.959
212	0.882	0.841

level analysis of Chapter 3 (Figures 3.8 and 3.9). These subjects and accompanying goodness-of-fit measures are shown in Table 5.10; the original correlation shows the goodness-of-fit measure obtained from Chapter 3 analyses for each of the twelve subjects.

Separate two-dimensional INDSCAL analyses were then made of groups a and b. The group stimulus spaces (in normalized form) appear in Figures 5.7 and 5.8, and supporting material is shown in Table C.52. It is of interest in Table 5.10 that the subjects' revised correlations, based on this further partitioning, do not necessarily exceed their original counterparts; for example, in group a the revised measures are lower than the original ones for subjects 152 and 182. Removing other subjects whose communality is high with some group a or group b members can lower the degree of fit for these individuals.[8]

The group stimulus spaces of Figures 5.7 and 5.8 differ somewhat from their group A and group B counterparts, but the presence of the sweetness and toast/nontoast dimensions is still apparent, although both configurations show reflected orientations (which are quite permissible) compared to Figures 3.8 and 3.9. In addition, we note some evidence of clustering in the stimulus space of group b.

The scenario-dependent preferences of each of the six subjects of group a and group b separately were then fitted by means of PREFMAP; in this partial replication only phases III and IV of the nonmetric version of the program were employed (see Tables C.53 and C.54). Moreover, the normalized group stimulus

[8]The two-dimensional solutions resulted in accounted-for variance of 0.63 for group a and 0.78 for group b.

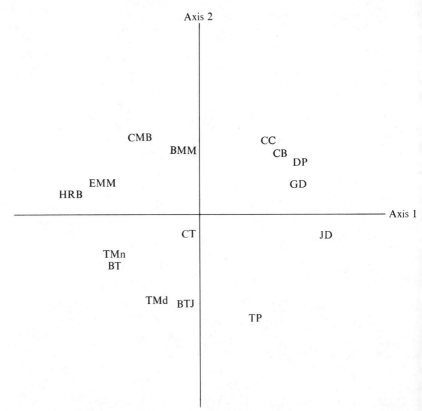

Figure 5.7   Two-space Stimulus Configuration of Group *a* **from INDSCAL Analysis (Projections scaled to unit sums of squares) (See Figure 5.2 for key.)**

spaces of Figures 5.7 and 5.8 (rather than configurations differentially stretched in accord with average-subject saliences) were used as input coordinates to PREFMAP.

For group *a* the root mean square of all 36 correlation coefficients (6 subjects × 6 scenario-dependent preferences) was 0.831 for the simple ideal-point model and 0.769 for the vector model. Corresponding values for group *b* were 0.867 and 0.842.

For illustration, only the vector model results are described here. However, supporting data for both phases appear in Tables C.55, C.56, and C.57. Figures 5.9 and 5.10 show the joint spaces of stimuli and vectors for group *a* and group *b*, respectively.

Examining Figure 5.9 first, we again find considerable heterogeneity, both

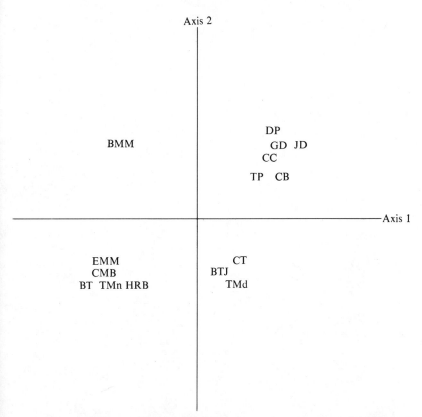

Figure 5.8   Two-space Stimulus Configuration of Group *b* from INDSCAL Analysis (Projection scaled to unit sums of squares) (See Figure 5.2 for key.)

among subjects and among scenarios within a subject.[9] Subjects 092 and 151 tend to exhibit preferences that are not highly dependent on scenario (with the exception of scenario 2). Other subjects show greater sensitivity to the preference context. Furthermore, intersubject heterogeneity is displayed *within* scenario; that is, subjects do not concur highly on preference orders even within narrowly defined entree-occasion situations.

Similar comments regarding heterogeneity pertain to Figure 5.10, which displays the joint space for group *b*. Some subjects, for example, 021, exhibit fairly high invariance over scenario (with the exception of scenario 2); but in

[9]It is interesting that the scenarios for light breakfasts and snacks exhibit some clustering in the upper right quadrant of Figure 5.9, while those for heavier breakfasts tend to group in the lower left quadrant.

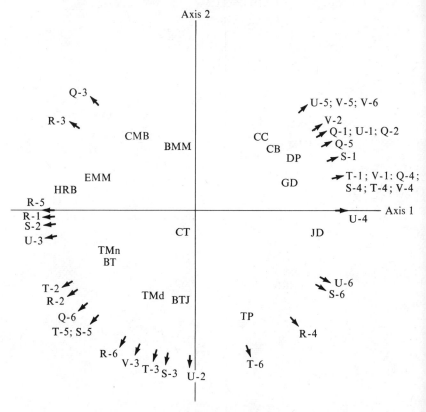

Figure 5.9 Phase IV Joint-space Configuration of Group *a* Scenario-dependent Preferences at the Individual-subject Level

Key

TP	Toast pop-up	DP	Danish pastry
BT	Buttered toast	GD	Glazed donut
EMM	English muffin and margarine	CC	Coffee cake
JD	Jelly donut	CMB	Corn muffin and butter
CT	Cinnamon toast		
BMM	Blueberry muffin and margarine	Q.1-V.1	Scenarios 1-6 of subject 092
HRB	Hard rolls and butter	Q.2-V.2	Scenarios 1-6 of subject 112
TMd	Toast and marmalade	Q.3-V.3	Scenarios 1-6 of subject 121
BTJ	Buttered toast and jelly	Q.4-V.4	Scenarios 1-6 of subject 151
TMn	Toast and margarine	Q.5-V.5	Scenarios 1-6 of subject 152
CB	Cinnamon bun	Q.6-V 6	Scenarios 1-6 of subject 182
		→	Ends of vectors

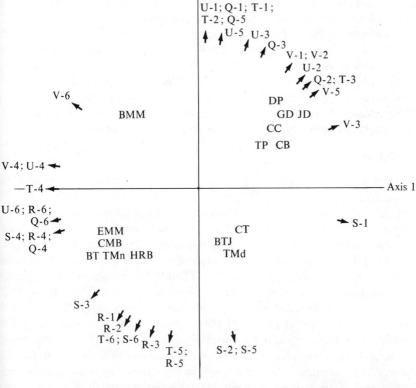

Figure 5.10   Phase IV Joint-space Configuration of Group *b* Scenario-dependent Preferences at the Individual-subject Level

Key

TP	Toast pop-up	DP	Danish pastry
BT	Buttered toast	GD	Glazed donut
EMM	English muffin and margarine	CC	Coffee cake
JD	Jelly donut	CMB	Corn muffin and butter
CT	Cinnamon toast		
BMM	Blueberry muffin and margarine	Q.1-V.1	Scenarios 1-6 of subject 021
HRB	Hard rolls and butter	Q.2-V.2	Scenarios 1-6 of subject 022
TMd	Toast and marmalade	Q.3-V.3	Scenarios 1-6 of subject 051
BTJ	Buttered toast and jelly	Q.4-V.4	Scenarios 1-6 of subject 061
TMn	Toast and margarine	Q.5-V.5	Scenarios 1-6 of subject 091
CB	Cinnamon bun	Q.6-V.6	Scenarios 1-6 of subject 212
		→	Ends of vectors

most cases individuals' preferences are context dependent. Moreover, we continue to note high variability across respondents within specific scenarios.[10]

The foregoing discussion is, of course, only illustrative of the ways in which PREFMAP can be used in the examination of scenario-dependent preference or other kinds of dominance data. We merely treat each preference order as an additional subject with no further changes in application of the technique. The sensitivity of a given individual's preferences can be displayed by changes in either ideal-point position, or, as shown here, vector direction. This approach seems quite useful as a systematic way to explore preference domains.

SUMMARY

In this chapter Carroll and Chang's PREFMAP method was used in conducting an external analysis of (a) overall preferences at the individual level and (b) scenario-dependent preferences at the average-subject level and then for subsets of subjects at the individual level. Both analyses were made along broadly similar lines employing metric and nonmetric versions of the program. However, the partial replication of individuals' scenario-dependent preferences utilized only the nonmetric version of PREFMAP and an INDSCAL group stimulus space in normalized (unit sums of squares point projections) form.

Analysis of individuals' overall preferences indicated that either a simple ideal-point or vector model (fitted to the Chapter 3 INDSCAL configurations for appropriate average subjects) was adequate in accounting for both group A and group B data. Four perceptual-preference segments, utilizing 34 of the 42 subjects, were identified. But an attempt to relate these segments to respondent background characteristics was not pragmatically successful. The four-group discriminant analysis resulted in only 59 percent correct classification.

The external analysis of averaged scenario-dependent preferences also indicated that a simple negative ideal-point model was appropriate for group A and a vector model for group B. In both cases preferences were somewhat sensitive to entree-occasion scenarios. In general, the sweet items (Danish pastry, coffee cake, and so on) were highly preferred for light breakfasts, while butter and margarine items were preferred for heavier breakfasts featuring egg dishes as entrees. In group A the negative ideal point representing overall preference was between the ideal points representing light and heavy breakfasts. In group B the overall preference vector was close to the vectors associated with light breakfasts or snacks.

The partial replication involving groups *a* and *b* indicated considerable intersubject preference heterogeneity, even within specific scenarios.

---

[10]Similar groupings of vectors for light breakfasts and snacks versus heavier breakfasts are observed in Figure 5.10. In general group *b* subjects exhibit greater clustering of vectors *and* stimuli than group *a* subjects.

CHAPTER 6

SUMMARY OF FINDINGS AND FUTURE RESEARCH AREAS

In line with the major objectives of the book, the preceding chapters have emphasized methodological aspects of the analysis. In this concluding chapter we first recapitulate the empirical findings of the various analyses, attempting to summarize and interrelate the methodological and content results.

Then we consider a variety of substantive areas that seem appropriate for future applications of multidimensional scaling and related techniques. Since little or no research has been carried on in many of these fields, our discussion must be more speculative and tentative. Indeed, our purpose is to help stimulate interest in these unexplored areas as a necessary step toward future investigation.

We conclude with some discussion of the types of predictive experiments in which multidimensional scaling methods might prove useful in the future.

SUMMARY OF METHODOLOGICAL FINDINGS

Discussion of methodological findings can be conveniently divided into two principal segments: (a) comparisons of scaling algorithms as applied to a common data set and (b) comparisons of approaches (with similar ultimate objectives) as applied to different data sets based on different measures of dissimilarity. The first type of comparison is illustrated in Chapter 2, in which several different algorithms are applied to the same data set, namely, average judgments of direct dissimilarity. Chapter 2 also contains an example of the second type of comparison, in which scaling analyses based on directly judged dissimilarities are compared, within algorithm, to those based on dissimilarities derived from ratings judgments. Finally, some comparisons are made across algorithm-data set combinations.

We first summarize findings based on comparing algorithms applied to common data sets, and then we discuss correspondences among alternative approaches to various kinds of data analysis.

COMPARISONS OF ALGORITHMS

In the data bank used in this study our findings, as related to the *two-dimensional* scaling solutions, indicate the following:

1. Little difference was found among algorithms used to scale either averaged judgments of direct dissimilarity or averaged derived dissimilarities, the latter being computed over ratings "space" (Chapter 2).
   a. In the case of averaged direct judgments of dissimilarity the algorithms compared were metric scaling, simple scaling (M-D-SCAL V), nonmetric analysis (TORSCA 8), and continuity analysis (Parametric Mapping).
   b. In the case of averaged derived measures of dissimilarity the algorithms compared were the four methods enumerated above, plus multiple discriminant analysis.
   c. The product-moment correlations of interpoint distances, across algorithms, were almost all in the 90s for both the direct and derived dissimilarities, considered separately.
   d. The nonmetric scaling results (TORSCA 8), at the two-space configuration level, were also consistent with cluster contours generated by Johnson's nonmetric and dimension-free clustering procedure, lending support to the

ability of the two-space scaling representations to preserve much of the information contained in the input matrices of dissimilarities, direct *or* derived.

e. When the four configurations of 1a were fitted to the INDSCAL target configuration, also obtained from direct dissimilarities (Chapter 3), high congruence was maintained. Individual pseudosubject correlations were in the mid-80s.[1]

2. Little difference was found among algorithms used in fitting property vectors based on bipolar scale ratings into common multidimensional scaling configurations, as obtained from INDSCAL analyses of group A's and group B's direct dissimilarities judgments (Chapter 3).

a. The algorithms used were the max "r" linear regression procedure, a monotone regression procedure, and Carroll and Chang's method based on optimizing an index of nonlinear correlation.

b. In general, the linear, monotone, and nonlinear algorithms yielded quite similar results insofar as direction cosines were concerned. While goodness-of-fit measures varied somewhat, in most cases these differences had no appreciable effect on the directions of best-fitting vectors.

3. Differences *were* noted in the algorithms used to derive stimulus spaces from overall preference data by means of internal analysis (Chapter 4).

a. The algorithms compared were MDPREF, a metric scalar products model, and three distance, or unfolding-type, procedures, namely, M-D-SCAL V row split option, M-D-SCAL V row comparability, and Parametric Mapping.

b. The interpoint distance correlations between the derived stimulus spaces and a common target (the INDSCAL average-subject space obtained from the Chapter 3 analysis of direct dissimilarities judgments) ranged from 0.47 to 0.78 for the three unfolding-type configurations. The root mean square correlation for the MDPREF congruence test was 0.77.

4. Some differences were noted among metric and nonmetric PREFMAP methods and models in the external analysis of (a) group A and group B's overall preference data and (b) these groups' averaged scenario-dependent preferences (Chapter 5). As will be recalled, groups A and B were formed on the basis of differences in dimension saliences, as obtained from an INDSCAL analysis of direct dissimilarities data in Chapter 3.

a. As might be expected, the nonmetric version of PREFMAP generally produced somewhat better fits to the data, holding type of preference model constant.

---

[1] As in Chapter 2, we caution that the high correspondences across algorithms and data sets may *not* be found in other applications. First, the linear component of the function relating dissimilarities to distances may not be as strong as found here. Second, manifest equal weighting of rating scales can lead to configurations quite different from those found by scaling direct judgments of dissimilarity.

b. Some subjects' overall preferences were fitted significantly better by the simple ideal-point model than by the vector model.

c. In general, however, the simpler models of PREFMAP (applied in phase III and phase IV of the program) provided adequate fits to the data. In particular, group A and group B's average-subject stimulus configurations obtained from INDSCAL did *not* require much rotation or differential stretching in order to accommodate the preference data.

COMPARISONS OF ALTERNATIVE APPROACHES AND ALGORITHM COMBINATIONS

In the data bank used in this study, our findings, again based on *two-dimensional* solutions, indicate the following:

1. At the aggregate level of analysis, solutions based on direct judgments of dissimilarity were quite similar to those obtained from derived measures of dissimilarity (Chapter 2).
   a. Within type of algorithm (with the exception of Parametric Mapping) the product-moment correlations between the interpoint distances of scaling configurations obtained from direct and derived dissimilarities were in the low 80s.
   b. Average cosine measures between configuration vectors obtained separately from direct and derived dissimilarities analysis, again within type of algorithm, were in the low 90s.
   c. Pseudosubject correlations obtained from the canonical decomposition analysis were mostly in the high 90s across all nine algorithm-data set combinations.
2. Aggregate-level configurations obtained from the nine Chapter 2 analyses were also generally congruent with the INDSCAL average-subject space, as developed from direct judgments of dissimilarity (Chapter 3).
3. At the disaggregate level of analysis, configurations obtained from group A and group B averaged ratings judgments were quite similar to each other even though these groups displayed appreciable differences in dimension salience in the case of direct judgments of dissimilarity (Chapter 3).
4. Stimulus spaces derived from overall preferences (Chapter 4) were not highly related, in a similarities transform sense, to the INDSCAL total-group solution (using an INDSCAL space that was differentially stretched in accord with the average subject's saliences) obtained from analyzing the direct dissimilarities judgments in Chapter 3.
   a. Product-moment correlations between derived and target interpoint distances fell in the range of 0.47 to 0.78; as might be expected, average cosine and canonical correlation measures were generally higher than these.

b. Still, correlations obtained from the INDSCAL congruence analysis (also conducted in Chapter 4) were sufficiently high to suggest that the INDSCAL coordinates constituted arguments of the preference functions.

A SYNTHESIS OF ALGORITHMS AND APPROACHES

At this stage it seems useful to describe a portmanteau type of congruence check on the foregoing discussion of algorithm-data set combinations. In this study 17 two-space configurations have been developed in line with various scaling objectives.[2] These are listed in Table 6.1 and have been discussed in preceding chapters.

As a capstone analysis we wished to see what the various configurations had in common and also to develop a synthesized configuration based on *all* 17 specific configurations. This was done by again using the INDSCAL model. First, Euclidean distances were computed between stimulus pairs for each of the 17 two-space configurations. The resulting $17 \times 15 \times 15$ three-way matrix was then submitted to INDSCAL for the purpose of finding a synthesized two-dimensional group stimulus space and a space of pseudosubjects (the 17 combinations of algorithm and data set in Table 6.1). In the four INDSCAL input solutions, interpoint distances were computed in the differentially stretched space of the appropriate average subject rather than the normalized stimulus space ordinarily produced by the program.

The group stimulus space is shown in Figure 6.1 and the pseudosubject space in Figure 6.2. Supporting numerical output (including, for comparison purposes, a 17×17 correlation matrix of interpoint distances across pseudosubjects) appears in Appendix Tables C.58, C.59, and C.60.

The INDSCAL model accounted for 82 percent of the variance in the three-way scalar products matrix. Table 6.1 shows individual goodness-of-fit measures (product-moment correlations), which range from 0.71 to 0.98, generally quite good fits. Their root mean square is 0.91.

An examination of the group stimulus space of Figure 6.1 shows that the horizontal axis is a type of sweet-nonsweet dimension, while the vertical axis represents the toast-nontoast dimension found in earlier analyses.[3] This result strongly confirms our previous discussions regarding the stability of these dimensions in three types of data: direct dissimilarity judgments, rating scale judgments, and preference data.

The pseudosubject space of Figure 6.2 shows a grouping of scaling results by type of data: direct or derived dissimilarities. The four configurations derived from the internal analysis of preference data show greater heterogeneity due to technique, as might be anticipated. The wide separation between group A and

---

[2] We omit the group *a* and group *b* configurations of Chapter 5 in this summary analysis in view of the small sample sizes on which they were based.

[3] In this case the dimensions were somewhat positively correlated ($r = 0.31$).

Table 6.1   17 Pseudosubject Two-space Configurations from INDSCAL Congruence Analysis

Pseudosubject	Discussion Section	Product-Moment Correlation
1. Metric Scaling (direct)	Figure 2.2	0.974
2. M-D-SCAL V (direct)	Figure 2.4	0.974
3. TORSCA 8 (direct)	Figure 2.6	0.978
4. Parametric Mapping (direct)	Figure 2.8	0.874
5. Metric Scaling (derived)	Figure 2.11	0.955
6. M-D-SCAL V (derived)	Figure 2.13	0.955
7. TORSCA 8 (derived)	Figure 2.15	0.953
8. Parametric Mapping (derived)	Figure 2.17	0.959
9. Discriminant Analysis (derived)	Figure 2.20	0.908
10. Total group INDSCAL (direct)	Figure 3.4*	0.862
11. Total group INDSCAL (derived)	Figure 3.6*	0.907
12. Group A INDSCAL (direct)	Figure 3.8*	0.888
13. Group B INDSCAL (direct)	Figure 3.9*	0.945
14. MDPREF (preferences)	Figure 4.2†	0.798
15. M-D-SCAL V Row Split (preferences)	Figure 4.3†	0.864
16. M-D-SCAL V Row Comparability (preferences)	Figure 4.5†	0.712
17. Parametric Mapping (preferences)	Figure 4.7†	0.886

*In all cases the normalized stimulus spaces shown originally in these figures were differentially stretched in accord with the average subject's saliences prior to computing interpoint distances.   †See also Table 4.2.

group B on the basis of differences in dimension saliences in the Chapter 3 INDSCAL analysis was also to be expected, given the basis on which these subgroups were constructed.

Finally, we note that the INDSCAL solutions based on direct and derived dissimilarities at the total-group level (pseudosubjects 10 and 11) give roughly equal weight to the dimensions, and the points plot quite close to each other.

Thus it appears that all 17 two-space configurations are rather closely related to each other if we allow for rotation followed by differential stretching of their axes along the particular dimensions obtained from the INDSCAL congruence procedure.[4]

SUMMARY OF SUBSTANTIVE FINDINGS

The main substantive findings of this study are listed on pages 139-141.

[4]One interesting type of analysis, mentioned in review by Wish (personal communication) would have been to analyze the set of 17 two-space solutions in *three* dimensions via INDSCAL. In particular, such an analysis might distinguish the similarities configurations from the configurations derived from an internal analysis of preference data.

1. The stimulus spaces obtained by various algorithms and approaches indicate two interpretable dimensions: a sweetness dimension and a toast/nontoast dimension.

   a. Similar interpretations were found for the aggregate-level analysis of direct judgments and derived measures of dissimilarity (Chapter 2). However, attempts to interpret the third axis of the stimulus configurations generally were not successful.

   b. The same two dimensions were noted in the unique orientations provided by the total-group INDSCAL analyses (Chapter 3) of both direct and derived dissimilarities. Moreover, this interpretation was supported by the results of three types of property-fitting procedures.

   c. Stimulus spaces at two types of subgrouping level—groups A and B (Chapter 3) and groups *a* and *b* (Chapter 5)—can be interpreted similarly.

   d. Stimulus spaces derived from the internal analysis of preference data (Chapter 4) also can be interpreted similarly.

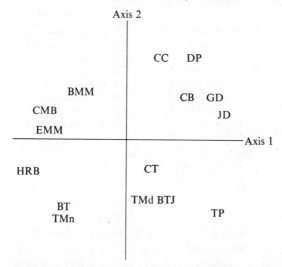

Figure 6.1   Synthesized Group Stimulus Configuration from INDSCAL Congruence Analysis of 17 Pseudosubjects (Projections scaled to unit sums of squares)

Key

TP	Toast pop-up	BTJ	Buttered toast and jelly
BT	Buttered toast	TMn	Toast and margarine
EMM	English muffin and margarine	CB	Cinnamon bun
JD	Jelly donut	DP	Danish pastry
CT	Cinnamon toast	GD	Glazed donut
BMM	Blueberry muffin and margarine	CC	Coffee cake
HRB	Hard rolls and butter	CMB	Corn muffin and butter
TMd	Toast and marmalade		

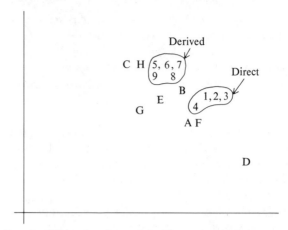

Figure 6.2   Pseudosubject Configuration from INDSCAL Congruence Analysis of 17 Pseudosubjects

Key

1	Pseudosubject 1*	A	Pseudosubject 10
2	Pseudosubject 2	B	Pseudosubject 11
3	Pseudosubject 3	C	Pseudosubject 12
4	Pseudosubject 4	D	Pseudosubject 13
5	Pseudosubject 5	E	Pseudosubject 14
6	Pseudosubject 6	F	Pseudosubject 15
7	Pseudosubject 7	G	Pseudosubject 16
8	Pseudosubject 8	H	Pseudosubject 17
9	Pseudosubject 9		

*See Table 6.1 for identification.

2. Individual differences in saliences of the INDSCAL perceptual dimensions (Chapter 3) were not highly correlated with respondent background characteristics.

3. Analysis of individual differences in overall preference data (Chapter 4) indicated only a modest statistical relationship with respondent background characteristics (a canonical correlation of 0.692). The "percentage overweight" variable appeared to be the most important predictor; overweight respondents tended to prefer sweet food items to a greater extent than those not overweight.

4. The external analysis of perceptual-preference segments (Chapter 5) continued to show only a modest statistical relationship with the background data. Thus, all in all, we are led to conclude that the particular background characteristics chosen here are not highly related to perception *or* preference, at least in the (rather homogeneous) student-type sample drawn for this study.

5. An analysis of husband-wife similarities judgments indicated significantly high correspondence with regard to homogeneity of direct dissimilarity

judgments. That is, husband-wife combinations tend to "see this particular breakfast food world" in a similar way.
6. No significantly high communality was observed between husband-wife combinations regarding overall preferences. That is, husband-wife combinations do *not* seem to "evaluate the breakfast food world" in a similar way.

In the light of the rather extensive methodological analysis conducted, our substantive findings may appear meager. Hence it should be reiterated that the primary focus of this book has been methodological rather than content-oriented. Had our interest centered on the substantive side, we would most certainly have desired to obtain a larger and more heterogeneous sample of respondents and stimuli. In addition, other background characteristics, including consumption behavior, would have been sought. Analyses would have been made at finer levels of disaggregation, and so on.

In summary, the paucity of content findings is not surprising, given the study design and major objectives. We do hope, however, that we have conveyed the *strategy* of such inquiry—particularly the emphasis on perceptual-preference segmentation—and the fact that the techniques used here to identify such segments are of interest beyond our illustrative data bank.

POTENTIAL RESEARCH AREAS

Before commenting on potential areas for future research, it seems appropriate first to discuss the kinds of applied research studies that have already been conducted—mostly on a pilot basis—using multidimensional scaling. While we attempt no extensive review of the literature, the following samples should give some idea of the versatility of these techniques when applied to problems in both the behavioral and administrative sciences.

PAST RESEARCH AREAS

Despite its recent development, multidimensional scaling has already been used in a variety of empirical applications.[5] The basic substantive assumption underlying applications of these models is that people react to stimuli on the basis of their internalized organization of events, or "perceptual map" as it were, and that a variety of judgmental or overt choice phenomena can be related to how the perceptual maps are used. Under this view, similarity and preference judgments, categorizations, unidimensional scale ratings of various kinds, and other classes of behavior can be represented as transformations of the respondent's perceptual map.

A number of researchers have already investigated a variety of phenomena in terms of such transforms. In the field of auditory perception, Shepard [119] and Wish [154, 155, 156] have used scaling procedures to discover the main

[5]This section, in part, has been drawn from [51].

dimensions along which people process nonverbal stimuli, such as Morse code signals, consonants, and vowels. In the area of impression formation Cliff and Young [23] and Rosenberg, Nelson, and Vivekananthan [114] have used multidimensional scaling methods as a major operational framework in the study of semantic descriptions of personality types. Rapoport [111] has used multidimensional scaling in the examination of semantic structures and Green, Maheshwari, and Rao [53] have examined its appropriateness for self-concept theory. In social psychology Runkel [117] and Isaac [72] have applied multidimensional scaling to the study of communications, and Gleason [46] has shown its relevance in the study of interpersonal relationships.

On even broader levels of social behavior, Bloombaum [6] has studied the social conditions underlying race riots in the United States, and McRae and Schwarz [97] the issues involved in legislative voting—all using one or more varieties of multidimensional scaling. In the field of international relations, Wish, Deutsch, and Biener [158] have employed an extensive array of multidimensional scaling methods in portraying individuals' similarities, preferences, and liking judgments of nations.

Nor has the field of business research been immune to the application of multidimensional scaling methods. A variety of studies, mostly in marketing research, have been reported by academics [106, 137], corporate researchers [39, 56], and business consultants [3, 74, 133]. Multidimensional scaling techniques have been applied even to such areas as how engineers view mathematics courses [83] and the citation network of psychology journals [29].

Individual Differences in Perception

Researchers in various fields are also examining the question of individual differences in perceptual judgments, as described in Chapter 3. In a ·highly controlled study (involving only six subjects) Tversky and Krantz [150] found strong evidence for individual differences in the "weights" that subjects applied to each of three stimulus attributes (shape of face, type of eyes, type of mouth) in arriving at judgments of overall similarity among a set of schematic drawings of faces. When also dealing with artificial stimuli, Shepard [122] found intraindividual differences, over trials, in the weights applied to each of two stimulus attributes. While one might argue in these cases that no culturally common composition rule exists for weighting the experimentally varied attributes in arriving at overall similarity judgments, a number of studies dealing with less analyzable (and less artificial) stimuli also have shown systematic individual differences in similarities judgments.

A study by Landis, Silver, Jones, and Messick [89], using air traffic descriptions as stimuli, produced four distinct subsets of subjects in terms of the dimensions used in making overall similarity judgments. Moreover, differences among subjects could be meaningfully related to differences in proficiency and training measures obtained independently from the subjects' superiors. Using photographs of various facial expressions as stimuli, Isaac [72] found reliable intersubject differences in similarity judgments and was able to relate these differences to encoding and decoding behavior in a communications task. In the domain of color perception Carroll and Chang [18] found that individual differences in perceptual judgments could be related to the extent of color deficiency exhibited by some of the subjects. With respect to speech perception, Wish [154] and Wish and Carroll [157] found that individuals with a background in music or phonetics perceived the rhythm and accent in English words along different dimensions than subjects who had no such training.

Systematic differences have been found among experts' similarity judgments of artistic drawings in studies by Skager, Schultz, and Klein [129]. Furthermore, differences in judges' points of view were correlated with other cognitive and achievement measurements. Finally, Wish [152, 153] and Wish, Deutsch, and Biener [158, 159], using the Carroll and Chang INDSCAL model, found systematic individual differences in conceptions of nations between "doves" and "hawks" (as determined by their views on the Vietnam war), males and females, and students from "developed" and "underdeveloped" countries.

Our own research on the problem of systematic individual differences has yielded instances of both reasonably homogeneous similarity judgments and systematic subgroup differences. For example, in a study with automobile models as stimuli [53], we and Maheshwari found evidence for a single, predominant point of view, coupled with unsystematic individual variation. In other instances Green and Carmone found [48] stable (and interpretable) differences in points of view.

FUTURE RESEARCH AREAS

As the preceding review indicates, multidimensional scaling and related techniques already have been employed in a variety of problems by researchers in several different disciplines. In our discussion of potential application areas we confine our speculations mainly to the administrative and behavioral sciences, even though the physical and life sciences are likely to find increasing use for the methodology as well.

Marketing and Public Opinion Research

Since the authors' substantive field is marketing, it seems only natural to speculate first about potential areas of application to this field. Actually, marketing researchers have been investigating the applicability of this methodology to consumer behavior and image research; and Green and Carmone [48] have listed a series of research problems such as market segmentation, product life cycle research, new product development, and advertisement measurement that could utilize multidimensional scaling.

It seems to us that market segmentation represents one of the most promising areas of application. Perceptual and preference measurements can be used to identify segments which, in turn, can be related to other consumer variables—socioeconomic, demographic, life style, brand usage. The effectiveness of sales effort can be portrayed in terms of its ability to change the saliences of dimensions or positions of brands in perceptual space. Similarly, sales effort effectiveness can also be related to changes in dimension saliences or ideal point-vector positions in perceptual-evaluative space.

Rao [110] has investigated the applicability of multidimensional scaling to the empirical measurement of price elasticity. He has also commented on how this early research can be extended to deal with elasticity measurements of advertising and other forms of sales effort.

New product development and testing, a field explored by Stefflre [133], Greenberg [57], Johnson [74], and others, also represents a promising area of application. Multidimensional scaling can be used to explore "gaps" or empty regions in the perceived structure of a product class and thus lead to the development of new combinations of brand attributes that could conceivably have buyer appeal. If coupled with segmentation analysis, multidimensional scaling could theoretically locate the groups of consumers most receptive to each new product candidate and the types of promotional appeals most appropriate for initial commercialization.

Public opinion research also represents a fruitful area of application. Multidimensional scaling could be used in political image measurement, including respondents' perceptions of candidate-issue relationships and their own position ("ideal" point) in regard to political issues [116]. Again, perceptual and preference structures might differ by segment; and background correlates with these different perceptual-preference structures could be utilized in designing political strategy.

In marketing, our ultimate interest centers on brand or supplier choice, in public opinion research on candidate or legislative choice. But from a research standpoint these behaviors are analogous. That is, models are needed to translate marketing or political strategies into changes in perceptual-preference structures and, ultimately, into predictions of choice. Green and Carmone [48] have speculated on the various forms that such models might take, but little has been done so far on their actual construction.

One of the major problems in the construction of these models is the paucity of research measuring the effect of policy variables on changes in perception and evaluation. It seems clear that additional research is needed to ascertain the reliability of similarities and preference judgments over time, and the impact of persuasive communications on changes in perceptual-evaluative structures.

Other Administrative Sciences

Multidimensional scaling seems potentially applicable to other areas of administrative science as well. For example, one of the major interests in managerial decision making is choosing among alternative courses of action whose outcomes are multidimensional; for example, a contemplated action may affect profits, market share, employee morale, community relations. With the increasing interest in the social responsibilities of business, it is apparent that naive models of profit maximization must be replaced with more complex models involving the consideration of tradeoffs among conflicting objectives. This may be called the evaluative function problem [29], that is, determining the implicit (or explicit) weights given to each component of a vector of outcomes in order to resolve partial orders into complete orders.

A number of lexicographic, conjunctive, disjunctive, and compensatory composition models have been proposed by psychologists and others interested in value theory. Multidimensional scaling provides a means both for explicating the models used in choosing among partially ordered alternatives and for estimating their parameter values.

Closely related to the evaluation function problem are the more general areas of decision theory and conflict theory. It seems probable that scaling methods will be utilized in the measurement of Bayesian prior distributions (statistical decision theory) where the probability assessor can only rank order outcomes and some of the intervals separating outcomes. In conflict theory, scaling could be used in the construction of joint payoff matrices and in various ancillary tasks related to differences in adversaries' perceptions and evaluations of the end-states of various negotiation situations.

Other areas of potential application include various long-range planning tasks in which administrators must consider the similarities and differences among "alternative futures" as well as their preferences for various possible futures. Similar tasks occur in the assessment of alternative research projects, job evaluation, personnel assignment, and investment portfolio selection. In short, scaling procedures seem applicable to a variety of administrative problems. In particular, we expect that multidimensional scaling will find increasing application in problem areas dealing with the public sector where evaluation of the benefits side of cost-benefit analysis has been traditionally limited to the use of economic tools.

Communications Research

The area of communications research, which currently draws from both the administrative and behavioral sciences, also appears amenable to the application of multidimensional scaling methods. Future research on the evaluation of message source, content, transfer medium, and receptor characteristics might well utilize scaling techniques. A number of problems, such as the effects on attitude change of prestige of source, message appeal, and congruence of appeal with the receptor's perceptions and evaluations, could be studied by means of scaling. Illustrative applications have already been commented upon in our discussion of past research.

The implications for advertising and public relations research also are apparent. Are messages whose content is congruent with perceived brand characteristics more effective than incongruent appeals? What kinds of arguments are most effective in bringing about desired changes in perception and evaluation of various political and social issues? What is the optimal number of arguments to include in a single appeal? How can "misperceptions" be corrected most effectively? Answers to these and similar questions could be sought through the application of scaling techniques.

Scaling methods and, more generally, conjoint measurement techniques [93] also seem potentially applicable to problems in measuring the joint impact of message and vehicle (the carrier of the message). For example, models of media selection could be developed in which the media scheduler is asked to rank, in order of effectiveness, all combinations of message and vehicle. Conjoint measurement models could then be used to find the separate contribution that each component makes to overall effectiveness. In this way judgmental estimates of message impact and vehicle appropriateness could be developed in a systematic fashion solely from rank-order data.

Similarly, these tools could be used to investigate the effects of message congruity (theme, vehicle, structure) on attitude change. This application appears particularly relevant in designing congruent components of a marketing or public relations mix.

The field of information storage and retrieval might also be researched in a similar fashion. Document classification based on perceived similarity could be more useful to the potential system user than less natural classification procedures such as the Dewey decimal system. Researchers interested in this problem area have started to employ subjective measures of document similarity in the development of information retrieval systems.

Behavioral Science

Multidimensional scaling methods seem to offer useful tools in the study of basic problems in perception, evaluation, learning, and social interaction. Multidimensional psychophysics (in which perceptual domains are related to physical domains) is an illustration of basic research in the perceptual-cognitive field. Scaling also might be useful in the study of learning processes and concept classification.

The field of personality theory, insofar as it relates to interpersonal differences in perception and evaluation, might also be researched by these methods. This would include the investigation of self-concept theory [76] and its relationship to overt behavior, such as one's choice of life style, associates and products.

Not surprisingly, the area of social psychology involving small-group interactions also appears amenable to scaling methodology. Clique formation, small group problem solving, joint decision making, and negotiation processes are only a few of the problem areas that might be researched. Multidimensional scaling might be applied also in the measurement of social costs and values, such as the seriousness of crimes, evaluations of alternative allocations of municipal funds, educational expenditures, public health programs, and the like.

For example, perceptions and preferences of various groups involved in medical activities—doctors, administrators, patients—could be measured in the context of alternate Medicare plans. Tradeoffs among conflicting objectives could then be estimated by various interest groups through conjoint measurement techniques.

Similarly, consumerism studies could be conducted to determine the value of additional information about brand or supplier characteristics in improving the "quality" of consumer choices. These findings could be used to formulate legislation leading to brand specifications that would enable the buyer to make better price-value decisions.

Cognitive anthropologists have also become interested in scaling and clustering methods in their attempts to understand how social experience is encoded and transferred to others. It seems likely that this type of research will also be expanded in the future.

Statistical Methodology

To this point we have emphasized substantive research areas. However, nonmetric scaling methods have a role to play in the development of statistical methodology itself, namely as nonparametric analogues to metric methods of multivariate analysis. Many of the researchers who have contributed to nonmetric scaling techniques have also developed nonmetric models for general multivariate analysis, including multiple regression, discriminant analysis, multivariate analysis of variance, and factor analysis.

Procedures for handling multivariate data expressed in rank form already exist, although knowledge about them has not yet been widely diffused through the research community. We expect to see much more methodological research in the area of nonparametric multivariate analysis in the future. It seems reasonable that the continued development of these techniques will culminate in nonmetric analogues to linear models that will be comparable in scope to the various nonparametric procedures that exist in univariate statistics.

TOWARD A SCHEMA FOR THE DESIGN
OF PREDICTIVE STUDIES

As we mentioned in the beginning of this chapter, one of our objectives was to describe programmatically the kinds of research that could be carried out using scaling procedures for predictive purposes. For illustrative purposes we emphasize the substantive field of marketing, although many of the same considerations would seem to apply to other disciplines. Green and Carmone [48] have discussed three general types of inquiry that might be utilized in marketing-type prediction studies:

1. Field-level studies, in which share of brand choices, either at the individual or group level are predicted by the longitudinal analysis of similarities and preference judgments of members of a consumer panel over some time period, for example, six months or a year
2. Computer simulation, in which actual market shares of brands in a product class are predicted from similarities and preference data obtained from a representative sample of the buying public
3. Laboratory investigation, in which various respondent choices are predicted from similarities and preference judgments obtained in a controlled setting

At this stage of methodological development, the third approach seems the most attractive procedure to implement. We believe this for two reasons. First, current scaling methodology is formulated at a microlevel, that is, *individual* similarities-preference configurations can be developed. This being the case, it would seem fruitful first to examine prediction at the individual respondent rather than aggregated level. Second, the differentiating feature of multi-dimensional scaling, compared to von Neumann-Morgenstern utility theory, is that the arguments of the preference function in multidimensional scaling are not the objects themselves, but the *properties* of the objects. This feature suggests the kinds of predictive experiments that may be most novel.

In contrast, field-level experiments raise serious questions of retaining experimental control over the influence of other variables (brand availability, price dealing, point-of-purchase display) on brand choice and the stability of estimated choice probability over time. Computer simulation procedures face the same problems and seem even less amenable to individual-respondent predictions. But laboratory experiments seem to provide the types of controls needed for exploiting the particular characteristics of the methodology. For example, individualized predictions can be made regarding new stimulus selection from an array of alternatives. These predictions can be based on observations of the similarity of the new stimulus to a subset of stimuli used in constructing the original space of stimulus and ideal-point or vector positions.

DESCRIPTION OF VARIOUS PREDICTIVE EXPERIMENTS

In prediction experiments, the experimenter has a number of choices to consider:

1. Nature of the stimulus set
   a. Domain of choice: what stimulus set should be used?

   b. Specific sampling from the chosen stimulus domain.

   c. Experimenter-defined characteristics of the stimuli.

   d. Description of stimuli to the respondent.

   e. Mode of stimulus presentation.

2. Nature of the respondent set

   a. Domain of choice: what types of respondents should be selected?

   b. Specific sampling of respondents.

   c. Measurements to be made on respondent.

3. Respondent task

   a. General background instructions.

   b. Specification of scenario.

These decisions depend on the specific type of predictive task. Assuming that a calibration set of similarities and preference judgments has been obtained from the respondent, we can illustrate the varied characteristics of task selection by enumerating the following studies which *could* be undertaken.

1. Predict the positioning of a new stimulus object by means of perceptual objective space transforms only, that is, the experimenter predicts positioning with no additional data from the respondent.

2. Predict a new object's positioning in perceptual space from the respondents unidimensional orderings of the (augmented) stimulus set according to a set of prespecified (and verbalized) dimensions.

3. Predict a new object's positioning in perceptual space from the respondent's single ranking of the original stimuli from the new object.

4. Predict a new object's positioning in perceptual space from a limited (but complete) set of dissimilarities developed by including the new object in a proper subset of the original stimuli.

5. Predict the respondent's preference for a new object (based on a previously obtained similarities-preference space), using

   a. Any of the procedures above, or

   b. Inclusion of the new object in a full similarities array of the augmented stimulus set.

6. Predict the respondent's new perceptual configuration under a change in scenario (problem-solving context) from

   a. Experimenter knowledge of scenario characteristics.

   b. Respondent's similarities judgments regarding the relationship of the new scenario with a core set of original scenarios.

7. Predict a similarities-preference configuration under a change in scenario from either of the above kinds of information.

8. Predict the respondent's perceptual configuration after receipt of a message about the stimuli from experimenter information regarding message content and source.

9. Predict a similarities-preference configuration after receipt of a message about the stimuli.
10. Predict choices for collections of stimuli from knowledge of a similarities-preference configuration as developed from single-choice preference alternatives.
11. Predict choices among single object "bundles" as a function of the congruence of the bundle (for example, package, descriptive content of message).
12. Predict choices of "best values" (best buys for the money) from knowledge of similarities-preference configurations and psychological versus objective price transforms.

This list is clearly not exhaustive of the ways in which various prediction experiments might be designed. However, it seems sufficient to point out two of the major problems associated with the current state of the art:

1. What is meant by *the* perceptual configuration and what is its relationship to
   a. Property or objective space?
   b. Problem-solving context (scenario)?
2. What is meant by *the* joint-space (perceptual evaluative) configuration based on similarities and preferences and what is its relationship to scenario?

Finally, no consideration has been given to intersubject differences. Another major class of prediction problems concerns respondent differences in personality, intelligence, stimulus set knowledge, and so on, as related to differences in perception and preference. In this case, a set of prediction experiments could be designed to emphasize individual differences in response to a common set or sets of stimuli.

For example, personality types may be developed by considering the common elements of their similarities or preference responses to several sets of stimuli. The concept of role may be articulated by appropriate choice of scenarios across a common stimulus set and respondent. Finally, prediction experiments theoretically could be designed to investigate both stimulus changes and individual differences in a manner not unlike the employment of covariates in experimental design procedures.

Clearly, a much more detailed elaboration could be made regarding the various types of prediction experiments that might be designed in the context of similarities and preference responses. However, we feel that the general nature of these classes of experiments has been conveyed by the illustrations included here.

SUMMARY

In this concluding chapter, we have tried first to summarize the various methodological and content findings of the study. Our results indicate generally high consistency over both algorithms and approaches to the scaling of similarities and preference data. Few surprises were found in terms of our substantive results.

We then turned to a discussion of past research and potential applications of scaling methodology in a variety of content areas—marketing and other administrative fields, communications, psychology, sociology, and so on. We then described some prototypical experiments in which multidimensional scaling procedures could be used predictively.

While our discussion about the future of these techniques is necessarily speculative, we hope we have conveyed at least enough of the excitement of working with this methodology to prompt the reader to consider its relevance to his own area of research.

QUESTIONNAIRE
AND BASIC DATA

The questionnaire used in this study is reproduced in its entirety so that the reader can observe the way in which the data of this monograph were obtained.

Similarly, all basic data for each subject is shown so that the reader may use some or all of this data bank for sample problem purposes. (Punch card decks of the basic data shown here are available upon request from the authors.)

QUESTIONNAIRE

Name:_____

Sex: _____ Male   _____ Female

FOOD ITEM STUDY—PART A

On the accompanying (separate) pages you will note a list of 15 food items, often used at breakfast or snack time. Take a few minutes to look over the list and think about what the items conjure up to you.

Each item will be singled out in turn. For each reference item please select, from those remaining, the item that *you* think is most similar, in a general way, to the reference item. Put its stimulus number in the rank-1 position. Then find the item that is next most similar to the reference item; put its stimulus number in the rank-2 position, and so on.

Try to maintain the same frame of reference throughout all comparisons. By "similar" we mean the item most likely to be substituted for the reference item if, for some reason, it is unavailable. However, the criteria of "general similarity" are up to you.

1. Toast Pop-up

1 ( )   8 ( )
2 ( )   9 ( )
3 ( )   10 ( )
4 ( )   11 ( )
5 ( )   12 ( )
6 ( )   13 ( )
7 ( )   14 ( )

2. Buttered Toast

1 ( )   8 ( )
2 ( )   9 ( )
3 ( )   10 ( )
4 ( )   11 ( )
5 ( )   12 ( )
6 ( )   13 ( )
7 ( )   14 ( )

3. English Muffin and Margarine

1 ( )   8 ( )
2 ( )   9 ( )
3 ( )   10 ( )
4 ( )   11 ( )
5 ( )   12 ( )
6 ( )   13 ( )
7 ( )   14 ( )

4. Jelly Donut

1 ( )   8 ( )
2 ( )   9 ( )
3 ( )   10 ( )
4 ( )   11 ( )
5 ( )   12 ( )
6 ( )   13 ( )
7 ( )   14 ( )

5. Cinnamon Toast

1 ( )   8 ( )
2 ( )   9 ( )
3 ( )   10 ( )
4 ( )   11 ( )
5 ( )   12 ( )
6 ( )   13 ( )
7 ( )   14 ( )

6. Blueberry Muffin and Margarine

1 ( )   8 ( )
2 ( )   9 ( )
3 ( )   10 ( )
4 ( )   11 ( )
5 ( )   12 ( )
6 ( )   13 ( )
7 ( )   14 ( )

7. Hard Rolls and Butter

1 ( )   8 ( )
2 ( )   9 ( )
3 ( )   10 ( )
4 ( )   11 ( )
5 ( )   12 ( )
6 ( )   13 ( )
7 ( )   14 ( )

8. Toast and Marmalade

1 ( )   8 ( )
2 ( )   9 ( )
3 ( )   10 ( )
4 ( )   11 ( )
5 ( )   12 ( )
6 ( )   13 ( )
7 ( )   14 ( )

9. Buttered Toast and Jelly

1 ( )   8 ( )
2 ( )   9 ( )
3 ( )   10 ( )
4 ( )   11 ( )
5 ( )   12 ( )
6 ( )   13 ( )
7 ( )   14 ( )

10. Toast and Margarine

1 ( )   8 ( )
2 ( )   9 ( )
3 ( )   10 ( )
4 ( )   11 ( )
5 ( )   12 ( )
6 ( )   13 ( )
7 ( )   14 ( )

11. *Cinnamon Bun*

1 ( )	8 ( )
2 ( )	9 ( )
3 ( )	10 ( )
4 ( )	11 ( )
5 ( )	12 ( )
6 ( )	13 ( )
7 ( )	14 ( )

12. *Danish Pastry*

1 ( )	8 ( )
2 ( )	9 ( )
3 ( )	10 ( )
4 ( )	11 ( )
5 ( )	12 ( )
6 ( )	13 ( )
7 ( )	14 ( )

13. *Glazed Donut*

1 ( )	8 ( )
2 ( )	9 ( )
3 ( )	10 ( )
4 ( )	11 ( )
5 ( )	12 ( )
6 ( )	13 ( )
7 ( )	14 ( )

14. *Coffee Cake*

1 ( )	8 ( )
2 ( )	9 ( )
3 ( )	10 ( )
4 ( )	11 ( )
5 ( )	12 ( )
6 ( )	13 ( )
7 ( )	14 ( )

15. *Corn Muffin and Butter*

1 ( )	8 ( )
2 ( )	9 ( )
3 ( )	10 ( )
4 ( )	11 ( )
5 ( )	12 ( )
6 ( )	13 ( )
7 ( )	14 ( )

FOOD ITEM STUDY—PART B

Now that you have completed the similarities task, we would like your judgments on the same set of 15 food items—this time their ratings on each of the following bipolar scales:

1. Easy to prepare/Hard to prepare
2. Simple flavor/Complex flavor
3. Mainly for adults/Mainly for kids
4. High calories/Low calories
5. Artificial flavor/Natural flavor
6. Dry texture/Moist texture
7. Expensive/Inexpensive
8. Highly filling/Not highly filling
9. Mostly eaten by itself/Mostly eaten with other foods
10. Simple shape/Complex shape

In each case we shall present one of the bipolar scales. We shall then ask you to rate each of the 15 food items on a 7-point intensity scale. For example, the first scale would range from "extremely easy to prepare" to "extremely hard to prepare." The full scale of *degrees of intensity* (illustrated for the first pair of phrases) is to be interpreted as

		Scale Value
"extremely"	Easy to prepare	1
"very"	Easy to prepare	2
"slightly"	Easy to prepare	3
"neither	Easy to prepare	4
nor"	Hard to prepare	
"slightly"	Hard to prepare	5
"very"	Hard to prepare	6
"extremely"	Hard to prepare	7

Try to "cover the range" of each scale in making your intensity judgments. Merely circle the direction and intensity level that best reflects your judgment regarding each of the food items.

	Easy to Prepare					Hard to Prepare	
Toast pop-up	1	2	3	4	5	6	7
Buttered toast	1	2	3	4	5	6	7
English muffin and margarine	1	2	3	4	5	6	7
Jelly donut	1	2	3	4	5	6	7
Cinnamon toast	1	2	3	4	5	6	7
Blueberry muffin and margarine	1	2	3	4	5	6	7
Hard rolls and butter	1	2	3	4	5	6	7
Toast and marmalade	1	2	3	4	5	6	7
Buttered toast and jelly	1	2	3	4	5	6	7
Toast and margarine	1	2	3	4	5	6	7
Cinnamon bun	1	2	3	4	5	6	7
Danish pastry	1	2	3	4	5	6	7
Glazed donut	1	2	3	4	5	6	7
Coffee cake	1	2	3	4	5	6	7
Corn muffin and butter	1	2	3	4	5	6	7

	Simple Flavor					Complex Flavor	
Toast pop-up	1	2	3	4	5	6	7
Buttered toast	1	2	3	4	5	6	7
English muffin and margarine	1	2	3	4	5	6	7
Jelly donut	1	2	3	4	5	6	7
Cinnamon toast	1	2	3	4	5	6	7
Blueberry muffin and margarine	1	2	3	4	5	6	7
Hard rolls and butter	1	2	3	4	5	6	7
Toast and marmalade	1	2	3	4	5	6	7
Buttered toast and jelly	1	2	3	4	5	6	7
Toast and margarine	1	2	3	4	5	6	7
Cinnamon bun	1	2	3	4	5	6	7
Danish pastry	1	2	3	4	5	6	7
Glazed donut	1	2	3	4	5	6	7
Coffee cake	1	2	3	4	5	6	7
Corn muffin and butter	1	2	3	4	5	6	7

	Mainly for Adults					Mainly for Kids
Toast pop-up	1	2	3	4	5	6	7
Buttered toast	1	2	3	4	5	6	7
English muffin and margarine	1	2	3	4	5	6	7
Jelly donut	1	2	3	4	5	6	7
Cinnamon toast	1	2	3	4	5	6	7
Blueberry muffin and margarine	1	2	3	4	5	6	7
Hard rolls and butter	1	2	3	4	5	6	7
Toast and marmalade	1	2	3	4	5	6	7
Buttered toast and jelly	1	2	3	4	5	6	7
Toast and margarine	1	2	3	4	5	6	7
Cinnamon bun	1	2	3	4	5	6	7
Danish pastry	1	2	3	4	5	6	7
Glazed donut	1	2	3	4	5	6	7
Coffee cake	1	2	3	4	5	6	7
Corn muffin and butter	1	2	3	4	5	6	7

	High Calories					Low Calories
Toast pop-up	1	2	3	4	5	6	7
Buttered toast	1	2	3	4	5	6	7
English muffin and margarine	1	2	3	4	5	6	7
Jelly donut	1	2	3	4	5	6	7
Cinnamon toast	1	2	3	4	5	6	7
Blueberry muffin and margarine	1	2	3	4	5	6	7
Hard rolls and butter	1	2	3	4	5	6	7
Toast and marmalade	1	2	3	4	5	6	7
Buttered toast and jelly	1	2	3	4	5	6	7
Toast and margarine	1	2	3	4	5	6	7
Cinnamon bun	1	2	3	4	5	6	7
Danish pastry	1	2	3	4	5	6	7
Glazed donut	1	2	3	4	5	6	7
Coffee cake	1	2	3	4	5	6	7
Corn muffin and butter	1	2	3	4	5	6	7

	Artificial Flavor						*Natural Flavor*
Toast pop-up	1	2	3	4	5	6	7
Buttered toast	1	2	3	4	5	6	7
English muffin and margarine	1	2	3	4	5	6	7
Jelly donut	1	2	3	4	5	6	7
Cinnamon toast	1	2	3	4	5	6	7
Blueberry muffin and margarine	1	2	3	4	5	6	7
Hard rolls and butter	1	2	3	4	5	6	7
Toast and marmalade	1	2	3	4	5	6	7
Buttered toast and jelly	1	2	3	4	5	6	7
Toast and margarine	1	2	3	4	5	6	7
Cinnamon bun	1	2	3	4	5	6	7
Danish pastry	1	2	3	4	5	6	7
Glazed donut	1	2	3	4	5	6	7
Coffee cake	1	2	3	4	5	6	7
Corn muffin and butter	1	2	3	4	5	6	7

	Dry Texture						*Moist Texture*
Toast pop-up	1	2	3	4	5	6	7
Buttered toast	1	2	3	4	5	6	7
English muffin and margarine	1	2	3	4	5	6	7
Jelly donut	1	2	3	4	5	6	7
Cinnamon toast	1	2	3	4	5	6	7
Blueberry muffin and margarine	1	2	3	4	5	6	7
Hard rolls and butter	1	2	3	4	5	6	7
Toast and marmalade	1	2	3	4	5	6	7
Buttered toast and jelly	1	2	3	4	5	6	7
Toast and margarine	1	2	3	4	5	6	7
Cinnamon bun	1	2	3	4	5	6	7
Danish pastry	1	2	3	4	5	6	7
Glazed donut	1	2	3	4	5	6	7
Coffee cake	1	2	3	4	5	6	7
Corn muffin and butter	1	2	3	4	5	6	7

	Expensive						*Inexpensive*
Toast pop-up	1	2	3	4	5	6	7
Buttered toast	1	2	3	4	5	6	7
English muffin and margarine	1	2	3	4	5	6	7
Jelly donut	1	2	3	4	5	6	7
Cinnamon toast	1	2	3	4	5	6	7
Blueberry muffin and margarine	1	2	3	4	5	6	7
Hard rolls and butter	1	2	3	4	5	6	7
Toast and marmalade	1	2	3	4	5	6	7
Buttered toast and jelly	1	2	3	4	5	6	7
Toast and margarine	1	2	3	4	5	6	7
Cinnamon bun	1	2	3	4	5	6	7
Danish pastry	1	2	3	4	5	6	7
Glazed donut	1	2	3	4	5	6	7
Coffee cake	1	2	3	4	5	6	7
Corn muffin and butter	1	2	3	4	5	6	7

	Highly Filling						*Not Highly Filling*
Toast pop-up	1	2	3	4	5	6	7
Buttered toast	1	2	3	4	5	6	7
English muffin and margarine	1	2	3	4	5	6	7
Jelly donut	1	2	3	4	5	6	7
Cinnamon toast	1	2	3	4	5	6	7
Blueberry muffin and margarine	1	2	3	4	5	6	7
Hard rolls and butter	1	2	3	4	5	6	7
Toast and marmalade	1	2	3	4	5	6	7
Buttered toast and jelly	1	2	3	4	5	6	7
Toast and margarine	1	2	3	4	5	6	7
Cinnamon bun	1	2	3	4	5	6	7
Danish pastry	1	2	3	4	5	6	7
Glazed donut	1	2	3	4	5	6	7
Coffee cake	1	2	3	4	5	6	7
Corn muffin and butter	1	2	3	4	5	6	7

	Mostly Eaten by Itself					Mostly Eaten with Other Foods	
Toast pop-up	1	2	3	4	5	6	7
Buttered toast	1	2	3	4	5	6	7
English muffin and margarine	1	2	3	4	5	6	7
Jelly donut	1	2	3	4	5	6	7
Cinnamon toast	1	2	3	4	5	6	7
Blueberry muffin and margarine	1	2	3	4	5	6	7
Hard rolls and butter	1	2	3	4	5	6	7
Toast and marmalade	1	2	3	4	5	6	7
Buttered toast and jelly	1	2	3	4	5	6	7
Toast and margarine	1	2	3	4	5	6	7
Cinnamon bun	1	2	3	4	5	6	7
Danish pastry	1	2	3	4	5	6	7
Glazed donut	1	2	3	4	5	6	7
Coffee cake	1	2	3	4	5	6	7
Corn muffin and butter	1	2	3	4	5	6	7

	Simple Shape					Complex Shape	
Toast pop-up	1	2	3	4	5	6	7
Buttered toast	1	2	3	4	5	6	7
English muffin and margarine	1	2	3	4	5	6	7
Jelly donut	1	2	3	4	5	6	7
Cinnamon toast	1	2	3	4	5	6	7
Blueberry muffin and margarine	1	2	3	4	5	6	7
Hard rolls and butter	1	2	3	4	5	6	7
Toast and marmalade	1	2	3	4	5	6	7
Buttered toast and jelly	1	2	3	4	5	6	7
Toast and margarine	1	2	3	4	5	6	7
Cinnamon bun	1	2	3	4	5	6	7
Danish pastry	1	2	3	4	5	6	7
Glazed donut	1	2	3	4	5	6	7
Coffee cake	1	2	3	4	5	6	7
Corn muffin and butter	1	2	3	4	5	6	7

FOOD ITEM STUDY—PART C

Now that you have supplied us with similarities and rating judgments, we would like to get some idea of your personal preferences for each of the food items under various types of eating occasions or menus. In each case merely place the stimulus number of the item you most prefer, next most prefer, and so on, in each of the rank positions under each eating occasion/menu description.

a. Overall preferences

(Highest)   Rank   1 ( )   9 ( )
                     2 ( )   10 ( )
                     3 ( )   11 ( )
                     4 ( )   12 ( )
                     5 ( )   13 ( )
                     6 ( )   14 ( )
                     7 ( )   15 ( )   (Lowest)
                     8 ( )

b. When I'm having a breakfast consisting of juice, bacon and eggs, and beverage

(Highest)   Rank   1 ( )   9 ( )
                     2 ( )   10 ( )
                     3 ( )   11 ( )
                     4 ( )   12 ( )
                     5 ( )   13 ( )
                     6 ( )   14 ( )
                     7 ( )   15 ( )   (Lowest)
                     8 ( )

c. When I'm having a breakfast consisting of juice, cold cereal, and beverage

(Highest)   Rank   1 ( )   9 ( )
                     2 ( )   10 ( )
                     3 ( )   11 ( )
                     4 ( )   12 ( )
                     5 ( )   13 ( )
                     6 ( )   14 ( )
                     7 ( )   15 ( )   (Lowest)
                     8 ( )

d. When I'm having a breakfast consisting of juice, pancakes, sausage, and beverage

(Highest)	Rank	1 ( )	9 ( )	
		2 ( )	10 ( )	
		3 ( )	11 ( )	
		4 ( )	12 ( )	
		5 ( )	13 ( )	
		6 ( )	14 ( )	
		7 ( )	15 ( )	(Lowest)
		8 ( )		

e. Breakfast, with beverage only

(Highest)	Rank	1 ( )	9 ( )	
		2 ( )	10 ( )	
		3 ( )	11 ( )	
		4 ( )	12 ( )	
		5 ( )	13 ( )	
		6 ( )	14 ( )	
		7 ( )	15 ( )	(Lowest)
		8 ( )		

f. At snack time, with beverage only

(Highest)	Rank	1 ( )	9 ( )	
		2 ( )	10 ( )	
		3 ( )	11 ( )	
		4 ( )	12 ( )	
		5 ( )	13 ( )	
		6 ( )	14 ( )	
		7 ( )	15 ( )	(Lowest)
		8 ( )		

FOOD ITEM STUDY—PART D

Now, to complete the interview we would like a little additional information about you.

1. Sex: Male _____   Female _____
2. Age, in years: _____
3. Marital Status: Single _____   Married _____
4. If married, number of children? _____
5. Do you consider yourself overweight? Yes _____   No _____
6. If yes, by what percentage of your normal weight? _____ percent
7. What does your typical weekday breakfast consist of?

   _____

   _____

   _____

8. What does your typical weekend breakfast consist of?

   _____

   _____

   _____

9. Please check the beverages below which you drink on a regular basis—at least once a day, normally. Coffee _____   Tea _____   Milk _____

BASIC DATA OF STUDY

The basic data used in this book are now listed. For every respondent the data matrix is printed in 15 rows, of which 14 have 60 positions and the last row, 37 positions. Thus, in all, there are $(14 \times 60) + 37 = 877$ entries in the data block for each respondent. Explanation of the entries is given below.

Position Number   *Item Description*

1-3   Respondent number (011, 012, and so on). The first two digits indicate the couple number, and the third digit indicates sex of spouse (1 = Male, 2 = Female).

4-5   Blank.

6-37   Anchor-point data when stimulus number 01 serves as reference. The entries are in 2-column (position) fields. The first entry is the number of the reference item. The remaining 14 entries are stimuli numbers judged as most similar to least similar to the reference item. The last entry of 2 positions is left blank.

38-69	Same as for 6-37 for stimulus number 2
70-101	Same as for 6-37 for stimulus number 3
102-133	Same as for 6-37 for stimulus number 4
134-165	Same as for 6-37 for stimulus number 5
166-197	Same as for 6-37 for stimulus number 6
198-229	Same as for 6-37 for stimulus number 7
230-261	Same as for 6-37 for stimulus number 8
262-293	Same as for 6-37 for stimulus number 9
294-325	Same as for 6-37 for stimulus number 10
326-357	Same as for 6-37 for stimulus number 11
358-389	Same as for 6-37 for stimulus number 12
390-421	Same as for 6-37 for stimulus number 13
422-453	Same as for 6-37 for stimulus number 14
454-485	Same as for 6-37 for stimulus number 15
486-489	The letters "ANCR" to indicate end of anchor-point data.
490-506	Ratings for the 15 stimuli on bipolar scale number 1. The entries are 15 one-digit numbers followed by 2 blanks.
507-523	Same as for 490-506 for construct number 2
524-540	Same as for 490-506 for construct number 3
541-557	Same as for 490-506 for construct number 4
558-574	Same as for 490-506 for construct number 5
575-591	Same as for 490-506 for construct number 6
592-608	Same as for 490-506 for construct number 7
609-625	Same as for 490-506 for construct number 8
626-642	Same as for 490-506 for construct number 9
643-659	Same as for 490-506 for construct number 10
660-663	The letters "RATE" to indicate end of ratings data.
664-695	Preference ranks for scenario number 1. The entries are 15 rank numbers in 2-digit fields for the stimuli 1 to 15. The last 2 positions are left blank.
696-727	Same as for 664-695 for scenario number 2
728-759	Same as for 664-695 for scenario number 3
760-791	Same as for 664-695 for scenario number 4
792-823	Same as for 664-695 for scenario number 5
824-855	Same as for 664-695 for scenario number 6
856-859	The letters "PREF" to indicate end of preference data.
860	Sex of respondent (1 = Male, 0 = Female).
861-862	Age of respondent in years.
863	Number of children.
864	Whether the respondent considers himself or herself overweight (Yes = 1, No = 0).
865-866	Percentage overweight; actual percentage reported.
867	Weekday breakfast type (Light = 1, Heavy = 0). Any

	combination of juice or fruit, beverage, toast or other bakery item, cheese, and cereal is coded as light breakfast.
868	Weekend breakfast type (Light = 1, Heavy = 0).
869	Coffee drinking habits (Regularly = 1, Otherwise = 0).
870	Tea drinking habits (Regularly = 1, Otherwise = 0).
871	Milk drinking habits (Regularly = 1, Otherwise = 0).
872-873	Blank.
874-877	Letters "CLAS" to indicate end of classification data.

```
BASIC DATA FOR SUBJECT NO. 011

011   0112080904051406131110030i0715   0210050908031115060712l
4011304   0310020908110515060112071413C4   0413121101140906150
5C€1CC7C203   C50i1C111214C10SC€030615070413   061514121102100
809070503011304   07021011141215060509080313040l   C8090210050
i111201040615071413   C9C8C21005030615140701111213C4   1002090
805030706151112141301C4   110512140413070609080103021015   120
4131114010906080507C2100315   13041211140109C80605150210030l7
 141106151201C4130908C210030507   1506C210031105141301090807l
204   ANCR477275377742167   6245i3255245262   422453255233323
123124432411235   252535555543346   354635355445332   153244533
6i1235   3342434432422324   362455545632325   624525222266354   R
ATE1312 7 3 5 4 8111015 2 1 6 S14   15 3 512 2 8 713 1 4 6101
1 S14   1410 9 3 7 61215 811 5 1 4 213   14 9 7 111 612151310
3 4 2 5 8   1012 8 4 9 6 7151413 3 1 5 211   1411 8 4 9 6 7151
012 3 2 5 113  PREF1261115101C1  CLAS

BASIC DATA FOR SUBJECT NO. 012

C12   01C80905021003040611120715l314   021003C9080501150607141
1121304   0310C205C90801071415l213040611   0413121409081002030
10615051107   05021009C8C311011i1406130415C7   061514121002050
8C9111304030107   07021003121114150109080513060x   08091002050
41i11141303C61501C7   C9C8C21CC5030111141206150x1307   1002090
5080301061114121513C4C7   110512141304061509C80210C30107   121
411C41308090603011505C21007   13041214110809060503011002150x7
 14121104130608090103050210150x7   15061403021007050908120111l
304   ANCR223135233211154   223433163256453   644543135432524
543132433431134   265243734532236   34464525543343x   564343656
63x335   543233533532235   266163533621213   212425611156635   R
ATE1511 6 310 514 8 912 7 1 4 i13   15 4 311 7 514 1 2 6 813
51210   15 8 2 310 114 5 6 91112 413 7   1512 7 111 214 91013
6 4 3 5 8   1513 6 311 512 8 91410 1 4 2 7   1513 8 712 311 91
014 4 1 5 2 6  PREF024100010101  CLAS

BASIC DATA FOR SUBJECT NO. 021

0i1   C1C412C809061114130502l0150703   02100703150609080511041
3011412   030715C61002C90508111304121401   0412130111060809051
00214150703   05080910021113041i140601071503   06150307C210090
8C5131112041401   C7031506C2100S0805111304121401   08091002010
7150306051104121314   C90802011CC7060315041211051314   1002090
8C7031506051113041214C1   110513140612040809011002071503   120
4131401C711060809C210C515C3   1304121114010608090510020703l5
 14111204130706080109C515C3021C   150603070210090805121304011
411   ANCR123145522265666   3223i3233344342   542443455354432
i363545335333i5   36666666565665   333534333355453   376663677
766645   47666566664443S   3235555333355S55   32242362225444x   R
ATE15101214 3 2 9 8 711 1 6 4 513   15 2 712 5 6 4 8 1 3 9101
11413   10 814 711 612 2 1 9 3 4 51315   61013 512 714 8 911
3 4 2 115   710 51113 614 8 91i 1 2 3 415   1310 6 71412 5 8
911 2 3 4 115  PREF124000C10101  CLAS
```

BASIC DATA FOR SUBJECT NO. 022

```
C22   01C51409C80612041311C31C021507   02100703150609080514110
1130412   030615C710C2C105141113120408C9   0413111214010908050
6C315C71002   C50908011104131214060315071002   C61503071002010
513C4111412CSC8   C7C315C610C2050109080413111412   08090502100
10413111412030607C15   C9C8C510C207150603141113040112   1002071
5C306C5C908140113041112   11120413140109080715030602100S   121
1141304C1C6C9C805C315C71002   13C4111214010509080615C307102
   14121113040809010506150307021C   15060303710C2C10908051413041
112   ANCR122525222144442   322233233234244   443443344444443
34323343342232   555665566565556   544545344443543   554554455
544444   565464566644444   544454355444454   332235433344525   R
ATE 61411  3 7 8121C 915  4  1  2  513     9 1 61210  8  5  4  3 214151
311 7     6  2  713  510  9  3  1  4111514  812     911  7  4  8 614121310
2  5  3  115     6  713  412111410  9  E  1  2  3  515     61310  215  9 7121
114  3  5  1  4  8   PREF023011C10100   CLAS
```

BASIC DATA FOR SUBJECT NO. 031

```
031   01C80511131204C61415C5C3C21007   02100305151406090801111
3120407   031002051514C609C8011113120407   0412131101080906141
5C503021007   C503C21015140609C8011113120407   061415050309080
210011113120407   C7021003051514C609080111131204   08090106111
31204141505030210C7   C9080106111312041415050302100S   1002030
5151406C908C111131204C7   11131204010809061415050302100S   121
3110401C8090614150503C210C7   13111204010809C614150503021007
14150605090803020100111113120407   151406050302100908011113120
4C7   ANCR122146233211112   312543135167543   732564154265543
167233723712245   175234733612346   542634156243113   176243754
711235   276143544711235   176113744711125   213613211175643   R
ATE15  9  61413  212  8  71C11  1  4  3  5   15  3  513  8  7  9  2  1  414111
210  6     15  9  61413  212  8  71C11  1  4  3  5   15  6  81210  214  5  4  71
3  111  3  9     15  9  61413  212  8  71C11  1  4  3  5   1511  8  714  21310
912  6  1  4  3  5   PREF13231  511011   CLAS
```

BASIC DATA FOR SUBJECT NO. 032

```
032   01051112141304C9C80615C31C0207   02100809050111121413040
6150307   030715060210C809050111112141304   0413141211010509080
61002150307   C508C91CC2C111121413040615030S7   061514121113040
105080910020307   C703C21015060E0905010413111214   08C90502100
11112141304061503C7   C9C80502100111121413040615030S7   1002080
9C50111121413040615035C7   11121413040105090806100215030S7   121
1141304010509080610021503C7   13041112140105090806100215030S7
   14121113040105C908061002150307   1503071002060809050113041S1
214   ANCR222136523271175   411536145157574   431653166133531
567233632711114   244356433452213   211523155133364   366373655
721314   476361755721314   472345755721214   113515322166573   R
ATE 91114  4  7  61510  812  5  2  3  113   11  114  6l0  41512  3  2  7  9
5  E13     91114  5  7  61510  812  2  9  4  113     91114  4  2  31510  112
6  7  5  813     91114  5  7  61510  812  2  3  4  113     91114  5  7  61510
812  2  3  4  113   PREF03131  21111C   CLAS
```

BASIC DATA FOR SUBJECT NO. 041

```
041   01100208050915070306111214I304   02011008050915070306111
2141304    03150710020111060413090805I214    0413080914060111051
2C71503C210   05111413C1C8120315C70904060210   060307151412110
50413091C080201   0715C210C1C90E081103141304 0512   08091304140
E1101051215070 30210   C902C1100E05150703061112141304    1002010
8C9C515C703061112141304    1105C615011214130 40803070 90210    121
4060113041508 05110307090210    1304060301110512151 40908070210
   1412130411050106031 5C908070210    150307100201110604130908051
214    ANCR123133223267263    213434233257562    424753155151442
564344544531226    275335755642326    233535244324343    675454655
E42424    675453566653424    376445666742326    213433211135454    R
ATE 914  5  6  8  413111215  7  2  1  310      1  31315  714  2  5  6  4  8121
0 911      7  81415  4  5  61213  9  31C  111  2      7  81415  5  4  6  91312
31C  111  2      914  5  6  8  413111215  7  2  1  310      914  6  5  8  412131
115  7  2  1  310    PREF125000C00C1C    CLAS
```

BASIC DATA FOR SUBJECT NO. 042

```
C42   01C40809021013051214060 3111507    021005090807C3150611140
1130412    03C61507111214080 9021005041301    0413011211080914050
6C302101507    05021009C811C3010E071512141304    060315071112140
8C9021005041301    07031502100611141205090813 0401    08090502100
1C412131114C6C70315    C9C8C5C21C0104121311140607 0315    1002050
9C80703150611140113041 2    1112130614150305021 00908070401    121
10413140603150509C8C2100107    13041108091002141206 0503150701
   1406111213030401150 5C908C2100 7    150306070210051114120908130
401    ANCR124135233256176    522435134346552    452632145423442
245133522411346    176446643633456    145647564573542    255343544
271345    553563244426543    274245633721223    115615322167654    R
ATE151012  6  9  213  8  711  3  1  5  414    15  41013  3  7  6  2  1  5  9141
1  E12    15  414  9  31011  1  2  5  712  8  613    151012  6  9  213  8  711
3  1  5  414    151012  6  9  213  8  711  3  1  5  414    151012  6  9  213  8
711  3  1  5  414    PREF025000010111    CLAS
```

BASIC DATA FOR SUBJECT NO. 051

```
C51   01C80904121311051406030 21C1507    021007150306080901 05111
3121404    03060210C715C501C8091113121404    0414111312090105060
3C80210C715    05141112C4C1C90603130802 10C715    060302100715050
1C8091113121404    C715C3060210141205111308090104    08090502100
1110603120413141507    C901C508C6C3111312 140402101507    1002071
50306080901051113121404    111314051209010408060302101507    121
4111305C409C1C80E03021C15C7    1312141105040901080603021 01507
   1412131105090104C8060302101507    150702100306051411120813090
4C1    ANCR234175534355165    626467135267473    723644124254551
47E245754723317    1562E76745323 27    237742124356561    475345266
731415    456447264542316    674164376755234    215314722167774    R
ATE1512  2  4  5  81011  313  7  9  6  114    15  8  211  3  414  7  1  9  5131
21C  6    1310  914  6  712  9  411  3  215  1  8    1113  5  1  4  61512  314
8  9  210  7    1513  410  5  6  812  714  3  211  1  9    1114  6  1  3  5  8  9
71510  4  21312    PREF12611  500111    CLAS
```

BASIC DATA FOR SUBJECT NO. 052

```
C52  C1C908C502101111412C41303C61507   02100703090105081306151
1041412   03100207C5C615C9C8C11311041412   04090812141111306150
1050302C710   051114120413C908C1061503020710   061511C50908010
302C71CC4131412   C70210C3C508090106151104131412   08090405011
2141113061503021007  C9C8C405C112141113061503021007  1002070
3C9C8050104111306151214  110509080104130615030207101214   121
4C4C61511C509C8011303C2071C   13C405110908011214061503020710
141204051113090801C61503C2071C   150611C51309080104141203020
710  ANCR125162233214172  412546233147576   744672155431612
47€155633741215  175453766341425  253743156517413   475372466
731312  375462344741512  375452266741412   521123422267673  R
ATE151310  7 6 4 9121114  5 2 8  1 3   15 8 513 4 210 7 6 9 3121
411 1   15131C 6 9 2 8121114 3 5 7 4 1   13 1 512 6 9 7 3 4 21
C151114 8   151211 7 9 4 5141C13 6 2 8 1 3   1511 9 3 6 2 710
€12 514 413 1  PREFC26100000011C  CLAS
```

BASIC DATA FOR SUBJECT NO. 061

```
061  01C8040911141305C61215C31CC2C7  0210507030609051412010
8111304  03150607C210C908C5140112131104  0413111412080905011
CC60315C207  C51201141113C4C603150908100207  060315070210080
911050112141304  C715C306C21CC50511141208011304  08090412140
11105130603151002C7  C90408011214111305060315100207  1002C71
5C3C6C9C108C514121113C4  111214041305010608091003150207  121
4130411010508090603151002C7  1311041214C501C809060315100207
1412111304010509060310150207  150307020610080905011112141
3C4  ANCR132122234311112  333244345366354  432543257353432
324144241312122  363243743455457  4656225646654326  334333232
322323  565674355545646  362222643511112  134434633346564  R
ATE 5 2 415 8 5 110 6 711131412 3   9 2 415 8 5 110 6 711131
412 3    9 2 415 8 5 110 6 711131412 3   9 1 515 8 6 310 7 21
1131412 4   9 2 515 8 6 112 7 310131411 4   9 6 315 8 4 114
7 510121311 2  PREF1271C0C101CC  CLAS
```

BASIC DATA FOR SUBJECT NO. 062

```
062  0114051203020713150411090€0810  02151006070314010512080
9C41113  031510140602070805090112041311  0411131214080906010
31C07050215  05C11CC8C3C5141113C21204060715  060310150902050
108120714130411  C715C203C809C60105101412111304  C8090401121
3C603C21005111415C7  C90801041205131114100215030607  1002090
1060308051512071413C411  111214130406010509081015070203  121
113140401050908100615030207  131104141208090605010302101507
14131112040€C901C515C710030602  150703020609100811010514121
304  ANCR122132233211112  323453344356462  532562154622421
435153343611114  364234635234136  2436544547643 2  554343444
621324  543643343511214  132122556411116  324545322256454  R
ATE11 1  21512 3 4 8 71410 913 5 6   11 1 21413 3 4 8 7 610121
5 5 9  11 1 315 5 7 210 8 6 9131412 4   11 1 515 6 8 210 7 3
5141312 4    5 2 515 8 7 114 4 311121310 6   311 11314 9 2121
510 5 7 8 6 4  PREFC26100011111  CLAS
```

BASIC DATA FOR SUBJECT NO. 071

```
071  0112131406110405C8C915021C0307  0209100307C815C50601111
4120413  031002071509C80506011114121304  0413121411010806050
S1502C31007  0506C80111141213C415091002 0307  060108051509141
112130410020307  C703C210C915CE0801051412111304  08090105150
6141211130403100207  C9080105150612141113040310 0207  1002030
7080501C9150612141113C4  1113C414120605090801151003 0207  121
40413110601050809151003 0207  13041112140601050809151003 0207
 1412041311C6C105C80915100030207  15060105080914111304 1210030
2C7  ANCR122132223211112  534245134332125  64455315644 4432
233745345466765  255664643422234  521534133245663  364343455
731324  566344355632224  365343234622223  122222322234254  R
ATE12 114 4 5 61113 21510 3 9 E 7  15 1 41011 7 914 3 212 61
3 5 8  15 1 41011 7 914 3 212 E13 5 8  15 1 41011 7 914 3 21
2 E13 5 E  15 1 4 511 7 914 3 212 61310 8  10 815 5 9 311131
214 6 1 7 2 4  PREF1270C0C100C1  CLAS
```

BASIC DATA FOR SUBJECT NO. 072

```
C72  0113121411040509 08C70206150310  0209080507150111141 3120
4C30610  0315020 7C806C91005011 114121304  04131211140509 08011
5C702060310  0511141213C415CSCEC70206030110  0615041112141 30
5C9C8C7C2010310  07020908100315060105111404 1312  0809041301 1
41211C51507C2C6031C  CSC8C4C11211131405150702060310  100209 0
3081506C705110104121314  11051412130401090815070206 0310  121
41113C4C509010815C702C6C310  13040112141105090802071506 0310
 1412130411C501C9C802C715C6C31C  150602C70803100511141 213040
1C9  ANCR223142233311122  544665223366564  74335323423 3332
233212332421112  242343444244344  355666455435534  34434 4544
633334  444234444522223  54445544445565  256565555466656  R
ATE131114 5 41210 8 715 3 2 6 1 9  13 114 6 31211 4 515 7 81
C S 2  13 114 3 212 6 4 515 7 8 91011  13 114 3 212 6 4 515
7 E 91011  131114 5 612 9 7 815 4 2 3 110  131114 5 612 9 7
E15 4 2 3 110  PREF02701 610001  CLAS
```

BASIC DATA FOR SUBJECT NO. 081

```
C81  C1C412141303080911050615 1C0207  02100715090806030511141
2130401  03100209C615C607C5131114120104  0413121411011009030
80506150207  0511C80902100103C7150614121304  06150307141 2021
CCSC8C111051304  C715060311011C02080905 14121304  080905021 00
103041311141206 15C7  C908C210050301041214061113 1507  100209 0
8C5010403121413110615C7  110514121306090108021003041507  121
4111304C601C5C9080310C215C7  130411141209080601050210031507
 14121104130601090805021 0C31507  150603111412130401050908021
CC7  ANCR135164233311122  213554122155354  62445424424 4534
311112111211112  276456566545456  233652233244453  26324 3554
567675  554344544566564  263224644632224  334544344456564  R
ATE1211 8 1 4 71410 913 5 2 6 315  12 3 5 9101314 2 1 4 8 61
1 715  101311 9 51215 7 614 3 2 4 1 8  101311 9 51215 7 614
3 2 4 1 8  81211 3 5 915 6 713 4 210 114  61312 1 71015 8
S14 3 4 2 511  PREF12300001111C  CLAS
```

BASIC DATA FOR SUBJECT NO. 082

```
C82  010409C8C612131114030510020715  021009081507C5060412131
1C11403  030615010412111314CCE09020705  0412130601151114020
9C810C50307  05111303060104151214090810020 7  060315090113110
512C414CE10C2C7  C715C309C20806011105130414121 0  08051002090
3C715C601041312141 1  C903C615070802100501121104131 4  1002090
8C71503C60511011204131 4  1105131204140603010908100215 07  121
40413110506C3C1C9C802101507  1304111214050601030908100215 07
 1412041311060105030 9C810C0215 07  150307021014080905010611130
412  ANCR123122222211122  212334122234241  544462144464434
434234343422224  364455666545446  333434233324433  434354544
432414  454444544443634  376445755744447  414555444456564  R
ATE1512  414  5  311  9  713  6  8  1  210   15  1  31412  8  5  7  6  213111
0  9  4   15  8  21410  113  7  6  911  5  4  312   15  4  11411  6  3  8  7  51
21013  9  2   1512  214  8  111  5  413  7  9  6  310   1512  514  6  411  9
E13  7  1  2  310  PREF02200C01001C  CLAS
```

BASIC DATA FOR SUBJECT NO. 091

```
091  C1120413140EC911C5C8C31CC21507  02100908050315070106141
1130412  03100209080715C5C1061411130412  0413121406010911050
8C3100215C7  C511C9081002031507010614130412  061412041311010
9C5080310021 5C7  C710C2C3C90815C501061411130412  08090510020
315C701C61114130412  09080510020315070106111413041 2  100209C
8C5C3150701061114130412  111413040612010905080310021507  120
4131406C10911C5080310C21507  130414120601C911C5080310021507
 141206010413110509080 310021507  15071002030908050106141113 0
412  ANCR122123222211111  22333232443353 42  433454224443423
443233443422223  166555666656545  345545245456654  465463446
634444  665564566643544  44444444443444  223324322235353  R
ATE  71C  E  313  6151211  9  5  1  4  214   15  2  313  8  9  5  4  112101
411  7   13  2  311  6  715  5  4  110  E12  914   15  2  313  8  9  7  5  4  11
21C1411  6   710  8  313  6151211  9  5  1  4  214   6  910  4  71315121
1  8  3  1  5  214  PREF126C0C01111C  CLAS
```

BASIC DATA FOR SUBJECT NO. 092

```
C92  010803091002150605110414121 3C7  021008090503150106110 41
2141307  03151002080901050612141104130 7  0413111412060105030
9C810C21507  051110C2C9C8C315C10414120613 07  061412110403051
301090802101507  C7151002C90803C106051411120413  C8090210031
5C1C506C71114120413  09080210040605010315141112130 7  1002080
9C315C5010611141204 13C7  11051214041306010315090802100 7  121
41104060113030515C908C21007  1304121411060103050 9C815021007
 141211C604C501031309150 8C21007  15030702100801090506141211 0
413  ANCR122135122211121  222225222255252  422462124222622
333233333322223  176666667666666  355656135365653  355553665
E53535  555352553522225  165252766622225  222223122223332  R
ATE  712  6  410  115  9  813  5  314  211   14  3  51311  8  7  2  1  412101
5  9  6   13  5  71112  915  4  3  610  114  2  8   13  1  512  9  715  3  4  2
E111410  6   712  6  410  115  9  813  5  314  211   812  6  114  515  91
01311  2  4  3  7  PREF02500001111C  CLAS
```

BASIC DATA FOR SUBJECT NO. 101

101 0112111304140309C805C615020710   0210070309080615050114
2111304   031007020908C61505011412111304   0413111201140506081
5C9C7100203 0511121314C4C6C1CEC91507020310 061503090801020
507101112141304 C70203091C15060805141201111304 C8090201050
7C60310151412111304 C90802010507060310151412111304 1003020
70SC81506051401121113C4 11130412140105080906150702031 121
4011311C405061508090702100 13041214011105060809070210031 5
  141213C40111050615C8C90702100 15060113041214110508090702 1
003 ANCR122123232321111 645556255435421 62154534433241 4
123133221512363 263653455364674 563524356573511 2351235 32
431233 343365233411267 176355355622325 41567662227654 5 R
ATE 2 9 8 51512 710 611 1 3 41314 11 1 41015 8 2 6 5 312 7
91314   6 1 310151311 5 4 2 8 7 91214   11314 510 912 8 715
2 3 4 611   51112 414 91C 8 713 2 1 3 615   11113 414 910 8
712 5 2 3 615 PREF1230115101CC CLAS

BASIC DATA FOR SUBJECT NO. 102

1C2 0112130414070315061008110C50902   0212130408071506110503 0
51C1401 03C708121304150614110509100201 0412131415060811050
70910020301 0511121304C81506C703C91014020 061507030812130
414110509100201 07030809121306150410141105020 08070312150
613041411051C090201 C9C8C3C71506121304110514100201 1008030
71506130414121105090201 11121415061304080705100903020 121
41311041506C807030509100201 1304121415061105080703100902 01
  1412130415C607081105C31CC9C2C1 15060413120814110703091005 0
201 ANCR233143233311112 712433241135463 43344325616463 3
232122331532122 176366777565657 322745234213111 475454 55
654454 653522144531323 176242777731215 12476541116776 6 R
ATE101115 6 9 414 21312 8 1 3 7 5   15 7 3 91012 2 1 5 41411
813 6   1514 7 911 4 1 2 5 61213 810 3   15 5 210 8 714 1 3 41
311 912 6 1514 8 9 4 31011121 6 1 2 5 7   1514 8 9 4 310111
213 6 1 2 5 7 PREF020000011111 CLAS

BASIC DATA FOR SUBJECT NO. 111

111 0112141104061513050BC903C71002   0210090807050314111304 1
5060112 03100207C515C608C9141113040112 0413141115060312010
50708091002 0511141201041506130308090207 061511C21401131
21C0304C509C807 0702C8091005031506111413040112 08020709100
40311C5150614130112 C9C8C2C31C07051506130414111201 1002070
8C903051314150611120401 11120114050615130408091007030 120
1111405C6C409C8151303100702 13040506031514110812011009070 2
14120111130406150510C9C8C70302 15060504130311011214090807 1
C02 ANCR233143323232223 533234233246354 62255533525464 3
133422433411213 365344656642226 365353555543332 16534364 5
721223 433432343453444 133222433321223 112213411133233 R
ATE12 1 210 315 5 6 413 711 8 514 15 1 214 312 5 6 7 81013
911 4   113 8 7 6111410 915 5 2 4 312   15 1 2 9 811 3 4 5 61
2141013 7   11510 6 5 814131211 4 2 7 3 9   2 111 7 6 915141
213 5 3 8 410 PREF12201 510111 CLAS

BASIC DATA FOR SUBJECT NO. 112

```
112  010905081210C203C715C413140611  021005090803150607011 41
3041211   03150210C908C605C7011213140411  0413111214090801060
21C05031507  05090802100311010€151407121304  061503071112140
SC8C41301050210  07031502100506090811131401 0412  08090502100
1C60315040712131114  C9C805C21CC61503C4010712111314  1002030
51508091101130607121404  111412130406150109080305070210  120
413140611011 5C908C503C70210  13041214110601 0908150305070210
  1411131204061503C908C10507021C  150306C71402101113090801051
2C4  ANCR222132222221122  63355645526644 3  633454444342444
243133433611223  16666645545 5446  255755266453433  355243445
611223  55335334452232 3  276545566722225  211514322156344  R
ATE141210  111  515  8  713  2  6  4  3  9  10  1  313  4  711  6  5  21215
914  8   13  2  €11  3  7  9  5  4  112141015  8   10  2  613  5  8  9  4  3  11
1141215  7   14  7  9  6  4  315  2  1  81013  51211   141113  1  7  61510
S12  3  5  2  4  8  PREF02301  810111  CLAS
```

BASIC DATA FOR SUBJECT NO. 121

```
121  C1C509C203C81006151412111 3C704  02080910070305010615131
4121104   03100207080915050613121114010 4  04 09011315060511121
4C8C3100207  0511C810C902010314120615130407  061503101214131
1C10405CS08C207  C702C308C61C1 5090501131214110 4  08091002010
3051506040713111214  C9080203010615101213050407111 4  1002080
3CSC1C5C7061511141312C4  1112131405061504010908030210 07  120
414C615011113C3C5C908C21007  13010412111415060908050302100 7
  141106151305120109080307100204  15061114130512010908030204 1
CC7  ANCR222142255212112  53464324546756 5  623632125252522
234134342411113  145245733321215  544645135324545  354342643
421212  243132232311112  344136744451156  524626523257656  R
ATE14  6  113  2  515  8  412  71C  S  311   12  8  1  9  2  313  6  510  4  71
11415   9  5  4  8  3  610  11112  213  71415   910  3  5  1  211  4  612
813  71514   12  8  2  6  7  1  9  3  513  414151110   1211  710  2  6  3  8
1  5  91315  414  PREF125011C101C1  CLAS
```

BASIC DATA FOR SUBJECT NO. 122

```
122  01C9100302050815040611121 41307  021007150506C8030901141
2111304   03020710150608090514111213 0401  04011309081406051 11
21502C31C07  0511C8C1C91413C3C4C61512021007  061501030913120
504111408020710  07021015C3C9C€C50106121 111141304  C8090203071
C150105C61411131204  09030210C€07051506011213140411  1002030
715C8091401050611120413  1105121413060108150904020310 07  121
406051113080915100401C20703  13041114120906010508150203100 7
  141211C6051304011503C9C8100207  15030210081112011406051309 0
407  ANCR233135222211123  42256624436566 3  644653112164532
254264634633235  166344757633456  544756155566774  364533776
643323  25423365452223  366223766533232  456456334466566  R
ATE1011  915  5  612  1  313  8  214  4  7   12  8  71410  9  6  1  31113  21
5  5  4   12  7  8141011  5  1  2  913  315  4  6   13  8  714  911  6  1  4101
2  315  2  5   11  8  7131510  5  1  4  S12  214  3  6   12  7  81315  9  6  2
41011  114  3  5  PREFC26000C101CC  CLAS
```

BASIC DATA FOR SUBJECT NO. 131

```
131   0109040208120506 13 10 1114C31507    C20903041213050611140IO
81C0715   0310091204020514081113060715O1    0413110914100812050
3C2C7C61501   0502C8C9C31CC41214131511060107   060302100408091
214051113150701   07090203121 5C51C08011306111404   08030410131
2C6C214C90511070115   C9C8031002051112141304061 50701   1002080
30504121309141506110IC7   11121314040308100206090515O701   120
4131103C8091402100506070115   131204081403110502090610150107
1413041112C81009C203C506150107   15060308050210071404I213010
911   ANCR122123333211113   211332133244443   642462144342422
221142343421122   377357754523227   454741166666521   272266666
721123   566364466732322   174165266721114   111512321167233   R
ATE15 8  7  5  91013  311  6  2  112  414   13  2  3  9  6  815  11C 4  7111
214 5   14  9  8  5101115  6  713  2  1  4  312   14  611  910  515  7  812
1  4  2  313   13  910  5111214  8  6  7  2  1  3  415    7  913  1  8  614151
210  5  4  3  211   PREF127000C1010C   CLAS
```

BASIC DATA FOR SUBJECT NO. 132

```
132   01020809100503070615111304141 2   021001090803C5070615111
3041412   03100206C915C70108051113041412   0412130911140615030
81C0502C701   05110208C9011C13C4141203061 5C7   061503100212080
911041314050107   0702031015010605141311080 91204   08091204051
11314061503C21C07C1   C9C812040511131406150307021001   1002010
9C803050706151113041412   110502080901101304141203061507   120
4131411C61503090805 10C20701   1304121406111503080509100 70201
140413121511C6030810C9C5C107C2   15060310021208091104131 4050
1C7   ANCR112132212111112   122234234235443   444445544445454
133544345257775   777677777666667   154545254545655   745344433
632213   765353455632224   775444366741114   222223322234243   R
ATE1513 8  510  7141211  6  4  1  3  29    5  3  610  7  815  2  1  414111
312 9    3  5  6  9  8  715  2  1  41411131210    5  1  611  8  715  4  3  21
4  9131210   1513  7  510  6141211  8  4  1  3  2  9   1513  7  410  614121
1  8  5  2  3  1  9   PREF024000010000   CLAS
```

BASIC DATA FOR SUBJECT NO. 141

```
141   01020508C91C1106C7141312030415   020910050 80111060714131
2030415   030607111501140 8C51C02C9130412   0413121401110603050
90208100715   05110902C8100106030 71514130412   060315111001080
5C209C714130412   0702C90810011 50306051114130412   08100902071
50306051101141213O4   C9080210150603050 7110114041312   1008090
2C50306150711 10114041312   1105C11412041303061 51008090207   121
40413011110503C6151008C90207   13C4120111051403061 51008090207
141201110504130306151 00C8C90207   15030610080902070501 11 14041
312   ANCR122632412267665   523543122267562   443543445466543
253645556567774   343454455352246   345635455436654   264353466
621234   544553455522314   654356655532245   324425533356543   R
ATE11 3  614  1  7  9  4  2  5 1C151312  8   11  1  614  2  7  9  4  3  510151
312  8   11  2  614  1  7  9  4  3  51015 1312  8   11  1  514  9  6  8  3  2  41
0151312  7   11  3  714  1  810  5  4  6  2151312  9    510  3  8  1  415121
113  2  9  7  614   PREF129000001010C   CLAS
```

```
                 BASIC DATA FOR SUBJECT NO. 142

142   010809C50604121114030713151002   02101513070314110601050
9C80412    0315C7061002051114CSC801130412    0401141112130908050
6C315071002    05111412130308090110020706 1504    060315111413050
4071CC2C8090112    C710C2031506051311080914040112    08050901120
4141113060315C71CC2    C908C4010514111312060315100207   1002070
315C611C513080914010412    110514071306150308090104100212   120
41411C1C809C513061507C31002    130406150307111405010809121002
  141112C5010408091306 1503C71CC2    150603071114041305010809121
CC2   ANCR122122222222122    512553255156162    444444344431434
233233322321313    277566766752257    343434344433234    244243344
421223    233233333322223    265253566621223    511411111146451   R
ATE 615   311  8  213  91014  5  712  1  4    11  6  214  4  3  7  8  9  512131
510  1      414  71012  815  1  213  5  911  3  6    10  2  513  9  8  3  6  7  11
1151412  4      314  711  6  515  91013  4  112  2  8      711  3  4  9  115121
31C  814  5  6  2    PREF027000010110   CLAS


                 BASIC DATA FOR SUBJECT NO. 151

151   C1C40908061214051315C7111C0203    02100905080306150411121
4C71301    030610150207C90804111213140501    0409010812141311031
50602100507    0509C210111214130403150807 0601    060315111213140
4090502C81007C1    C703061510C205090804111412 1301    08090502100
615031112131404 0701    C90210080506031504121413110701   1002050
5CEC306130412111 41507C1    11121413050403061509021008 0701   121
4111304030C6150210C905C807C1    13041412111 03061509021005080701
  141211041303060715100209050801    150306121114041307090210050
EC1   ANCR455145446511114    534556256366665    74444444444444
2221322113111 12    144444444444444    14462445544444444    332242332
322222    332332332333333    143133422311113    2111111111111111   R
ATE15  71C   212  913  8  5  611  1  3   414    15  210  512  913  8  3  111  4
6  714    15  710  212  913  8  5  611  1  3   414    15  710  212  913  8  5  61
1  1  3   414    15  710  212  913  8  5  611  1  3   414    15  710  212  913  8
5  611  1  3   414   PREF12401 4101CC   CLAS


                 BASIC DATA FOR SUBJECT NO. 152

152   0104090806121411C31513C7C5C210    021005C90803C6130411121
4C71501    030210070605C81509111214130401    0413121411060315070
5C5021CC801    C509C210C611121413C40315080701    060315111214130
409050210080701    C703C615C210C905080411141213 01    08090502100
6C315111213140407C1    C902100805060315120413141107 01   1002050
9C80306130411121 4C715C1    11121413040503 0615090210080701   121
4111304030615090210 05C80701    13041412111 03061509021005080701
  141211041303C6150709C210050801    150306121114130407090210050
8C1   ANCR123135223211115    513225123235125    64344443 4443424
121121221211121    155556555555553    355654455333334    243342343
432323    333333333333333    177651667655577    112313311124243   R
ATE1510  7  2  9  61412  811  5  3  1  413    15  4  214  9  7  8  6  3  511  11
21C13    15  1  6  9  3  713  5  4  21011  81214    15  1  6  9  3  713  5  4  21
011  81214    1510  6  212  71413  911  5  4  1  3  8    1510  6  212  71413
911  5  3  1  4  8    PREF021000C1010C   CLAS
```

BASIC DATA FOR SUBJECT NO. 161

161 0105110715030610020909C813C41214   0210C9C80701C5150311061
2130414   031506090210C80704120114051113   0406090812130210031
5C7C1051114   C511C11314C71215C3C6C408C021009   060315130401051
41210020809C711   C711021510C3C6C05011314C8C91204   C8090210150
6C30413121407051101   C908C210040612150314C113050711   1002090
6150308C412140713050111   110514C11213070315060410020809   121
4130405110106031507021008C9   1311140405120106031510020809C7
141213C61503C4C511C1C7100208C9   J50306131105011412040710020
809 ANCR325636142216675   235646234217575   534345343554534
423342221231412   374342766541324   265623277615345   453232544
651314   563453267621313   545544355461525   435635233326563   R
ATE11 4 91015 8 6 5 11314 212 3 7   11 7 9 313 814 5 61512 1
4 210 1310 9 614 511 4 31512 1 7 2 8   5 21210 611 7 3 1 41
5 614 913 11 4 9 613 712 5 11415 210 3 8 1210 6 313 411 9
81415 1 7 2 5 PREF12600001111C CLAS

BASIC DATA FOR SUBJECT NO. 162

162 0115060311120405131410092020708   0207080910121314150104C
6C30511   03061502C708C91012131401040511   0412131415060207080
91C01030511   05111502C7C8C91C12131401040603   060304151102070
8C9101213140105   070102080910121314150304050611   08010209071
C1213141503C4050611   C9C10208C71C12131415030405061   1001020
80709121314150304050611   11051501030406100207080912131 4   121
314C201C8071C09150304050611   13121415020108071009030405061 1
141213C115C2C80710C5C304C5C611   151413120603010208071009040
511 ANCR222121122211112   11777711363536   4441444444444444
141142444411111   171111777611111   145642444465331   242242444
421111   135554444523333   111155111351111   515515511156667   R
ATE 9 310131411 1 2 4 515 6 7 612   9 110131411 5 2 3 415 6
7 612   9 31C131411 1 2 4 515 6 7 812   9 110131411 5 2 3 41
5 6 7 812   9 310131411 1 2 4 515 6 7 812   4 8 51314 612 91
C1115 1 2 3 7 PREF026000011111 CLAS

BASIC DATA FOR SUBJECT NO. 171

171 C1C205C8C91C11112 04C61303141507   0210031507010908060511 0
4131214   0315C607021CC809C511C412130114   0413111214060105090
21CC8150307   0508090104121111 31C 14060703   061503071114131
204C5C8C901C210   07031506111413120508040910010 2   08091214011
30411C5061503070210   C9010812141113040605150307100 2   1002070
3C61508C511091412130401   111413120401050809150603020710   121
4111304010 8C5C5061503C7C210   13140412110605150809071002030 1
141112130406031509 08C105C71C02   151112061413040108090503070
21C ANCR112433511157543   423653434344523   4444444444444444
221223323311153   3435 5564565666   326523255432345   356654546
543266   434424634232233   322227433222222   222222242222222   R
ATE15 8 11110 2 41314 9 6 512 3 7   8 2 411 5 6 1 910 3 7151
21413 14 2 312 8 4 5 6 7 113 5101511   15 2 711 313 6 4 5 1
8 9121014 1510 8 7 5 412131411 3 2 6 1 9 1512 3 1 2 710 5
613 8 411 914 PREF123011010111 CLAS

BASIC DATA FOR SUBJECT NO. 172

```
172  01C5110413121406C80902100031507   0210031507130908C511040
1120614   03150706C210C9C8C511C413011214   0413111214060105080
90210150307   C5C8C901041311121406150307C210   061503071114131
2C40508C9010210   C7031506111413120405080901 1002   08090112141
3041105C61503C71002   C9C8C1121411113 0405 061503071002   1002070
30615C5C8091114121304C1   1114121304010508090615030702 10   121
4111304C108C905061503 C7C210   13041412110615050809010307 0210
  1412111304C61505C809010307021C   15061112141304010809050307 0
21C  ANCR124455411145544   5236 56425166575   243434422524112
732444346343623   16745E645434367   326251435434354   355674356
764657   453433465461211   36734576634726 5   212523611167453  R
ATE15 8  31110  2  41314  9  6  512  1  7     8  3  211  5  6  110  9  4  7131
21415     9  2  314  8  4  5  6  7  11011131215   15  2  711  313  6  4  5  1
8  9121014   1510  8  7  5  412131411  3  2  6  1  9   151110  313  7  9  5
612  8  1  2  414   PREFC23011011111   CLAS
```

BASIC DATA FOR SUBJECT NO. 181

```
181  01C509081412041311C6C315021C07   C2100908050701111214150
3061304   03150614110105121002C709081304   0413121114060109031
5C51C020807   05111412C103C61502100709081304   061201031504141
1C50908130210C7   C71215031411C21005090806011304   08090210050
1120714111503061304   C9080210050112040714111503 0613   1002050
9C8C7C112141115030613C4   1114120503150601090810021304 07   121
41101130406031505C9C81002C7   13041211011406031505C9C810020 7
  141112C6031501C513040908100207   1503061114120105130908100020
4C7  ANCR35615636563511116   61553625613512 3   713414414144534
232253152522131   16623676665325 7   625616433235333   263363765
753353   162171165722121   17616645565417 7   513113111157663  R
ATE15 61C1412  8  2  4  3  511  113  7  5   15  1  81411  7  3  5  4  212  91
310  6   1511  3  814  11310  912  6  4  7  5  2   15  9  41211  214  8  710
5  113  6  3   1510  41312  2  5  9  811  6  114  7  3   15' 613  9  81114  5
4  7  2  110  312   PREF13S311CCC1CC   CLAS
```

BASIC DATA FOR SUBJECT NO. 182

```
182  01C50210C90807141211113C4150306   0210090805070112141104 1
3060315   0315060114120711091002080504 13   0413061503111214090
8C507C1C210   C5110C801C21CC912141304C7061503   060315110504131
412090802100107   07021001121 4C EC9051113041503 06   08090210001 1
214C413C511061503C7   C9C804021C0105111214130615030 7   1002010
70511120908141304C315C6   11051214130409080210061503010 7   121
41105130403061509C9080 2100107   13040615030908121411050210010 7
  1412110513041503C6C9C8021001 07   1503121406051113040908021 00
1C7  ANCR235144234213135   42435634517646 3   712442444141414
233335233511215   272333763632322   533636267253325   362313736
711312   253133553622122   464364262377272   115325122166265  R
ATE12 21311  915  3  1  4  5  6  810  714   7  11312  515  2  4  6  3  8  91
11014     91014  6  81312  3  211  1  5  7  415   10  914  4  813  5  1  212
7  611  315   121115  8  61013  1  4  5  3  5  7  214   13  914  5  712  8  4
611  1  310  215   PREFO3S311C101CC   CLAS
```

BASIC DATA FOR SUBJECT NO. 191

```
191  010205080911100315070612131404   0208091001050311150607l
3121404   0302010908100512150607111314C4   0413121114150603050
7C9C8100102   05111213C21CC8C9C11503060704l4   060311150113080
709020405101214   0712C615111303140501080910C204   08090210010
3051115060712130414   09C810020103051511060712131404   1002010
8C9C50311150607121403413   1105131215060908100102030407l4   121
31106150414050301021C0908C7   131112140415010209081006030705
  140512111315C6C2C901C810040307   1506030511090810020112C4130
714  ANCR212145122113224   223244332244324   433633244435623
334234443422243   35456465536423C4   355644466535434   665445666
644566   543244333342344   43446544435654   343343233345434   R
ATE 5 1 6111210 7 4 3 213 9 81415   5 1 61512 9 7 4 3 21113
81410   6 1 51411 9 8 4 3 21512 71310   5 1 61512 9 7 4 3 21
113 81410   5 1 6 8151110 4 3 214 7 91312   9 510 4151211 8
7 614 3 1 213  PREF12201 8101CC  CLAS
```

BASIC DATA FOR SUBJECT NO. 192

```
192  010502100908030615070411131412   021009080105030615070C41
1131412   03C615021009C50801070411131412   0412111408091306051
50102100703   05141109C804C6150112100302130C7   C6110315021007C
908010405121314   0715030602100105080911141312C4   08090403020
1121314C615C71C11C5   C9C8C412010210C611131415070305   1002030
70615010508091104121314   1113120414050908010203C6071510   120
4111413060908C501C215C31007   13110412140509080601C30207151C
  140511121304090102080C60315071C   150706030210010809110412131
405  ANCR122144234311115   344564335366564   443754245443613
333133462322353   466376744663345   344544234355534   564343665
621323   554144542432324   47444376673345C4   433445633336345   R
ATE1511 713 4 6 914 812 110 3 2 5   5 2 314 8 7 4 910 111151
213 6   10 2 91412 8 5 4 3 1151311 6 7   10 2 61411 8 5 4 3 11
51312 7 9   14 91312 6 515 8 71C 1 4 3 211   14 91312 6 515 8
71C 1 4 3 211  PREF02101 510001  CLAS
```

BASIC DATA FOR SUBJECT NO. 201

```
201  C1C205CE1C11C903C4061214131507   0204081012140103151l1130
5C706C9   0302100104081506C5C71409111312   0407091302061001150
81103051412   050803121501C406C9100207111314   060709140802041
CC1C31105121513   C710C8150206C91113010314120405   08090214120
6C70311050104131015   C907100814060511020112041503l3   1013120
2010407C611090314051508   110903151304100205120701061408   121
4C51303C607110204C80115l005   13081040712010914030211050615
  14060311100804070915C102121305   15110312010507020804101306l
4C9  ANCR123545212246543   232355122345453   121645125242532
132435312135533   563663753454563   455636146322314   124234122
135443   553352454632345   222334654132232   124325221136544   R
ATE 6 112 515 9 2 711 3 810 41413   6 112 514 9 2 711 3 815
41013   7 1 4 81014 215 3 9 511 61213   4 1 3 61215 7 9 510
2 8111314   5 814 610 113 2 9 312 4 71511   9 811 1 314 615
41310 5 212 7  PREF150312C0100C  CLAS
```

BASIC DATA FOR SUBJECT NO. 202

```
202   010409C603081211C2050710131415   020307090405101508011111
2131406   030205C710C9C8C113040611121514   0401061211131403100
91502050708   05111312140906040115020308100 7   060315141201040
8C913C205071011   C7021008C915050306121114130401   08090603010
51015020414111213C7   C901C615040305080207101114121 3   1002060
8C305070915141211130401   111214130406010903101505080207   121
114C413C1031506C9C502C81007   131204111409060103150508100207
   141211130401061503090805 02071C   150306080910141213110705020
1C4   ANCR121131222211112   413435133256553   515435123256653
4542524624111 14   673454777364436   755634455444445   233174455
611122   133133344411112   71744361447777 4   314517311147657   R
ATE14 1 515  4 6 3 8 9 21211131C 7   15 1 713 614  8 2 3 411101
2  9 5   15 1 714 6 810  9 5 2121113 4 3   15 1 610 9 7 8 2 3 41
4121311 5   15 2 81410 9 3 4 5 6131112 1 7   15 2 81410 9 3 4
5 6131112 1 7  PREF04931121010C  CLAS
```

BASIC DATA FOR SUBJECT NO. 211

```
211   01C5020810090312C4111314C61507   02100803090501071511130
6041214   03060208091001051112130414150 7   0412091311051406080
31501C21007   0511C208C910030112130414061507   061512090401130
81002030511C714   C715C210C603C511131404080912 01   08091005110
20114130615120403 07   0908100502011112041314030615 07   1002010
8C9C511C703041312140615   110512130401090802030706101415   121
3C40905C814110615C110C203C7   13120409C811050106141003021507
   141204130615020310080901110507   15060702100301140809121105 0
413   ANCR123125222211133   211144322214 5451   542654236464643
43313243333111 12   177555765522247   133534355435423   675454766
743436   76624256664222 5   776247766631137   113514211145453   R
ATE10  3 214 9 1 81213 411  515 6 7   10 1 214 9 4 81213 711 61
5 3 5   10 1 314 9 4 81213 211  715 5 6   10 3 214 9 1 81213 41
1 515 6 7   10 1 314 9 6 81213 211  515 4 7   9 4 71011 2 8121
3 514 615 1 3  PREF12400CC1101C  CLAS
```

BASIC DATA FOR SUBJECT NO. 212

```
212   0109111214080403C6C51302C71015   021003070908C5150611121
4130401   031502100607090805111214041301   0413011211140509080
61507C31C02   050211C1C9C8121314C304061007 15   061503100205090
807141211130401   070210031514120609C811130501 04   08090105131
4121104C21003061507   C908011413121105040602100315 07   1002030
715C6C9C8051214130411C1   111312140401060503090810020715   121
4110501C8090603150410C21307   130401111412050609080310020715
   141213110401050615080903C21007   15060302100714120508091113 0
401   ANCR122136622211116   112244122134345   542332226432524
433122543522223   177445623743226   455656256544433   443332244
531212   664622255623322   175246722734246   224324522256665   R
ATE13  3 114 410 515 6 211  712 6 9   13 3 114 410 515 6 211  71
2  8 9   15 1 310 513 6 9 4 211  712 814   15 1 310 513 6 9 4 21
1 712 814   13 3 114 410 515 6 211  712 8 9   1510 112 2 6 8141
311 9 3 4 5 7  PREF02300CC000CC  CLAS
```

DETAILS OF
THE PROGRAM USED

Here we present various details of the programs used in the book. The discussion covers salient aspects of their theoretical bases and computational procedures as well as several facets of the various input and output options and their use in this book. The titles of the programs and their developers are given below:

TRICON, F. J. Carmone and P. E. Green [10]
DISTAN, V. R. Rao [110]
M-D-SCAL V, J. B. Kruskal and F. J. Carmone [87]
TORSCA 8, F. W. Young and W. S. Torgerson [163]
PARAMAP, J. D. Carroll and J. J. Chang [126]
JOHNSON CLUSTER, S. C. Johnson [75]
C-MATCH, Norman Cliff [22] and R. J. Pennell and F. W. Young [108]
INDSCAL, J. D. Carroll and J. J. Chang [15]
HOWARD-HARRIS CLUSTER, Nigel Howard and Britton Harris [71]
PROFIT, J. J. Chang and J. D. Carroll [21]
MDPREF, J. J. Chang and J. D. Carroll [20]
PREFMAP, J. D. Carroll and J. J. Chang [13]

The programs used here represent University of Pennsylvania versions. Thus, various options may *not* agree completely in detail with other versions of these programs—whether formulated by the original developers or converted by other applications researchers.

TRICON

The method for collecting direct dissimilarities data involved asking the respondent to rank strictly, by degree of overall similarity to a reference stimulus, i, all of the $n - 1$ remaining stimuli. Each of the n stimuli in turn served as a reference item, yielding n rank orders for each respondent.

Such data are called conjoint because all pairwise dissimilarities have a stimulus in common. Coombs [29] proposed a triangularization procedure for converting such data to a complete order of ranks over all pairs of stimuli. This procedure has been computerized and is known as TRICON [10], an acronym for "TRIangularization of CONjoint data." This method produces a weak order of all possible pairs. The method is illustrated with the aid of data for respondent 011. (The number of stimuli is 15.)

The original rank-order data for this respondent are reproduced in Table B.1. The entries are stimulus numbers and the columns represent rank positions. To illustrate further the meaning of the entries, consider the first row. The subject ranked stimulus 12 as most similar to the reference item (stimulus 1), stimulus 8 as next most similar, and stimulus 15 as least similar. Similar meanings can be given to the entries of the other rows. However, for all rows the entry of 0 (corresponding to the reference item) is for positional purposes only and should be ignored.

The first step in the TRICON algorithm is to develop an n $(n-1)/2 \times n$ $(n-1)/2$ matrix of all possible tetradic comparisons from the input data. All direct comparisons are derived in this step. In the illustration this matrix is of size 105×105. The entries of this matrix are either 1 or 0, according to whether the row pair is considered more dissimilar than the

Table B.1   Original Matrix for Subject 011

Reference							Rank Position							
Item	1	2	3	4	5	6	7	8	9	10	11	12	13	14	15
1	0	12	8	9	4	5	14	6	13	11	10	3	2	7	15
2	10	0	5	9	8	3	11	15	6	7	12	14	1	13	4
3	10	2	0	9	8	11	5	15	6	1	12	7	14	13	4
4	13	12	11	0	1	14	9	6	15	5	8	10	7	2	3
5	2	10	11	12	0	14	1	9	8	3	6	15	7	4	13
6	15	14	12	11	2	0	10	8	9	7	5	3	1	13	4
7	2	10	11	14	12	15	0	6	5	9	8	3	13	4	1
8	9	2	10	5	3	11	12	0	1	4	6	15	7	14	13
9	8	2	10	5	3	6	15	14	0	7	1	11	12	13	4
10	2	9	8	5	3	7	6	15	11	0	12	14	13	1	4
11	5	12	14	4	13	7	6	9	8	1	0	3	2	10	15
12	4	13	11	14	1	9	6	8	5	7	2	0	10	3	15
13	4	12	11	14	1	9	8	6	5	15	2	10	0	3	7
14	11	6	15	12	1	4	13	9	8	2	10	3	5	0	7
15	6	2	10	3	11	5	14	13	1	9	8	7	12	4	0

Table B.2   First 10 Rows and 10 Columns of the 105 × 105 Pairwise Comparison Matrix

					Pair					
Pair	1, 2	1,3	1, 4	1, 5	1, 6	1, 7	1, 8	1, 9	1, 10	1, 11
1, 2	0	1	1	1	1	0	1	1	1	1
1, 3	0	0	1	1	1	0	1	1	1	1
1, 4	0	0	0	0	0	0	1	1	0	0
1, 5	0	0	1	0	0	0	1	1	0	0
1, 6	0	0	1	1	0	0	1	1	0	0
1, 7	1	1	1	1	1	0	1	1	1	1
1, 8	0	0	0	0	0	0	0	0	0	0
1, 9	0	0	0	0	0	0	1	0	0	0
1, 10	0	0	1	1	1	0	1	1	0	1
1, 11	0	0	1	1	1	0	1	1	0	0

column pair. Only the first 10 rows and 10 columns of this 105 × 105 matrix are reproduced in Table B.2. In the original data the respondent judged the pair (1, 4) as more similar than the pair (1, 5). Accordingly, in Table B.2 the entry in the cell (1, 4), (1, 5) is 0 and that in the (1, 5), (1, 4) cell is 1.

The second step is to compute the row sums of this pairs-by-pairs matrix. The sum for any row represents the number of times the pair corresponding to that row was judged by the respondent as more dissimilar than the other pairs. The rows and columns of the pairs-by-pairs matrix are permuted so that the row sums are in decreasing order. Ties are taken in

Table B.3   Row Sums for the Illustrative TRICON Data

Pair	Row Sum	Pair	Row Sum	Pair	Row Sum
3, 4	26	11, 15	17	5, 8	9
2, 4	25	1, 11	17	1, 5	9
12, 15	25	9, 11	17	3, 15	9
1, 7	25	9, 13	17	1, 8	8
7, 12	24	4, 8	17	2, 7	8
3, 13	24	1, 6	17	14, 15	8
4, 9	23	7, 9	16	6, 12	8
4, 6	23	7, 15	16	3, 8	7
2, 13	22	2, 11	16	2, 15	7
10, 13	22	5, 14	16	7, 11	7
1, 2	22	9, 12	16	3, 9	6
3, 14	22	13, 15	16	11, 13	6
1, 10	21	7, 14	16	12, 14	6
5, 13	21	6, 8	15	1, 4	6
3, 12	21	5, 15	15	7, 10	6
1, 15	21	9, 15	15	2, 3	5
4, 15	20	3, 11	14	4, 11	5
4, 5	20	9, 14	14	8, 10	4
3, 7	20	6, 7	14	1, 12	4
10, 11	20	8, 11	13	3, 10	4
8, 15	20	7, 12	13	5, 10	4
10, 14	20	3, 5	13	2, 8	4
8, 14	20	8, 12	13	9, 10	3
10, 12	20	6, 9	12	2, 9	3
7, 8	20	5, 12	11	11, 12	3
6, 13	19	6, 9	11	5, 11	2
8, 13	19	2, 6	11	11, 14	2
2, 14	19	1, 13	11	12, 13	2
2, 12	19	1, 9	11	6, 14	2
4, 6	19	5, 8	10	2, 5	1
1, 3	18	10, 15	9	4, 12	1
5, 7	18	4, 14	9	8, 9	0
4, 19	18	6, 11	9	6, 15	0
5, 6	18	13, 14	9	4, 13	0
3, 6	17	1, 14	9	2, 10	0

any order.[1] In Table B.3 the row sums for the illustrative data are shown in decreasing order.

If the subject were perfectly consistent in his judgments, there would be no 1s below the major diagonal in the permuted matrix of pairs-by-pairs. A 1 below

[1] More recent versions of the program handle ties in a more efficient manner, for example, by evaluating the effect on intransitivities by permuting all rows in a specific block of ties. The row permutation leading to the lowest number of intransitivities is chosen for subsequent computation.

the major diagonal indicates an intransitive pair. In our illustration there are 103 intransitivies, which are listed in Table B.4. In the algorithm two options are available for removing intransitivities: (a) remove intransitivity with no symmetric entry, that is, just ignoring the 1 in the lower half or (b) remove the 1 in the lower half and place a 1 in the corresponding upper half of the matrix. In this book the first option was chosen.

After removing intransitivities, it is possible to power the matrix of pairs-by-pairs to obtain higher-order (assumed to be transitive) connections between the pairs. Powering is continued in the program until no further relationships can be deduced. (In this book the powering option was not executed.)

Table B.4   Intransitive Pairs Found in the Illustrative TRICON Data

4,7 7,13	2,11 1,11	1,9 6,9
1,15 1,7	2,11 9,11	5,8 5,14
1,15 1,2	13,15 5,13	5,8 5,12
1,10 10,13	13,15 6,13	10,15 6,10
4,15 12,15	13,15 8,13	1,14 1,9
4,15 1,15	13,15 9,13	5,9 5,14
3,7 3,12	13,14 11,15	5,9 5,12
10,14 10,12	9,15 1,15	1,5 5,14
8,14 7,8	9,15 11,15	1,5 5,12
8,15 1,15	9,15 13,15	1,5 1,9
8,13 7,8	5,15 5,6	3,15 3,11
8,13 8,14	5,15 11,15	3,15 3,5
8,13 8,15	5,15 5,14	3,15 10,15
2,14 8,14	6,8 4,8	6,12 9,12
1,3 1,10	3,11 1,11	1,8 8,12
11,15 10,11	3,11 9,11	1,8 8,11
1,6 5,6	9,14 9,15	1,8 5,8
3,6 5,6	6,7 7,15	2,7 2,11
4,8 4,5	6,7 7,14	2,7 2,6
4,8 4,15	6,7 6,8	14,15 11,15
4,8 4,6	7,12 9,12	14,15 5,15
4,8 4,9	7,12 7,14	14,15 10,15
9,12 9,11	3,5 5,14	14,15 3,15
7,9 5,7	3,5 3,11	3,8 5,8
7,15 1,15	8,12 9,12	2,15 2,11
7,15 8,15	8,11 9,11	7,11 2,7
7,15 11,15	6,9 6,8	12,14 14,15
7,14 3,14	5,12 9,12	1,4 1,9
7,14 10,14	5,12 8,12	1,4 1,8
7,14 8,14	2,6 2,11	7,10 2,7
7,14 2,14	1,13 1,6	3,9 5,9
5,14 3,14	1,9 7,9	1,12 12,14
5,14 10,14	1,9 9,15	11,14 11,12
5,14 8,14	1,9 9,14	5,11 5,10
5,14 2,14		

Table B.5 Ranks Assigned to the Pairs in the TRICON Illustration for Subject 011

	1	2	3	4	5	6	7	8	9	10	11	12	13	14
2	96.0													
3	71.5	23.5												
4	17.5	103.0	105.0											
5	30.0	6.5	48.5	89.0										
6	67.5	44.5	67.5	92.5	76.0									
7	103.0	30.0	82.5	96.0	76.0	48.5								
8	23.5	17.5	30.0	60.0	38.0	62.5	89.0							
9	35.0	12.5	23.5	76.0	35.0	48.5	64.5	2.5						
10	89.0	2.5	17.5	99.0	17.5	48.5	23.5	17.5	12.5					
11	71.5	62.5	55.0	23.5	6.5	41.5	30.0	55.0	71.5	89.0				
12	12.5	82.5	92.5	6.5	41.5	35.0	48.5	55.0	64.5	89.0	12.5			
13	44.5	96.0	100.5	2.5	92.5	82.5	100.5	67.5	71.5	96.0	30.0	9.5		
14	38.0	76.0	96.0	41.5	55.0	9.5	55.0	82.5	60.0	82.5	6.5	23.5	41.5	
15	82.5	30.0	30.0	76.0	55.0	2.5	60.0	82.5	55.0	38.0	67.5	103.0	48.5	17.5

The pairs are then ranked in a decreasing order of row sums. Ranks are split for tied pairs. The resulting rank order of the pairs is reproduced in Table B.5 as a lower-half matrix. The output can also be obtained as a vector of ranks for the $n(n-1)/2$ pairs. Lower ranks in Table B.5 represent greater similarity.

The resulting weak order of all possible pairs is used as the set of direct measures of dissimilarity in further analysis by multidimensional scaling procedures.

DISTAN

The DISTAN program [110] computes a matrix of interpoint distances from a data matrix of stimuli-by-variables "scores." The program can handle up to 75 points (stimulus objects) and 75 variables. The distances can be computed for any number of such data matrices (that is, for any number of subjects). An option exists for standardizing the data matrix by columns before computing distances. An average-distance matrix across all subjects can also be computed. The relevant formulas are given below:

Let
$$X^{(i)} = \left(x_{jt}^{(i)}\right); \; i = 1, 2, \ldots, m$$
$$j = 1, 2, \ldots, n; \; t = 1, 2, \ldots, r$$

represent the data matrix for the ith subject of r observations on n stimuli. We assume there are m such matrices. Let $D^{(i)} = (d_{jk}^{(i)})$ represent the matrix of interpoint distances between the pair of points j and k for the ith subject. Let $\bar{D} = (\bar{d}_{jk})$ represent the matrix of interpoint distances for the average subject.

If the data are standardized,

let
$$Z^{(i)} = \left(z_{jt}^{(i)}\right); \; i = 1, 2, \ldots, m$$
$$j = 1, 2, \ldots, n; \; t = 1, 2, \ldots, r$$

represent the standardized data matrix for the ith subject. This is computed simply by the formula

$$z_{jt}^{(i)} = \left[x_{jt}^{(i)} - \bar{x}_t^{(i)}\right] / s_t^{(i)}$$

where $\bar{x}_t^{(i)}$ and $s_t^{(i)}$ are, respectively, the mean and standard deviation for the tth variable of the ith subject. With no standardization the distance $d_{jk}^{(i)}$ is given by the formula

$$d_{jk}^{(i)} = \sqrt{\sum_{t=1}^{r} \left(x_{jt}^{(i)} - x_{kt}^{(i)}\right)^2}$$

In the case of standardization the z values take the place of x values. The distance, $\bar{d}_{jk}$, for the average subject is computed by the formula:

$$\bar{d}_{jk} = \sqrt{\left[\sum_{i=1}^{m} d_{jt}^{(i)2}\right] \Big/ m}$$

M-D-SCAL V

Kruskal's multidimensional scaling program, known as M-D-SCAL V, is highly versatile in that it can be used for a varied number of scaling problems. The program has gone through five versions so far and the discussion here relates to the fifth version, called M-D-SCAL V. The original discussion of the program can be found in Kruskal [84].

DISCUSSION OF COMPUTATIONAL PROCEDURE

The problem tackled by Kruskal is that of deriving a configuration of objects in a prespecified number of dimensions, given a set of proximities data among pairs of objects. Let δ_{ij} represent the original measure of dissimilarity between pairs of objects i and j. Assume for the moment that the dissimilarities can be strongly rank ordered. (The way that ties are handled by the program will be discussed later.) The objective is to represent the n objects by n points in a t-dimensional space, such that the rank order of distances between pairs of points best reproduces the rank order of the δs. Let the coordinates of the ith point be $x_i = (x_{i1}, \ldots, x_{it})$. Let d_{ij} denote the distance from x_i to x_j.

The criterion used for obtaining the best configuration of xs is one of minimizing the function called stress (S) given by the formula, currently known as stress formula 2:

$$S = \sqrt{\sum_{i<j} (d_{ij} - \hat{d}_{ij})^2 \Big/ \sum_{i<j} (d_{ij} - \bar{d})^2}$$

where $\bar{d}$ is the average of all d_{ij} values. The $\hat{d}_{ij}$ are a set of numerical values chosen to be as close to their d_{ij} counterparts as possible, subject to being monotone with the original δ_{ij}. The $\hat{d}_{ij}$ take on the role of fitted values in the monotone regression procedure. The procedure used for obtaining the xs is the numerical method of steepest descent. Briefly stated, the method involves improving the starting configuration a bit by moving it around slightly. The method of steepest descent ascertains in which direction in the configuration space stress is decreasing most quickly and moves a short step in that direction. This direction is called the (negative) gradient and is determined by evaluating the partial derivatives of the function S. When a new set of xs is found, the d_{ij}s are computed and the procedure is repeated until a minimum value of S is achieved.

SPECIAL FEATURES OF THE M-D-SCAL PROGRAM

The M-D-SCAL program can cope with a variety of problems arising in the original dissimilarities data. These include missing data, nonsymmetry, ties, and non-Euclidean distances.

Missing Data

The program can be set to identify missing observations by reading in a cutoff value below which data are treated as missing. The stress function is modified by simply omitting, both in the numerator and denominator, the terms which correspond to the missing cells.

Nonsymmetry

Either because of inherent nonsymmetry of measurement procedures or errors in measurement, the values of δ_{ij} and δ_{ji} may not be equal in some cases. In such a situation the stress function is computed over all cells (that is, i, j and j, i) and minimized in the algorithm.

Ties

Two approaches are possible for resolving ties which arise between dissimilarities whenever $\delta_{ij} = \delta_{kl}$. These approaches are called primary and secondary.

In the primary approach, when $\delta_{ij} = \delta_{kl}$, no restriction is placed on the corresponding computed distances (that is, no correction is made in the configuration when d_{ij} is not equal to d_{kl}). This is done by choosing a monotone transform so that whenever $\delta_{ij} < \delta_{kl}$, then $\hat{d}_{ij} \leqslant \hat{d}_{kl}$.

The secondary approach is appropriate when $\delta_{ij} = \delta_{kl}$ suggests that d_{ij} *ought* to be equal to d_{kl}. This equality is accomplished by imposing the constraint $\hat{d}_{ij} = \hat{d}_{kl}$. Then if $d_{ij} \neq d_{kl}$ the terms $(d_{ij} - \hat{d}_{ij})^2$ and $(d_{kl} - \hat{d}_{kl})^2$ cannot be zero, and stress can be lowered by making a correction to the configuration. The constraints used in the secondary approach are

Whenever $\delta_{ij} < \delta_{kl}$, then $\hat{d}_{ij} \leqslant \hat{d}_{kl}$
Whenever $\delta_{ij} = \delta_{kl}$, then $\hat{d}_{ij} = \hat{d}_{kl}$

Non-Euclidean Distances

The user of M-D-SCAL can choose any Minkowski p-metric, by specifying the value of p ($\geqslant 1.0$), thus causing the program to use the following formula for computing d_{ij}:

$$d_{ij(p)} = \left[\sum_{t=1}^{r} |x_{it} - x_{jt}|^p \right]^{1/p}$$

This option enables one to use certain non-Euclidean distances.

INPUT PARAMETERS

M-D-SCAL can be used for scaling up to 100 objects up to six dimensions and down to one dimension. The total number of data values read may not exceed 1800. Many options exist in the program. The most commonly used are mentioned below.

Options for Regression

Four basic options exist for performing the regression of d_{ij} on δ_{ij}. These are:

1. Ascending regression provides for performing monotone regression when the original data are dissimilarities.
2. Descending regression provides for performing monotone regression when the original data are similarities.
3. Polynomial regression provides a specified integer (degree of polynomial). If the degree of polynomial is equal to 1 it becomes a linear regression. An integer from 1 through 4 can be used. In the linear case one has the option of including or excluding a constant term.
4. Multivariate regression provides an integer (number of variates) for performing a prespecified regression by supplying a separate Fortran subroutine for same.

Options for Data Input

The input matrices can be in one or more of these forms:

1. Full matrix
2. Lower-half matrix, diagonal present
3. Lower-half matrix, diagonal absent
4. Upper-half matrix, diagonal present
5. Upper-half matrix, diagonal absent
6. Lower-corner matrix
7. Upper-corner matrix

Initial Configuration

The user may supply a starting configuration for scaling the objects. If not, two varieties of a random start can be used.

Splitting Data

Four options exist for using parts of the data as separate sublists for performing separate regressions if desired:

1. Split by rows
2. Split by groups
3. Split by decks
4. Split no more

The first three options make each row, each group, or each data deck a separate sublist. The split-no-more option is relevant only when several data decks are used; it causes all subsequent data decks to be joined into a single sublist until further indication.

Data Saving

It is possible to use the same data for performing different methods of scaling by using the SAVE DATA option.

Parameters Controlling Convergence of Iteration

Four parameters, namely, SFGRMN, SRATST, STRMIV, and Number of Iterations, control the iterative process in M-D-SCAL V.

SFGRMN is the minimum of the scale factor of the gradient. If the scale factor is less than or equal to this criterion, the program decides that a local minimum has been reached. The standard value of this parameter is 0.0.

SRATST ("stress ratio stop") is a criterion by which both stress ratio (ratio of the stress value for one iteration to that of the previous iteration) and weighted average stress ratio are judged. If these two values are between SRATST and 1.0, then the criterion is met. The standard value of SRATST is 0.999.

STRMIN is the preset minimum value of stress. If the stress reaches this value, the iterations terminate. The standard value of STRMIN is 0.01.

No internal limit is placed on the number of iterations. However, the standard (externally supplied) value is 50.

Weighting of Data

The program allows for differential weighting of the original data values. This can be done either by supplying a deck of cards containing weights in the same way as the data are laid out or by using a Fortran subroutine for generating weights internally. The standard weights are taken as 1.0 for each observation.

OUTPUT DETAILS

A typical run using the M-D-SCAL program generates the following output:

1. A complete listing of control cards read in, including the user-supplied starting configuration, if any, and the original data values and their corresponding weights.
2. A complete history of computation, showing the value of stress and other related computer values for each iteration.
3. Final configuration in the specified dimensionality.
4. Shepard diagram showing the relationship between d_{ij} and $\hat{d}_{ij}$ versus original δ_{ij}s.
5. Plot of the first two dimensions of the configuration.

USE IN THE BOOK

The M-D-SCAL program has been used in four situations in the book:

1. For scaling the direct dissimilarities data at the group level using the linear regression (polynomial = 1, no intercept term) option.

2. For scaling the derived dissimilarities data at the group level using the linear regression option.
3. For nonmetrically scaling the overall preference data (read in as a lower-corner matrix) to derive a joint space of respondents and stimuli using the row split option.
4. For nonmetrically scaling the overall preference data (read in as a lower-corner matrix) to derive a joint space of respondents and stimuli using the row comparability option.

In all cases a "rational" starting configuration was used. It is a principal components solution in cases of 1 and 2. In the cases of 3 and 4 it is computed by the method discussed in Chapter 4. The options for regression were linear (polynomial = 1) for cases 1 and 2 and monotone-ascending for cases 3 and 4. Other control parameters were set at their standard values in [87].

TORSCA 8

TORSCA 8 is version 8 of Young and Torgerson's program for the multi-dimensional scaling of proximities data [163]. The program performs two methods of scaling, namely, metric (principal components) and non-metric, the latter incorporating a modification of one of Shepard's algorithms. These two methods are used in separate stages, the first stage yielding the metric principal components solution. If desired, the initial principal components solution can be modified by a quasi-nonmetric procedure before (or instead of) using the nonmetric method.

THEORETICAL DISCUSSION

Given a rank order of proximity data on a set of stimulus pairs, the objective of the TORSCA algorithm is to find a spatial configuration of the points in a specified number of dimensions whose rank order of interpoint distances best reproduces the original rank order of input data. Stated mathematically, given the matrix of dissimilarities,

$$\Delta = (\delta_{ij}); \ i = 1, 2, \ldots, n; \ j = 1, 2, \ldots, n; \ i \neq j; \ \delta_{ij} = \delta_{ji}; \ \delta_{ii} = 0$$

between pairs of n points, the objective is to find a matrix X where x_i is the row vector $(x_{i1}, x_{i2}, \ldots, x_{ir})$ so that some prespecified optimality criterion is satisfied. Let $D = (d_{ij})$ represent the matrix of computer interpoint distances from the configuration X in r dimensions. The manner in which the X matrix is computed is described in the next section. Let $(\hat{d}_{ij})$ be a set of real numbers monotone with the original dissimilarities (δ_{ij}) so that $\hat{d}_{ij} \leq \hat{d}_{kl}$ whenever $\delta_{ij} < \delta_{kl}$.

The optimization criterion used in both stages of the TORSCA algorithm is called the Index of Agreement. According to this criterion the set of derived distances is compared with the monotone transform of the original dissimilarities to test the assumption of linearity between $\hat{d}_{ij}$ and d_{ij}, which are both referred to a common natural origin by evaluating the degree to which a plot of d_{ij} versus $\hat{d}_{ij}$ can be fitted by an equation of the form $y = bx$. Interest is primarily in the degree of relationship rather then in the prediction of one variable from the other.

$$I = 1/2 + 1/2 \; \frac{\Sigma d_{ij} \Sigma \hat{d}_{ij}}{\sqrt{(\Sigma d_{ij}{}^2)(\Sigma \hat{d}_{ij}{}^2)}}$$

The index varies from 0.5 to 1.0 and is called "squariance" by Torgerson.

The algorithm also computes, as a stopping criterion, Kruskal's stress[2] criterion, S [84], defined as follows:

$$S = \left[\left[\sum_{\substack{i, j = 1 \\ i \neq j}}^{n} (d_{ij} - \hat{d}_{ij})^2 \right] \Bigg/ \sum_{\substack{i, j = 1 \\ i \neq j}}^{n} d_{ij}^2 \right]^{1/2}$$

COMPUTATIONAL PROCEDURE

The steps in the TORSCA algorithm may now be stated.

Step 1. The original dissimilarities (or similarities) are transformed by a series of steps into a matrix of scalar products.

Step 2. The matrix $U = (u_{ij})$ of scalar products is factor analyzed and the r largest eigenroots and the corresponding eigenvectors are found. Each (unit-length) eigenvector is multiplied by the square root of its eigenroot. Let $V = (v_{ia})$; $i = 1, 2, \ldots, n$; $a = 1, 2, \ldots, r$ represent the scaled eigenvectors. This matrix represents the principal components solution.

Step 3. Distances, d_{ij}, are computed from the matrix V for a prespecified Minkowski metric, p, according to the formula:

$$d_{ij(p)} = \left[\sum_{a = 1}^{r} |v_{ia} - v_{ja}|^p \right]^{1/p}$$

Usually, however, p is set at 2 to yield Euclidean distances.

Step 4. The best possible monotone transform $(\hat{d}_{ij})$ of the original dissimilarities (δ_{ij}) is obtained. (The set of numbers $\hat{d}_{ij}$ are used in iterations of stage 1 to improve the Index of Agreement.) The index, I, is computed using the set of numbers $\hat{d}_{ij}$ and d_{ij}.

---

[2]This formulation of Kruskal's criterion is known as stress formula 1. Kruskal's M-D-SCAL V program allows the user to specify stress formula 1 or 2 (as described earlier).

Step 5. The new "distances," $\hat{d}_{ij}$, are used in a second principal components factor analysis in the same manner as were the original distances, and the process is repeated; this procedure (called stage 1) is a quasi-nonmetric method. After each iteration the Index of Agreement is computed. The iterative process stops when the index either no longer increases (according to a criterion value) or the number of iterations reaches the maximum allowed by the investigator.

Step 6. The sixth step, called stage 2, involves nonmetric improvement of the result of the iterative process of step 5 using a modification of one of Shepard's algorithms. Alternatively, stage 1 (after an initial principal components analysis) can be bypassed completely. At each iteration of stage 2 each point is moved to a new position, the extent and direction of the move depending on its original position relative to that of the other points and on the size of the discrepancies between the distances (d_{ij}) to the other points as given by the configuration and the values $(\hat{d}_{ij})$ as obtained from the monotone transform of original dissimilariites.

Consider a particular point, i, and its relation to all other points, j ($j = 1, 2, \ldots, n; j \neq i$), in turn. If $d_{ij} > \hat{d}_{ij}$, then i is moved toward j by an amount proportional to the size of the discrepancy $|d_{ij} - \hat{d}_{ij}|$. If, however, $d_{ij} < \hat{d}_{ij}$, i is moved away from j by an amount proportional to the size of the discrepancy. For each of the $(n - 1)$ points in the configuration there will be $(n - 1)$ corrections of each dimension. For the ath dimension, the new value of the average correction is computed by the equation

$$\bar{c}_{(ia)} = \frac{a}{n - 1} \sum_{\substack{j = 1 \\ j \neq i}} \left[1 - \frac{\hat{d}_{ij}}{d_{ij}} \right] (x_{ja} - x_{ia})$$

where a is the step size in the correction process. Except for details, the above formula (with stress formula 1) is equivalent to Kruskal's gradient method (with stress formula 1).

Step 7. Such corrections are computed for each of n points and added algebraically to the old coordinates of the configuration. This step thus yields a new configuation of points. The value of the Index of Agreement is computed for the new configuration and the iterative process is continued until either no improvement is possible, or stress is below a critical value (CRIT), or the maximum number of stage-2 iterations is reached. If there is no improvement the program adjusts the proportionality constant a (ALPHA) by the factor of (ALPDIV) and tries again. This process is repeated until a minimum value (ALPMIN) is reached for a, the maximum number of iterations is reached, or until the stress is less than CRIT.

The algorithm works from a maximum to a minimum number of dimensions as set by the user. Solutions are provided for each dimensionality between and including these two parameter values.

PASSIVE CELLS

If any of the entries is blank (that is, represents a passive cell), it is replaced by the average dissimilarity measure and does not enter into the computation of stress.

INPUT PARAMETERS

The program can handle up to 75 stimuli in up to 9 dimensions. The maximum number of stage-1 or stage-2 iterations is 50. (The stage-2 iterations are known as jiggles.) The proximities data can be either dissimilarities or similarities. This input can be in one of three forms: (a) full matrix, (b) lower-half matrix without the diagonal, or (c) ordered vector of $n(n-1)/2$ values in the order $(1, 2), (1, 3), \ldots, (1, n), (2, 3), \ldots, (2, n), \ldots, (n-1, n)$.

For the stage-2 algorithm four parameters control the iterative process, namely, CRIT, ALPHA, ALPDIV, and ALPMIN. The user can read in values for these parameters at his discretion. The default values, however, are, respectively, 0.0, 1.0, 0.05, and 2.0 .

OUTPUT DETAILS

The full output of this program includes

1. Listing of input options selected and the original matrix of dissimilarities or similarities. If the original data are similarities, their reciprocals are used in the algorithm as dissimilarities.
2. Normalized matrix of dissimilarities. Normalization is done by dividing each entry by the root mean square of all entries in the matrix of dissimilarities.
3. Principal components analysis (iteration 1 of stage 1) of eigenroots and scaled eigenvectors.
4. Best monotone transform of the original dissimilarities, derived distances based on the principal components solution and associated eigenvalues and scaled eigenvectors.
5. Shepard diagram between original data and best monotone transform and derived distances and the associated stress for the principal components solution.
6. Plots of the principal components solution between all pairs of dimensions.
7. History of calculations, showing stress and the Index of Agreement.
8. Final solution of stage 2, before rotation to principal components.
9. Final solution of stage 2, rotated to principal components.

10. Shepard diagram.
11. Plots of final solution between all pairs of dimensions.

USE IN THE MONOGRAPH

The TORSCA 8 algorithm has been used to derive principal components and nonmetric solutions at the group level for both direct and derived dissimilarities in Chapter 2. In the metric runs only iteration 1 of stage 1 was used. In the nonmetric runs the iterations of stage 1 and stage 2 were each set at 25, and default options for the parameters CRIT, ALPHA, ALPDIV, and ALPMIN were used.

PARAMAP

PARAMAP [126], or Parametric Mapping, is a computer program developed by Carroll and Chang to perform multidimensional scaling of a rectangular data matrix of objects by variables (or a symmetric matrix of dissimilarities). Its chief feature is the continuity assumption made for relating observed proximities to derived proximities.

THEORETICAL DISCUSSION

Let $Y = (y_{ik})$; $i = 1, 2, \ldots, n$; $k = 1, 2, \ldots, m$, represent the matrix of data on n objects measured on m variables. Further, let y_i represent the row-vector of observations on the ith object, $(y_{i1}, y_{i2}, \ldots, y_{im})$ and $y^{(k)}$ represent the kth variable so that $y_i^{(k)} = y_{ik}$.

Using this notation, the basic model of Parametric Mapping can be stated as follows. Assume the existence of r underlying or "latent" variables

$$x^{(k')}, \; k' = 1, 2, \ldots, r \; (r < m)$$

and a set of continuous functions f_k such that

$$y^{(k)} = f_k \left(x^{(1)}, x^{(2)}, \ldots, x^{(r)} \right)$$

so that

$$y_{ik} = y_i^{(k)} = f_k \left(x_i^{(1)}, x_i^{(2)}, \ldots, x_i^{(r)} \right)$$

or, restating in vector notation,

$$y = F(x)$$
$$y_i = F(x_i)$$

where F is a continuous mapping from the x to the y space. It is this mapping from the solution to the data space that we want to be optimally "smooth," or "continous," in the sense of Carroll's starred kappa measure, K*, to be defined. Given this measure of continuity, the objective of Parametric Mapping is to find the "solution space" (in a prespecified dimensionality) that optimizes it.

MEASURES OF CONTINUITY

The measure of "continuity" proposed by Carroll has the general form:

$$K^* = \left[\sum_{i \neq j} \sum (d_{ij}^2)^a \Big/ (D_{ij}^2)^b \right] \Big/ \left[\sum_{i \neq j} \sum (D_{ij}^2)^c \right]^{-b/c}$$

where

$$d_{ij}^2 = \sum_{k=1}^{m} (y_{ik} - y_{jk})^2$$

and

$$D_{ij}^2 = \sum_{k'=1}^{r} (x_{ik'} - x_{jk'})^2 + Ce^2.$$

e^2 is a parameter that can be roughly identified with "unique variance," and C is a normalizing constant.

The rationale for K^* as a measure of continuity can be found in Carroll [126]. In Parametric Mapping a numerical procedure based on the method of steepest descent is used to find the values of $\{x_{ik'}\}$ and e^2 that optimize K^*.

The values $a = 1$, $b = 2$, and $c = -1$ are most often used in practice for this measure.[3] For this special case the measure, called K (kappa), is of the form:

$$K = \left[\sum_{i \neq j} \sum d_{ij}^2 \Big/ D_{ij}^4 \right] \Big/ \left[\sum_{i \neq j} \sum \frac{1}{D_{ij}^2} \right]^2$$

This index measures continuity *inversely*; smoother functional relations are indicated by *smaller* values of K. The following discussion will be limited to this special case.

COMPUTATIONAL PROCEDURE

As mentioned before, the PARAMAP algorithm uses the method of steepest descent to optimize the value of K. For any arbitrary starting X matrix of order $n \times r$ the program computes the associated measure K, which measures continuity inversely. Since K is an inverse measure of continuity, the (negative) gradient of K is used as the basis for an iterative process in which the x values are repeatedly adjusted by the method of steepest descent until an X configuration is reached for which K is stationary. The stationary X configuration thus attained in the prespecified

[3] Provision is made in the algorithm to choose other values for the three parameters that enter into the index of continuity.

number of dimensions is taken as the reduced parametric representation of the original $n \times m$ matrix of Y data.

The possibility of reaching a local minimum does exist when no control is exercised on the starting configuration. One way of reducing the incidence of local minima is to read in a starting configuration which is itself a solution obtained from multidimensional scaling under more stringent assumptions (for example, metric scaling using principal components).

INPUT PARAMETERS

The limitations on problem size, as applicable to the current version of the program, are as follows:

Number of points (stimuli) $\leqslant 150$
Number of variables $\leqslant 500$
Number of mapping dimensions $\leqslant 10$
Number of iterations $\leqslant 100$

The program accepts both types of input, namely, rectangular matrices or proximity matrices. In the latter case the input can be distances, squared distances, correlation or covariance measures, read in as a lower half (without diagonal) of a square matrix.

For computation of the K measure, the parameters a, b, c, and Ce^2 can be altered by the user. Default values are respectively 1, 2, -1, and 25. The user can also alter the value of initial step size (CALF), the critical terminating value of kappa (GCRIT), and the cutback in step size (PCUT) when the value of kappa in the ith iteration is greater than its value in the $(i - 1)$ iteration. The default values for these parameters are, CALF = 0.05, GCRIT = 0.0, and PCUT = 0.5. Provision is also made for not normalizing the X matrix, the default option being one of normalization.

OUTPUT DETAILS

The following are some important elements of output for a run using PARAMAP:

1. Listing of input options selected and the original matrix of either Y or proximities (interpreted as d^2s, that is, squared interpoint distances).
2. Initial X configuration and its plot.
3. History of computation showing kappa and other internal measures.
4. Normalized solution (X matrix) rotated to principal components and its plot.
5. Plot of the value of kappa at each iteration.
6. Computed interpoint distances in the solution space and a plot showing their relationship to the original data expressed as proximities.

The above output is printed for each dimensionality of the mapping.

USE IN THE BOOK

The PARAMAP program has been used in Chapters 2 and 4 to obtain the following scaling solutions:

1. Group scaling of direct dissimilarities (Chapter 2)
2. Group scaling of derived dissimilarities (Chapter 2)
3. Stimulus space from overall preference data using internal analysis methods (Chapter 4)

In the case of solutions 1 and 2 the input is a matrix of dissimilarities, while for solution 3 it is a rectangular matrix (of order 15 × 42). The maximum number of iterations was set at 50 in all three cases. The remaining computational parameters discussed above were set at their respective default values.

A rational starting configuration has been used for these runs. In cases 1 and 2 the appropriate factor analysis (principal components) solution for the same data was used. In case 3 a principal components solution obtained from scaling the matrix of interstimulus distances (computed from the overall preference ranks) was used.

JOHNSON HIERARCHICAL CLUSTER PROGRAM

Johnson's program [75] performs cluster analysis on a hierarchical basis, using as input a dissimilarity matrix of stimuli (or people). The method used is invariant under monotone transformations of the input proximities.

THEORETICAL DISCUSSION

Let $d(i,j)$ represent the measure of dissimilarity between the pair of objects i and j $(i, j = 1, 2, \ldots, n; i \neq j)$. If the data are "perfect," the dissimilarity measures obey the *ultrametric* inequality, namely, $\delta(x, z) \leqslant \max(\delta(x, y), \delta(y, z))$. The real problem of clustering hierarchically can be reduced to finding a set of real numbers $a_0, a_1, a_2, \ldots, a_m$ associated with $m + 1$ clusterings, $c_0, c_1, c_2, \ldots, c_m$ such that

$$0 = a_0 < a_1 < \ldots < a_m$$

$$c_{k-1} < c_k \ (k = 1, 2, \ldots, m)$$

and the a numbers obey the ultrametric inequality. Johnson [75] proves the existence of a hierarchical clustering scheme for every matrix of distance (dissimilarity) measures among all pairs of n objects.

Two versions of the general hierarchical clustering scheme are used in the program. These methods use two functions, namely, MIN and MAX. The procedure using the MIN function is called the connectedness method, while that using the MAX function is known as the diameter method. The principles underlying the two methods can be described as follows.

Min Method

Given a dissimilarity function on n objects, the steps involved in building a hierarchical clustering scheme (HCS) are

1. Cluster c_0 with value 0 to represent the weak clustering where every object is a cluster by itself.
2. Assuming we are given the clustering c_{j-1} with the dissimilarity function, defined for all objects or clusters c_{j-1}, let a_j be the smallest nonzero entry in the matrix. Merge all pairs of points and/or clusters with distance a_j to create c_j, of value a_j.
3. Create a new similarity function for c_j in the following manner; if x and y are clustered in c_j and not in c_{j-1}, define the "distance" from cluster $\{x, y\}$ to any third object, z, by

$$d \{(x, y), z\} = \text{MIN} \{d(x, z), d(y, z)\}$$

4. This step results in a new dissimilarity function d for c_j.

Repeat steps 2 and 3 until all objects are clustered in one cluster.

Max Method

The MAX method is the same as the MIN method, except that in step 3, the MIN function is replaced by the MAX function, that is

$$d \{(x, y), z\} = \text{MAX} \{d(x, z), d(y, z)\} .$$

INPUT OPTIONS AND OUTPUT DETAILS

The program can cluster up to 75 stimuli. The input may be either similarities or dissimilarities. The output consists of a tree diagram connecting the stimuli into clusters hierarchically for both methods of connectedness and diameter. For each level of clustering the associated value of a is printed.

USE IN THE BOOK

Johnson's cluster program has been used in Chapter 2 to form clusters of the 15 stimuli on the basis of both direct and derived group dissimilarities.

C-MATCH

C-MATCH, or CLIFF-MATCH, is an algorithm conceptualized by Cliff [22] and programmed by Pennell and Young [108], designed to orthogonally rotate two matrices (for example, multidimensional scaling solutions) to congruence, either by rotating them simultaneously to a compromise position or by taking one of the two as a target (or using a hypothesized target) and rotating the other to maximum congruence to it. These two variations are referred to as case I and case II, respectively.

THEORETICAL DISCUSSION

Case I—Factor Matching

Let $A = (a_{ij})$; $i = 1, 2, \ldots, n$; $j = 1, 2, \ldots, r$ be one solution of n points in r dimensions, and $F = (f_{ij})$; $i = 1, 2, \ldots, n$; $j = 1, 2, \ldots, s$ be another solution for the same n points in s dimensions. The problem of simultaneously matching the two solutions is equivalent to finding directions in r space and directions in s space such that the projections of the n points on these axes are as similar as possible and repeating the process for successive directions until the orthogonal directions of r or s (whichever is fewer) are found. The direction cosines of each axis constitute a rotation of the original basis. We thus have two orthogonal rotations Λ_A and Λ_F such that

$$A\Lambda_A = P_A$$
$$F\Lambda_F = P_F$$

where corresponding columns of P_A and P_F are as similar as possible. The problem is one of determining the Λs.

If we wish to determine the columns of Λ_A and Λ_F one at a time, taking the sum of products of corresponding columns of P_A and P_F as the measure of similarity, then

$$\Phi = \sum_{i=1}^{n} P_{ikA}\, P_{ikF}$$

the problem is equivalent to finding a column of Λ_A and a column of Λ_F which maximize the trace of $A\Lambda_A \Lambda'_F F'$. In terms of Eckart-Young decomposition [40], the problem simplifies to finding two orthogonal matrices, U and V, and a diagonal matrix, S such that

$$A'F = USV$$

The entries in S correspond to successive values of Φ. Thus the solution to simultaneous matching is one of finding eigenroots and eigenvectors and applying those transformations (U and V') to A and F.

Case II—Fixed Target

Suppose A is the target matrix which is taken as fixed and we wish to find an orthogonal transformation, T which when applied to F, results in a matrix, $\hat{A}$, which is as similar as possible to A:

$$FT = \hat{A}$$

Using the degree of collinearity between corresponding rows of $\hat{A}$ and A as a measure of congruence, the problem is to maximize

$$\psi = \sum_{i=1}^{n} \sum_{k=1}^{r} \hat{a}_{ik} a_{ik}$$

or to maximize the trace of $AT'F'$. This is equivalent to finding two other transformations X and Y, where X is an orthogonal $r \times r$ matrix and Y is an $r \times s$ matrix $(r \leqslant s)$ so as to maximize $\Psi = \text{tr } AXYF'$.

The two matrices Λ_A and Λ_F found in Case I satisfy the above requirement, since this is the same trace we maximize by getting a complete solution for Case I. Therefore,

$$T = \Lambda_F \, \Lambda'_A = V'U'$$

The above discussion requires that U and V both have inverses.

INPUT PARAMETERS

The program C-MATCH can handle a target matrix of up to 50 rows and up to 50 columns, and a data matrix with the same limitations. The program can fit any number of data matrices to a given target matrix and can perform both cases in the same run.

OUTPUT DETAILS

The output for a typical run using C-MATCH consists of the following:

1. Original target matrix, including its eigenroots and eigenvectors.
2. Target matrix translated to zero mean, rotated to principal axes and scaled to result in a mean distance from the origin of unity.
3. Same as 1 and 2 for each data matrix.
4. Transformation matrix for the target and the resulting transformed target (only for the case of simultaneous transformations).
5. Transformation matrix for the data and the resulting transformed data matrix (for both cases).
6. Plot showing the transformed target and data matrices in the first two dimensions. In simultaneous transformation both sets of points refer to transformed matrices, and in the case of fitting data to a fixed target the points refer to original (normalized) target and transformed data.
7. Two measures of goodness of fit, namely, average cosine of the angle between corresponding vectors and the product moment correlation of interpoint distances between target and data.

USE IN THE BOOK

The C-MATCH program has been used in Chapters 2 and 4 of the monograph for:

1. Testing the congruence of two-dimensional solutions of direct and derived dissimilarities (at the group level) as obtained by the same method of scaling, that is, principal components, M-D-SCAL V (polynomial = 1), TORSCA, and PARAMAP.
2. Obtaining normalized matrices of all nine solutions of Chapter 2, prior to the CANDECOMP analysis.
3. Testing the congruence between each of the solutions obtained from the internal analysis of overall preference data of Chapter 4 and the INDSCAL solution of direct dissimilarities of Chapter 3. The solutions were M-D-SCAL (row split option), M-D-SCAL (row comparability option), and PARAMAP.

In all these runs there were 15 rows and two columns in both data and target matrices. The control paramaters for running this program do not require further elaboration.

INDSCAL

The INDSCAL approach to scaling of proximities data by means that retain individual differences was developed by Carroll and Chang [15]. Two basic options for scaling stimuli exist in this program: (a) INDIFF analysis, when symmetric matrices of proximity measures are available for a number of individuals and (b) CANDECOMP analysis, when stimulus measurements are available on a number of variables (that is, the input matrices are rectangular). Carroll's method of canonical decomposition of N-way tables is employed in both options of the program.

THE INDSCAL MODEL

THE INDSCAL model of individual differences in perception is based on three major assumptions.

Common Space

A set of r dimensions, or "factors," underlie the n stimuli. These dimensions are assumed to be common for all m individuals making similarity judgments. Let $X = (x_{jt})$ represent the matrix of stimulus coordinates in the common, or group, space; x_{jt} is the coordinate value for the jth stimulus on the tth dimension; $j = 1, 2, \ldots, n$; and $t = 1, 2, \ldots, r$.

Linearity

The similarity judgments for each individual are related in a simple way to a "modified" Euclidean distance in the group stimulus space, and the relationship is assumed to be linear. That is, the dissimilarity measure, $\delta_{jk}^{(i)}$, given by the ith individual for the pair of stimuli j and k is related to the modified Euclidean distance $d_{jk}^{(i)}$ by

$$\delta_{jk}^{(i)} = L\,(d_{jk}^{(i)})$$

where L is a linear function with a positive slope. The subscripts j and k range from $1, 2, \ldots, n$; and the subscript i ranges from $1, 2, \ldots, m$.

Modified Distance

The "modified" Euclidean distance for the ith subject is given by the formula

$$d_{jk}^{(i)} = \sqrt{\sum_{t=1}^{r} w_{it}(x_{jt} - x_{kt})^2}$$

This formula differs from the usual Euclidean distance formula only in the presence of the weights w_{it}, which represent the saliences or importances which the ith individual gives to the tth dimension of the group perceptual space, represented by the matrix X. Another way of looking at it is to note that $d_{jk}^{(i)}$s are ordinary Euclidean distances computed in a space whose coordinates are

$$y_{jk}^{(i)} = w_{it}^{\frac{1}{2}} x_{jt}$$

This is a space that is like the X space except that the configuration has been expanded or contracted (differentially) in directions corresponding to the coordinate axes.

The above model is sufficiently general to accommodate individuals with widely divergent perceptions of a set of stimuli in terms of a common perceptual space. For example, consider a two-dimensional perceptual space of a set of automobile brands whose axes are identified as luxuriousness and sportiness. Let us now imagine two individuals, P and Q, who view the brands entirely differently, P considering the brands only on one dimension (luxuriousness), while Q views them only on the other (sportiness). The INDSCAL model has the capability of accommodating the judgments of both persons P and Q. The model will produce axis weights of $(1, 0)$ for P and $(0, 1)$ for Q.

ESTIMATION OF PARAMETERS

We now discuss the procedures by which the parameters of the model, the $n \times r$ elements of the X matrix and the $m \times r$ elements of the matrix $W = (w_{it})$, are estimated from dissimilarities judgments on all possible n $(n - 1)/2$ distinct pairs of stimuli by m individuals.

The first step in the method of estimation is to convert the dissimilarities judgments into distance estimates. In view of the linearity assumptions made above, this is done using the standard procedure described in Torgerson [141, pp. 268-276]. This method entails estimation of an additive constant which converts the comparative distances (that is, the original dissimilarities judgments) into absolute distances between pairs of stimuli. The method estimates the value of the constant that guarantees satisfaction of the triangle inequality for all triples of points. The distance estimates are then converted for each subject to scalar products of vectors. This is done by double centering the matrix whose entries are $-\frac{1}{2}\left(d_{jk}^{(i)}\right)^2$. Let us denote by $b_{jk}^{(i)}$, the resulting numbers, which are regarded as the scalar products between the vectors $(y_{j1}^{(i)}, y_{j2}^{(i)}, \ldots, y_{jr}^{(i)})$. Algebraically, this relation can be shown by the equation

$$b_{jk}^{(i)} = \sum_{t=1}^{r} y_{jt}^{(i)} y_{kt}^{(i)} = \sum_{t=1}^{r} w_{it} x_{jt} x_{kt}$$

Thus the three-way matrix of individual by stimulus pairs, whose general entries are the values of $b_{jk}^{(i)}$, can be generated from the similarities data. The problem now is one of estimating values of the X matrix and the W matrix, whose elements enter into the right-hand side of the preceding equation so that the estimates satisfy the equation. This estimation procedure is called CANDECOMP "canonical decomposition of N-way tables," and is described in [15].

NORMALIZATION OF DATA AND SOLUTION

In the algorithm for the INDIFF part of the program the original data and final solutions are normalized. The scalar product matrices of the original data are normalized so that the sum of squares of the scalar product matrix is set equal to unity for each subject. In the INDIFF analysis the final stimulus space is normalized so that the sum of squares of projections of stimuli on the coordinate axes is equal to unity and the centroid is at the origin. The appropriate companion normalization is applied to the subject matrix. This procedure has one interesting outcome: the square of the Euclidean distance of a subject's point from the origin can be (approximately) interpreted as the (proportion of) total variance accounted for in the scalar products data for that subject. If the dimensions of the stimulus space are orthogonal, then the square of the Euclidean distance of the subject's point will exactly equal the proportion of variance accounted for. No such normalization is done for the CANDECOMP option.

INPUT PARAMETERS

Data input options for INDSCAL are controlled by a parameter called IRDATA. Eight alternatives are provided in the program, corresponding to integer values of 0 to 7 for IRDATA.

IRDATA	Input Option
0	Rectangular matrices (CANDECOMP option)
1	Lower half of similarities matrix without diagonal
2	Lower half of dissimilarities matrix without diagonal
3	Lower half of Euclidean distance matrix without diagonal
4	Lower half of correlation matrix without diagonal
5	Lower half of covariance matrix without diagonal
6	Full symmetric matrix of similarities
7	Full symmetric matrix of dissimilarities

In cases 1 through 5 the matrix can also be read as an ordered vector.

The user can obtain either a simultaneous or a successive dimensional solution. In the simultaneous case all dimensions in the matrices are computed at one time, whereas in the successive case only one dimension is estimated at a time. The user can control the iterative process by two parameters, MAXIT (maximum number of iterations) and CRIT (a cutoff value).

An option exists for not setting matrix 2 equal to matrix 3. In the CANDECOMP analysis this option must always be chosen, since, in general, the input matrices are different. In INDIFF analysis, however, matrix 2 *is* set equal to matrix 3, since these input matrices are equal.

The INDSCAL program can also be used to solve for the weights assigned by subjects to a prespecified configuration. The program also can use a prespecified configuration as a rational start even in the case in which all matrices are to be solved for.

The limits currently imposed on the program are:

Number of matrices $\leqslant 7$

Number of dimensions $r \leqslant 10$

$N_1 \cdot N_2 \cdot N_3 \cdot N_4 \cdot N_5 \cdot N_6 \cdot N_7 \leqslant 1800$ where N_i refers to the size of the ith matrix

MAX $(N_i) \leqslant 100; i = 1, \ldots, 7$

MAX $(r \cdot N_i) \leqslant 300; i = 1, \ldots, 7$

Number of iterations $\leqslant 50$

OUTPUT DETAILS

Typical output for an INDSCAL run for a three-way matrix consists of the following:

1. Listing of the options chosen for the run.

2. Initial matrices for the group stimulus and subject spaces.
3. Estimates of the group stimulus and subject spaces at each iteration and the corresponding error sum of squares.
4. History of computation, showing the correlation between data and estimates and the normalized residual variance at each iteration.
5. Final estimates of the matrices.
6. Sums of squares and products matrix for all pairs of dimensions.
7. Two-dimensional plots of the matrices for all pairs of dimensions.
8. Correlation between computed and original scalar products data for subjects.

USE IN THE BOOK

The INDIFF feature of the INDSCAL algorithm has been used in Chapters 3 and 5 to scale both direct and derived dissimilarities for all respondents and to scale direct dissimilarities for the subgroups A and B and a and b. This feature has also been used to analyze differences in the subgroup average ratings data in Chapter 3 and to compare scaling methods in Chapters 3, 4, and 6. The CANDECOMP option has been used to compare the two-dimensional solutions of the nine methods of group scaling in Chapter 2.

HOWARD-HARRIS CLUSTER PROGRAM

The Howard-Harris cluster program forms groups of objects using an objects-by-variables matrix [71] as data. The program uses the criterion of minimum within-group variance at each level of clustering.

THEORETICAL DISCUSSION

Let the number of objects being clustered be n, each of which is measured on N variables. Let the objects be denoted by $x_1, x_2, \ldots, x_n$, each x_i being a vector $(x_{i1}, \ldots, x_{iN})$ in an N-dimensional space. Let P $(S,\ p)$ represent a p-fold partitioning of the set S into disjoint subsets, A, B, and so on.

With this notation the problem of hierarchical clustering may be stated as follows. Given a set of objects $(x_1,\ x_2, \ldots, x_n | x_i \in S)$, each characterized by a number of variables, partition S into subsets that are as internally homogeneous and at the same time as mutually dissimilar as possible. The dissimilarity between any two objects, x_i and x_j, in S can be defined as

$$|x_i - x_j|^2 = \sum_{k=1}^{N} (x_{ik} - x_{jk})^2$$

For a set n_A members in any group A, it can be shown that the sum of all squared interpoint distances is directly comparable with the sum of all interpoint deviations from the mean of the group. Mathematically stated,

$$\sum_{(x_i \epsilon A)}^{n_A} |x_i - \overline{x}_A|^2 = \frac{1}{2n_A} \sum_{(x_i, x_j \epsilon A)}^{n_A} \Sigma |x_i - x_j|^2$$

where $\overline{x}_A$ is the centroid of A.

The total variance, V_T, of all n members in S can be written as

$$V_T = \frac{1}{2n} \sum_{i=1}^{} \sum_{j=1}^{} |x_i - x_j|^2$$

For any p-fold partition into p groups this variance can be divided into two components: a within-group variance, V_W, and a between-group variance, V_B. The total within-group variance, V_W, can be obtained by

$$V_W = \sum_{A \epsilon P(S,p)} V_A$$

The criterion of optimally partitioning S into p groups is stated as follows: find $P(S, p)$ so that V_W is a minimum.

Unfortunately, no algorithm presently exists for finding such a split in N dimensions. However, a locally optimal solution can be found by choosing a good split and then shifting points until a minimum V_W is found by a procedure to be described subsequently. The result will be at least locally optimal, given the initial split. In the Howard-Harris program an initial split[4] is made on the basis of the maximum variance component of the vectors in the group being split.

COMPUTATIONAL PROCEDURE

The steps involved in finding a $(p + 1)$-fold partitioning of S so that V_W is minimum, given that one already has a p-fold partition of S, are as follows:

1. A group A is chosen for splitting on the basis of maximum within-group variance.
2. A component of the vectors x_i in A is chosen to serve as the splitting variable on the basis of maximum variance.
3. New group membership for the vectors x_i (formerly in A) is found on the basis of splitting at the mean value of the maximum variance component of x_i in A.

---

[4] A superior method, also suggested by Howard, would be to extract the first principal component and then partition on the basis of the scores on that component. However, this method is not followed in the present version of the algorithm.

4. Finally a local optimization is carried out by comparing the distance from each $x_i \epsilon S$ to the centroid of each of the $p + 1$ existing groups. Points are shifted and centroids recomputed until group reassignments are represented by minimum squared distance to the centroid of each cluster.

It can be shown, using proof by counterexample [71], that the solution obtained in step 4 is locally optimal. The property of the locally optimal solution is: should any single point be moved from its assigned group to any other group, total within-group variance would be increased.

The actual test for final group membership is made by testing for changes in within-group variance that would accompany a hypothetical shift of $x_i \epsilon A$ to any other group, B. If the shift would result in decreased variance, it is made.

INPUT PARAMETERS

The limits on the parameters in the standard version of this program are

Number of objects $\leqslant 120$
Number of variables $\leqslant 16$

Two other versions exist which can handle up to 2000 objects with the same number of variables and up to 200 objects with a maximum of 25 variables.

The input data can be standardized by column at the user's option. Furthermore, different scaling factors for each variable can be read in. The user can also specify the maximum number of groups to be formed.

OUTPUT DETAILS

The output of a typical run, using the Howard-Harris program, consists of the following:

1. Listing of parameter values selected.
2. Listing of original data and means and standard deviations by columns.
3. Listing of standardized data (if no standardization is requested, the original data will be listed again).
4. Table showing the final assignment of objects to various levels of grouping, up to the maximum level selected.
5. Table showing the minimum within-group sum of squares attained for each level of grouping.

USE IN THE BOOK

The Howard-Harris cluster program has been used in Chapter 3 to form clusters of respondents based on their saliences assigned to the three-dimensional INDSCAL configuration of direct dissimilarities data. In this run the number of people (objects) was 42, each measured on 3 variables. The data were not standardized, and a grouping of up to 10 levels was selected.

PROFIT

PROFIT is a computer algorithm developed by Chang and Carroll [21] for fitting outside property vectors into stimulus spaces.[5] The program can perform two of the methods of property fitting employed in the book: the max "r" procedure [102] and the nonlinear correlation procedure [13].

THEORETICAL DISCUSSION

The problem of property fitting one property vector at a time can be stated mathematically as follows. Given a prespecified stimulus configuration, $X = (x_{jk})$; $j = 1, 2, \ldots, n$; $k = 1, 2, \ldots, r$; of n stimuli in r dimensions and ratings of the stimuli on an attribute, $p = (p_j)$; $j = 1, 2, \ldots, n$; determine a vector of direction cosines, (t_k), $k = 1, 2, \ldots, r$ for portraying the property vector according to some prespecified criterion function. Let $h = (h_j)$; $j = 1, 2, \ldots, n$; represent the projections of the n stimuli on the fitted property vector.

Max "r" Linear Regression

The criterion in the max "r" procedure is the minimum sum of squares of differences between the original ratings, P, and the fitted ratings, H, in the space of stimuli. The origin of the stimulus space is set equal to the centroid of the n points. The solution for the transformation, t, can be obtained by familiar regression procedures and is given by

$$t = (X'X)^{-1} X'p$$

and the stimulus ratings on the fitted vector are obtained from the equation

$$h = Xt = X(X'X)^{-1} X'p$$

The vector of direction cosines is obtained by normalizing t to unit length.

Nonlinear Regression

The criterion for nonlinear regression can be best explained for the unidimensional case. It is one of minimizing the value of K=(Kappa) defined by

$$K = S^{1/2} \sum_{\substack{i=1 \\ i \neq j}} \sum_{j=1} w_{ij}(x_i - x_j)^2$$

---

[5] There is no constraint that these spaces be obtained by multidimensional scaling analysis.

where w_{ij} is a monotonically decreasing function of the absolute difference between the original ratings for the ith and jth stimuli, $|p_i - p_j|$, and

$$S^2 = \frac{1}{n} \sum_{i=1}^{n} (x_i - \bar{x})^2$$

Usually $w_{ij} = 1/[(p_i - p_j)^2 + a]$ where a is a constant.

To find the direction cosines (t) of the fitted vector, the $r \times r$ symmetric matrix $X'AX$ (where X has been orthonormalized) is first constructed where the elements of A are defined by

$$A_{ij} = -w_{ij} \text{ for } i \neq j$$
$$A_{ii} = \sum_{j \neq i}^{n} w_{ij}$$

The smallest nonzero characteristic root of $X'AX$ is the minimum value of K, and the corresponding characteristic vector gives the direction cosines (t) of the fitted vector. The projections (h) are obtained, as before, by $h = Xt$.

COMPUTATIONAL PROCEDURE

The computation procedure is quite straightforward for linear regression. The X matrix is first normalized by columns. The direction cosines for each property vector are computed from the regression coefficients, and ratings on the fitted vector are then obtained. In addition, the program computes the product moment correlation between the projections of the n points onto the fitted vector and the original ratings on the property vector.

In nonlinear regression, the first step is to transform the stimulus configuration into a set of orthonormal vectors. The $(r \times r)$ symmetric matrix $X'AX$ is then computed, and its eigenvalues and eigenvectors extracted. The smallest eigenvalue will yield the minimum value of K, and the corresponding eigenvector will define the direction cosines of the fitted vector. The projections, h, are computed according to the formula $h = Xt$. The configuration is then transformed back to the original coordinates, and the direction cosines for the original coordinates are also computed.

OUTPUT DETAILS

This program can perform only linear regression or only nonlinear regression, or both, for a set of up to 20 properties for a configuration of up to 150 stimuli in a maximum of 10 dimensions.

In the nonlinear regression procedure, however, the input parameter IWGT and the associated constant BCO become relevant. In the present version of the program three options are available for IWGT, which determine the manner of computing the w_{ij}s.

The following are some important elements of output for a run using the PROFIT algorithm:

1. Normalized configuration of stimuli.
2. Original ratings and projections onto fitted vector for each property.
3. Moments and standardized index of nonlinear correlation (in nonlinear regression).
4. Plot showing the fitted vector versus the original vector for each property.
5. Correlation between fitted and original vector.
6. Summary tables showing the degree of fit, cosines of angles between property vectors, and direction cosines in the normalized and original spaces.
7. Plot showing the original stimulus coordinates and the directions of fitted vectors.

USE IN THE BOOK

The PROFIT program has been used in Chapter 3 to fit the 10 product-attribute average ratings in the (direct) stimulus spaces for groups A and B. For the runs involving nonlinear correlations, the parameters IWGT and BCO were respectively set at 0 and 0.01 (see [21] for details).

MDPREF

MDPREF is a computer program developed by Chang and Carroll [20] to perform an internal analysis of preference (or any other type of dominance) data. The program develops simultaneously the vector directions for the subjects and configuration of stimuli in a common space. The preferences are assumed to be described by a vector model.

THEORETICAL DISCUSSION

In MDPREF the dominance judgments can be either paired comparisons or rankings of stimuli. The following discussion is for the former case; the development is quite similar for the latter.

$$\text{Let } P = (p_{i,jk}); i = 1, 2, \ldots, m \; ; jk = 1, 2, \ldots, n(n - 1)/2$$

represent the matrix of paired comparisons for the ith subject for a set of n stimuli. We assume that there are m subjects making such judgments. The entries $p_{i,jk}$ take the values +1, −1, or 0 according to whether individual i judges stimulus j as more preferred, less preferred, or indifferent compared to stimulus k.

The model assumes that stimulus points are projected onto subject vectors and that preference judgments are in agreement with these projected values. Let $x_j = (x_{j1}, \ldots, x_{jr})$ represent the r-dimensional vector emanating from the origin to the jth stimulus and $y_i = (y_{i1}, \ldots, y_{ir})$ represent the unit-length vector for subject i. Then $\hat{S}_{ij}$, the estimated preference scale value of stimulus j for subject i is defined by the scalar product

$$\hat{S}_{ij} = y_i \cdot x_j' = \sum_{t=1}^{r} y_{it} \, x_{jt}$$

Let $X = (x_{jt})$ be the $n \times r$ matrix of stimulus coordinate values and $Y = (y_{it})$ the $m \times r$ matrix of the termini of subject vectors; then

$$\hat{S} = (\hat{S}_{ij}) = YX'$$

The problem is to determine the matrices Y and X' from the set of paired comparison judgments so that the P matrix will agree as nearly as possible with the $\hat{S}$ matrix. Carroll [17] describes an iterative procedure and one utilizing Eckart-Young decomposition [40] to accomplish this task.

If the input data are already scale values of preference (this matrix S is called the first-score matrix), the program proceeds to decompose S by the Eckart-Young procedure which involves the matrices $S'S$ and SS'. If the input data are paired comparisons, they are first converted to a matrix of scale values. (Monte Carlo analyses by Carroll and Chang indicated that the simpler Eckart-Young procedure worked as well with errorful data as the iterative one. Therefore, MDPREF utilizes only the Eckart-Young procedure.)

INPUT OPTIONS

The current limits on the parameters of this program are as follows:

Number of subjects $(NP) \leqslant 100$
Number of stimuli $(NS) \leqslant 100$
Maximum $(NP \times NS) = 5000$
Number of dimensions (NF) $\leqslant$ MIN (NP, NS)
Maximum (NP $\times$ NF) = 1000

As noted, the program has two input options: paired comparisons and direct judgments of preference scale values. In paired comparisons, options exist for reading in weight matrices specific to each subject and for handling missing data. In direct preference judgments (for example, rankings) two options exist for normalization: (a) subtracting row means or (b) subtracting row means and dividing entries by the standard deviation of values for that row.

OUTPUT DETAILS

The following are the major output categories entailed in a typical run of MDPREF:

1. First-score matrix normalized as in above option (chosen in the case of direct judgments) and as computed in the case of paired comparisons.
2. Cross-products matrix of subjects.
3. Cross-products matrix of stimuli.
4. Eigenroots of the first score matrix.
5. Estimates of the first-score matrix after the factorization. (This is called the second-score matrix.)
6. Coordinates of stimuli and vector directions for subjects in the user-specified dimensionality.
7. Plot of the first two dimensions of stimuli and subject vectors.

USE IN THE BOOK

The MDPREF program has been used to derive a joint stimulus-subject space from the overall preference data in Chapter 4. The application is quite straightforward. The input parameters were 42 subjects and 15 stimuli. The first-score matrix of preference ranks was read in and the second normalization option chosen. Solutions were obtained in two and three dimensions.

PREFMAP

The set of multidimensional preference models developed by Carroll and Chang [13] is a generalization of the basic Coombsian unfolding model of preference [30]. These models, known as PREFMAP, utilize a known configuration of stimuli and attempt to portray an individual's preference data via a hierarchy of four models, which are analyzed by four corresponding phases. The phases are referred to as phases I, II, III, and IV; as one goes from phase I to phase IV the underlying assumptions and model complexity are considerably reduced.

ASSUMPTIONS OF THE MODELS

The assumptions underlying these models follow:

1. A group of individuals share the same perceptual configuration of r dimensions for a set of n stimuli. Let $X = (x_{jt})$; $j = 1, 2, \ldots, n$; $t = 1, 2, \ldots, r$ represent the common perceptual space.
2. The preference value (or utility function) for the jth stimulus of any individual, say, the ith, is (at least) monotonically related to the squared distance between the individual's ideal point (the most desired location in the perceptual space) and the location of the stimulus in the space. Let the matrix $S = (s_{ij})$; $i = 1, 2, \ldots, m$; $j = 1, 2, \ldots, n$ represent the scale values of preference of m individuals for the n stimuli. Each row of the S matrix represents the scale values of individual i's preference for n

stimuli. (For convenience, we assume that smaller values on the scale represent higher preferences.)

TWO VERSIONS OF THE PREFMAP MODELS

Two versions of PREFMAP models may be distinguished: metric and nonmetric. In the metric version the monotone function is assumed to be linear, while a general monotonic form, not specified *a priori*, is permitted in the nonmetric case. Thus, the preference scale values are assumed to be interval scaled in the metric version, while only their ordinal relationships are utilized in the nonmetric version.

METRIC VERSION OF THE PREFMAP ALGORITHM

In the metric version of the PREFMAP algorithm it is assumed that the scale value of preference is *linearly* related (excluding an error term) to the *square* of the Euclidean distance, that is,

$$s_{ij} \approx a_i d_{ij}^2 + b_i$$

where a_i and b_i are constants ($a_i \geqslant 0$).

Let $x_j = (x_{j1}, \ldots, x_{jr})$ represent the row vector of coordinates of the jth stimulus ($j = 1, 2, \ldots, n$) and $y_i = (y_{i1}, \ldots, y_{ir})$ represent the coordinates of the ideal point for the ith individual ($i = 1, 2, \ldots, m$). Given the relationship shown above for the scale values of the ith individual, the PREFMAP model solves for the coordinate values of the vector y_i.

Four alternative models for relating preference data to a given stimulus space, called phases I, II, III, and IV, have been developed by Carroll and Chang. These models range in a decreasing order of complexity. Phase I fits a highly generalized unfolding model of preference; phase II is a particular case of phase I; phase III fits the simple unfolding model; and phase IV fits the linear, or vector, model. Phases I, II and III differ in the way the term d_{ij}^2 is formulated, that is, in the definition of the metric.

All four models utilize quadratic or linear regression procedures to estimate the s_{ij}s, which are then parameterized in various ways, as described in detail in [13].

Phase I assumes that both x_j and y_i are operated on by an orthogonal transformation matrix, t_i—which is idiosyncratic for each subject—and then squared distances are computed from the *transformed values*. Thus, phase I defines

$$x_j^* = x_j T_i$$
$$y_i^* = y_i T_i$$

and then computes the (weighted) Euclidean squared distances, d_{ij}^2, by the formula

$$d_{ij}^2 = \sum_{t=1}^{r} w_{it}(x_{jt}^* - y_{it}^*)^2$$

Phase II

Unlike phase I, phase II does not assume a different orthogonal transformation for each individual, although it assumes a differential weighting of dimensions, so that squared distances are computed by a formula similar to the immediately preceding one.

Phase III

Phase III is the simple unfolding model. But since it allows some or all of the dimensions to have negative weight, Phase III is equivalent to Phase II, with weights $w_{it} = \pm 1$.

Phase IV

Phase IV utilizes the vector model in which preference scale values are related by a regression equation (excluding the error term) of the form:

$$s_{ij} \approx b_i X_j' + C_i$$

This regression equation contains only linear terms. After estimation of the coefficients $b_{i1}, b_{i2}, \ldots, b_{ir}$, the direction cosines of the vector for the ith individual are obtained by normalizing his b_i to unit length.

NONMETRIC VERSION OF THE PREFMAP ALGORITHM

The nonmetric version of PREFMAP fits monotonic functions between the preference scale values, and the squared Euclidean distances between ideal point and the stimulus points. This is accomplished by the following steps:

1. Solve for the parameters of the appropriate regression equation (quadratic or linear) to predict the s_{ij}s. This is essentially the metric version of the PREFMAP model.
2. Estimate the monotone function $M_i^{(1)}$ that relates the estimates (the $\hat{s}_{ij}$s) to the original s_{ij}s, using the procedure described by Kruskal [84] for least squares monotone regession.
3. Replace s_{ij} with $s_{ij}^{(1)}$ to compute a new set of predicted values.
4. Using the new set of $\hat{s}_{ij}$s, compute a new monotone function $M_i^{(2)}$ and a new set of $\hat{s}_{ij}$s, namely, $\hat{s}_{ij}^{(2)}$.
5. Continue this iterative procedure until the process converges (that is, until no more changes occur in the monotone function or regression coefficients). The process is terminated by a parameter called CRIT. If CRIT is greater than or equal to the sum of squares of differences in the predicted s_{ij}s for the Ith and $(I-1)$th iterations, the process stops at the Ith iteration.

INPUT PARAMETERS

PREFMAP can analyze preference data up to a maximum of 49 subjects for a set of up to 100 stimuli in as many as 5 dimensions. The preference input data can be expressed in (a) smaller values indicating higher preferences or (b) larger values indicating higher preferences. The program can start with any prespecified phase and can work its way down to any model of lower complexity.

The input options for the linear or monotone versions of the algorithm are controlled by the LFITSW parameter, which refers to the way in which d^2 is assumed to be related to the preference values. LFITSW can take any one of four integer values from 0 to 3:

LFITSW = 0   Linear option (d^2 is linearly related to s_{ij})

LFITSW = 1   Nonblock monotone option (d^2 is monotonically related to s_{ij} and there are no ties)

LFITSW = 2   Block monotone option with ordering within blocks

LFITSW = 3   Block monotone option with equality within blocks

Other options include (a) normalization (or otherwise) of original scale values and (b) computing each subject's scale values for each new phase or, alternatively, using the estimates of the previous phase as the original values for the following phase.

OUTPUT DETAILS

A typical run of PREFMAP produces the following output:

1. Listing of all input parameters selected and the original configuration of stimuli.
2. For each subject the printout of the original vector of scale values, regression coefficients and estimates of d^2 or s_{ij} for each phase and for each iteration in the monotone version.
3. For phase I (only) the direction cosines of each subject's idiosyncratic rotation.
4. Coordinates (or direction cosines for phase IV) of ideal point and weights of the dimensions specific to each subject.
5. Plot, showing the relationship between the monotone transform of the scale values and original scale values (optional).
6. Plot, showing the positions of ideal points (or vector directions) for phases III and IV of all subjects as well as stimulus positions.
7. A summary table showing the correlation coefficients for each subject by each phase and corresponding F-ratios, including F-ratios associated with the inclusion of additional parameters, as utilized in the more complex phases of the hierarchy.

USE OF THE PREFMAP PROGRAM IN THE BOOK

The external analysis of preference data in Chapter 5 is based exclusively on the PREFMAP program. In addition, the program has been used to fit the 10 average ratings as properties in the stimulus spaces of groups A and B, utilizing the monotone regression procedure (Chapter 3).

In all of the above runs the options chosen for the various parameters are shown below:

1. LFITSW was set at 0 for linear runs and 1 for monotone runs.
2. The preference scale values were always normalized.
3. The maximum number of iterations was set at 15 and the value of CRIT at 0.001 for all monotone runs.
4. At the beginning of a new phase the $\hat{s}_{ij}$ values of the previous phase were used in the monotone runs.
5. Average subject values, for monotone runs, were computed anew for each phase.

SUPPORTING MATERIAL FOR CHAPTER DISCUSSIONS

Here we present a variety of tables and charts that support chapter discussions. The material is organized by chapter and presented in chronological order to agree with the textual presentation. Where appropriate, each table or figure is referenced to a table or figure in the text. This procedure is to aid the reader who desires to look at supporting material as he reads each chapter.

219

In this section we present supporting computer output for material covered in Chapter 2.

Table C.1   Basic Data on Directly Judged Dissimilarities from TRICON for First Three Subjects (see Table 2.2)

96.0						Subject 011							
71.5	23.5												
17.5	103.0	105.0											
30.0	6.5	48.5	89.0										
67.5	44.5	67.5	82.5	76.0									
103.0	30.0	82.5	96.0	76.0	48.5								
23.5	17.5	30.0	60.0	38.0	62.5	89.0							
35.0	12.5	23.5	76.0	35.0	48.5	64.5	2.5						
89.0	2.5	17.5	99.0	17.5	48.5	23.5	17.5	12.5					
71.5	62.5	55.0	23.5	6.5	41.5	30.0	55.0	71.5	89.0				
12.5	82.5	92.5	6.5	41.5	35.0	48.5	55.0	64.5	89.0	12.5			
44.5	96.0	100.5	2.5	92.5	82.5	100.5	67.5	71.5	96.0	30.0	9.5		
38.0	76.0	96.0	41.5	55.0	9.5	55.0	82.5	60.0	82.5	6.5	23.5	41.5	
82.5	30.0	30.0	76.0	55.0	2.5	60.0	82.5	55.0	38.0	67.5	103.0	48.5	17.5

33.5						Subject 012							
38.5	6.5												
49.0	76.5	76.5											
33.5	12.0	28.0	92.0										
82.0	49.0	99.0	86.5	55.0									
63.0	28.0	22.5	105.0	99.0	104.0								
38.5	22.5	55.0	33.5	28.0	71.5	96.0							
17.0	12.0	33.5	55.0	22.5	71.5	92.0	3.0						
38.5	3.0	17.0	59.5	8.5	42.5	42.5	17.0	12.0					
86.5	86.5	102.0	45.0	12.0	42.5	63.0	55.0	49.0	67.0				
67.0	96.0	71.5	12.0	67.0	28.0	49.0	42.5	59.5	89.0	6.5			
92.0	99.0	82.0	3.0	76.5	55.0	102.0	49.0	76.5	92.0	28.0	17.0		
82.0	82.0	63.0	17.0	67.0	22.5	67.0	49.0	59.5	82.0	8.5	3.0	22.5	
92.0	33.5	33.5	96.0	76.5	3.0	22.5	86.5	71.5	49.0	59.5	76.5	102.0	38.5

86.5						Subject 021							
105.0	25.0												
11.5	75.5	99.0											
69.0	39.5	81.0	45.5										
69.0	32.0	16.0	57.5	59.5									
103.0	20.5	4.0	96.0	75.5	20.5								
20.5	35.5	54.0	61.5	20.5	57.5	45.5							
20.5	25.0	50.0	54.0	39.5	45.5	39.5	4.0						
96.0	4.0	32.0	69.0	32.0	45.5	32.0	11.5	11.5					
45.5	75.5	86.5	28.0	4.0	39.5	81.0	61.5	69.0	69.0				
20.5	91.5	100.5	4.0	64.0	64.0	50.0	75.5	64.0	86.5	32.0			
35.5	86.5	91.5	8.0	50.0	54.0	86.5	75.5	81.0	69.0	11.5	11.5		
39.5	100.5	96.0	28.0	59.5	69.0	54.0	81.0	91.5	103.0	4.0	16.0	25.0	
91.5	28.0	11.5	86.5	81.0	4.0	16.0	45.5	54.0	39.5	103.0	75.5	96.0	96.0

Table C.2   Basic Data on Derived Distances (DISTAN) from Ratings for First Three Subjects (see Table 2.3)

2.02							Subject 011						
1.26	1.51												
1.34	1.59	1.74											
1.36	1.41	1.29	1.71										
1.64	0.95	1.30	1.22	1.40									
1.99	1.07	1.45	1.87	1.43	1.05								
1.59	1.32	1.36	1.40	0.88	1.12	1.45							
1.53	1.17	1.53	1.17	0.90	1.11	1.55	0.52						
2.21	0.73	1.51	2.02	1.41	1.02	0.73	1.38	1.44					
0.90	1.53	1.29	0.84	1.55	1.17	1.69	1.52	1.35	1.88				
0.91	1.93	1.42	0.86	1.84	1.52	2.03	1.74	1.63	2.28	0.62			
1.23	1.55	1.25	1.40	1.45	1.34	1.23	1.57	1.55	1.70	1.04	1.19		
1.17	1.65	1.10	1.43	1.56	1.28	1.63	1.54	1.50	1.78	0.91	1.16	1.37	
2.11	1.35	1.62	2.13	1.48	1.12	0.89	1.48	1.61	0.89	1.84	2.30	1.70	1.66
1.28							Subject 012						
1.39	0.75												
1.83	1.93	1.50											
1.31	0.82	0.20	1.44										
1.72	1.62	1.07	1.28	1.01									
1.84	1.31	1.55	2.51	1.61	1.90								
1.37	1.12	0.83	1.24	0.76	1.00	1.85							
1.18	0.91	0.83	1.32	0.80	1.22	1.87	0.63						
1.13	0.35	0.88	1.97	0.90	1.64	1.33	1.15	0.98					
1.50	1.62	1.23	1.22	1.18	1.26	1.77	1.13	1.42	1.63				
2.19	2.28	1.78	1.29	1.72	1.50	2.33	1.59	1.95	2.31	0.80			
1.73	1.89	1.41	0.68	1.34	1.25	2.24	1.37	1.44	1.93	0.90	0.97		
1.72	1.79	1.32	1.64	1.27	0.95	1.96	1.06	1.44	1.80	1.06	1.30	1.51	
1.25	1.20	1.17	2.08	1.22	1.43	1.11	1.45	1.38	1.18	1.38	2.01	1.81	1.35
2.04							Subject 021						
2.05	0.82												
1.82	1.59	1.57											
1.81	1.13	1.03	1.14										
1.70	1.75	1.36	1.20	1.01									
1.97	1.26	1.28	1.43	1.27	1.43								
1.67	1.04	1.35	1.15	0.93	1.52	1.39							
1.67	1.04	1.35	1.15	0.93	1.52	1.39	0.00						
1.63	0.84	0.79	1.32	0.88	1.43	1.36	0.91	0.91					
2.00	2.16	2.10	1.19	1.46	1.32	1.59	1.58	1.58	1.83				
1.69	2.05	1.89	1.07	1.33	1.16	1.65	1.50	1.50	1.53	0.60			
1.81	1.79	1.59	1.08	1.05	0.94	1.25	1.29	1.29	1.44	0.72	0.73		
1.97	2.42	2.09	1.44	1.67	1.04	1.92	1.88	1.88	1.95	0.93	0.82	0.91	
1.86	1.63	1.10	1.56	1.14	1.00	1.16	1.71	1.71	1.30	1.72	1.50	1.15	1.62

Table C.3   Stimulus Coordinates from Metric Scaling of Direct Dissimilarities in Two and Three Dimensions (see Figure 2.2)

Stimulus	Dimension				
	1	2	1	2	3
1	−0.193	−0.474	−0.193	−0.474	−0.091
2	0.740	−0.226	0.740	−0.226	0.063
3	0.616	0.277	0.616	0.277	−0.071
4	−0.738	−0.110	−0.738	−0.110	−0.367
5	−0.051	−0.380	−0.051	−0.380	0.529
6	0.036	0.516	0.036	0.516	−0.237
7	0.772	0.380	0.772	0.380	0.035
8	0.160	−0.502	0.160	−0.502	−0.131
9	0.171	−0.488	0.171	−0.488	−0.208
10	0.760	−0.202	0.760	−0.202	0.011
11	−0.574	0.129	−0.574	0.129	0.365
12	−0.690	0.108	−0.690	0.108	−0.004
13	−0.709	0.084	−0.709	0.084	−0.034
14	−0.608	0.278	−0.608	0.278	0.103
15	0.307	0.611	0.307	0.611	0.037

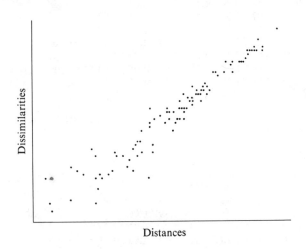

Figure C.1   Shepard Diagram from Metric Scaling of Direct Dissimilarities in Three Dimensions (see Figure 2.3)

Table C.4   Stimulus Coordinates from M-D-SCAL V Analysis of Direct
Dissimilarities in Two and Three Dimensions (see Figure 2.4)

| Stimulus | Dimension | | | | |
	1	2	1	2	3
1	−0.192	−0.864	−0.366	−0.764	−0.257
2	1.127	−0.265	1.076	−0.290	0.089
3	0.844	0.391	0.811	0.398	−0.335
4	−1.207	−0.046	−1.051	−0.069	−0.331
5	−0.148	−0.536	−0.076	−0.487	0.639
6	0.154	0.774	0.037	0.756	−0.339
7	1.274	0.431	1.189	0.504	0.261
8	0.250	−0.643	0.300	−0.725	−0.092
9	0.309	−0.642	0.296	−0.707	−0.168
10	1.191	−0.208	1.117	−0.275	−0.008
11	−0.841	0.052	−0.780	0.051	0.541
12	−1.034	0.216	−0.998	0.215	0.116
13	−1.251	0.086	−1.119	0.074	−0.288
14	−0.952	0.471	−0.854	0.474	0.191
15	0.475	0.783	0.418	0.845	−0.020

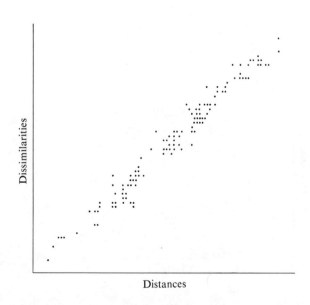

Figure C.2   Shepard Diagram from M-D-SCAL V Analysis of Direct Dissimilarities in Three Dimensions (see Figure 2.5)

Table C.5   Stimulus Coordinates from TORSCA 8 Analysis of Direct Dissimilarities in Two and Three Dimensions (see Figure 2.6)

Stimulus	Dimension 1	2	1	2	3
1	−0.137	−0.560	−0.244	−0.510	−0.170
2	0.713	−0.179	0.710	−0.188	0.081
3	0.532	0.256	0.532	0.278	−0.170
4	−0.767	−0.066	−0.689	−0.061	−0.241
5	−0.088	−0.341	−0.042	−0.321	0.432
6	0.088	0.502	0.025	0.500	−0.213
7	0.810	0.294	0.797	0.331	0.139
8	0.169	−0.424	0.202	−0.483	−0.081
9	0.208	−0.425	0.190	−0.461	−0.150
10	0.759	−0.125	0.740	−0.166	−0.032
11	−0.528	0.051	−0.516	0.031	0.363
12	−0.657	0.142	−0.656	0.132	0.092
13	−0.800	0.048	−0.743	0.049	−0.155
14	−0.604	0.315	−0.567	0.303	0.106
15	0.301	0.511	0.261	0.567	−0.002

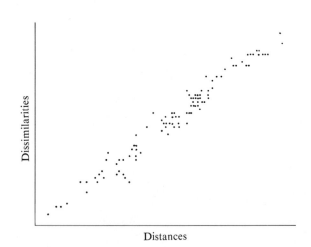

Figure C.3   Shepard Diagram from TORSCA 8 Analysis of Direct Dissimilarities in Three Dimensions (see Figure 2.7)

Table C.6   Stimulus Coordinates from Parametric Mapping of Direct
Dissimilarities in Two and Three Dimensions (see Figure 2.8)

	Dimension				
Stimulus	1	2	1	2	3
1	−0.13213	−0.30938	−0.14616	−0.17838	−0.10214
2	0.21343	−0.10200	0.18081	−0.12652	0.00164
3	0.28290	0.08677	0.29993	0.04711	0.00818
4	−0.29939	0.14242	−0.12414	0.14297	0.01494
5	−0.15200	−0.12566	−0.15740	−0.16351	0.10580
6	0.19489	0.26620	0.22361	0.24285	−0.00598
7	0.15768	0.02950	0.16691	0.02137	−0.02553
8	0.02793	−0.21064	0.00228	−0.22813	0.00806
9	0.02895	−0.21088	0.00481	−0.22647	0.00536
10	0.23087	−0.13466	0.21832	−0.12963	0.00734
11	−0.19920	−0.00201	−0.29028	0.15703	0.02301
12	−0.17463	0.10383	−0.21967	0.07012	−0.01983
13	−0.26829	0.15048	−0.15581	0.15334	0.01509
14	−0.12796	0.12765	−0.26623	0.04856	−0.03572
15	0.21695	0.18837	0.26301	0.16930	−0.00021

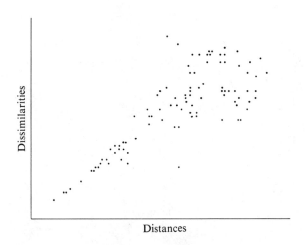

Dissimilarities

Distances

Figure C.4   Shepard Diagram from Parametric Mapping of Direct Dissimilarities
in Three Dimensions (see Figure 2.9)

Table C.7 Stimulus Coordinates from Metric Scaling of Derived Dissimilarities in Two and Three Dimensions (see Figure 2.11)

Stimulus	Dimension				
	1	2	1	2	3
1	0.069	0.595	0.069	0.595	-0.578
2	-0.573	0.005	-0.573	0.005	0.086
3	-0.241	-0.140	-0.241	-0.140	0.009
4	0.368	0.300	0.368	0.300	0.281
5	-0.174	0.121	-0.174	0.121	0.150
6	0.080	-0.215	0.080	-0.215	0.014
7	-0.416	-0.401	-0.416	-0.401	-0.271
8	-0.346	0.143	-0.346	0.143	0.173
9	-0.253	0.200	-0.253	0.200	0.251
10	-0.588	0.038	-0.588	0.038	0.017
11	0.430	0.003	0.430	0.003	-0.016
12	0.731	-0.171	0.731	-0.171	0.060
13	0.478	0.140	0.478	0.140	0.036
14	0.543	-0.305	0.543	-0.305	-0.066
15	-0.108	-0.314	-0.108	-0.314	-0.147

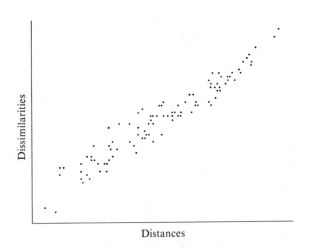

Figure C.5 Shepard Diagram from Metric Scaling of Derived Dissimilarities in Three Dimensions (see Figure 2.12)

Table C.8   Stimulus Coordinates from M-D-SCAL V Analysis of Derived
             Dissimilarities in Two and Three Dimensions (see Figure 2.13)

Stimulus	Dimension				
	1	2	1	2	3
1	0.087	1.467	0.137	1.113	−0.810
2	−1.047	−0.037	−1.058	0.006	0.085
3	−0.443	−0.260	−0.446	−0.272	0.095
4	0.790	0.533	0.725	0.586	0.423
5	−0.313	0.265	−0.367	0.149	0.540
6	0.146	−0.575	0.131	−0.586	0.345
7	−1.120	−0.762	−0.976	−0.669	−0.483
8	−0.645	0.240	−0.612	0.317	0.048
9	−0.531	0.306	−0.495	0.392	0.109
10	−1.149	0.042	−1.161	0.049	0.063
11	0.841	−0.007	0.816	0.040	−0.251
12	1.499	−0.302	1.458	−0.231	0.068
13	0.916	0.227	0.895	0.248	0.098
14	1.188	−0.586	1.135	−0.572	−0.103
15	−0.219	−0.552	−0.183	−0.569	−0.228

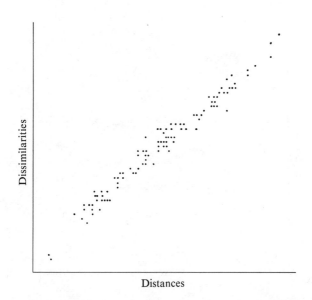

Distances

Figure C.6   Shepard Diagram from M-D-SCAL V Analysis of Derived Dissimilar-
              ities in Three Dimensions (see Figure 2.14)

Table C.9   Stimulus Coordinates from TORSCA 8 Analysis of Derived
Dissimilarities in Two and Three Dimensions (see Figure 2.15)

Stimulus	Dimension				
	1	2	1	2	3
1	0.130	0.928	0.128	0.837	−0.410
2	−0.674	0.003	−0.699	0.001	0.141
3	−0.289	−0.158	−0.291	−0.184	0.057
4	0.516	0.334	0.488	0.262	0.405
5	−0.204	0.199	−0.225	0.265	−0.080
6	0.071	−0.370	0.086	−0.387	0.189
7	−0.721	−0.481	−0.687	−0.440	−0.297
8	−0.407	0.177	−0.407	0.199	0.118
9	−0.334	0.232	−0.313	0.221	0.225
10	−0.738	0.050	−0.779	0.018	0.056
11	0.542	−0.031	0.542	0.034	−0.183
12	0.946	−0.240	0.975	−0.192	0.022
13	0.584	0.129	0.598	0.141	0.102
14	0.722	−0.431	0.711	−0.414	−0.158
15	−0.145	−0.340	−0.126	−0.360	−0.186

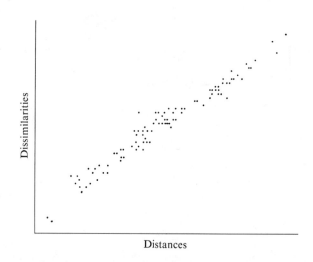

Figure C.7   Shepard Diagram from TORSCA 8 Analysis of Derived Dissimilarities in Three Dimensions (see Figure 2.16)

Table C.10   Stimulus Coordinates from Parametric Mapping of Derived Dissimilarities in Two and Three Dimensions (see Figure 2.17)

Stimulus	Dimension				
	1	2	1	2	3
1	0.02684	0.28841	0.01248	0.25092	−0.12852
2	−0.18818	0.01976	−0.20279	0.01190	−0.00072
3	−0.08626	−0.04717	−0.09264	−0.07760	0.00951
4	0.15949	0.09944	0.14435	0.10540	0.11126
5	−0.05453	0.06845	−0.07260	−0.01086	0.15593
6	0.01712	−0.13313	0.03318	−0.15201	0.08023
7	−0.21558	−0.14948	−0.15975	−0.07722	−0.17332
8	−0.12062	0.05024	−0.12375	0.05806	0.04428
9	−0.09210	0.05995	−0.09619	0.06899	0.05951
10	−0.20539	0.02581	−0.22273	0.01287	−0.00250
11	0.16461	−0.00573	0.15419	0.03477	−0.05404
12	0.25490	−0.07234	0.27301	−0.04779	−0.01684
13	0.17556	0.03931	0.17666	0.05863	0.03860
14	0.20919	−0.12498	0.21062	−0.10310	−0.08252
15	−0.04504	−0.11856	−0.03404	−0.13297	−0.04084

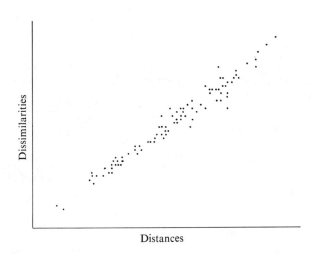

Distances

Figure C.8   Shepard Diagram from Parametric Mapping Analysis of Derived Dissimilarities in Three Dimensions (see Figure 2.18)

Table C.11   Stimulus Coordinates from Discriminant Analysis of Ratings Data in Three Dimensions (see Figure 2.20)

Stimulus	Dimension		
	1	2	3
1	0.24967	−1.95449	1.32171
2	−1.84557	0.27254	−0.02977
3	−0.53983	0.53083	−0.03068
4	0.69737	−1.07548	−0.64027
5	−0.53802	−0.53890	−0.39262
6	0.47761	0.62517	−0.68271
7	−0.66799	1.76110	0.85616
8	−1.14095	−0.33908	−0.43177
9	−1.00891	−0.84526	−0.84607
10	−1.83168	−0.07214	0.45906
11	1.22016	−0.06851	−0.09070
12	2.17698	0.37416	−0.21548
13	1.14569	−0.66558	0.50001
14	1.51604	0.76880	0.14951
15	0.08943	1.22685	0.07362

Table C.12   Canonical Weights from Discriminant Analysis of Ratings Data in Three Dimensions (see Figure 2.20)

Original Variable	Coefficient for Canonical Variable		
	1	2	3
1	−0.15407	0.28807	−0.29630
2	0.41873	−0.17585	−0.64438
3	0.06785	−0.74879	−0.05900
4	−0.06780	0.10516	0.10615
5	−0.01732	0.59384	−0.61607
6	−0.23375	−0.24182	−0.75767
7	−0.30992	−0.05918	−0.06820
8	−0.32174	−0.32400	−0.13049
9	−0.34989	0.09917	−0.03447
10	0.68606	0.50396	0.03863

Table C.13   Two-Space Stimulus Coordinates Orthogonally Rotated to Best
Congruence with Metric Scaling Configuration Obtained from Direct
Dissimilarities (see Figure 2.21)

Stimulus	Metric Scaling (Target)		M-D SCAL V (Direct Dissimilarities)		TORSCA 8 (Direct Dissimilarities)	
1	−0.300	−0.737	−0.486	−1.215	−0.222	−0.896
2	1.151	−0.351	1.205	−0.339	1.140	−0.290
3	0.957	0.430	0.588	0.157	0.853	0.407
4	−1.147	−0.171	−0.948	−0.422	−1.227	−0.102
5	−0.079	−0.591	0.298	−0.355	−0.143	−0.545
6	0.056	0.802	−0.046	0.499	0.144	0.803
7	1.200	0.590	1.107	0.607	1.299	0.466
8	0.249	−0.781	0.648	−0.500	0.268	−0.679
9	0.265	−0.758	0.419	−0.567	0.330	−0.681
10	1.181	−0.314	1.218	−0.417	1.214	−0.204
11	−0.892	0.200	−0.909	0.240	−0.845	0.085
12	−1.072	0.168	−1.444	0.779	−1.051	0.231
13	−1.102	0.131	−1.088	−0.022	−1.280	0.081
14	−0.944	0.432	−0.970	0.954	−0.965	0.507
15	0.477	0.949	0.408	0.600	0.485	0.816

Stimulus	Parametric Mapping (Direct Dissimilarities)		Metric Scaling (Derived Dissimilarities)		M-D-SCAL V (Derived Dissimilarities)	
1	−0.532	−1.468	−0.194	−0.887	−0.477	−1.498
2	1.098	−0.237	1.158	−0.269	1.095	−0.238
3	0.526	0.158	0.865	0.404	0.528	0.153
4	−0.956	−0.367	−1.239	−0.051	−0.959	−0.344
5	0.264	−0.395	−0.150	−0.551	0.255	−0.357
6	0.012	0.628	0.156	0.795	0.000	0.634
7	1.341	0.536	1.306	0.446	1.362	0.495
8	0.603	−0.429	0.259	−0.659	0.605	−0.419
9	0.465	−0.493	0.319	−0.658	0.470	−0.457
10	1.186	−0.336	1.223	−0.210	1.180	−0.346
11	−0.873	0.237	−0.863	0.051	−0.870	0.229
12	−1.460	0.717	−1.062	0.219	−1.474	0.708
13	−0.997	−0.009	−1.284	0.085	−1.009	0.006
14	−1.029	0.952	−0.979	0.481	−1.077	0.920
15	0.353	0.505	0.485	0.805	0.372	0.514

SUPPORTING MATERIAL FOR CHAPTER 3

In this section we present supporting computer output for material covered in Chapter 3.

Table C.13   (Concluded)

Stimulus	TORSCA 8 (Derived Dissimilarities)		Parametric Mapping (Derived Dissimilarities)		Discriminant Analysis (Derived Dissimilarities)	
1	−0.139	−1.335	−0.467	−1.554	−0.738	−1.173
2	0.934	−0.137	1.012	−0.317	1.258	−0.373
3	0.976	0.664	0.526	0.164	0.501	0.179
4	−1.309	0.190	−0.986	−0.369	−0.763	−0.479
5	−0.431	−0.658	0.223	−0.437	0.184	−0.503
6	0.429	1.245	0.054	0.750	−0.119	0.540
7	0.567	0.298	1.350	0.582	0.948	0.925
8	0.355	−0.770	0.607	−0.409	0.627	−0.554
9	0.359	−0.770	0.439	−0.432	0.393	−0.838
10	1.039	−0.241	1.100	−0.369	1.147	−0.589
11	−0.757	−0.242	−0.898	0.214	−0.798	0.318
12	−0.788	0.190	−1.320	0.680	−1.278	0.883
13	−1.200	0.258	−1.008	−0.021	−0.928	−0.085
14	−0.638	0.336	−1.011	0.918	−0.739	0.939
15	0.605	0.974	0.379	0.602	0.306	0.809

Table C.14   Individual-subject Correlation Coefficients from Aggregate-level INDSCAL Analysis of Direct Dissimilarities in Two and Three Dimensions (see Table 3.1)

Subject	Correlation 2 Dimensions	Correlation 3 Dimensions	Subject	Correlation 2 Dimensions	Correlation 3 Dimensions
011	0.681579	0.729967	121	0.728526	0.833790
012	0.773622	0.805039	122	0.669985	0.822491
021	0.703208	0.811365	131	0.552923	0.586364
022	0.819969	0.858527	132	0.795524	0.813062
031	0.747295	0.747297	141	0.594755	0.731785
032	0.791853	0.819479	142	0.775582	0.780482
041	0.768560	0.849226	151	0.698254	0.782791
042	0.828093	0.831276	152	0.669394	0.742979
051	0.835294	0.885165	161	0.461562	0.716408
052	0.732317	0.767095	162	0.398500	0.467105
061	0.885497	0.928459	171	0.859681	0.870329
062	0.799956	0.841655	172	0.816372	0.832050
071	0.689715	0.766934	181	0.699702	0.725995
072	0.777362	0.859737	182	0.732595	0.751617
081	0.738437	0.775965	191	0.664499	0.778352
082	0.468984	0.682728	192	0.786277	0.879236
091	0.641242	0.700249	201	0.277371	0.281537
092	0.630586	0.764461	202	0.583610	0.762107
101	0.597931	0.779505	211	0.789382	0.800719
102	0.315227	0.577547	212	0.839367	0.858019
111	0.440272	0.588893	Average		
112	0.816059	0.861351	subject	0.873253	0.947330

Table C.15   Individual-subject Dimension Saliences from Aggregate-level INDSCAL Analysis of Direct Dissimilarities in Two and Three Dimensions (see Figure 3.3)

	Salience on Dimension				
Subject	1	2	1	2	3
011	0.54326	0.41057	0.49186	0.38113	0.26798
012	0.55556	0.53731	0.51176	0.51222	0.22836
021	0.63037	0.31048	0.55076	0.26487	0.41502
022	0.77662	0.26161	0.72658	0.23294	0.26086
031	0.73740	0.11979	0.73702	0.11957	0.00200
032	0.68350	0.39852	0.64201	0.37475	0.21634
041	0.56731	0.51743	0.49626	0.47672	0.37042
042	0.62643	0.54040	0.61214	0.53221	0.07453
051	0.80531	0.22026	0.74770	0.18725	0.30036
052	0.66561	0.30411	0.62070	0.27838	0.23415
061	0.88303	0.06442	0.82812	0.03297	0.28625
062	0.76446	0.23420	0.71300	0.20472	0.26828
071	0.64843	0.23381	0.58247	0.19602	0.34390
072	0.73597	0.24888	0.66374	0.20751	0.37655
081	0.57939	0.45673	0.53250	0.42987	0.24445
082	0.36587	0.29270	0.26829	0.23680	0.50876
091	0.54926	0.32987	0.49393	0.29817	0.28849
092	0.40888	0.47928	0.32388	0.43059	0.44314
101	0.53537	0.26525	0.43701	0.20890	0.51281
102	0.22703	0.21826	0.13185	0.16373	0.49623
111	0.34371	0.27449	0.26679	0.23043	0.40103
112	0.53713	0.61334	0.48292	0.58229	0.28263
121	0.41292	0.59942	0.33316	0.55373	0.41583
122	0.53397	0.40365	0.44014	0.34989	0.48921
131	0.46490	0.29844	0.42651	0.27645	0.20015
132	0.60182	0.51912	0.56878	0.50019	0.17223
141	0.41693	0.42336	0.33307	0.37532	0.43718
142	0.73594	0.24340	0.71876	0.23356	0.08954
151	0.43215	0.54763	0.36256	0.50776	0.36283
152	0.33823	0.57702	0.27482	0.54069	0.33057
161	0.32360	0.32851	0.21584	0.26678	0.56182
162	0.21564	0.33471	0.16771	0.30725	0.24988
171	0.66096	0.54846	0.63427	0.53317	0.13917
172	0.70918	0.40304	0.67756	0.38493	0.16484
181	0.38570	0.58306	0.34762	0.56125	0.19854
182	0.24739	0.68909	0.21434	0.67016	0.17229
191	0.25214	0.61433	0.17242	0.56866	0.41560
192	0.72681	0.29858	0.64942	0.25424	0.40347
201	0.18228	0.20871	0.17279	0.20328	0.04948
202	0.45068	0.36994	0.35429	0.31472	0.50256
211	0.57251	0.54238	0.54611	0.52725	0.13767
212	0.79623	0.26411	0.76124	0.24406	0.18245
Average subject	0.72185	0.48991	0.64834	0.44781	0.37689

Table C.16   Stimulus Coordinates from Aggregate-level INDSCAL Analysis of Direct Dissimilarities in Two and Three Dimensions (see Figure 3.4)

Stimulus	1	2	1	2	3
1	0.13205*	−0.34766*	0.13205	−0.34766	0.10673
2	−0.28440	−0.32395	−0.28440	−0.32395	0.15632
3	−0.34168	0.06387	−0.34168	0.06387	0.26267
4	0.34489	0.20219	0.34489	0.20219	−0.02802
5	0.05608	−0.34615	0.05608	−0.34615	−0.39787
6	−0.20603	0.32174	−0.20603	0.32174	0.13973
7	−0.39019	0.04713	−0.39019	0.04713	0.17461
8	0.24872	−0.24674	0.24872	−0.24674	0.27268
9	0.22994	−0.23202	0.22994	−0.23202	0.32503
10	−0.27864	−0.30509	−0.27864	−0.30509	0.21306
11	0.14865	0.10381	0.14865	0.10381	−0.46388
12	0.25016	0.24465	0.25016	0.24465	−0.24484
13	−0.25478	0.23934	−0.25478	0.23934	−0.25492
14	0.15518	0.27481	0.15518	0.27481	−0.33853
15	−0.31952	0.30406	−0.31952	0.30406	0.07726

*Option used to constrain two-dimensional solution coordinates to equal sub-space coordinates of three-dimensional solution.

Table C.17   Results of Max "r" Property Fitting of Average Ratings in the Three-dimensional INDSCAL Stimulus Space of Direct Dissimilarities Data

Property	1	2	3	Correlation Coefficient
1	−0.9429	0.3030	−0.1382	0.4736
2	0.7240	0.5380	−0.4318	0.8577
3	0.9155	−0.4003	−0.0388	0.7795
4	−0.8641	−0.4645	0.1941	0.9176
5	−0.9634	−0.1013	0.2483	0.6714
6	0.7992	0.2201	0.5593	0.6795
7	−0.5449	−0.7905	0.2795	0.8879
8	−0.3195	−0.8885	0.3294	0.9572
9	−0.7584	−0.5428	0.3608	0.8896
10	0.0957	0.9218	−0.3755	0.9570

Table C.18   Individual-subject Correlation Coefficients from Aggregate-level
INDSCAL Analysis of Derived Dissimilarities in Two and Three
Dimensions (see Table 3.2)

Subject	Correlation		Subject	Correlation	
	2 Dimensions	3 Dimensions		2 Dimensions	3 Dimensions
011	0.710594	0.803208	121	0.781565	0.872007
012	0.825912	0.839537	122	0.700738	0.750415
021	0.707267	0.819549	131	0.765495	0.897506
022	0.584700	0.632077	132	0.892946	0.895444
031	0.851130	0.876619	141	0.808780	0.859032
032	0.738354	0.786022	142	0.682786	0.882298
041	0.807779	0.835761	151	0.653092	0.691583
042	0.757142	0.770129	152	0.431031	0.638024
051	0.715743	0.787794	161	0.482301	0.541052
052	0.574234	0.796713	162	0.394192	0.706657
061	0.643982	0.675571	171	0.376298	0.386609
062	0.773195	0.843109	172	0.551164	0.617798
071	0.797754	0.903256	181	0.436052	0.785900
072	0.679694	0.747007	182	0.543747	0.594301
081	0.713454	0.751323	191	0.387476	0.395365
082	0.767666	0.789420	192	0.710442	0.728126
091	0.770161	0.839460	201	0.625633	0.628435
092	0.673665	0.736743	202	0.563948	0.830070
101	0.622687	0.643948	211	0.864876	0.872814
102	0.662126	0.798896	212	0.694334	0.711082
111	0.620220	0.812612	Average		
112	0.691065	0.854959	subject	0.834470	0.925955

Table C.19   Individual-Subject   Dimension   Saliences   from   Aggregate-level INDSCAL Analysis of Derived Dissimilarities in Two and Three Dimensions (see Figure 3.5)

Subject	Salience on Dimension				
	1	2	1	2	3
011	0.17758	0.67343	0.09978	0.60488	0.38966
012	0.56807	0.55413	0.53677	0.52655	0.15676
021	0.56468	0.38148	0.47865	0.30567	0.40389
022	0.43761	0.35308	0.38772	0.30912	0.24986
031	0.19774	0.81156	0.15414	0.77313	0.21839
032	0.54695	0.45258	0.49094	0.40323	0.28053
041	0.68250	0.37902	0.63794	0.33976	0.22318
042	0.28602	0.67765	0.25675	0.65187	0.14656
051	0.44311	0.52643	0.37472	0.46617	0.34252
052	0.49831	0.24690	0.38356	0.14578	0.57474
061	0.49792	0.36907	0.45550	0.33169	0.21246
062	0.64760	0.37198	0.57775	0.31044	0.34983
071	0.64801	0.41450	0.55999	0.33694	0.44086
072	0.52074	0.39564	0.45635	0.33890	0.32250
081	0.49349	0.47584	0.44455	0.43271	0.24510
082	0.38621	0.63209	0.34796	0.59840	0.19153
091	0.70009	0.26797	0.63070	0.20682	0.34757
092	0.48590	0.42794	0.42392	0.37333	0.31040
101	0.24860	0.55060	0.21450	0.52055	0.17078
102	0.38241	0.50966	0.28952	0.42781	0.46520
111	0.24261	0.55098	0.13351	0.45485	0.54640
112	0.53647	0.39329	0.43187	0.30112	0.52385
121	0.33621	0.67814	0.25585	0.60734	0.40245
122	0.19119	0.65844	0.13540	0.60928	0.27941
131	0.46726	0.56872	0.36990	0.48293	0.48760
132	0.88223	0.08286	0.86834	0.07062	0.06956
141	0.71271	0.32761	0.65255	0.27461	0.30127
142	0.31721	0.57882	0.20110	0.47651	0.58153
151	0.48335	0.40084	0.43607	0.35919	0.23676
152	0.38940	0.15523	0.29166	0.06911	0.48955
161	0.45313	0.13173	0.40218	0.08684	0.25518
162	0.34295	0.16790	0.22109	0.06052	0.61036
171	0.28010	0.22906	0.26167	0.21282	0.09231
172	0.41653	0.32795	0.35854	0.27685	0.29045
181	0.14629	0.39879	0.01043	0.27908	0.68043
182	0.37152	0.36733	0.32168	0.32342	0.24962
191	0.18330	0.32647	0.16697	0.31208	0.08178
192	0.43458	0.52704	0.40144	0.49783	0.16598
201	0.60872	0.10246	0.59641	0.09161	0.06168
202	0.44399	0.31275	0.31743	0.20123	0.63386
211	0.64935	0.51981	0.62494	0.49831	0.12222
212	0.50962	0.43109	0.47774	0.40300	0.15966
Average subject	0.58467	0.54878	0.50108	0.47597	0.41755

Table C.20   Stimulus Coordinates from Aggregate-level INDSCAL Analysis of Derived Dissimilarities in Two and Three Dimensions (see Figure 3.6)

Stimulus	Dimension				
	1	2	1	2	3
1	−0.51900*	−0.29090*	−0.51900	−0.29090	−0.42022
2	−0.22880	0.22710	−0.22880	0.22710	0.33340
3	−0.11933	0.24117	−0.11933	0.24117	0.09368
4	0.11267	−0.40438	0.11267	−0.40438	−0.07927
5	−0.13589	−0.04719	−0.13589	−0.04719	0.36169
6	0.05687	0.17373	0.05687	0.17373	−0.02211
7	−0.00715	0.47111	−0.00715	0.47111	−0.04783
8	−0.12624	−0.00639	−0.12624	−0.00639	0.31017
9	−0.11818	−0.08986	−0.11818	−0.08986	0.28494
10	−0.26984	0.23714	−0.26984	0.23714	0.31505
11	0.23014	−0.24176	0.23014	−0.24176	−0.20495
12	0.49305	−0.26476	0.49305	−0.26476	−0.32241
13	0.21285	−0.28519	0.21285	−0.28519	−0.22068
14	0.43055	−0.05263	0.43055	−0.05263	−0.28959
15	−0.01170	0.33281	−0.01170	0.33281	−0.09187

*Option used to constrain two-dimensional solution coordinates to equal sub-space coordinates of three-dimensional solution.

Table C.21   Means, Standard Deviations, and Pairwise Correlation Matrix of the 10 Background Characteristics (see Table 3.4)

Variable	Mean	Standard Deviation
Sex	0.500	0.506
Age	26.810	6.500
NChild	0.571	1.063
Ovrwgt	0.452	0.504
Pctowt	4.048	5.387
Wdaybf	0.881	0.328
Wendbf	0.262	0.445
Coffee	0.786	0.415
Tea	0.476	0.505
Milk	0.405	0.497

	Correlation Matrix									
	1	2	3	4	5	6	7	8	9	10
Variable	Sex	Age	NChild	Ovrwgt	Pctowt	Wdaybf	Wendbf	Coffee	Tea	Milk
Sex	1.000									
Age	0.089	1.000								
NChild	0.000	0.828	1.000							
Ovrwgt	0.144	0.325	0.417	1.000						
Pctowt	0.197	0.498	0.426	0.837	1.000					
Wdaybf	−0.074	−0.057	−0.150	0.039	0.072	1.000				
Wendbf	−0.054	−0.100	0.037	−0.215	−0.280	0.219	1.000			
Coffee	0.058	0.138	0.118	0.125	0.223	0.166	0.047	1.000		
Tea	−0.095	−0.254	−0.110	−0.196	−0.322	−0.091	0.625	0.033	1.000	
Milk	−0.049	−0.232	−0.125	0.225	0.093	0.153	0.060	−0.042	0.185	1.000

Table C.22   Euclidean Distances Based on Direct Dissimilarities between Husbands and Wives

Subject*	011 121	021 131	031 141	041 151	051 161	061 171	071 181	081 191	091 201	101 211	111
012	22.81 25.91	27.36 29.28	30.86 29.90	28.52 27.94	27.50 33.19	29.21 28.35	29.21 28.86	24.37 29.27	25.57 41.29	32.44 24.19	34.87
022	26.51 29.00	21.83 35.17	30.08 26.16	25.71 29.41	20.24 33.35	19.00 25.98	24.51 29.19	25.36 33.16	25.27 42.16	23.96 27.29	29.75
032	26.10 27.98	21.51 33.87	31.82 26.14	26.62 28.01	25.10 34.13	25.07 27.05	24.72 27.01	24.15 29.96	20.33 41.89	28.38 24.23	31.03
042	24.63 26.28	25.14 31.27	30.39 28.66	28.33 22.61	26.19 35.57	27.61 27.24	32.45 25.89	22.95 31.58	27.75 39.61	33.56 27.10	36.00
052	34.11 29.24	31.46 38.24	32.00 34.30	27.74 33.34	27.13 35.25	25.45 26.08	24.84 34.01	31.09 33.37	34.42 42.69	27.17 31.14	32.29
062	30.20 30.53	26.26 31.50	28.90 27.92	28.12 31.54	23.11 34.01	20.02 27.30	29.45 33.29	26.39 34.50	28.42 40.23	29.85 28.77	36.29
072	28.16 29.45	22.71 35.14	30.73 29.43	25.38 30.99	23.92 32.59	21.97 28.18	25.77 30.82	27.95 34.16	25.96 42.65	24.57 30.65	29.54
082	30.20 30.33	25.00 35.92	36.70 23.44	30.50 29.08	29.33 31.73	30.74 36.57	28.48 29.32	30.79 32.21	24.98 43.61	28.00 31.80	30.80
092	26.36 23.65	26.39 34.07	32.60 23.66	26.53 27.41	29.28 31.84	30.98 32.48	28.15 25.91	27.57 27.81	18.03 39.84	29.84 26.43	31.97
102	39.34 36.25	35.32 39.35	43.47 38.87	38.34 34.07	39.07 38.05	38.39 36.04	36.53 39.76	38.84 39.22	39.65 44.30	32.85 42.11	34.22
112	23.28 21.57	22.98 32.53	29.29 24.68	24.81 22.89	26.33 31.77	27.39 24.98	27.52 27.04	21.26 26.98	22.94 40.89	27.93 24.92	33.65
122	28.25 22.69	26.32 37.32	33.02 26.32	23.78 27.45	26.33 28.84	27.03 28.14	24.88 26.90	27.57 29.58	24.24 40.72	25.09 27.67	28.29
132	33.11 29.60	31.60 33.69	33.42 31.23	27.50 31.37	29.59 32.93	30.35 25.83	31.87 35.38	30.24 31.01	31.99 42.37	33.46 22.89	37.72
142	31.00 32.96	29.66 40.35	30.87 34.79	29.49 31.51	26.24 36.30	24.65 24.76	30.08 32.17	29.78 37.51	33.23 44.14	31.29 33.82	33.06
152	26.76 25.27	24.91 32.96	34.03 28.97	32.89 15.07	30.58 34.63	34.00 30.35	31.04 26.16	24.65 30.08	27.91 42.91	28.34 30.69	28.76
162	37.44 35.50	37.24 43.50	41.85 34.76	37.11 38.35	39.96 35.68	40.97 39.74	38.26 33.67	34.99 36.52	37.72 41.52	33.36 37.91	35.24
172	29.09 28.66	27.05 38.30	30.33 35.23	28.83 29.45	24.01 34.26	23.43 13.75	25.18 31.54	27.52 33.91	31.69 41.27	26.16 30.46	32.19
182	35.23 28.74	37.02 39.15	38.40 32.63	30.23 30.63	36.73 33.27	37.56 31.80	36.27 25.58	33.79 32.25	36.93 42.09	36.95 30.94	35.60
192	30.73 28.33	26.88 32.34	31.59 28.68	24.01 31.38	22.99 31.56	21.21 27.09	28.89 33.82	28.93 29.58	30.41 40.44	29.32 26.98	35.44
202	27.74 24.11	24.85 34.05	30.63 25.83	31.42 26.01	27.08 30.72	29.00 30.39	23.96 28.24	30.29 31.96	24.29 43.00	24.53 30.19	29.78
212	24.55 30.19	22.33 33.54	27.09 31.32	30.25 28.38	16.84 35.61	19.21 24.77	26.44 30.38	25.18 35.19	28.66 41.80	25.22 27.69	32.16

*Rows represent wives and columns husbands.

Table C.23   Subgroup Compositions at Ten Levels of Hierarchical Clustering of the 42 Respondents (see Table 3.7)

Subject	Group Level								
	2	3	4	5	6	7	8	9	10
011	2*	3	3	3	3	7	7	7	7
012	2	3	3	3	3	7	7	7	10
021	2	2	2	2	6	6	6	6	6
022	2	2	2	2	6	6	6	6	6
031	2	2	2	2	2	2	2	2	2
032	2	2	3	3	3	3	3	3	3
041	1	3	3	3	3	7	7	7	10
042	2	3	3	3	3	3	3	3	3
051	2	2	2	2	6	6	6	6	6
052	2	2	2	2	6	6	6	6	6
061	2	2	2	2	2	2	2	2	2
062	2	2	2	2	6	6	6	6	6
071	2	2	2	2	6	6	6	6	6
072	2	2	2	2	6	6	6	6	6
081	2	3	3	3	3	7	7	7	10
082	1	1	4	4	4	4	4	4	4
091	2	2	3	3	6	7	7	7	7
092	1	1	4	4	4	4	8	9	9
101	1	1	4	4	4	4	8	8	8
102	1	1	4	4	4	4	4	4	4
121	1	1	4	4	4	4	4	4	4
122	1	3	3	3	3	7	7	7	10
131	1	3	1	5	5	5	5	9	9
132	1	1	4	4	4	4	8	8	8
141	2	3	3	1	1	7	7	7	7
142	2	3	3	3	3	3	3	3	3
151	1	1	4	4	4	4	8	8	8
152	2	2	2	2	2	2	2	2	2
161	1	3	1	5	5	5	5	9	9
162	1	3	1	5	5	5	5	9	9
171	1	1	4	4	4	4	4	4	4
172	1	1	1	1	1	1	1	1	1
181	2	3	3	3	3	3	3	3	3
182	2	2	3	3	3	3	3	3	3
191	1	3	1	5	5	5	5	5	5
192	1	3	1	5	5	5	5	5	5
201	1	1	1	5	5	5	5	9	9
202	2	2	2	2	6	6	6	6	6
211	1	1	1	1	1	1	1	1	1
212	1	1	4	4	4	4	8	8	8
221	2	3	3	3	3	3	3	3	3
222	2	2	2	2	2	2	2	2	2

*Group assignment.

Table C.24   Individual-subject Correlation Coefficients from Group A and B
INDSCAL Analysis of Direct Dissimilarities in Two Dimensions
(see Table 3.9)

Group A		Group B	
Subject	Correlation	Subject	Correlation
041	0.709212	011	0.783921
082	0.688394	012	0.683012
092	0.800253	021	0.885833
101	0.749620	022	0.889764
102	0.425502	031	0.711632
111	0.675219	032	0.874761
112	0.831968	042	0.739796
121	0.805586	051	0.876313
122	0.760859	052	0.635218
141	0.775378	061	0.879043
151	0.785728	062	0.790245
152	0.781771	071	0.835863
161	0.510602	072	0.847318
162	0.485741	081	0.750681
181	0.732004	091	0.912088
182	0.856493	131	0.550752
191	0.641527	132	0.588966
201	0.218143	142	0.749181
202	0.742025	171	0.736083
Average		172	0.813369
subject	0.933193	192	0.738330
		211	0.677648
		212	0.882585
		Average	
		subject	0.933643

Table C.25   Individual-subject Dimension Saliences and Stimulus Coordinates
from Group A INDSCAL Analysis of Direct Dissimilarities in Two
Dimensions (see Figure 3.8)

| | Salience | | | Coordinate | |
| | Dimension | | | Dimension | |
Subject	1	2	Stimulus	1	2
041	0.57346	0.44343	1	0.06210	0.24813
082	0.67419	0.25774	2	−0.23456	0.33820
092	0.65668	0.37568	3	−0.30538	−0.18011
101	0.79982	0.16955	4	0.20859	−0.13853
102	0.55572	0.14746	5	0.24472	0.27412
111	0.62100	0.25617	6	−0.09989	−0.34652
112	0.54702	0.50200	7	−0.33265	−0.02090
121	0.59190	0.50549	8	−0.19974	0.34439
122	0.71277	0.30595	9	−0.24291	0.31028
141	0.68819	0.35432	10	−0.26674	0.29333
151	0.46617	0.52555	11	0.37506	−0.12675
152	0.48539	0.53689	12	0.31752	−0.20391
161	0.55405	0.28991	13	0.29752	−0.21015
162	0.30366	0.34506	14	0.32080	−0.24126
181	0.37969	0.60491	15	−0.14446	−0.34033
182	0.20088	0.69238			
191	0.47715	0.49810			
201	0.09544	0.16638			
202	0.69723	0.26677			
Average					
subject	0.72692	0.50086			

Table C.26   Individual-subject Dimension Saliences and Stimulus Coordinates from Group B INDSCAL Analysis of Direct Dissimilarities in Two Dimensions (see Figure 3.9)

| | Salience | | | Coordinate | |
| | Dimension | | | Dimension | |
Subject	1	2	Stimulus	1	2
011	0.29591	0.53608	1	0.23015	−0.06915
012	0.28623	0.48526	2	−0.30177	0.27497
021	0.28978	0.68959	3	−0.31292	0.29596
022	0.47950	0.55760	4	0.30637	−0.29631
031	0.59757	0.29749	5	0.04744	−0.07430
032	0.36314	0.58766	6	−0.19558	0.05601
042	0.48210	0.30795	7	−0.43914	0.22999
051	0.55750	0.47783	8	0.31044	0.18059
052	0.56308	0.25805	9	0.28342	0.17731
061	0.63127	0.47630	10	−0.30190	0.26658
062	0.43769	0.53296	11	0.05683	−0.38432
071	0.34118	0.64099	12	0.25432	−0.29004
072	0.43553	0.56367	13	0.15850	−0.38448
081	0.36944	0.42881	14	0.13267	−0.28103
091	0.15441	0.75425	15	−0.22883	0.29820
131	0.21608	0.41205			
132	0.38833	0.34854			
142	0.75763	0.11177			
171	0.53205	0.30903			
172	0.59660	0.32168			
192	0.39681	0.56328			
211	0.34117	0.41192			
212	0.60488	0.39968			
Average subject	0.54706	0.56799			

Table C.27   Average Ratings on the 10 Rating Scales for Group A

	Stimulus														
Property	1	2	3	4	5	6	7	8	9	10	11	12	13	14	15
1	1.79	2.47	3.00	1.74	3.32	3.58	2.16	2.53	3.00	2.32	1.84	2.47	1.89	2.42	3.32
2	3.95	2.05	3.42	4.11	4.00	4.95	1.89	3.26	3.37	2.26	4.53	5.47	3.89	4.63	3.32
3	5.11	2.68	3.05	4.53	4.11	3.58	2.53	3.26	4.16	2.63	4.47	3.37	4.84	3.00	3.21
4	2.32	3.37	2.89	2.21	3.42	3.16	3.26	3.26	2.58	4.05	2.00	1.95	2.21	2.37	3.05
5	2.16	5.95	4.26	3.84	4.47	4.26	6.05	5.42	5.37	4.68	4.42	3.32	3.58	3.74	4.84
6	3.47	4.26	4.26	5.79	3.47	4.58	2.74	4.58	5.05	3.68	3.63	4.05	3.89	3.32	3.37
7	2.95	4.84	3.84	2.89	4.11	3.11	5.00	4.47	4.37	5.21	3.00	2.05	2.89	2.53	3.21
8	3.58	4.47	3.37	3.00	4.16	2.84	3.37	4.32	3.84	4.68	2.58	2.05	2.68	2.53	3.42
9	2.63	4.95	4.79	2.95	4.21	4.00	5.00	4.63	4.58	4.79	3.79	2.79	2.79	3.53	4.42
10	2.79	1.74	3.53	3.95	2.63	4.37	3.00	1.89	1.95	1.79	4.16	5.42	4.32	4.58	4.21

Table C.28   Average Ratings on the 10 Rating Scales for Group B

	Stimulus														
Property	1	2	3	4	5	6	7	8	9	10	11	12	13	14	15
1	1.30	2.26	2.91	1.48	3.61	3.87	2.87	2.57	2.83	2.26	2.43	2.35	1.70	3.22	3.39
2	3.39	1.91	2.70	4.00	4.13	4.00	1.91	3.17	3.83	2.04	4.52	5.35	3.70	5.00	3.30
3	4.96	3.57	2.83	4.70	4.61	3.26	2.09	3.91	4.65	3.43	3.74	3.17	4.30	2.87	2.65
4	3.09	3.65	3.65	2.00	3.22	3.22	4.00	3.30	2.91	4.26	2.17	2.00	2.43	2.61	3.70
5	2.30	5.96	5.26	3.96	4.96	5.09	6.04	4.78	4.57	4.87	4.00	3.43	3.35	3.96	5.83
6	2.91	3.78	3.96	5.43	3.78	4.00	2.52	4.35	4.65	3.96	4.09	4.35	4.04	3.52	3.22
7	3.48	5.52	4.43	3.35	4.70	3.43	4.57	4.74	4.83	5.83	3.30	2.26	3.22	2.87	4.22
8	4.57	5.30	4.61	3.52	4.43	3.43	4.13	4.70	4.43	5.26	3.13	2.52	3.13	2.48	3.78
9	3.26	5.70	4.09	2.65	4.04	4.17	4.78	4.57	4.61	5.57	2.87	2.39	2.39	2.70	4.09
10	2.43	1.91	2.96	3.91	2.22	3.74	3.83	2.22	2.09	1.91	4.78	5.57	4.35	4.78	3.70

Table C.29   Stimulus Coordinates from Group A and Group B INDSCAL Analysis of Average Ratings Data in Two Dimensions (see Figure 3.16)

	Coordinate on Dimension	
Stimulus	1	2
1	−0.46273	0.11586
2	0.29258	−0.41498
3	0.16771	−0.10047
4	−0.36709	0.21356
5	0.00888	−0.10873
6	0.08039	0.10858
7	0.47921	−0.25488
8	0.07516	−0.22741
9	−0.04169	−0.16970
10	0.22460	−0.39618
11	−0.15404	0.24221
12	−0.22757	0.46615
13	−0.30804	0.25848
14	−0.03522	0.29817
15	0.26784	−0.03066

SUPPORTING MATERIAL FOR CHAPTER 4

In this section we present supporting computer output for material covered in Chapter 4.

Table C.30 Stimulus and Subject Coordinates from MDPREF Analyses in Two and Three Dimensions (see Figure 4.2)*

Dimensions

			Subjects			
1	−1.0000	−0.9962	−0.8508	−0.9025	−0.6676	−0.9680
	0.7875	0.2633	−0.9606	−0.9961	−0.9956	−0.7588
	0.6824	−0.9912	−0.4251	−0.4911	−0.9901	−0.9993
	−0.0688	0.9980	−0.3194	−0.3807	0.4067	0.9918
	0.2219	0.5008				
2	0.0060	0.0868	0.5254	−0.4307	0.7445	−0.2510
	0.6163	0.9647	0.2781	−0.0878	−0.0940	0.6513
	0.7309	−0.1323	0.9052	0.8711	0.1400	0.0384
	0.9976	0.0628	0.9476	0.9247	0.9135	−0.1281
	0.9751	0.8656				
			Stimuli			
1	−0.2639	−0.3225	−0.0540	0.2492	0.0153	0.1893
	0.2635	0.3829	0.2454	0.3810	−0.1623	
2	0.4650	−0.1353	−0.3772	0.5016	−0.1449	−0.3239
	0.0751	−0.0137	0.3201	−0.2920	−0.1496	
			Subjects			
1	−0.9985	−0.9550	−0.8242	−0.9024	−0.6420	−0.9559
	0.7830	0.2610	−0.6800	−0.9612	−0.9832	−0.7581
	0.4110	−0.9893	−0.4227	−0.4533	−0.7525	−0.9971
	−0.0334	0.5483	−0.3138	−0.3763	0.2293	0.3807
	0.2206	0.4887				
2	0.0060	0.0832	0.5090	−0.4306	0.7160	−0.2478
	0.6128	0.9561	0.1969	−0.0847	−0.0928	0.6507
	0.4402	−0.1320	0.9001	0.8040	0.1064	0.0383
	0.4848	0.0345	0.9311	0.9139	0.5151	−0.0492
	0.9691	0.8447				
3	0.0538	0.2847	0.2481	−0.0172	0.2743	0.1577
	−0.1068	0.1332	0.7063	0.2624	0.1574	−0.0444
	0.7983	0.0615	0.1057	0.3849	0.6499	0.0657
	0.8740	0.8356	−0.1859	−0.1524	0.8259	0.9234
	−0.1108	0.2182				
			Stimuli			
1	−0.2639	−0.3225	−0.0540	0.2492	0.0153	0.1893
	0.2635	0.3829	0.2454	0.3810	−0.1623	
2	0.4650	−0.1353	−0.3772	0.5016	−0.1449	−0.3239
	0.0751	−0.0137	0.3201	−0.2920	−0.1496	
3	0.3755	−0.3770	0.1813	0.0287	0.2126	0.2072
	0.1392	−0.3346	−0.0315	−0.0399	0.4722	

*Vector directions in Figure 4.2 represent reflections of subject coordinate values. This table should be read row-wise.

Table C.30   (Concluded)

Dimensions

	Subjects			
1	−0.9997	−0.9966	−0.9112	−0.8950
	−0.9570	−0.9733	−0.2962	−0.9371
	0.8076	−0.7485	−0.9598	−0.9981
	0.9719	−0.7322	0.6542	0.6875
2	0.0252	0.0821	0.4120	0.4461
	−0.2902	0.2294	−0.9551	−0.3490
	0.5898	0.6631	−0.2807	−0.0616
	−0.2352	0.6811	−0.7563	0.7262
	Stimuli			
1	−0.3762	−0.1299	−0.0827	−0.3351
2	−0.0854	0.1132	−0.0419	0.0888
	Subjects			
1	−0.9732	−0.9212	−0.8926	−0.8679
	−0.9511	−0.9605	−0.2851	−0.9362
	0.7929	−0.5737	−0.6390	−0.9733
	0.7281	−0.6793	0.5760	0.6767
2	0.0245	0.0759	0.4036	0.4326
	−0.2884	0.2264	−0.9192	−0.3486
	0.5791	0.5082	−0.1869	−0.0601
	−0.1762	0.6319	−0.6658	0.7148
3	−0.2285	0.3816	0.2010	−0.2442
	0.1106	−0.1616	0.2716	0.0443
	0.1896	−0.6423	0.7462	0.2214
	0.6625	−0.3732	0.4742	0.1765
	Stimuli			
1	−0.3762	−0.1299	−0.0827	−0.3351
2	−0.0854	0.1132	−0.0419	0.0888
3	−0.0795	−0.3001	−0.3660	−0.0881

Table C.31   Stimulus and Subject Coordinates for Rational Starting
Configuration M-D-SCAL V Analysis in Three Dimensions
(see Figures 4.3 and 4.5)

	Dimension				Dimension		
Stimulus	1	2	3	Subject	1	2	3
1	0.4237	0.5015	0.3257	011	−0.4793	0.2023	−0.0482
2	0.5179	−0.1457	−0.3269	012	−0.5423	0.0704	−0.1000
3	0.0867	−0.4068	0.1572	021	−0.2505	−0.1415	0.1616
4	−0.4002	0.5408	0.0249	022	−0.4697	0.2904	−0.0975
5	−0.0246	−0.1562	0.1842	031	−0.5102	−0.2262	−0.0484
6	−0.3040	−0.3491	0.1797	032	−0.5402	0.0052	−0.1174
7	0.6041	−0.0920	−0.0690	041	−0.5402	0.0052	−0.1174
8	0.2086	0.1220	−0.2603	042	−0.4473	−0.0943	0.0034
9	0.1328	−0.0452	−0.3173	051	−0.1308	−0.2556	−0.0649
10	0.5380	0.0957	−0.0765	052	−0.3220	−0.1637	0.0282
11	−0.4230	0.0809	0.1208	061	0.4609	−0.1330	0.0045
12	−0.6148	−0.0147	−0.2902	062	0.1002	−0.3005	0.0033
13	−0.3941	0.3451	−0.0272	071	0.0120	−0.0685	−0.3115
14	−0.6118	−0.3149	−0.0347	072	−0.5499	−0.0829	−0.0680
15	0.2607	−0.1614	0.4095	081	−0.5423	0.0704	−0.1000
				082	−0.4366	−0.1063	0.0393
				091	−0.5423	0.0704	−0.1000
				092	−0.5102	−0.2262	−0.0484
				101	−0.2047	0.1892	0.0521
				102	−0.2668	0.1508	−0.1926
				111	0.1933	−0.2362	0.0048
				112	−0.4783	0.1023	0.0370
				121	−0.1832	−0.2926	0.1022
				122	−0.0911	0.0207	−0.2893
				131	−0.2764	0.0627	−0.1432
				132	−0.5402	0.0052	−0.1174
				141	0.2087	−0.1157	−0.1533
				142	−0.2764	−0.3569	0.1007
				151	−0.4697	0.2904	−0.0975
				152	−0.4697	0.2904	−0.0975
				161	−0.3646	−0.1249	−0.2141
				162	0.4435	−0.0386	−0.2187
				171	−0.2764	−0.3569	0.1007
				172	−0.2764	−0.3569	0.1007
				181	0.0407	−0.0506	−0.2255
				182	0.4435	−0.0366	−0.2187
				191	0.3962	−0.0317	−0.2402
				192	−0.4763	0.0370	0.0196
				201	0.5533	−0.0473	−0.1575
				202	0.5533	−0.0473	−0.1575
				211	0.1002	−0.3005	0.0033
				212	0.3809	−0.1523	−0.0821

Table C.32   Stimulus and Subject Coordinates from M-D-SCAL V Analysis (Row Split Option) in Two and Three Dimensions (see Figure 4.3)*

Stimulus	Dimension 1	2	1	2	3
1	0.033	−2.021	0.029	−1.683	−0.592
2	1.251	0.413	1.307	0.081	−0.136
3	0.264	1.288	0.247	0.564	−1.081
4	−1.093	−0.464	−1.206	−0.300	0.714
5	−0.518	−1.038	−0.182	−0.452	−1.107
6	−0.799	0.917	−0.546	0.714	−0.902
7	1.250	0.692	1.368	0.273	−0.018
8	0.416	−1.134	0.579	−0.970	0.672
9	0.547	−1.066	0.650	−0.917	0.535
10	1.282	0.513	1.416	0.349	0.253
11	−1.143	−0.205	−0.914	−0.638	−0.465
12	−0.957	−0.499	−0.575	0.017	1.037
13	−1.006	−0.579	−0.820	−0.861	−0.291
14	−1.055	0.369	−0.932	0.213	−0.671
15	−0.230	1.333	−0.310	0.368	−1.433

Subject	Dimension 1	2	1	2	3
011	−0.833	−0.328	−0.335	0.102	0.437
012	0.056	0.054	−0.319	0.366	0.348
021	0.095	0.062	0.085	0.040	0.023
022	−1.234	−0.763	−0.831	−0.496	0.341
031	0.075	0.092	−0.078	0.339	0.183
032	−1.059	−0.267	−0.758	−0.294	0.242
041	−0.850	0.033	−0.619	0.061	0.019
042	0.058	0.045	−0.080	0.134	0.252
051	0.069	0.076	−0.063	0.079	0.042
052	−0.345	0.255	−0.516	0.238	−0.076
061	1.123	0.784	1.056	0.128	−0.847
062	0.327	1.062	0.521	0.588	−0.582

*Also, see Figure C.9 on page 249.

Table C.32   (Concluded)

| Subject | Dimension | | | | |
	1	2	1	2	3
071	-0.524	0.018	-0.413	-0.030	-0.024
072	-0.623	-0.478	-0.231	-0.268	0.131
081	-0.792	-0.288	-0.669	0.114	0.385
082	0.072	0.069	-0.011	0.008	-0.110
091	-1.126	-0.069	-0.892	-0.058	0.262
092	-1.041	0.364	-0.867	0.644	0.364
101	0.939	-0.576	0.397	-0.552	0.570
102	-0.643	-0.060	-0.721	0.085	0.195
111	0.877	-0.370	-0.206	-0.237	-0.159
112	-1.044	0.089	-0.845	0.097	0.154
121	-0.008	-0.006	0.055	-0.123	-0.195
122	0.207	-0.468	0.190	-0.533	0.900
131	0.083	0.054	-0.010	0.168	0.209
132	0.069	0.075	-0.476	0.074	0.299
141	0.567	-0.399	0.483	-0.478	-0.672
142	-0.693	1.061	-0.834	0.517	-0.749
151	0.083	0.054	-0.144	0.322	0.486
152	-0.670	0.027	-0.376	0.152	0.162
161	0.478	-0.428	0.214	-0.090	0.759
162	1.296	-0.394	1.220	-0.293	0.631
171	0.069	0.184	-0.048	0.747	-0.031
172	0.071	0.169	-0.059	0.616	-0.020
181	0.121	0.088	0.456	0.175	0.560
182	1.196	-0.398	1.026	-0.332	0.407
191	1.477	-0.619	1.253	-0.585	0.632
192	0.087	0.089	-0.402	-0.037	-0.745
201	1.375	0.393	1.370	0.236	-0.026
202	1.243	0.365	1.076	0.163	-0.491
211	0.382	1.124	0.255	1.050	-0.384
212	0.746	0.708	0.625	0.406	-0.396

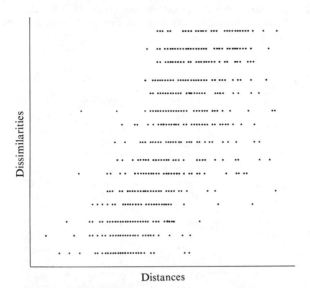

Figure C.9   Shepard Diagram Based on Three-space Solution from M-D-SCAL V Row Split Analysis (see Figure 4.4)

Figure C.10 Shepard Diagram Based on Three-space Solution from M-D-SCAL V Row Comparability Analysis (see Figure 4.6)

Table C.33   Stimulus and Subject Coordinates from M-D-SCAL V Analysis (Row Comparability Option) in Two and Three Dimensions (see Figure 4.5)*

Stimulus	Dimension				
	1	2	1	2	3
1	0.980	1.861	0.856	1.236	0.661
2	1.259	−0.144	1.222	−0.085	−0.004
3	0.399	−1.178	0.337	−1.109	0.471
4	−0.982	1.116	−0.757	1.147	−0.494
5	0.531	−1.324	0.475	−0.085	1.129
6	−0.454	−1.029	−0.247	−0.699	0.855
7	1.500	0.106	1.206	0.215	0.559
8	1.063	0.727	0.529	0.542	−1.241
9	1.102	0.158	0.500	−0.154	−1.270
10	1.528	0.488	1.186	0.490	0.491
11	−0.680	1.036	−0.251	0.548	0.974
12	−0.533	0.445	−0.542	0.423	−0.454
13	−0.770	1.021	−0.181	0.820	0.790
14	−0.720	−0.449	−0.747	−0.601	0.141
15	0.146	−1.744	0.485	−0.283	1.322

Subject	Dimension				
	1	2	1	2	3
011	−0.556	0.407	−0.602	0.526	0.043
012	−0.741	0.106	−0.692	0.117	−0.232
021	−0.399	−0.185	−0.577	0.142	0.629
022	−0.592	0.489	−0.610	0.629	−0.003
031	−0.527	−0.559	−0.405	−0.502	−0.105
032	−0.744	0.299	−0.758	0.282	0.030
041	−0.712	−0.003	−0.707	0.037	0.072
042	−0.644	0.203	−0.691	0.124	−0.009
051	−0.459	−0.353	−0.252	−0.670	−0.325
052	−0.745	−0.474	−0.679	−0.382	0.131
061	1.121	−0.694	1.083	−0.707	0.234
062	0.261	−0.594	0.613	−0.881	−0.019

*Also, see Figure C.10 on page 249.

Table C.33   (Concluded)

Subject	Dimension				
	1	2	1	2	3
071	0.022	−0.055	0.105	−0.093	−0.560
072	−0.602	0.209	−0.719	0.189	0.030
081	−0.692	0.168	−0.715	0.277	−0.023
082	−0.524	−0.580	−0.472	−0.444	0.362
091	−0.610	0.413	−0.681	0.375	−0.132
092	−0.658	−0.120	−0.629	−0.205	−0.093
101	−0.155	1.102	−0.065	1.074	0.134
102	−0.465	0.336	−0.400	0.404	−0.345
111	0.839	−0.318	0.788	−0.455	−0.314
112	−0.826	0.257	−0.789	0.357	0.204
121	0.189	−0.679	0.126	−0.805	−0.044
122	0.030	−0.197	−0.003	−0.155	−0.663
131	−0.378	0.361	−0.483	0.308	−0.372
132	−0.639	0.309	−0.686	0.245	−0.022
141	0.959	−0.475	0.800	−0.393	−0.389
142	−0.559	−0.527	−0.494	−0.606	0.227
151	−0.492	0.374	−0.525	0.422	−0.418
152	−0.785	0.228	−0.718	0.441	0.043
161	0.243	0.046	0.082	−0.207	−0.696
162	1.092	0.345	0.894	0.138	−0.552
171	−0.398	−0.680	−0.157	−0.843	0.103
172	−0.512	−0.613	−0.367	−0.727	0.108
181	0.710	0.214	0.496	0.019	−0.600
182	0.988	0.564	0.909	0.211	−0.596
191	1.150	0.760	0.993	0.192	−0.493
192	−0.532	−0.479	−0.498	0.135	0.790
201	0.677	0.988	0.987	0.633	−0.087
202	1.256	−0.542	1.256	−0.308	0.115
211	0.110	−0.571	0.278	−0.757	−0.025
212	0.931	−0.570	0.895	−0.543	−0.070

Table C.34   Stimulus Coordinates for Rational Starting Configuration from Parametric Mapping Analysis in Two and Three Dimensions (see Figure 4.7)

Stimulus	Dimension				
	1	2	1	2	3
1	0.11177	0.13229	0.13513	0.15995	0.10388
2	0.13662	-0.03843	0.16518	-0.04647	-0.10426
3	0.02287	-0.10731	0.02765	-0.12974	0.05014
4	-0.10557	0.14266	-0.12764	0.17248	0.00794
5	-0.00649	-0.04120	-0.00785	-0.04982	0.05875
6	-0.08019	-0.09209	-0.09696	-0.11134	0.05731
7	0.15936	-0.02427	0.19267	-0.02934	-0.02200
8	0.05503	0.03218	0.06653	0.03891	-0.08302
9	0.03503	-0.01192	0.04235	-0.01442	-0.10120
10	0.14192	0.02525	0.17159	0.03052	-0.02440
11	-0.11158	0.02134	-0.13491	0.02580	0.03853
12	-0.16218	-0.00388	-0.19608	-0.00469	-0.09255
13	-0.10396	0.09104	-0.12569	0.11006	-0.00867
14	-0.16139	-0.08307	-0.19512	-0.10043	-0.01106
15	0.06877	-0.04258	0.08315	-0.05148	0.13061

Table C.35   Stimulus Coordinates from Parametric Mapping in Two and Three Dimensions (see Figure 4.7)

Stimulus	Dimension				
	1	2	1	2	3
1	0.14630	0.21307	0.15540	0.19563	0.05783
2	0.19271	-0.01278	0.17944	-0.05570	-0.07623
3	-0.00108	-0.15642	0.02665	-0.16796	0.04353
4	-0.15137	0.16502	-0.15935	0.17966	-0.00931
5	-0.01219	-0.06336	-0.01867	-0.01984	0.12143
6	-0.12575	-0.10685	-0.11969	-0.12488	0.03051
7	0.21634	-0.02901	0.21780	-0.05763	-0.03056
8	0.08636	0.05398	0.06863	0.04130	-0.09950
9	0.05976	0.02072	0.04489	-0.00663	-0.09986
10	0.21846	0.01015	0.22721	0.01726	-0.03199
11	-0.13863	0.02658	-0.14771	0.02945	0.04286
12	-0.24783	-0.01537	-0.23762	-0.04665	-0.07585
13	-0.14198	0.12048	-0.15516	0.12566	-0.00960
14	-0.20160	-0.06544	-0.20222	-0.09126	-0.01104
15	0.10050	-0.16078	0.12039	-0.01841	0.14777

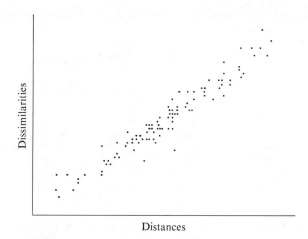

Figure C.11   **Shepard Diagram Based on Three-space Solution from Parametric Mapping (see Figure 4.8)**

Table C.36   First Six Subjects' Dissimilarities in Overall Preference Rankings (see Figure 4.10)

Subject	011	012	021	022	031	032
011	0.0	12.880	15.620	12.000	21.540	14.900
012	12.880	0.0	17.780	13.110	15.360	11.140
021	15.620	17.780	0.0	18.490	18.440	16.250
022	12.000	13.110	18.490	0.0	21.860	8.370
031	21.540	15.360	18.440	21.860	0.0	19.490
032	14.900	11.140	16.250	8.370	19.490	0.0

Table C.37   Stimulus Coordinates from TORSCA 8 Analysis in Two and Three Dimensions

Subject	Dimension				
	1	2	1	2	3
011	0.453	−0.003	0.477	−0.016	−0.218
012	0.371	0.044	0.402	0.053	0.048
021	0.142	−0.121	0.148	−0.169	−0.318
022	0.576	0.171	0.599	0.214	−0.057
031	0.035	−0.222	0.042	−0.176	0.323
032	0.483	0.147	0.509	0.167	−0.037
041	0.506	−0.095	0.527	−0.120	0.047
042	0.321	0.079	0.343	0.097	−0.009
051	0.262	−0.134	0.263	−0.094	−0.384
052	0.366	−0.259	0.360	−0.300	0.092
061	−0.826	−0.310	−0.856	−0.278	0.104
062	−0.482	−0.355	−0.520	−0.358	0.162
071	−0.051	0.324	−0.033	0.289	−0.390
072	0.366	0.215	0.384	0.161	−0.292
081	0.451	0.090	0.468	0.101	−0.134
082	0.194	−0.295	0.196	−0.348	−0.182
091	0.491	0.189	0.485	0.200	0.167
092	0.479	−0.211	0.418	−0.185	0.284
101	0.144	0.717	0.134	0.761	0.063
102	0.478	0.359	0.423	0.207	0.419
111	−0.572	0.188	−0.473	0.124	−0.500
112	0.505	0.050	0.535	0.051	−0.002
121	−0.101	−0.308	−0.093	−0.325	−0.353
122	−0.173	−0.126	−0.187	−0.278	−0.171
131	0.155	0.252	0.132	0.307	0.125
132	0.452	−0.047	0.447	0.008	0.146
141	−0.837	−0.097	−0.780	−0.133	−0.375
142	0.291	−0.513	0.263	−0.555	0.163
151	0.198	0.361	0.200	0.417	0.028
152	0.427	0.067	0.454	0.084	−0.032
161	−0.327	0.161	−0.329	0.138	0.353
162	−0.692	0.376	−0.690	0.385	0.199
171	−0.087	−0.494	−0.109	−0.459	0.261
172	−0.034	−0.472	−0.056	−0.442	0.261
181	−0.499	0.061	−0.531	0.127	0.211
182	−0.545	0.461	−0.556	0.466	−0.218
191	−0.788	0.424	−0.778	0.470	0.008
192	0.200	−0.410	0.198	−0.449	−0.228
201	−0.511	0.743	−0.510	0.742	0.230
202	−0.769	−0.243	−0.807	−0.217	−0.020
211	−0.413	0.490	−0.428	−0.407	0.350
212	−0.640	−0.273	−0.672	−0.263	−0.124

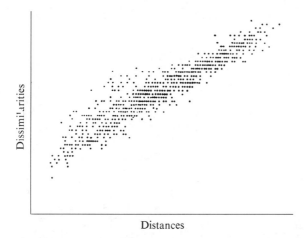

Distances

Figure C.12 Shepard Diagram Based on Three-space Solution from TORSCA 8 Analysis (see Figure 4.11)

Table C.38 Product-Moment Correlations by Subject from Three-way CANDECOMP Analysis in Two and Three Dimensions (see Figure 4.12)

Subject	Correlation 2 Dimensions	Correlation 3 Dimensions	Subject	Correlation 2 Dimensions	Correlation 3 Dimensions
011	0.713411	0.720411	112	0.633021	0.633606
012	0.705902	0.722291	121	0.218081	0.229899
021	0.591398	0.637834	122	0.449404	0.455061
022	0.593537	0.605702	131	0.686758	0.683920
031	0.704123	0.739255	132	0.645987	0.688149
032	0.765924	0.793133	141	0.658567	0.657086
041	0.520107	0.603501	142	0.337366	0.549693
042	0.762127	0.783299	151	0.609436	0.772495
051	0.505310	0.517428	152	0.735171	0.751966
052	0.360639	0.562698	161	0.265208	0.360271
061	0.819075	0.888011	162	0.464280	0.638570
062	0.637484	0.719572	171	0.585109	0.623227
071	0.578587	0.580066	172	0.618517	0.636709
072	0.564671	0.627508	181	0.532615	0.534579
081	0.746155	0.776888	182	0.380957	0.692048
082	0.698418	0.767048	191	0.582325	0.717842
091	0.741245	0.735440	192	0.667416	0.675148
092	0.689199	0.710221	201	0.053706	0.304449
101	0.441469	0.599115	202	0.789611	0.796023
102	0.562966	0.632097	211	0.511895	0.698050
111	0.331532	0.320135	212	0.618572	0.642097

Table C.39 Stimulus Coordinates from Three-way CANDECOMP Analysis in Two and Three Dimensions (see Figure 4.12)

Stimulus	Dimension				
	1	2	1	2	3
1	-0.31241	0.05869	-0.30642	0.07882	0.32540
2	-0.00353	0.40987	-0.04230	0.44206	0.00397
3	-0.10335	0.23875	-0.20840	0.14656	-0.01921
4	-0.42613	-0.32973	-0.34762	-0.28751	0.48064
5	-0.22064	0.06170	-0.26195	0.02069	0.16208
6	-0.21782	-0.01633	-0.29242	-0.11969	0.10182
7	-0.13544	0.31007	-0.20269	0.28194	0.08051
8	-0.15668	0.15178	-0.13377	0.21602	0.20587
9	-0.11590	0.16897	-0.09931	0.22856	0.15819
10	-0.06965	0.36732	-0.11871	0.37914	0.04341
11	-0.35775	-0.24970	-0.33240	-0.26482	0.35089
12	-0.35481	-0.33503	-0.30234	-0.33170	0.37581
13	-0.39637	-0.31120	-0.32987	-0.28555	0.44361
14	-0.32415	-0.26084	-0.31355	-0.29900	0.29565
15	-0.19172	0.19138	-0.30653	0.07903	0.04184

Table C.40 Dimension "Loading" Matrices, Subjects, and Scenarios from Three-way CANDECOMP Analysis in Two and Three Dimensions (see Figure 4.12)

Subject	Dimension				
	1	2	1	2	3
011	77.95180	-61.09013	62.92732	-53.93456	-15.78437
012	80.11575	-56.86232	60.79747	-50.80865	-20.44292
021	79.80812	-53.08878	88.70235	-38.17557	11.37928
022	79.65230	-53.54469	81.49303	-41.06398	3.66828
031	83.51917	-45.73740	48.17947	-43.91119	-38.03197
032	76.55714	-64.86208	91.80975	-48.46815	17.94225
041	77.65662	-54.89073	52.23471	-52.08046	-27.45834
042	81.51489	-55.86966	84.73586	-42.56084	4.97368
051	79.60791	-50.27275	53.88618	-45.25661	-27.32008
052	79.99005	-43.38551	31.47495	-45.87781	-52.89037
061	84.01019	-3.35707	22.24963	-7.97112	-66.44649
062	83.86421	-14.15328	27.83507	-17.48636	-60.30952
071	83.76424	-35.44487	54.92403	-30.54494	-30.33594
072	78.45694	-54.94624	92.02588	-38.73276	16.42500
081	77.22897	-63.29662	91.77315	-47.04840	17.25877
082	84.40628	-40.06804	36.61971	-41.84578	-51.77907
091	83.68552	-47.10342	68.13010	-39.28232	-15.65367
092	83.17482	-46.54359	58.06839	-42.02737	-26.59900
101	78.20000	-51.18610	103.81612	-31.01753	30.35390
102	81.77264	-45.96049	50.00623	-44.10092	-34.18948
111	80.22150	-41.16565	65.67665	-32.71735	-14.48474
112	83.88429	-38.89085	64.89864	-31.84880	-19.33771
121	80.40392	-30.26311	61.73203	-22.38414	-19.09354
122	82.84160	-29.53291	64.74483	-21.05066	-18.21753
131	79.34813	-57.69167	86.05119	-42.75211	8.93965
132	82.40074	-47.58842	66.97469	-40.96335	-15.96851

Table C.40   (Concluded)

Subject	Dimension				
	1	2	1	2	3
141	84.88113	−18.93336	53.98199	−14.44053	−32.16472
142	80.75209	−38.94302	30.18605	−42.27209	−54.99142
151	79.95216	−53.43156	109.40323	−31.28873	34.33694
152	82.97708	−49.89229	70.85295	−41.42529	−12.14569
161	79.49586	−41.03780	84.90889	−26.26689	7.44827
162	82.90608	−24.33728	94.59659	−7.28638	15.25948
171	83.72652	−36.31931	49.14107	−34.59625	−36.93872
172	83.58026	−39.94328	54.79825	−36.39001	−30.45418
181	83.06865	−37.28476	50.13847	−33.25237	−34.87001
182	79.87218	−44.64149	114.27141	−21.02533	40.23389
191	83.96199	−19.79111	93.08438	−2.57124	12.86302
192	84.31090	−38.39474	53.15430	−35.40724	−32.96297
201	78.64177	−32.53654	94.05246	−14.82920	19.17102
202	85.70383	−11.55242	54.44844	−6.56045	−32.47597
211	83.17119	−20.71880	19.17763	−26.11282	−69.40820
212	84.64346	−22.24756	46.85164	−20.12309	−40.13165

Scenario	Dimension				
	1	2	1	2	3
1	−0.40508	−0.47049	−0.40929	−0.49291	−0.40071
2	−0.42043	−0.16970	−0.41886	−0.09562	−0.39630
3	−0.41386	−0.33900	−0.41430	−0.30653	−0.40508
4	−0.41789	−0.32715	−0.40728	−0.28028	−0.44802
5	−0.40275	−0.49712	−0.40460	−0.51958	−0.41247
6	−0.38862	−0.52987	−0.39473	−0.55265	−0.38398

SUPPORTING MATERIAL FOR CHAPTER 5

In this section we present supporting computer output for material covered in Chapter 5.

Table C.41   Ideal-point Coordinates and Dimension Weights for Group A
               Overall Preferences (see Figure 5.2)

	Ideal Point		Dimension Weight*	
Subject	1	2	1	2
041	0.30020	-0.36891	1.10168	1.10168
082	0.01471	0.01758	-11.14547	-11.14547
092	-1.10979	1.07900	-0.25905	-0.25905
101	0.10026	0.00486	4.17659	4.17659
102	0.13568	-0.03432	3.17098	3.17098
111	0.00778	-0.10539	-4.25365	-4.25365
112	-0.25877	0.24096	-1.36649	-1.36649
121	-0.00268	0.00475	-9.36559	-9.36559
122	0.01614	-0.01555	-7.17034	-7.17034
141	0.04980	-0.14993	-3.42377	-3.42377
151	1.63450	-0.87628	0.20758	0.20758
152	-0.22169	0.13020	-1.86550	-1.86550
161	0.10639	0.09253	-3.74811	-3.74811
162	0.08738	-0.08429	-3.83162	-3.83162
181	0.02554	0.01922	-11.02543	-11.02543
182	-0.00954	-0.05133	-8.60096	-8.60096
191	0.21552	-0.28153	-1.49337	-1.49337
201	0.17783	-0.05129	-1.88461	-1.88461
202	0.07580	-0.01058	-5.83506	-5.83506

*Only the algebraic sign of the dimension weights is relevant for the simple ideal-point model.

Table C.42   Ideal-point Coordinates and Dimension Weights for Group B
Overall Preferences (see Figure 5.3)

Subject	Ideal Point		Dimension Weight*	
	1	2	1	2
011	1.88737	4.37258	−0.15640	−0.15640
012	−0.05876	0.22990	−2.03339	−2.03339
021	−0.10163	−0.15516	4.21886	4.21886
022	4.45101	−15.25669	0.03610	0.03610
031	−0.13957	−0.32393	1.40075	1.40075
032	0.23473	−0.63532	0.78984	0.78984
042	0.49166	3.10912	−0.20127	−0.20127
051	−0.05244	−0.31034	1.47234	1.47234
052	−0.12952	−0.29469	2.09878	2.09878
061	−0.15248	0.39357	1.32329	1.32329
062	−0.57351	0.05812	0.91435	0.91435
071	0.01383	−0.18730	1.68520	1.68520
072	−1.18628	−18.47569	0.03427	0.03427
081	−0.10983	−0.66834	0.99643	0.99643
091	0.00151	0.30803	−2.07886	−2.07886
131	−0.12362	0.11112	−2.30624	−2.30624
132	−0.00639	0.22675	−2.71408	−2.71408
142	−0.07438	−0.06483	5.46289	5.46289
171	2.55139	1.70472	−0.29968	−0.29968
172	2.51116	1.68349	−0.30439	−0.30439
192	−0.19404	−0.26494	2.41332	2.41332
211	−0.18694	−0.04217	3.83097	3.83097
212	−0.53648	0.07362	0.96738	0.96738

*Only the algebraic sign of the dimension weights is relevant for the simple ideal-point model.

Table C.43   Vector Model Direction Cosines for Group A and Group B
Overall Preferences (see Figures 5.2 and 5.3)

	Direction Cosines of Fitted Subject Vectors				
Group A	Dimension		Group B	Dimension	
Subject	1	2	Subject	1	2
041	0.6272	−0.7789	011	−0.4079	−0.9130
082	−0.1382	−0.9904	012	0.1186	−0.9929
092	0.7265	−0.6871	021	−0.3847	−0.9230
101	0.9998	0.0213	022	0.2880	−0.9576
102	0.9336	−0.3583	031	−0.3145	−0.9492
111	−0.2285	0.9735	032	0.3858	−0.9226
112	0.7375	−0.6754	042	−0.1900	−0.9818
121	0.9236	0.3833	051	−0.0561	−0.9984
122	−0.6247	0.7809	052	−0.3609	−0.9326
141	−0.2856	0.9584	061	−0.2944	0.9557
151	0.8800	−0.4750	062	−0.9933	0.1159
152	0.8574	−0.5147	071	0.2827	−0.9592
161	−0.7789	−0.6271	072	−0.0726	−0.9974
162	−0.7012	0.7130	081	−0.1293	−0.9916
181	−0.9057	−0.4240	091	−0.0846	−0.9964
182	0.4855	0.8742	131	0.5851	−0.8110
191	−0.6065	0.7951	132	−0.1577	−0.9875
201	−0.9798	0.1998	142	0.9617	−0.2742
202	−0.9827	0.1852	171	−0.8310	−0.5563
			172	−0.8307	−0.5567
			192	−0.5177	−0.8556
			211	−0.9984	−0.0558
			212	−0.9888	0.1493

Table C.44 Supporting Output for Four-way Discriminant Analysis, Perceptual-Preference Segments versus Background Characteristics (see Figure 5.4)

Step Number	Variable Entered	F Value to Enter or Remove	Number of Variables Included	U-Statistic
1	2	3.2031	1	0.7574
2	3	1.6784	2	0.6453
3	8	1.2563	3	0.5688
4	7	0.9200	4	0.5160
5	5	0.7289	5	0.4760
6	10	0.7030	6	0.4390
7	6	0.6116	7	0.4078
8	4	0.4632	8	0.3846
9	1	0.3088	9	0.3690
10	9	0.3755	10	0.3502

	Eigenvalues	
0.84367	0.36153	0.13746
	Cumulative Proportion of Total Dispersion	
0.62836	0.89762	1.00000
	Canonical Correlations	
0.67646	0.51530	0.34764

Coefficients for Canonical Variable

Original Variable	1	2	3
1	−0.40556	−0.76270	−0.07308
2	−0.24705	0.11026	−0.18500
3	0.60347	−1.29109	0.83368
4	−1.58418	−0.22333	0.06188
5	0.21597	0.14500	−0.05245
6	−0.59691	0.26628	1.63865
7	0.69906	0.14972	−2.30176
8	−1.52619	0.08621	0.34136
9	0.59993	1.16143	0.82942
10	−0.18439	−1.29625	−1.39050

Group	Canonical Variables Evaluated at Group Means		
1	−1.47565	0.44657	−0.19290
2	0.53400	0.63172	0.51926
3	1.27020	0.37835	−0.62143
4	0.01604	−0.62931	0.05484

Table C.45   Multiple Correlation Coefficients and F-Ratios between Phases for the Linear Model of Group A Scenario-dependent Preferences

Scenario	Correlation Coefficient for Phase			
	1	2	3	4
1	0.7223	0.7110	0.7089	0.1023
2	0.9678	0.9676	0.9575	0.8431
3	0.8684	0.8642	0.8611	0.4847
4	0.9277	0.9156	0.9145	0.7832
5	0.6786	0.6773	0.6548	0.2658
6	0.8475	0.8375	0.8259	0.7160

	F-Ratios between Phases					
	F12	F13	F14	F23	F24	F34
Scenario	D.F.1 9	2 9	3 9	1 10	2 10	1 11
1	0.3071	0.1813	3.2074	0.0596	5.0044	10.8792
2	0.0479	1.4080	10.6831	3.0593	17.6844	27.2146
3	0.2668	0.2327	6.3367	0.2144	10.1132	21.5510
4	1.4420	0.7844	5.3204	0.1214	6.9522	14.9796
5	0.0285	0.2650	2.1677	0.5554	3.5856	6.8945
6	0.5412	0.5769	2.1905	0.6421	3.1601	5.8691

Table C.46   Multiple Correlation Coefficients and F-Ratios between Phases for the Linear Model of Group B Scenario-dependent Preferences

Scenario	Correlation Coefficient for Phase			
	1	2	3	4
1	0.6304	0.6304	0.6258	0.5990
2	0.8459	0.8419	0.8401	0.7953
3	0.5323	0.5218	0.5217	0.3540
4	0.3906	0.3906	0.3868	0.2289
5	0.7088	0.7016	0.7016	0.6800
6	0.8267	0.8223	0.8195	0.8155

	F-Ratios between Phases					
	F12	F13	F14	F23	F24	F34
Scenario	D.F.1 9	2 9	3 9	1 10	2 10	1 11
1	0.0001	0.0433	0.1919	0.0961	0.3197	0.5921
2	0.2168	0.1572	0.8764	0.1059	1.3088	2.7338
3	0.1389	0.0700	0.6614	0.0012	1.0095	2.2194
4	0.0000	0.0154	0.3546	0.0342	0.5910	1.2583
5	0.1817	0.0908	0.2409	0.0000	0.2947	0.6482
6	0.2078	0.1697	0.1743	0.1429	0.1711	0.2161

Table C.47   Multiple Correlation Coefficients and F-Ratios between Phases for the Monotone Model of Group A Scenario-dependent Preferences

| | Correlation Coefficient for Phase | | | F-Ratios between Phases | | |
| | | | | F23 | F24 | F34 |
Scenario	2	3	4	D.F.1 10	2 10	1 11
1	0.8239	0.8249	0.3644	-0.0477*	8.5031	18.8492
2	0.9875	0.9884	0.9090	-0.7107*	29.9523	71.7783
3	0.9696	0.9518	0.7965	5.7349	25.5484	31.7116
4	0.9816	0.9514	0.8984	15.9874	21.4322	11.3765
5	0.8291	0.8117	0.6059	0.9124	5.1227	9.4080
6	0.8438	0.8205	0.8019	1.3465	1.1964	1.0142

| | Correlation Coefficient for Phase | | F-Ratios between Phases F34 |
Scenario	3	4	D.F.1 11
1	0.8249	0.3283	19.7089
2	0.9881	0.9090	69.8664
3	0.9507	0.7965	30.7883
4	0.9498	0.8981	10.7296
5	0.8029	0.6059	8.5952
6	0.8199	0.7999	1.0919

*Negative F-ratios are due to rounding error and should be read as zero.

Table C.48   Multiple Correlation Coefficients and F-Ratios between Phases for the Monotone Model of Group B Scenario-dependent Preferences

| | Correlation Coefficient for Phase | | | F-Ratios between Phases | | |
| | | | | F23 | F24 | F34 |
Scenario	2	3	4	D.F.1 10	2 10	1 11
1	0.8107	0.7816	0.7787	1.3499	0.7421	0.1301
2	0.9406	0.9316	0.9303	1.4634	0.8422	0.2120
3	0.7689	0.7371	0.6643	1.1689	1.8325	2.4584
4	0.6791	0.6773	0.3206	0.0469	3.3265	7.2328
5	0.8610	0.8513	0.8403	0.6454	0.6814	0.7413
6	0.9687	0.9359	0.9245	10.1171	6.7790	1.8815

| | Correlation Coefficient for Phase | | F-Ratios between Phases F34 |
Scenario	3	4	D.F.1 11
1	0.8082	0.7787	1.4884
2	0.9408	0.9304	1.8632
3	0.6710	0.6650	0.1603
4	0.6146	0.6035	0.2393
5	0.8512	0.8404	0.7231
6	0.9594	0.9245	9.0657

Table C.49 Ideal-point Coordinates and Dimension Weights for Group A
Scenario-dependent Preferences (see Figure 5.5)

	Ideal Point		Dimension Weight*	
Scenario	1	2	1	2
1	0.01242	0.02760	−9.65257	−9.65257
2	0.06569	−0.04252	−6.03123	−6.03123
3	0.02957	−0.00573	−10.08162	−10.08162
4	0.06260	−0.04613	−5.82858	−5.82858
5	0.00410	0.03324	−8.98296	−8.98296
6	−0.08017	0.06103	−4.04044	−4.04044

*Only the algebraic sign of the dimension weight is relevant for the simple ideal-point model.

Table C.50 Ideal-point Coordinates and Dimension Weights for Group B
Scenario-dependent Preferences (see Figure 5.6)

	Ideal Point		Dimension Weight *	
Scenario	1	2	1	2
1	−0.17660	−0.36222	1.81202	1.81202
2	−0.09540	0.44925	1.23499	1.23499
3	0.37645	0.53551	1.02617	1.02617
4	−0.11334	0.20967	1.42385	1.42385
5	−0.26554	−0.61837	1.12285	1.12285
6	−0.00568	0.24156	−2.56758	−2.56758

*Only the algebraic sign of the dimension weight is relevant for the simple ideal-point model.

Table C.51 Vector Model Direction Cosines for Group A and Group B
Scenario-dependent Preferences (see Figures 5.5 and 5.6)

	Group A Dimension		Group B Dimension	
Scenario	1	2	1	2
1	−0.4259	−0.9048	−0.3704	−0.9289
2	−0.8418	0.5398	−0.1596	0.9872
3	−0.6685	0.7437	0.6074	0.7944
4	−0.8128	0.5825	−0.3407	0.9402
5	0.3688	−0.9295	−0.3511	−0.9363
6	0.8804	−0.4742	−0.1981	0.9802

Table C.52   Subject Saliences and Stimulus Coordinates from INDSCAL
Analysis of Groups *a* and *b* in Two Dimensions (see Figures 5.7
and 5.8)

Subject	Group *a* Saliences		Subject	Group *b* Saliences	
092	0.73050	0.36158	021	0.60364	0.39596
112	0.69749	0.49831	022	0.73655	0.27516
121	0.65800	0.50175	051	0.81823	0.09069
151	0.57624	0.54704	061	0.90295	0.02747
152	0.57375	0.50723	091	0.29892	0.79551
182	0.26346	0.56373	212	0.79370	0.10107

Stimulus	Group *a* Coordinates			Group *b* Coordinates	
1	0.17107	−0.44259		0.19507	0.18559
2	−0.27926	−0.19573		−0.33471	−0.26760
3	−0.31235	0.13188		−0.30292	−0.16453
4	0.39392	−0.10718		0.31215	0.30447
5	−0.02448	−0.08061		0.14992	−0.18800
6	−0.01089	0.25071		−0.26862	0.29751
7	−0.41501	0.07568		−0.30951	−0.27298
8	−0.13936	−0.36218		0.09092	−0.27902
9	−0.04139	−0.37574		0.06279	−0.22013
10	−0.28102	−0.17567		−0.31836	−0.25743
11	0.26723	0.29118		0.25408	0.17564
12	0.31749	0.20321		0.23954	0.37254
13	0.32986	0.13061		0.28585	0.29498
14	0.21905	0.32386		0.24713	0.26088
15	−0.19485	0.33258		−0.30335	−0.24190

Table C.53   Multiple Correlation Coefficients and F-Ratios between Phases for the Monotone Model of Group *a* Scenario-dependent Preferences

Subject and Scenario	Correlation Coefficient for Phase		F-Ratio between Phases F 34
	3	4	D.F. 1 11
092-1	0.7944	0.7894	0.2355
2	0.9170	0.9080	1.1293
3	0.4496	0.5826	−1.8934†
4	0.7536	0.7475	0.2331
5	0.7944	0.7894	0.2355
6	0.8593	0.8519	0.5292
112-1	0.9396	0.9347	0.8542
2	0.9554	0.8708	19.5006
3	0.9850	0.9119	51.3819
4	0.9811	0.9459	19.8510
5	0.8631	0.6303	14.9981
6	0.9919	0.9749	22.7063
121-1	0.7909	0.4460	12.5333
2	0.8131	0.4016	16.2247
3	0.6756	0.6500	0.6863
4	0.8774	0.5767	20.8869
5	0.5520	0.5531	−0.0199†
6	0.6924	0.5675	3.3238
151-1	0.7659	0.7649	0.0383
2	0.6715	0.4441	5.0813
3	0.7659	0.7649	0.0383
4	0.7659	0.7649	0.0383
5	0.7659	0.7649	0.0383
6	0.7659	0.7649	0.0383
152-1	0.9402	0.9406	−0.0679†
2	0.7839	0.6524	5.3899
3	0.9462	0.7523	34.5854
4	0.9462	0.7523	34.5854
5	0.9495	0.9424	1.5018
6	0.9495	0.9424	1.5106
182-1	0.7970	0.7874	0.4618
2	0.8989	0.8970	0.2015
3	0.8858	0.8819	0.3480
4	0.7176	0.7179	−0.0094†
5	0.8780	0.8010	6.2107
6	0.7117	0.6850	0.8316

†Minus value is due to rounding error and should be read as zero.

Table C.54   **Multiple Correlation Coefficients and F-Ratio between Phases for the Monotone Model of Group _b_ Scenario-dependent Preferences**

| Subject and Scenario | Correlation Coefficient for Phase | | F-Ratio between Phases F 34 |
	3	4	D.F. 1 11
021-1	0.6794	0.6452	0.9232
2	0.7837	0.7837	0.0028
3	0.6298	0.6211	0.1981
4	0.9826	0.9829	−0.1500†
5	0.8480	0.7915	3.6293
6	0.7376	0.7160	0.7570
022-1	0.9993	0.9993	0.6569
2	0.9652	0.9631	0.6484
3	0.9411	0.8112	21.8891
4	0.9431	0.9430	0.0210
5	0.9609	0.9390	5.9366
6	0.9531	0.9179	7.9277
051-1	0.6701	0.6409	0.7659
2	0.7776	0.6295	5.8003
3	0.6934	0.5700	3.3048
4	0.8008	0.7495	2.4399
5	0.5922	0.5885	0.0728
6	0.7845	0.7130	3.0595
061-1	0.9899	0.9629	28.8389
2	0.9899	0.9629	28.8389
3	0.9899	0.9629	28.8389
4	0.9961	0.9963	−0.7494†
5	0.9931	0.9958	−4.3323†
6	0.9943	0.9947	−0.6221†
091-1	0.9951	0.9934	3.6968
2	0.9853	0.9835	1.3540
3	0.7520	0.7438	0.3115
4	0.9852	0.9835	1.2994
5	0.9951	0.9934	3.6968
6	0.9573	0.9459	2.8652
212-1	0.7690	0.7632	0.2367
2	0.7690	0.7632	0.2367
3	0.7617	0.7427	0.7482
4	0.7617	0.7427	0.7482
5	0.7690	0.7632	0.2367
6	0.6650	0.5484	2.7896

†Minus value is due to rounding error and should be read as zero.

Table C.55   Ideal-point Coordinates and Dimension Weights for Group a
Scenario-dependent Preferences

Subject and Scenario	Ideal Point		Dimension Weight*	
	1	2	1	2
092-1	0.55590	0.25065	0.61538	0.61538
2	0.55805	0.03946	-0.82287	-0.82287
3	0.00349	0.01531	2.30907	2.30907
4	-0.16002	-0.09623	1.66157	1.66157
5	0.55590	0.25065	0.61538	0.61538
6	-0.33134	-0.11181	-1.10237	-1.10237
112-1	0.62168	0.30110	0.64077	0.64077
2	-0.09417	-0.08419	2.85491	2.85491
3	-0.10611	-0.05562	2.99099	2.99099
4	-0.17464	-0.13266	1.90095	1.90095
5	0.02867	-0.07621	4.10501	4.10501
6	0.21813	0.07823	1.97417	1.97417
121-1	-0.00160	0.00943	4.10473	4.10473
2	0.01044	-0.01466	4.48784	4.48784
3	-0.02623	-0.30385	1.09544	1.09544
4	0.02510	-0.03822	4.79750	4.79750
5	-0.22163	0.04261	1.07418	1.07418
6	-0.01535	-0.06368	3.18514	3.18514
151-1	-1.59435	-0.42990	-0.22064	-0.22064
2	0.06415	-0.02477	3.38604	3.38604
3	-1.59435	-0.42990	-0.22064	-0.22064
4	-1.59435	0.42990	-0.22064	-0.22064
5	-1.59435	-0.42990	-0.22064	-0.22064
6	-1.59435	-0.42990	-0.22064	-0.22064
152-1	1.23311	0.63586	0.31854	0.31854
2	-0.10637	-0.02242	2.50266	2.50266
3	-0.03679	-0.07212	3.84535	3.84535
4	-0.03679	-0.07212	3.84535	3.84535
5	-0.47993	-0.47397	-0.64458	-0.64458
6	-0.47993	-0.47192	-0.64591	-0.64591
182-1	0.32015	0.25966	-0.88156	-0.88156
2	-0.63251	-1.12460	0.32604	0.32604
3	0.95046	-0.52803	0.45026	0.45026
4	-1.83525	4.24182	-0.08247	-0.08247
5	0.21361	-0.11466	2.01243	2.01243
6	-0.19680	-0.19668	-1.12646	-1.12646

*Only the algebraic sign of the dimension weight is relevant for the simple ideal-point model.

Table C.56   Ideal-point Coordinates and Dimension Weights for Group *b* Scenario-dependent Preferences

Subject and Scenario	Ideal Point		Dimension Weight*	
	1	2	1	2
021-1	−0.08173	0.22523	2.07542	2.07542
2	2.19943	3.70015	−0.07281	−0.07281
3	−0.55018	0.16468	−0.72876	−0.72876
4	−0.46074	−1.96637	−0.21268	0.21268
5	−0.10135	0.23724	2.57560	2.57560
6	−0.17170	−0.07830	−1.53938	−1.53938
022-1	−3.29777	−2.74295	−0.09111	−0.09111
2	−0.44393	−0.58695	0.50991	0.50991
3	−0.06968	−0.01272	4.27967	4.27967
4	−0.20855	−1.25525	−0.33175	−0.33175
5	−0.20970	−0.07088	−1.81031	−1.81031
6	−0.16187	−0.05151	−2.29439	−2.29439
051-1	0.01851	0.23877	1.36441	1.36441
2	−0.05879	−0.00406	3.93096	3.93096
3	−0.10957	0.03097	3.40539	3.40539
4	−0.01079	0.12565	3.18576	3.18576
5	−0.06807	0.11197	3.55452	3.55452
6	−0.13297	0.03802	−3.45297	−3.45297
061-1	−0.22323	0.00335	2.29148	2.29148
2	−0.22323	0.00335	2.29148	2.29148
3	−0.22323	0.00335	2.29148	2.29148
4	−0.43129	−0.01533	1.16231	1.16231
5	−0.60132	0.09290	0.93401	0.93401
6	−11.90599	1.89486	0.04625	0.04625
091-1	−0.10909	−0.48468	−0.84908	−0.84908
2	0.12388	0.81539	−0.55660	−0.55660
3	0.06906	−0.48796	0.77358	0.77358
4	0.12785	0.82056	−0.55151	−0.55151
5	−0.10909	−0.48468	−0.84908	−0.84908
6	−0.27816	−0.10986	−1.32817	−1.32817
212-1	0.38454	0.18580	−0.71139	−0.71139
2	0.38454	0.18580	−0.71139	−0.71139
3	0.01107	0.19050	−1.94101	−1.94101
4	0.01107	0.19050	−1.94101	−1.94101
5	0.38454	0.18580	−0.71139	−0.71139
6	0.03326	−0.03158	−2.96782	−2.96782

*Only the algebraic sign of the dimension weight is relevant for the simple ideal-point model.

Table C.57   Vector Model Direction Cosines for Group a and b Scenario-
dependent Preferences (see Figures 5.9 and 5.10)

| | Group a | | | Group b | |
| Subject and Scenario | Dimensions | | Subject and Scenario | Dimensions | |
	1	2		1	2
092–1	0.8721	0.4894	021–1	0.1585	0.9874
2	−0.9970	−0.0779	2	−0.5302	−0.8479
3	0.9424	0.3346	3	0.9792	−0.2028
4	−0.7055	−0.7087	4	0.1634	0.9866
5	0.8721	0.4894	5	0.0986	0.9951
6	0.9724	0.2335	6	0.6267	0.7792
112–1	0.8695	0.4939	022–1	0.7576	0.6528
2	−0.8447	−0.5352	2	−0.4931	−0.8700
3	−0.9925	−0.1221	3	0.2537	−0.9673
4	−0.8646	−0.5024	4	0.0631	0.9980
5	−0.0002	−1.0000	5	0.7175	0.6966
6	0.8492	0.5281	6	0.6168	0.7871
121–1	−0.7010	0.7131	051–1	0.4621	0.8869
2	−0.8360	0.5488	2	−0.3356	−0.9420
3	−0.1923	−0.9813	3	−0.7187	−0.6953
4	−0.2380	−0.9713	4	0.7299	0.6836
5	−0.9827	−0.1851	5	0.3372	0.9414
6	−0.3916	−0.9201	6	0.9242	0.3820
151–1	0.9693	0.2458	061–1	−0.9541	−0.2996
2	0.6813	−0.7320	2	−0.9541	−0.2996
3	0.9693	0.2458	3	−0.9541	−0.2996
4	0.9693	0.2458	4	−0.9998	−0.0220
5	0.9693	0.2458	5	−0.9897	0.1435
6	0.9693	0.2458	6	−0.9870	0.1606
152–1	0.8831	0.4691	091–1	0.0669	0.9978
2	−0.9997	−0.0248	2	−0.1957	−0.9807
3	−0.6778	−0.7352	3	0.2406	−0.9706
4	−0.6778	−0.7352	4	−0.1971	−0.9804
5	0.7482	0.6635	5	0.0669	0.9978
6	0.7488	0.6628	6	0.7735	0.6338
182–1	−0.7485	−0.6631	212–1	−0.9803	−0.1975
2	−0.4951	−0.8688	2	−0.9803	−0.1975
3	0.8752	−0.4837	3	−0.4289	−0.9033
4	0.3841	−0.9233	4	−0.4289	−0.9033
5	0.9052	−0.4250	5	−0.9803	−0.1975
6	0.7425	0.6698	6	−0.8360	0.5488

SUPPORTING MATERIAL FOR CHAPTER 6

In this section we present supporting computer output for material covered in Chapter 6.

Table C.58   Correlation Matrix of Interpoint Distances across 17 Pseudosubjects (see Table 6.1)

Pseudosubject	1	2	3	4	5	6	7	8	9	10	11	12	13	14	15	16	17
1	1.000																
2	0.980	1.000															
3	0.982	0.999	1.000														
4	0.815	0.840	0.840	1.000													
5	0.804	0.822	0.828	0.602	1.000												
6	0.763	0.801	0.806	0.596	0.979	1.000											
7	0.765	0.799	0.805	0.594	0.981	0.999	1.000										
8	0.775	0.810	0.816	0.633	0.966	0.993	0.993	1.000									
9	0.772	0.759	0.770	0.560	0.953	0.922	0.929	0.920	1.000								
10	0.873	0.841	0.843	0.802	0.624	0.588	0.590	0.614	0.632	1.000							
11	0.729	0.774	0.775	0.640	0.883	0.907	0.905	0.912	0.811	0.618	1.000						
12	0.846	0.810	0.819	0.740	0.735	0.701	0.704	0.726	0.759	0.846	0.577	1.000					
13	0.889	0.851	0.854	0.760	0.637	0.600	0.605	0.614	0.624	0.763	0.618	0.698	1.000				
14	0.543	0.617	0.620	0.564	0.694	0.728	0.723	0.734	0.581	0.412	0.721	0.516	0.423	1.000			
15	0.807	0.801	0.805	0.789	0.595	0.616	0.618	0.639	0.623	0.769	0.595	0.721	0.756	0.494	1.000		
16	0.542	0.575	0.577	0.617	0.552	0.575	0.568	0.599	0.475	0.485	0.528	0.592	0.443	0.695	0.569	1.000	
17	0.688	0.740	0.742	0.626	0.803	0.826	0.816	0.818	0.717	0.572	0.779	0.672	0.519	0.876	0.653	0.743	1.000

Table C.59   Stimulus Coordinates from INDSCAL Analysis of Group Stimulus Space in Two Dimensions (see Figure 6.1)

Stimulus	Dimension	
	1	2
1	0.31386	−0.31312
2	−0.26501	−0.30746
3	−0.32205	0.00196
4	0.36740	0.13963
5	0.08042	−0.11846
6	0.19165	0.23579
7	−0.40519	−0.13141
8	−0.05519	−0.28136
9	0.05090	−0.25777
10	−0.25530	−0.34268
11	0.22202	0.22865
12	0.24095	0.39496
13	0.31114	0.22001
14	0.11041	0.40738
15	−0.31308	0.12387

Table C.60   Pseudosubject Saliences of INDSCAL Scaling of 17 Algorithm-Data Set Combinations in Two Dimensions (see Figure 6.2)

Pseudo-subject	Dimension	
	1	2
1	0.75328	0.54891
2	0.75960	0.54099
3	0.75990	0.54540
4	0.69217	0.46983
5	0.57294	0.71057
6	0.58520	0.69998
7	0.59288	0.69036
8	0.60550	0.68695
9	0.53074	0.68717
10	0.68979	0.45401
11	0.64896	0.57331
12	0.43693	0.73164
13	0.90370	0.20162
14	0.55465	0.52175
15	0.69945	0.44434
16	0.47842	0.48240
17	0.48595	0.69460

REFERENCES

The following list of references is primarily illustrative of applied research using multidimensional scaling. More extensive bibliographical material can be found in C.H. Coombs' *A Theory of Data* (New York: John Wiley & Sons, Inc., 1964) and P.E. Green and F.J. Carmone's *Multidimensional Scaling and Related Techniques in Marketing Analysis* (Boston: Allyn and Bacon, Inc., 1970).

1. Abelson, R.P., "A Technique and a Model for Multidimensional Attitude Scaling," *Public Opinion Quarterly*, vol. 18 (1954-1955), pp. 405-418.
2. Attneave, Fred, "Dimensions of Similarity," *American Journal of Psychology*, vol. 63 (1950), pp. 516-556.
3. Barnett, N.L., "Beyond Market Segmentation," *Harvard Business Review*, vol. 47 (1969), pp. 152-156.
4. Beals, R.W., D.H. Krantz, and Amos Tversky, "The Foundations of Multidimensional Scaling," *Psychological Review*, vol. 75 (1968), pp. 127-142.
5. Bennett, J.F., and W.L. Hays, "Multidimensional Unfolding: Determining the Dimensionality of Ranked Preference Data," *Psychometrika*, vol. 25 (1960), pp. 27-43.
6. Bloombaum, Milton, "The Conditions Underlying Race Riots as Portrayed by Multidimensional Scalogram Analysis: A Re-analysis of Lieberson and Silverman's Data," *American Sociological Review* (1969), pp. 76-91.
7. Bloxom, Bruce, "Individual Differences in Multidimensional Scaling," *Research Bulletin 68-45*. Educational Testing Service, Princeton, N.J., October 1968.
8. Boulding, K.E., *The Image*. Ann Arbor, Mich.: University of Michigan Press, 1968.
9. Boyd, J.E., and D.N. Jackson, "The Perceived Structure of Social Attitudes and Personality: A Multidimensional Scaling Approach," *Multivariate Behavioral Research*, vol. 2 (1967), pp. 281-297.
10. Carmone, F.J., P.E. Green, and P.J. Robinson, "TRICON—An IBM 360/65 Fortran IV Program for the Triangularization of Conjoint Data," *Journal of Marketing Research*, vol. 5 (1968), pp. 219-220.
11. Carroll, J.D., "A General Method for Preference Mapping of Perceptual Space," *Bulletin of the Operations Research Society of America*, vol. 16 (1968), pp. 227-228.
12. Carroll, J.D., "A Generalization of Canonical Correlation Analysis to Three or More Sets of Variables," *Proceedings of 76th Annual Convention of the American Psychological Association* (1968), pp. 227-228.
13. Carroll, J.D., "Individual Differences and Multidimensional Scaling," in R.N. Shepard, A.K. Romney, and S. Nerlove, eds., *Multidimensional Scaling: Theory and Application in the Behavioral Sciences*. New York: Academic Press, 1972, in press.
14. Carroll, J.D., "Polynomial Factor Analysis," *Proceedings of the 77th Annual Convention of the American Psychological Association* (1969), pp. 103-104.
15. Carroll, J.D., and J.J. Chang, "Analysis of Individual Differences in Multidimensional Scaling via an *N*-way Generalization of Eckart-Young Decomposition," *Psychometrika*, vol. 35 (1970), pp. 283-319.
16. Carroll, J.D., and J.J. Chang, "A General Index of Nonlinear Correlation

and Its Application to the Interpretation of Multidimensional Scaling Solutions," *American Pyschologist*, vol. 19 (1964), p. 540.

17. Carroll, J.D., and J.J. Chang, "Nonmetric Multidimensional Analysis of Paired Comparisons Data," paper presented at the Joint Meeting of the Psychometric and Psychonomic Societies, Niagara Falls, N.Y., October 1964.

18. Carroll, J.D. and J.J. Chang, "Reanalysis of Some Color Data of Helm's by the INDSCAL Procedure for Individual Differences Multidimensional Scaling," *Proceedings of the 78th Annual Convention of the American Psychological Association* (1970), pp. 137-138.

19. Carroll, J.D. and J.J. Chang, "Relating Preference Data to Multidimensional Scaling Solutions via a Generalization of Coombs' Unfolding Model," Bell Telephone Laboratories, Murray Hill, N.J., 1967 (mimeographed).

20. Chang, J.J., and J.D. Carroll, "How to Use MDPREF, a Computer Program for Multidimensional Analysis of Preference Data," Bell Telephone Laboratories, Murray Hill, N.J., 1969 (mimeographed).

21. Chang, J.J., and J.D. Carroll, "How to Use PROFIT, A Computer Program for Property Fitting, by Optimizing Nonlinear or Linear Correlation," Bell Telephone Laboratories, Murray Hill, N.J., 1970 (mimeographed).

22. Cliff, Norman, "Orthogonal Rotation to Congruence," *Psychometrika*, vol. 31 (1966), pp. 33-42.

23. Cliff, Norman, and F.W. Young, "On the Relation between Unidimensional Judgments and Multidimensional Scaling," *Organizational Behavior and Human Performance*, vol. 3 (1968), pp. 269-285.

24. Coombs, C.H., "Inconsistency of Preferences as a Measure of Psychological Distance," in C.W. Churchman and P. Ratoosh, eds., *Measurement: Definition and Theories*. New York: John Wiley & Sons, Inc., 1959.

25. Coombs, C.H., "Mathematical Models in Psychological Scaling," *Journal of the American Statistical Association*, vol. 46 (1951), pp. 480-489.

26. Coombs, C.H., "A Method for the Study of Interstimulus Similarity," *Psychometrika*, vol. 19 (1954), pp. 183-194.

27. Coombs, C.H., "Psychological Scaling without a Unit of Measurement," *Psychological Review*, vol. 57 (1950), pp. 148-158.

28. Coombs, C.H., "Theory and Methods of Social Measurement," in L. Festinger and D. Katz, eds., *Research Methods in the Behavioral Sciences*. New York: Holt, Rinehart and Winston, Inc., 1953.

29. Coombs, C.H., *A Theory of Data*. New York: John Wiley & Sons, Inc., 1964.

30. Coombs, C. H., "A Theory of Psychological Scaling," *Engineering Research Institute Bulletin no. 23*. Ann Arbor, Mich.: University of Michigan Press, 1952.

31. Coombs, C.H., Robyn Dawes, and Amos Tversky, *Mathematical Psychol-*

ogy: An Elementary Introduction. Englewood Cliffs, N.J., Prentice-Hall, Inc., 1970.

32. Day, R.L., "Systematic Paired Comparisons in Preference Analysis," *Journal of Marketing Research*, vol. 2 (1965), pp. 406-412.

33. Degerman, Richard, "Multidimensional Analysis of Complex Structure: Mixtures of Class and Quantitative Variation," unpub. Ph.D. thesis, Johns Hopkins University, 1968.

34. de Leeuw, Jan, "Canonical Discriminant Analysis," *RN 007-68*, Faculty of Social Sciences, University of Leiden, Netherlands, April 1968.

35. de Leeuw, Jan, "Nonmetric Discriminant Analysis," *RN 006-68*, Faculty of Social Sciences, University of Leiden, Netherlands, April 1968.

36. de Leeuw, Jan, "Nonmetric Multidimensional Scaling," *RN 010-68*, Faculty of Social Sciences, University of Leiden, Netherlands, April 1968.

37. de Leeuw, Jan, "The Positive Orthant Method for Nonmetric Multidimensional Scaling," mimeographed report, Department of Data Theory for the Social Sciences, University of Leiden, Netherlands, 1969.

38. Dixon, W.J., ed., "Biomedical Computer Programs," Education and Health Sciences Facility, University of California, 1965.

39. Doehlert, D.H., "Similarity and Preference Mapping: A Color Example," in R.L. King, ed., *Proceedings of the Denver Conference of the American Marketing Association.* Chicago: American Marketing Association, 1968, pp. 250-258.

40. Eckart, Charles and Gale Young, "The Approximation of One Matrix by Another of Lower Rank," *Psychometrika*, vol. 1 (1936), pp. 211-218.

41. Ekman, G., and L. Sjoeberg, "Scaling," *Annual Review of Psychology*, vol. 16 (1965), pp. 451-474.

42. Fenker, R.M., and D.R. Brown, "Pattern Perception, Conceptual Spaces and Dimensional Limitations on Information Processing," *Multivariate Behavioral Research*, vol. 4 (1969), pp. 257-269.

43. Fishburn, P.C., "Methods of Estimating Additive Utilities," *Management Science*, vol. 13 (1967), pp. 435-453.

44. Fishburn, P.C., "A Note on Recent Developments in Additive Utility Theories for Multiple-Factor Situations," *Operations Research*, vol. 14 (1966), pp. 1143-1148.

45. Frank, R.E., and P.E. Green, "Numerical Taxonomy in Marketing Analysis: A Review Article," *Journal of Marketing Research*, vol. 5 (1968), pp. 83-94.

46. Gleason, T.C., "A General Model for Nonmetric Multidimensional Scaling," *Michigan Mathematical Psychology Program 67-3.* University of Michigan, June 1967.

47. Green, P.E., and F.J. Carmone, "Multidimensional Scaling: An Introduction and Comparison of Nonmetric Unfolding Techniques," *Journal of Marketing Research*, vol. 6 (1969), pp. 330-341.

48. Green, P.E., and F.J. Carmone, *Multidimensional Scaling and Related Techniques in Marketing Analysis.* Boston: Allyn and Bacon, Inc., 1970.
49. Green, P.E., and F.J. Carmone, "The Performance Structure of the Computer Market: A Multivariate Approach," *Economics and Business Bulletin,* vol. 21 (1968), pp. 1-11.
50. Green, P.E., and F.J. Carmone, "Selected Studies in Multidimensional Scaling and Cluster Analysis," Marketing Science Institute, August 1968.
51. Green, P.E., and F.J. Carmone, "Stimulus Context and Task Effects on Individuals' Similarities Judgments," paper delivered at American Marketing Association's Attitude Research Conference, Mexico City, March 2-4, 1970.
52. Green, P.E. and Arun Maheshwari, "A Note on the Multidimensional Scaling of Conditional Proximity Data," *Journal of Marketing Research,* vol. 7 (1970), pp. 106-110.
53. Green, P.E., Arun Maheshwari, and V.R. Rao, "Self Concept and Brand Preference: An Empirical Application of Multidimensional Scaling," *Journal of the Market Research Society,* vol. 11 (1969), pp. 343-360.
54. Green, P.E., and V. R. Rao, "Configuration Invariance in Multidimensional Scaling," *Proceedings of the 129th Annual Meeting of the American Statistical Association, 1969.*
55. Green, P.E., and D.S. Tull, *Research for Marketing Decisions,* 2nd ed. Englewood Cliffs, N.J., Prentice-Hall, Inc., 1970.
56. Greenberg, M.G., "Some Applications of Nonmetric Multidimensional Scaling," *Proceedings of the 129th Annual Meeting of the American Statistical Association,* 1969.
57. Greenberg, M.G., "A Variety of Approaches to Nonmetric Multidimensional Scaling," paper presented at the 16th International Meeting of the Institute of Management Sciences, New York, March 1969.
58. Gulliksen, H., "Linear and Multidimensional Scaling," *Psychometrika,* vol. 26 (1961), pp. 9-25.
59. Gulliksen, H., and S.J. Messick, eds. *Psychological Scaling.* New York: John Wiley & Sons, Inc., 1960.
60. Guttman, L., "A Basis for Scaling Qualitative Data," *American Sociological Review,* vol. 9 (1944), pp. 139-150.
61. Guttman, L., "The Development of Nonmetric Space Analysis: A Letter to Professor John Ross," *Multivariate Behavioral Research,* vol. 2 (1967), pp. 71-82.
62. Guttman, L., "A General Nonmetric Technique for Finding the Smallest Coordinate Space for a Configuration of Points," *Psychometrika,* vol. 33 (1968), pp. 469-506.
63. Guttman, L., "The Nonmetric Breakthrough for the Behavioral Sciences," Automatic Data Processing Conference of the Information Processing Association of Israel, Jerusalem, 1966, pp. 1-16.

64. Harris, B., "An IBM 360 Program for Ward-Berry Hierarchical Grouping," University of Pennsylvania Computer Center, November 1967.
65. Hays, W.L., and J.R. Bennett, "Multidimensional Unfolding: Determining Configuration from Complete Rank Ordering of Preference Data," *Psychometrika*, vol. 26 (1961), pp. 221-238.
66. Horan, C.B., "Multidimensional Scaling: Combining Observations when Individuals Have Different Perceptual Structures," *Psychometrika*, vol. 34 (1969), pp. 139-165.
67. Horst, P., "Relations among *m* Sets of Measures," *Psychometrika*, vol. 26 (1961), pp. 129-149.
68. Hotelling, H., "Relations between Two Sets of Variates," *Biometrica*, vol. 28 (1936), pp. 321-377.
69. Householder, A.S., and Gale Young, "Matrix Approximation and Latent Roots," *American Mathematical Monthly*, vol. 45 (1938), pp. 165-171.
70. Howard, J.A., and J.N. Sheth, *The Theory of Buyer Behavior*. New York: John Wiley & Sons, Inc., 1969.
71. Howard, N. and B. Harris, "A Hierarchical Grouping Routine, IBM 360/65 FORTRAN IV Program," University of Pennsylvania Computer Center, October 1966.
72. Isaac, P.D., "Dissimilarity Judgments and Multidimensional Scaling Configuration as Indices of Perceptual Structure: A Study of Intra-Individual Consistencies," *Michigan Mathematical Psychology Program 68-3*, University of Michigan, 1968.
73. Jackson, D.N., and S.J. Messick, "Individual Differences in Social Perception," *British Journal of Social and Clinical Psychology*, vol. 2 (1963), pp. 1-10.
74. Johnson, R.M., "Market Segmentation: A Comparison of Techniques," paper presented at the 16th International Meeting of the Institute of Management Sciences, New York, March 27, 1969.
75. Johnson, S.C., "Hierarchical Clustering Schemes," *Psychometrika*, vol. 32 (1967), pp. 241-254.
76. Kelly, G.A., *Psychology of Personal Constructs*. New York: W.W. Norton & Company, Inc., 1955.
77. King, C., and D. Tigert, eds., *Attitude Research Reaches New Heights* Chicago: American Marketing Association, 1971.
78. Klahr, D., "Decision Making and Search in Multidimensional Environments," paper presented at the Institute of Management Sciences, April 16, 1967.
79. Klahr, D., "Decision Making in a Complex Environment: The Use of Similarity Judgments to Predict Preferences," *Management Science*, vol. 15 (1969), pp. 595-618.
80. Klahr, D., "A Monte Carlo Investigation of the Statistical Significance of

Kruskal's Nonmetric Scaling Procedure," *Psychometrika*, vol. 34 (1969), pp. 319-333.

81. Klingberg, F.L., "Studies in Measurement of the Relations among Sovereign States," *Psychometrika*, vol. 6 (1941), pp. 335-352.

82. Kruskal, J.B., "Analysis of Factorial Experiments by Estimating Monotone Transformations of the Data," *Journal of the Royal Statistical Society*, ser. B, vol. 27 (1965), pp. 251-263.

83. Kruskal, J.B., "How Engineers View Mathematics Courses," Bell Telephone Laboratories, Murray Hill, N.J., 1970 (mimeographed).

84. Kruskal, J.B., "Multidimensional Scaling by Optimizing Goodness of Fit to a Nonmetric Hypothesis," *Psychometrika*, vol. 29 (1964), pp. 1-27.

85. Kruskal, J.B., "Nonmetric Multidimensional Scaling: A Numerical Method," *Psychometrika*, vol. 29 (1964), pp. 115-129.

86. Kruskal, J.B., "Transformations of Data," *International Encyclopedia of the Social Sciences*. New York: Crowell-Collier and Macmillan, Inc., 1968.

87. Kruskal, J. B., and F. J. Carmone, "How to Use M-D-SCAL (Version 5M) and Other Useful Information," Bell Telephone Laboratories, Murray Hill, N.J., March 1969 (mimeographed).

88. Kruskal, J.B. and J.D. Carroll, "Geometric Models and Badness of Fit Functions," in P. R. Krishnaiah, ed., *Multivariate Analysis*. New York: Academic Press, Inc., 1969, vol. ii pp. 639-671.

89. Landis, D., C.A. Silver, J.M. Jones, and S.J. Messick, "Level of Proficiency and Multidimensional Viewpoints about Problem Similarity," *Journal of Applied Psychology*, vol. 51 (1967), pp. 216-222.

90. Lingoes, J.C., "A General Nonparametric Model for Representing Objects and Attributes in a Joint Metric Space," in J.D. Garden, ed., *Les Compte-rendus de Colloque International sur L'emploi des Calculateurs en Archeologie: Problemes Semiologiques et Mathematiques*. Marseilles: Centre National de La Recherche Scientifique, 1969.

91. Lingoes, J. C., "An IBM 7090 Program for Guttman-Lingoes Smallest Space Analysis," *Behavioral Science*, vol. 10 (1965): SSA I, pp. 183-184; SSA II, p. 487; vol 11 (1966): SSA III, pp. 75-76; SSA IV, p. 407; SSAR I, p. 322; SSAR II, p. 323; vol. 12 (1967): SSAR IV, pp. 74-75.

92. Lingoes, J.C., and L. Guttman, "Nonmetric Factor Analysis: A Rank Reducing Alternative to Linear Factor Analysis," *Multivariate Behavioral Research*, vol. 2 (1967), pp. 485-505.

93. Luce, R.D. and J.W. Tukey, "Simultaneous Conjoint Measurement: A New Type of Fundamental Measurement," *Journal of Mathematical Psychology*, vol. 1 (1964), pp. 1-27.

94. McGee, V.E., "CEMD/DEMD: Nonmetric Individual Differences Model for (Elastic) Multidimensional Data Reduction to Handle N Sets of Multivariate Data," *Journal of Marketing Research*, vol. 5 (1968), p. 322.

95. McGee, V.E., "EMD: A Fortran IV Program for Nonmetric (Elastic)

Multidimensional Data Reduction," *Journal of Marketing Research*, vol. 5 (1968), p. 321.

96. McGee, V.E., "Multidimensional Scaling of *N* Sets of Similarity Measures: A Nonmetric Individual Differences Approach," *Multivariate Behavioral Research*, vol. 3 (1968), pp. 233-248.

97. McRae, Duncan, and S.B. Schwarz, "Identifying Congressional Issues by Multidimensional Models," working paper, University of Chicago (n.d.).

98. Messick, S.J., "Dimensions of Social Desirability," *Journal of Consulting Psychology*, vol. 24 (1960), pp. 279-287.

99. Messick, S.J., "The Perceived Structure of Political Relationships," *Sociometry*, vol. 24 (1961), pp. 270-278.

100. Messick, S.J. and R.P. Abelson, "The Additive Constant Problem in Multidimensional Scaling," *Psychometrika*, vol. 21 (1956), pp. 1-15.

101. Messick, S.J., and J. Ross, *Measurement in Personality and Cognition*. New York: John Wiley & Sons, Inc., 1962.

102. Miller, J.E., R.N. Shepard, and J.J. Chang, "An Analytical Approach to the Interpretation of Multidimensional Scaling Solutions," *American Psychologist*, vol. 19 (1964), pp. 579-580.

103. Myers, J.G., *Consumer Image and Attitude*, Institute of Business and Economic Research, University of California at Berkeley, 1968 (monograph).

104. Myers, J.G., and F.M. Nicosia, "On the Study of Consumer Typologies," *Journal of Marketing Research*, vol. 5 (1968), pp. 182-193.

105. Neidell, L.A., "Physicians' Perceptions and Evaluations of Selected Ethical Drugs: An Application of Nonmetric Multidimensional Scaling to Pharmaceutical Marketing," unpub. Ph.D. thesis, University of Pennsylvania, December 1968.

106. Neidell, L.A., "The Use of Nonmetric Multidimensional Scaling in Marketing Analysis," *Journal of Marketing*, vol. 33 (1968), pp. 37-43.

107. Osgood, C.E., G.J. Suci, and P.H. Tannenbaum, *The Measurement of Meaning*. Urbana, Ill.: University of Illinois Press, 1957.

108. Pennell, R.J. and R.W. Young, "An IBM System 360 Program for Orthogonal Least-Squares Matrix Fitting," *Behavioral Science*, vol. 19 (1967), p. 165.

109. Phillips, J.P.N., "A Procedure for Determining Slater's *i* and All Nearest Adjoining Orders," *British Journal of Mathematical and Statistical Psychology*, vol. 20 (1967), pp. 217-255.

110. Rao, V.R., "The Salience of Price in the Perception and Evaluation of Product Quality: A Multidimensional Measurement Model and Experimental Test," unpub. Ph.D. thesis, University of Pennsylvania, May 1970.

111. Rapoport, Ammon, "A Comparison of Two Tree-Construction Methods for Obtaining Proximity Measures among Words," *Journal of Verbal Learning and Verbal Behavior*, vol. 6 (1967), pp. 884-890.

112. Richardson, M.W., "Multidimensional Psychophysics," *Psychological Bulletin*, vol. 35 (1938), pp. 659-660.

113. Robinson, J.P., and R. Hefner, "Perceptual Maps of the World," *The Public Opinion Quarterly*, vol. 32 (1968), pp. 273-280.

114. Rosenberg, S., C. Nelson, and P.S. Vivekananthan, "A Multidimensional Approach to the Structure of Personality Impressions," *Journal of Personality and Social Psychology*, vol. 9 (1968), pp. 283-294.

115. Roskam, E.E., "A Comparison of Principles for Algorithm Construction in Nonmetric Scaling," *Michigan Mathematical Psychology Program 69-2*, University of Michigan, February 1969.

116. Roskam, E.E., *Metric Analysis of Ordinal Data in Psychology*. Voorschoten, Holland: VAM Press, 1968.

117. Runkel, P.J., "Cognitive Similarity in Facilitating Communication," *Sociometry*, vol. 19 (1956), pp. 178-191.

118. Schonemann, P.H., "On Metric Multidimensional Unfolding," *Psychometrika*, vol. 35 (1970), pp. 349-366.

119. Shepard, R.N., "Analysis of Proximities as a Technique for the Study of Information Processing in Man," *Human Factors*, vol. 5 (1963), pp. 33-48.

120. Shepard, R.N., "The Analysis of Proximities: Multidimensional Scaling with an Unknown Distance Function: Part One," *Psychometrika*, vol. 27 (1962), pp. 125-139.

121. Shepard, R.N., "The Analysis of Proximities: Part Two," *Psychometrika*, vol. 27 (1962), pp. 219-246.

122. Shepard, R.N., "Attention and the Metric Structure of the Stimulus," *Journal of Mathematical Psychology*, vol. 1 (1964), pp. 54-87.

123. Shepard, R.N., "Metric Structures in Ordinal Data," *Journal of Mathematical Psychology*, vol. 3 (1966), pp. 287-315.

124. Shepard, R.N., "On Subjectively Optimum Selection among Multiattribute Alternatives," in G.L. Bryan and N.W. Shelley, eds., *Human Judgments and Optimality*. New York: John Wiley & Sons, Inc., 1964, pp. 257-281.

125. Shepard, R.N., "Similarity of Stimuli and Metric Properties of Behavioral Data," in H. Gulliksen and S. Messick, eds., *Psychological Scaling: Theory and Application*. New York: John Wiley & Sons, Inc., 1960.

126. Shepard, R.N., and J.D. Carroll, "Parametric Representation of Nonlinear Data Structures," in P.R. Krishnaiah, ed., *Multivariate Analysis*. New York: Academic Press, Inc., 1966, pp. 561-592.

127. Shepard, R.N. and Kruskal, J.B., "Nonmetric Methods for Scaling and for Factor Analysis," *American Psychologist*, vol. 19 (1964), pp. 557-558 (abstract).

128. Sherman, C.R. and F.W. Young, "Nonmetric Multidimensional Scaling: A Monte Carlo Study," *Proceedings of the 76th Annual Convention of the American Psychological Association* (1968), pp. 207-208.

129. Skager, R.W., C.G. Schultz, and S.P. Klein, "The Multidimensional Scaling

of a Set of Artistic Drawings: Perceived Structure of Scale Correlates," *Multivariate Behavioral Research,* vol. 1 (1966), pp. 425-436.

130. Slater, Patrick, "The Analysis of Personal Preferences," *British Journal of Statistical Psychology,* vol. 13 (1960), pp. 119-135.

131. Slater, Patrick, "Inconsistencies in a Schedule of Paired Comparisons," *Biometrica,* vol. 48 (1961), pp. 303-312.

132. Sokal, R. R. and P. H. A. Sneath, *Principles of Numerical Taxonomy.* San Francisco: W. H. Freeman and Company, 1963.

133. Stefflre, V.J., "Market Structure Studies: New Products for Old Markets and New Markets (Foreign) for Old Products," in F.M. Bass, C.W. King, and E.A. Pessemier, eds., *Proceedings of the Purdue Symposium: Application of the Sciences in Marketing Management.* New York: John Wiley & Sons, Inc., 1968, pp. 251-268.

134. Stenson, H.H., and R.L. Knoll, "Goodness of Fit for Random Rankings in Kruskal's Nonmetric Scaling Procedure," *Psychological Bulletin,* vol. 71 (1969), pp. 122-126.

135. Taylor, J.R., "Alternative Methods for Collecting Similarities Data," paper presented to the American Marketing Association, Cincinnati, Ohio, August 1969.

136. Taylor, J.R., "An Empirical Evaluation of Coombs' Unfolding Theory," unpub. Ph.D. thesis, University of Minnesota, July 1967.

137. Taylor, J.R., "The Meaning and Structure of Data Related to Scaling Models," paper presented at the Denver Meeting of the Education Division of the American Marketing Association, August 1968.

138. Torgerson, W.S., "Multidimensional Scaling: I—Theory and Method," *Psychometrika,* vol. 17 (1952), pp. 401-419.

139. Torgerson, W.S., "Multidimensional Scaling of Similarity," *Psychometrika,* vol. 30 (1965), pp. 379-393.

140. Torgerson, W.S., "A Theoretical and Empirical Investigation of Multidimensional Scaling," unpub. Ph.D. thesis, Princeton University, 1951.

141. Torgerson, W.S., *Theory and Methods of Scaling.* New York: John Wiley & Sons Inc., 1960.

142. Tucker, L.R., "Description of Paired Comparison Preference Judgments by a Multidimensional Vector Model," *RM55-7.* Educational Testing Service, Princeton, N.J., 1960.

143. Tucker, L. R., "Dimensions of Preference," *RM-60-7.* Educational Testing Service, Princeton, N.J., 1960.

144. Tucker, L.R., "The Extension of Factor Analysis to Three-Dimensional Matrices," in N. Fredericksen and H. Gulliksen, eds., *Contributions to Mathematical Psychology,* New York: Holt, Rinehart and Winston, Inc., 1964. Pp. 109-127.

145. Tucker, L.R., "Factor Analysis of Double Centered Score Matrices," *RM-56-3,* Educational Testing Service, Princeton, N.J., October 1956.

146. Tucker, L.R. and S. Messick, "An Individual Differences Model for Multidimensional Scaling," *Psychometrika*, vol. 28 (1963), pp. 333-367.

147. Tversky, Amos, "Additivity, Utility, and Subjective Probability, *Journal of Mathematical Psychology*, vol. 4 (1967), pp. 175-201.

148. Tversky, Amos, "A General Theory of Polynomial Conjoint Measurement," *Journal of Mathematical Psychology*, vol. 4 (1967), pp. 1-20.

149. Tversky, Amos, "Elimination by Aspects: A Probabilistic Theory of Choice," MMPP 71-12, University of Michigan, July 1971.

150. Tversky, Amos, and D.H. Krantz, "Similarity of Schematic Faces: A Test of Interdimensional Additivity," *Perception and Psychophysics*, vol. 5 (1969), pp. 124-128.

151. Wind, Yoram, P.E. Green, and P.J. Robinson, "The Determinants of Vendor Selection: The Evaluation Function Approach," *Journal of Purchasing*, vol. 4 (1968), pp. 29-41.

152. Wish, Myron, "Comparisons among Multidimensional Structures of Nations Based on Different Measures of Subjective Similarity," in A. Rapoport, ed., *General Systems*. Ann Arbor, Mich.: Society for General Systems Research, 1970, vol. 15, pp. 55-65.

153. Wish, Myron, "Individual Differences in Perceptions and Preferences among Nations," in C.W. King and D. Tigert, eds. *Attitude Research Reaches New Heights*. Chicago: American Marketing Association, 1971.

154. Wish, Myron, "Individual Differences in Perceived Dissimilarity among Stress Patterns of English Words," paper presented at Psychonomic Society meetings, St. Louis, October 1969.

155. Wish, Myron, "An INDSCAL Analysis of the Miller-Nicely Consonant Confusion Data," paper presented at meetings of the Acoustical Society of America, Houston, November 1970.

156. Wish, Myron, "A Model for the Perception of Morse Code-like Signals," *Human Factors*, vol. 9 (1967), pp. 529-540.

157. Wish, Myron, and J.D. Carroll, "Multidimensional Scaling with Differential Weighting of Dimensions," in D.A. Kendall, R.G. Hodson, and P. Tautu, eds., *Mathematics in the Archaeological and Historical Sciences*. Edinburgh: Edinburgh University Press, 1971.

158. Wish, Myron, Morton Deutsch, and L. Biener, "Differences in Conceptual Structures of Nations: An Exploratory Study," *Journal of Personality and Social Psychology,* vol. 16 (1970), pp. 361-373.

159. Wish, Myron, Morton Deutsch, and L. Biener, "Differences in Perceived Similarity of Nations," in R.N. Shepard, A.K. Romney, and S. Nerlove, eds., *Multidimensional Scaling: Theory and Applications in the Behavioral Sciences*. New York, Academic Press, 1972.

160. Young, F.W., "Nonmetric Multidimensional Scaling: Development of an Index of Metric Determinancy," *Report No. 68*, Psychometric Laboratory, University of North Carolina, August 1968.

161. Young, F.W., "TORSCA, An IBM Program for Nonmetric Multidimensional Scaling," *Journal of Marketing Research*, vol. 5, (August 1968), pp. 319-321.

162. Young F.W., and R.J. Pennell, "An IBM System/360 Program for Points of View Analysis," *Behavioral Science*, vol. 12 (1967), p. 166.

163. Young, F.W., and W.S. Torgerson, "TORSCA, A Fortran IV Program for Shepard-Kruska Multidimensional Scaling Analysis," *Behavioral Science*, vol. 12 (1967), p. 498.

164. Young, G. and A.S. Householder, "Discussion of a Set of Points in terms of Their Mutual Distances," *Psychometrika*, vol. 3 (1938), pp. 19-22.

INDEX

Administrative sciences, future research areas, 145

Aggregate analysis, disaggregate vs. 7-8

Aggregate-level analysis, dissimilarities data, 17-48

Aggregate-level analysis (cont.)

canonical decomposition analysis, 45-47

conditional rank-order data, preprocessing, 24-25

Aggregate-level analysis (cont.)
  configurations, comparing, 22
  configuration interpretation, 34
  congruence testing, 41-43
    via orthogonal rotation, 44-45
  data collection procedures, prepro-
    cessing steps and, 22-26
  derived, preprocessing, 25-26
  derived measures of dissimilarity,
    scaling, 19-20
  direct, scaling, 26-34
  direct measures of dissimilarity,
    scaling, 19
  discriminant analysis, 38-41
  flow diagram, 20-21
  hierarchical cluster analysis, 37-38
  metric analysis, 28
  nonmetric analysis, 32
  nonmetric cluster analysis, 33-34
  outline of the analysis, 18-22
  parametric mapping analysis, 32-33
  preprocessing steps, 18-19
  ratings data scaling, 34-47
  simple scaling analysis, 28-32
Algorithms, alternative, 11-12
  approaches and, synthesis of, 137-
    138
  combinations, alternative approaches
    and, comparison of, 136-137
  comparison of, 134-136
  M-D-SCAL V, 86, 87
  metric, nonmetric vs., 8, 10
  nonmetric, 6; metric vs., 8, 10
  parametric mapping, 79, 105,
    108-109

Background characteristics, respon-
    dent differences in perception,
    62
Behavioral science, future research
    area, 146-147
Bennett, J. F., 83
Biener, L., 142, 143
Bipolar scales, food items and, used in
    pilot study, 4
Bloombaum, Milton, 142

C-MATCH program, 44, 182, 200-203
CANDECOMP program, 43, 45, 46, 47
Canonical correlation, 95
Canonical decomposition analysis,
    45-47
  of scenario-dependent preferences,
    101-103
Carmone, F. J., 2, 10, 143, 144, 182
Carroll, J. D., 9, 10, 32, 33, 43, 45,
    53, 55 n., 79, 82, 83, 99 n., 101,
    105, 132, 143, 182, 210, 214
Chang, J. J., 10, 32, 43, 45, 53, 55 n.,
    79, 82, 83, 89, 101, 105, 132,
    143, 182, 210, 214
Chapter discussions, supporting mate-
    rial for, 219-272
Cliff, Norman, 22, 44, 142, 182
Cluster analysis, hierarchical, 19, 33,
    37-38, 134, 144, 182, 199-203
  nonmetric, 33-34
Communications, future research area,
    145-146
Comparative analysis, preference data,
    scaling of, 11
  similarities data, scaling of, 8
Conceptual approaches, alternative,
    5-11
  scaling of preference data, 8-11
    comparative analysis, 11
    internal analysis, external vs., 10
    metric algorithms, nonmetric vs.,
      10
    point-point representation, point-
      vector vs., 10
  scaling of similarities data, 5-8
    aggregate vs. disaggregate analysis,
      7-8
    comparative analysis, 8
    direct vs. derived similarities, 7
Configuration interpretation, 34
Conflict theory scaling, 145
Congruence, INDSCAL, 95-97
  with INDSCAL stimulus space, tests
    for, 90-92
  orthogonal rotation to, 92-95
  testing, 41-43, 58-62

Congruence testing (cont.)
  via orthogonal rotation, 44-45
Conjoint tetrads, 23-24
Coombs, C. H., 1, 2, 24, 108
Correlation, canonical, 95
  procedure, nonlinear, 69-73

Data, basic, collection procedures, preprocessing steps and, 22-26
  methods, alternative, 22-24
  conditional rank-order, prepro-
    cessing, 24-25
  profile, 24
  See also Dissimilarities data; Pref-
    erence data; Questionnaire; Rat-
    ings data
Data bank, 3-5
Data base, comments on, 12-13
de Leeuw, Jan, 12
Derived dissimilarities, 57-58
  data, preprocessing, 25-26
Derived measures of dissimilarity,
  scaling, 19-20
  of similarity, 5
Derived similarities, direct vs., 7
Deutsch, Morton, 142, 143
Differences in perception, respondent,
  analysis of, 62-66
Dimensional saliences, segmentation
  based on, 63-65
Direct dissimilarities, analysis of,
  55-57
  INDSCAL analysis of, 67
Direct measures of dissimilarity, scaling, 19
Direct similarities, derived vs., 7
Disaggregate analysis, aggregate versus,
  7-8
Disaggregate-level analysis, dissimilarities data, 49-77
  congruence testing, 58-62
  derived dissimilarities, 57-58
  dimensional saliences, segmentation
    based on, 63-65
  direct dissimilarities analysis, 55-57

Disaggregate-level analysis (cont.)
  husband-wife differences, 63-65
  individual differences, approaches
    to, 53-55
  INDSCAL analysis at subgroup level,
    65-66
  at total group level, 55-62
  max "r" linear regression procedure,
    67-69
  monotone regression procedure, 69
  nonlinear correlation procedure,
    69-73
  outline of the analysis, 50
  property fitting at subgroup level,
    66-76
  respondent differences in percep-
    tion, analysis of, 62-66
  subgroup analysis, 51-53
  subgroup differences based on
    ratings data, analysis of, 73-76
  total group-level analysis, 50-51
Discriminant analysis, 38-41
  external analysis of overall pre-
    ferences, 120-121
Disjoint tetrads, 23
Dissimilarities, derived measures of,
  scaling, 19
  direct measures of, scaling, 19
  See also Derived dissimilarities; Di-
    rect dissimilarities
Dissimilarities data, aggregate-level
  analysis of, 17-48
  canonical decomposition analysis,
    45-47
  conditional rank-order data, pre-
    processing, 24-25
  configuration interpretation, 34
  configurations, comparing, 22
  congruence testing, 41-43
  congruence testing via orthogonal
    rotation, 44-45
  data collection procedures, pre-
    processing steps and, 22-26
  derived, preprocessing, 25-26
  derived measures of, scaling, 19-20
  direct, scaling, 26-34

Dissimilarities data, derived measures of (cont.)
  direct measures of dissimilarity, scaling, 19
  discriminant analysis, 38-41
  flow diagram, 20-21
  hierarchical cluster analysis, 37-38
  metric analysis, 28
  nonmetric analysis, 32
  nonmetric cluster analysis, 33-34
  outline of the analysis, 18-22
  parametric mapping analysis, 32-33
  preprocessing steps, 18-19
  ratings data scaling, 34-47
  simple scaling analysis, 28-32
disaggregate-level analysis of, 49-77
  congruence testing, 58-62
  derived dissimilarities, 57-58
  dimensional saliences, segmentation based on, 63-65
  direct dissimilarities analysis, 55-57
  husband-wife differences, 63-65
  individual differences, approaches to, 53-55
  INDSCAL analysis at subgroup level, 65-66
  INDSCAL analysis at total group level, 55-62
  max "r" linear regression procedure, 67-69
  monotone regression procedure, 69
  nonlinear correlation procedure, 69-73
  outline of the analysis, 50
  property fitting at subgroup level, 66-76
  respondent differences in perception, analysis of, 62-66
  subgroup analysis, 51-53
  subgroup differences based on ratings data, analysis of, 73-76
  total group-level analysis, 50-51
DISTAN program, 50, 182, 187

Eckart-Young decomposition, 82, 83
Evaluative space, 81
External analysis, internal vs., 10
  overall preferences, 109-121
    average-subject coordinates from INDSCAL analysis, 110
    discriminant analysis, 120-121
    metric analysis, 111-114
    nonmetric analysis, 114-120
    rankings at individual-subject level, 110
  preference data, 104-132
    flow diagram of the analysis, 107
    market segmentation, 106-108
    outline of the analysis, 105-106
    PREFMAP algorithm, 108-109
    segment identification, utilizing PREFMAP for, 109
  scenario-dependent preferences, 121-132
    replication at individual level, partial, 126-132

Findings, see Methodological findings; Substantial findings
Flow diagrams, analysis at aggregate level, 52
  analysis at disaggregate level, 54
  external analysis of preference data, 107
  internal analysis, 80
Food item study, part A, 153-155
  part B, 156-161
  part C, 162-163
  part D, 164-166
Food items, bipolar scale and, used in pilot study, 4

Gleason, T. C., 142
Green, P. E., 2, 142, 143, 144, 182
Greenberg, M. G., 144
Group-level analysis, total, 50-51
  INDSCAL analysis at, 55-62
Guttman, L., 1, 12, 28 n., 83

Harris, Britton, 51, 77, 182
Hays, W. J., 83

Hierarchical cluster analysis, 19, 33, 37-38, 134, 144, 182, 199-203
Howard, Nigel, 7, 51, 77, 182
Howard-Harris Cluster program, 182, 207-210
Husband-wife analysis, preference data, internal analysis, 99-101
Husband-wife differences, 63-65

Individual differences, approaches to, 53-55
INDSCAL program, 50, 51, 53, 57, 60, 73, 77, 79, 85, 86, 101, 105, 106, 110, 123, 128, 129, 135, 136, 137, 138, 143, 182, 203-207
  analysis of derived dissimilarities, 59
  analysis of direct dissimilarities, 68
  analysis at subgroup level, 65-66
  at total group level, 55-62
  congruence, 95-97
  stimulus space, tests for congruence with, 90-92
Internal analysis, external analysis vs., 10
  overall preferences, 83-90
    M-D-SCAL V analysis, 86-89
    MDPREF analysis, 83-86
    rankings by individual subject, 84
    row comparability option, 87-89
    row split option, 87
  preference data, 78-103
    alternative procedures in, 81-83
    canonical correlation, 95
    canonical decomposition of scenario-dependent preferences, 101-103
    congruence, tests for, with INDSCAL stimulus space, 90-92
    differences in overall preferences, individual, 97-99
    flow diagram of, 80
    husband-wife analysis, 99-101
    INDSCAL congruence, 95-97
    orthogonal rotation to congruence, 92-95

Internal analysis, preference data (cont.)
  outline of the analysis, 79-81
  parametric mapping analysis, 89-90
  point-point models, 82-83
  point-vector models, 82
Isaac, P. D., 142, 143

Johnson, S. C., 19, 33, 134, 144, 182
Johnson Hierarchical Cluster program, 19, 33, 134, 144, 182, 199-203
Jones, J. M., 142

Kappa values, 33
Klein, S. P., 143
Krantz, D. H., 142
Kruskal, J. B., 10, 11, 27, 28, 79, 82, 83, 89, 182, 188

Landis, D., 142
Linear regression procedure, max "r," 67-69
Lingoes, J. C., 12, 83

M-D-SCAL V program, 18 n., 28, 30, 31, 36, 37, 38, 79, 86-89, 108, 134, 182, 188-192
  overall preferences analysis, 86-89
  row comparability analysis, Shepard diagram based on two-space solution from, 91
    two-space configuration from, 90
  row split analysis, Shepard diagram based on two-space solution from, 89
    two-space configuration from, 88
Maheshwari, Arun, 142, 143
Market segmentation, external analysis of, 106-108
Marketing, 2
  future research area, 143-144
Max "r" linear regression procedure, 67-69
McGee, V. E., 12
McRae, Duncan, 142

MDPREF program, 82, 113, 135, 182, 212-214
  analysis, 83-86
  two-space point-vector configuration from, 85
Messick, S. J., 53, 142
Methodological findings, summary of, 134-138
  algorithms, comparison of, 134-136
  algorithms and approaches, synthesis of, 137-138
  alternative approaches and algorithm combinations, comparison of, 136-137
Methodology, statistical, future research area, 147
Metric analysis, aggregate-level analysis of dissimilarities data, 28
  external analysis of overall preference, 111-114
Monotone regression procedure, 69

Nelson, C., 142
Nonlinear correlation procedure, 69-73
Nonmetric analysis, 32
  cluster analysis, 33-34
  external analysis of overall preference, 114-120

Objectives of the study, 3
Orthogonal rotation, congruence testing via, 44-45
  to congruence, 92-95
Overall preferences, external analysis of, 109-121
  average-subject coordinates from INDSCAL analysis, 110
  discriminant analysis, 120-121
  metric analysis, 111-114
  nonmetric analysis, 114-120
  rankings at individual-subject level, 110
  individual differences in, 97-99
  internal analysis of, 83-90
  M-D-SCAL V analysis, 86-89
  MDPREF analysis, 83-86

Overall preferences, internal analysis of (cont.)
  rankings by individual subject, 84
  row comparability option, 87-89
  row split option, 87

PARAMAP program, 32, 33, 34, 36, 40, 42, 135, 136, 182, 196-199
  algorithm, 79
  analysis, 32-33; preference data, 89-90
  Shepard diagram based on two-space solution from, 92
  two-space configuration from, 91
Pennell, R. J., 44, 182
Perception, individual differences in, 142-143
  respondent differences in, analysis of, 62-66
Point-point models, 82-83
Point-point representation, point-vector vs., 10
Point-vector models, 82
Point-vector representation, point-point vs., 10
Points of View model, 53
Predictive experiments, description of various, 148-150
Predictive studies, design of, toward a schema for, 147-148
Preference data, 14
  external analysis of, 104-132
    flow diagram of the analysis, 107
    market segmentation, 106-108
    outline of the analysis, 105-106
    overall preferences, 109-121
    PREFMAP algorithm, 108-109
    scenario-dependent preferences, 121-132
    segment identification, utilization of PREFMAP for, 109
  internal analysis of, 78-103
    alternative procedures in, 81-83
    canonical correlation, 95
    canonical decomposition of scenario-dependent preferences, 101-103

Preference data, internal analysis of (cont.)
  congruence, tests for, with INDSCAL stimulus space, 90-92
  differences in overall preferences, individual, 97-99
  flow diagram of the analysis, 80
  husband-wife analysis, 99-101
  INDSCAL congruence, 95-97
  orthogonal rotation to congruence, 92-95
  outline of the analysis, 79-81
  overall preferences, 83-90
  parametric mapping analysis, 89-90
  point-point models, 82-83
  point-vector models, 82
scaling of, alternative approaches to, 8-11
  comparative analysis, 11
  internal analysis, external vs., 10
  metric algorithms, nonmetric vs., 10
  point-point representation, point-vector vs., 10
Preferences, overall, see Overall preferences
  scenario-dependent, see Scenario-dependent preferences
PREFMAP program, 182, 214-218
  algorithm, 105, 108-109
  model, utilization of, for segment identification, 109
Profile data, 24
PROFIT program, 182, 210-212
Programs used, details of, 181-218
  C-MATCH, 44, 182, 200-203
  DISTAN, 50, 182, 187
  Howard-Harris Cluster, 182, 207-210
  INDSCAL, 50, 51, 53, 57, 60, 73, 77, 79, 85, 86, 101, 105, 106, 110, 123, 128, 129, 135, 136, 137, 138, 143, 182, 203-207
  Johnson Hierarchical Cluster, 37-38, 134, 144, 182, 199-203
  M-D-SCAL, 18 n., 28, 30, 31, 36, 37, 38, 79, 86-89, 108, 134, 135, 182, 188-192

Programs used (cont.)
  MDPREF, 135, 182, 212-214
  PARAMAP, 32, 33, 34, 36, 40, 42, 135, 136, 182, 196-199
  PREFMAP, 182, 214-218
  PROFIT, 182, 210-212
  TORSCA 8, 19, 31, 32, 36, 39, 98, 134, 182, 192-196
  TRICON, 18, 19, 24, 25, 28, 50, 182-187
Property fitting at subgroup level, 66-76
Public opinion, future research area, 143-144

Questionnaire, basic data and, 152-166
  basic data for subjects no. 011-212, 167-180
  food item study, part A, 153-155
  part B, 156-161
  part C, 162-163
  part D, 164-166

Rank-order data, conditional, preprocessing of, 24-25
Rao, V. R., 142, 144, 182
Rapoport, Ammon, 142
Ratings data, 13
  discriminant analysis of, stimulus configuration of, 42
  input matrix of derived dissimilarities from, 27
  scaling, 34-47
  subgroup differences based on, analysis of, 73-76
Regression procedures, linear, max "r," 67-69
  monotone, 69
Research areas, future, 143-147
  administrative sciences, 145
  behavioral science, 146-147
  communications, 145-146
  marketing and public opinion, 143-144
  statistical methodology, 147
  potential, 141-143

Research areas, potential (cont.)
  perception, individual differences in, 142-143
  predictive experiments, description of various, 148-150
  predictive studies, design of, toward a schema for, 147-148
Respondent background data, preference scenarios and, 4
Respondent differences in perception, analysis of, 62-66
Rosenberg, S., 142
Roskam, E. E., 12, 82
Row comparability option, 87-89
Row split option, 87
Runkel, P. J., 142

Saliences, dimensional, segmentation based on, 63-65
Scaling analysis, comments on, 15
Scenario-dependent preferences, canonical decomposition of, 101-103
  external analysis of, 121-132
  replication at individual level, partial, 126-132
  respondent background data and, 4
Schoneman, P. H., 83
Schultz, C. G., 143
Schwarz, S. B., 142
Segment identification, utilization of PREFMAP for, 109
Shepard, R. N., 1, 141, 142
Shepard diagrams, 28, 29, 30, 31, 32, 34, 35, 36, 37, 38, 39, 40, 87, 89, 90, 91, 92
Sheth, J. N., 7
Silver, C. A., 142
Similarities, direct vs. derived, 7
Similarities data, scaling of, alternative approaches to, 5-8
  aggregate vs. disaggregate analysis, 7-8
  comparative analysis, 8

Similarities data, scaling of (cont.)
  direct vs. derived similarities, 7
Simple scaling analysis, 28-32, 83 n.
Skager, R. W., 143
Slater, Patrick, 10, 82
Statistical methodology, future research area, 147
Stefflre, V. J., 7, 144
Stimulus space, INDSCAL, tests for congruence with, 90-92
Subgroup analysis, 51-53
  differences based on ratings data, 73-76
Subgroup level, INDSCAL analysis at, 65-66
  property fitting at, 66-76
Substantive findings, summary of, 138-141
Summary of findings, see Methodological findings; Substantive findings

Tetrads, conjoint, 23-24
  disjoint, 23
Torgerson, W. S., 1, 2, 27 n., 32, 182
TORSCA 8 program, 19, 31, 32, 36, 39, 98, 134, 182, 192-196
Total group-level analysis, 50-51
  INDSCAL analysis, 55-62
Tree diagrams, 35, 41
TRICON program, 18, 19, 24, 25, 28, 50, 182-187
  input matrix of direct dissimilarities from, 26
Tucker, L. R., 53, 82
Tversky, Amos, 142

Vivekananthan, P. S., 142

Wharton School of Finance, 2, 3
Wish, Myron, 141, 142, 143

Young, F. W., 32, 44, 83, 142, 182